The Dove and the Dragon

Praise for *The Dove and the Dragon*

Ed Simon is the prolific cultural historian for our apocalyptic age, and his latest work is as ambitious as it is intimate. From the Dead Sea Scrolls to medieval Cathars and Fraticelli to the fiery rhetoric of modern politics, *The Dove and the Dragon* unfurls a tapestry of ideas where angels whisper and prophets roar. It's a lucid and learned encyclopedia that leaves you at once awed and grounded—a reminder that every era, not just ours, is fraught with crises and hope.

—**Andrew Hui**, author of *The Study: The Inner Life of Renaissance Libraries*

Intellectual history at its finest, this book traces the evolution of an idea that underpins the vexing moment we are living in, from the Zoroastrians to the evangelicals of today. Whether you support Trumpism or are aghast at it, you will never see the movement the same way after reading this book.

—**Rick Shenkman**, founder of the History News Network, and author of *Political Animals: How Our Stone-Age Brain Gets in the Way of Smart Politics*

In this ambitious volume, Simon considers a religious concept that has "merited the attention of billions": the end of the world. Simon is the perfect guide for such an expansive subject. His schema for apocalyptic thinking—the dove and the dragon—is a brilliant lens through which to engage a massive subject. Simon demonstrates that apocalypticism is neither fringe thinking nor historical footnote; he expertly reveals that wonder and worry over the end of time fuels religion, literature, art, and politics.

—**Nick Ripatrazone**, culture editor, *Image* journal, and author of *Longing for an Absent God*

How did the apocalypse become a theological idea that wields more cultural influence over modernity than God? Ed Simon seeks an answer to this question, tracing the elusive double-edged sword of apocalyptic thought: gentle like a dove, yet violent as a dragon. His ambitious and insightful apocalyptic history illuminates our enduring, and yet never more relevant, obsession with the end of the world.

—**Beatrice Marovich**, associate professor of theology, Hanover College, and author of *Sister Death: Political Theologies for Living and Dying*

Ed Simon is one of our most insightful and prolific commentators on religion and culture. In *The Dove and the Dragon*, Simon turns to the West's fascination with the end of time. "Apocalyptic thinking," in Simon's terms, has given us an entire vocabulary and grammar to decode humanity's successive cataclysms, as well as the enduring problems of evil and inequality. Few have the breadth of knowledge necessary for a history of the apocalypse from ancient Judea to the Anthropocene—fortunately we have Ed Simon.

—**Simon Rabinovitch**, author of *Sovereignty and Religious Freedom: A Jewish History*

Ed Simon is up to his old tricks, getting ahead of us, showing us how to think better in the present by reading for the ending. In this case, that ending is the one that comes when time has run out and the meaning of history is revealed, in retrospect, as the purification of all that has come before. But Armageddon is not the only path to apocalypse, Simon demonstrates, because purification by fire is not the only way to imagine perfection: If we let it, the dove will have as much to say as the dragon in our designs of and for the future. The importance of this book, another tour de force, resides in the recognition that the task now before us is not to choose between these two figures but to realize that there will never be an ending that is already a foregone conclusion.

—**James Livingston**, professor emeritus, Department of History, Rutgers University–New Brunswick

The Dove and the Dragon

A Cultural History of the Apocalypse

Ed Simon

FORTRESS PRESS
Minneapolis

THE DOVE AND THE DRAGON
A Cultural History of the Apocalypse

30 29 28 27 26 25 1 2 3 4 5 6 7 8 9

Library of Congress Cataloging-in-Publication Data

Names: Simon, Ed, author.
Title: The dove and the dragon : a cultural history of the apocalypse / Ed Simon.
Description: Minneapolis : Fortress Press, [2025] | Includes bibliographical references and index.
Identifiers: LCCN 2024061909 (print) | LCCN 2024061910 (ebook) | ISBN 9798889834618 (paperback) | ISBN 9798889834625 (ebook)
Subjects: LCSH: Eschatology--Comparative studies. | Apocalyptic literature--History and criticism.
Classification: LCC BL500 .S556 2025 (print) | LCC BL500 (ebook) | DDC 202/.3--dc23/eng/20250324
LC record available at https://lccn.loc.gov/2024061909
LC ebook record available at https://lccn.loc.gov/2024061910

Cover image: Then war broke out in heaven: Michael and his angels fought against the dragon, and the dragon and his angels fought back. (Revelation, Chapter 12, 7). Woodcut engraving after a drawing by Julius Schnorr von Carolsfeld (German painter, 1794–1872), published in 1877. Sourced from ZU_09/Getty Images
Cover design: Kris E. Miller

Print ISBN: 979-8-8898-3461-8
eBook ISBN: 979-8-8898-3462-5

Dedicated to all future generations, hopefully

For every second of time was the strait gate through which the Messiah might enter.

—Walter Benjamin, *Theses on the Philosophy of History*

CONTENTS

Introduction

The Eternal Prelude to Armageddon

When British field marshal Edmund Allenby—the 1st Viscount Allenby and ultimate recipient of the Knight Grand Cross of the Order of St. Michael and St. George—conquered the city of Jerusalem in December of 1917, he first entered on foot. Dismounting from his horse, the properly comported Nottinghamshire-born officer, with his slight frame, neatly parted brown hair, and regimental-clipped mustache, took off his cap and crossed underneath the famed Jaffa Gate, one of the seven historical entrances into the city.[1] For several months during World War I Allenby had led the British and their Arab allies in bloody fighting against the Ottomans and Germans throughout Palestine, and now that Jerusalem itself was under his control the field marshal was cognizant of the symbolic implications that would be conveyed if he triumphally bestrode into the Holy City sacred to Judaism, Christianity, and Islam.

So, rather like a supplicating pilgrim, Allenby simply walked into the city that had housed Solomon and Herod's Temple, the hill of Golgotha where Christ was crucified, and where the prophet Muhammad underwent his ascent unto heaven. "To the Inhabitants of Jerusalem the Blessed and the People Dwelling in its Vicinity," read the proclamation of martial law written by Allenby, "since your city is regarded with affection by the adherents of three of the great religions of mankind and its soil has been consecrated by the prayers and pilgrimages of multitudes of devout people of these three religions for many centuries, therefore do I make it known to you that every sacred building, monument, holy spot, shrine . . . will be maintained and protected."[2]

With little concern for alienating their Arab allies, the British press were less sanguine. Despite a private memorandum from the British government released only a month before Allenby's entry into Jerusalem, which instructed reporters not to use language that described "military operations against Turkey in any sense as a Holy War, [or] a modern crusade," *Punch* magazine still ran an article with the headline "The Last Crusade." The piece featured a cartoon of the medieval English king Richard the Lionheart, the crusader who'd failed to take Jerusalem from the Muslims, looking down from heaven with tears in his eyes and crying "My dream comes true!"[3] A few years after the occupation of Jerusalem, popular novels would be published in Britain such as F. H. Cooper's *Khaki Crusaders* (1919), R. E. C. Adams's *The Modern Crusaders* (1920), and John N. Moore's *With Allenby's Crusaders* (1923).

Soon the British Department of Information's initial reticence to speak in religious terms faded, with it first releasing a telegram to the press which claimed that the "commanders who have played a great part in the South Palestine campaign are descended from the knights who fought in the wars of the crusades," and later premiering a forty-minute propaganda film entitled *The New Crusades: With the British Forces on the Palestinian Front.* John Paterson Smyth claimed in *A People's Life of Christ*, published four years after the capture of Jerusalem, that Allenby himself had said "England has sent out the eighth, a new Crusade. And England has won! . . . The Last Crusade is fought. The Holy Land is free."[4]

Such problematic enthusiasms seemed to be unavoidable in the Levant. The Great War was inevitably discussed by diplomats and journalists, politicians and generals alike in providential terms, an apocalyptic battle that was the "war to end all wars," as US president Woodrow Wilson termed it. Conquering Jerusalem opened a northern front in Palestine, and Allenby pursued the Ottomans throughout the Levant, eventually taking the ancient cities of Aleppo and Damascus. The battles which made that possible occurred around an ancient fortification site on an arid plain in the north of what is today Israel, a place in Hebrew named Tel Megiddo, but which is far better known by its Greek adaptation—Armageddon. Allenby and the British didn't miss the symbolic importance of that name either. The field marshal didn't discount the association with that mythic battle of Armageddon spoken of in the New Testament book of Revelation, which holds that at the end of the world a great conflagration would be fought here between the forces of good and evil, before ushering in a millennium of peace and the second coming of Christ.[5] British readers, raised on the King James Version of the Bible and *The Book of Common Prayer*, thrilled to the battle of Megiddo, even though very little fighting actually took place at that desolate spot. World War I was portrayed as many things—a fight against German militarism, a battle on behalf of democracy, a war for security and peace.

But despite all of those ostensibly modern aims, both propagandists and citizens couldn't help but still hear those ancient martial hoofbeats of imagined wars of the past, of prophecy from scripture. Translating from the Hebrew as "Mount of the Governor," today Tel Megiddo is home to a small Israeli kibbutz founded by Polish Holocaust survivors. During antiquity it was at a crucial trading crossroads; first as a Canaanite fortification, a way station between Mesopotamia and Egypt, later a minor royal city in the kingdom of the Israelites. The sands of Megiddo were stained with blood centuries before Allenby's campaign; some 3,500 years ago Pharaoh Thutmose III fought the Canaanites there, a millennium after that Pharaoh Necho II defeated the ruler of Judea, King Josiah, at that crossroads.[6]

However, Tel Megiddo isn't celebrated for any battle that happened there in the past—including the British victory—but rather for a war which is supposed to be fought there in the future. Other than for a handful of biblical references, Tel Megiddo has little reason to be famous, even while in the Western imagination the settlement has become synonymous with the end of the world. Within the Hebrew Scriptures (known as the Old Testament by Christians, who arrange its individual books differently), Megiddo is mentioned only twelve times, and none of those references have to do with the apocalypse. There is even less reference to Tel Megiddo in the New Testament, but the one passage which does mention what would otherwise be a forgotten corner of the desert comes from the complicated, baroque, disquieting, and surreal book of Revelation. Describing the final days, John of Patmos writes in Revelation 16:16–17 that God "gathered them together into a place called in the Hebrew tongue Armageddon . . . and there came a great voice out of the temple of heaven, from the throne, saying, it is done."[7] Notably the passage doesn't actually say anything about warring armies fighting on that desolate plain, save for earlier in Revelation when Patmos writes that the "spirits of devils, working miracles, which go forth unto the kings of the earth and of the whole world, [were] to gather them to the battle of that great day of God Almighty."[8]

From that congruence many have assumed that said war would be fought at Tel Megiddo itself. Sometimes those armies are identified with the cryptically imprecise satanic soldiers of Gog and Magog, who at the end of days would "gather them for battle" as in "number they are like the sand on the seashore."[9] They are also described in the Hebrew Scriptures, but it's their role in the Christian story about the end of days that has long made Gog and Magog—and the correct identification of who exactly they're supposed to be—a source of obsession. For ancient Roman Christians, they were identified with the Huns, Vandals, Visigoths, and Goths bearing down on the Eternal City; medieval Europeans feared that they were the Mongols; their Renaissance descendants thought they could be the Ottomans, while during the nineteenth century Napoleon's troops were conflated with them (and the general with the antichrist). By the twentieth century, some evangelical Christians saw Gog and Magog as representing the Soviet Union.[10] Apocalyptic thought is ever thus, an often-confusing morass of complex symbols and ambiguous passages, differing interpretations and theological positions battling like armies in the desert.

Armageddon and *apocalypse* are not technically synonymous, though they're related by connotation and certainly conflated together in the wider culture. While Armageddon refers to a specific location, apocalypse denotes a particular spiritual action, one that doesn't necessarily have to do with the end of the world at all. Derived from a koine Greek term that means "unveiling," *apocalypse* is used to describe visions, prophecies, and revelations, synonymous with the impartation of secret knowledge, of invisible things being made visible and unknown things being made known. Such is the meaning in Revelation itself, when John of Patmos was initiated into hidden things in the form of a symbolically mediated account of how the world would end. Henceforth, both Armageddon and apocalypse would be connected to one another, shorthand for discussing what it would mean when history is no more.

John of Patmos didn't invent the idea of apocalypse—such thinking is threaded through the Hebrew Scriptures; the Jews themselves drew much inspiration from their experiences with other Near-Eastern peoples. Nor should it be said that the concept of some kind of epoch-shattering, violent conflagration was foreign to other cultures; the vagaries of life in the ancient world were such that people were more than familiar with the idea of famine, drought, pandemic, and marauding armies burning settlements to the ground. Such experiences must have colored peoples' conception of history, and the mythic systems of most cultures explain destruction and creation to be cyclical aspects of history, from the Hindu Kali Yuga to the Norse Ragnarök. What apocalypse as mediated through Jewish understanding, and then through that of Christian and Islamic thinking, signified was something new in religious thought. Not just that the world could end—but that the world could end *forever*. Apocalypse introduced termination, finality, and the writing of a conclusion to the affairs of humanity. The apocalyptic imagination offered a certain symmetry to the idea of the world being created out of nothing. Both of these were innovations of ancient Jewish thinking. From nothing came everything and to nothing should everything return (in a manner of speaking). More than just that, apocalyptic thinking—Revelation with its Great Dragon and its seven seals, the Whore of Babylon, and the Four Horsemen—was a mechanism for introducing a potent significance, a new meaning, to the otherwise mundane details of everyday life.

No Western religious concept has been as socially, culturally, economically, and politically significant as that of the apocalypse. Neither heaven nor hell, sin nor salvation, even God and the devil, have so merited the attention of billions of people in the manner that belief in the end of the world has. Theologians and historians use words like "apocalypse," "millennium," and "eschatology" in particular ways, but the contours of the day of judgment—it's broad history as a metaphor in culture and its rhetoric appearing in unexpected places—can't be circumscribed by sect or denomination. The implications of history's conclusions are far larger than any particular faith's assortments of theologies, requiring an admission that the word "apocalypse" encompasses a broader set of associated concepts than merely the meaning deployed by theologians.

From abstract theology derives tangible consequences in the affairs of humans, for the twinned affirmation that the world shall either be destroyed or that a perfectibility awaits us in a millennial future (or a combination therein) has long dominated the dreams and nightmares of the faithful, even when they're not always aware that what they're adhering to is a faith, even while apocalyptic thinking endures among the ostensibly secular as well. Obviously apocalypse has meant the reign of the antichrist, the arrival of the messiah, and the purging of sinners and the elevation of the saved, but it's also meant the inevitability of revolution, of the establishment of political utopia, and the fantasies of an advanced technocratic future. Particularly in our present moment, which can feel so intrinsically apocalyptic, it becomes crucial to understand how the cultural thinking of the end of the world has had a profound impact on the affairs of people, giving them a standard by which to judge their experience, to circumscribe both those dreams and nightmares. From the ashes of the obliterated world come two visages—*the dove and the dragon*. Apocalyptic thinking is riven by a fruitful—and at times dangerous—binary between the hopes for a coming millennium when all shall be perfected or a fiery deluge when the earth shall be destroyed. Obviously most religious thinking countenances some kind of relationship between those two scenarios, though there are crucial implications derived from the various presumed timelines about those events. What I argue is that the dove and the dragon are convenient ciphers for categories of apocalyptic thinking which endure across religions and secular ideologies. As a critical neologism, the dove and the dragon offer a means of classifying and explicating the tremendous diversity of apocalyptic thinking, especially as manifested in secular thinking where the traces of the eschatological might be more difficult to discern, because despite sublimation many ideologies from Marxism to fascism are simply veiled faiths. Within my schema, the gentle dove is representative of apocalyptic thinking which presumes some idealized future, when inequities are leveled, injustices are rectified, and the oppressed are liberated, while the vengeful dragon is an emissary of destruction, a creature of fire who comes to annihilate.

The dove and the dragon need not be mutually exclusive, for both signal a rupture to normal history; they are "apocalyptic" precisely because they assume a certain finality to history, whether or not what follows is heavenly or hellish. They are potent archetypes with long connotative histories: the dove evoking the creature whom Noah sent to find dry land following the deluge or the indwelling presence of the Christian Holy Spirit; the fearsome dragon displaying glimmers of that rough beast rising in Revelation. They are inextricable and often intermixed; it can be difficult to separate the two. Often they can be confused for one another—sometimes the dragon has feathers and frequently the dove arrives breathing fire. The history of apocalyptic thinking is then a question of parsing the nature of this binary, of the interactions between the millennial dove and the dragon of Armageddon.

The eighteenth-century Romantic poet William Blake referred to Scripture as a "great code" of literature, a set of symbols, images, metaphors, and phrases that, regardless of our own beliefs, underscores our culture in the subsequent millennia. Nowhere is this more obvious than in the idea of apocalypse, for all of us alike drink from that reservoir which imagines an end of days; dreams and nightmares alike born out of that sense of fire and brimstone raining down upon us and erasing all that we've produced. That the world could end, that either nothingness, hell, or paradise could follow, that humanity works from a script which the adept divinator can parse—this is a way of thinking that's not just religious, but now secular as well, the purview of futurists, analysts, and political scientists as much as prophets. Furthermore, apocalyptic thinking merged divine time with regular time. In many traditions broadly labeled as "pagan," such as the classical Greek belief system, there was a disjuncture between the time of the gods and the time of mortals, neither being synonymous with each other.[11] The imposition of divine providence coupled with a clearly delineated account of human affairs meant that divine time and human time became in some sense equivalent.

Admittedly there is something of the literal about apocalypticism, the way in which interpreting history as providential removes the divine from the mythopoeic realm and inserts it into material existence, but it's also what gives people the ability to envision a future different from the present. Ancient apocalyptic thinkers, unlike their pagan contemporaries, conceived of history as changing in a manner made possible by a belief in the end of the world—it opened a space for them to imagine us. There are, to be sure, a multitude of different understandings, approaches, and theologies that have evolved over the centuries. Combined with the inextricably related concept of millennialism, apocalypticism was a means of envisioning the world as purged of inequity and injustice, of an upending of social expectations and a radical releveling of the social order. Since the apocalypse was first introduced as a concept, we've been able to understand history as a story that has a final conclusion. As the Canadian literary theorist Northrop Frye writes in a study whose title is drawn from Blake's contention, *The Great Code: The Bible and Literature*, "Man creates what he calls history as a screen to conceal the workings of the apocalypse from himself," for such endings "may break on anyone at any time."[12]

To which I would add that, as storytelling creatures, it is the sense of a narrative ending to which (whether it's real or not) our minds naturally incline. Being able to imagine an apocalypse, an end to all things, was an innovation in storytelling first and foremost, but as this book will attest, one with a profound influence on the affairs of humans. No religious concept—not even God—has had a more crucial impact on culture, giving us the language to describe both the dreams of a millennial kingdom and the nightmares of an apocalyptic wilderness, of the realm of both the dove and the dragon.

CHAPTER ONE

In the Beginning Was the End

Judaism and the Prophets

Beginning of the End

The Earliest of Apocalypses

FIRST THE BABYLONIANS gave the ancient Jews the experience of an apocalypse and then after their liberation the Persians gave them the language with which to understand that apocalypse. For almost two generations during the seventh century BCE, following the Babylonian invasion of the kingdom of Judea and the destruction of Solomon's Temple, thousands of the faithful suffered exile in Mesopotamia, true to the plaintive mourning of Psalm 137 with its evocation that "By the rivers of Babylon, there we sat down, yea, we wept, when we remembered Zion. . . . How shall we sing the Lord's song in a strange land?" Only fifty years separate the destruction of the First Temple in 588 BCE and the return of exilic Jews to Judea in 538 BCE after their deliverance by the Persians, but the trauma of the Babylonian captivity had an indelible effect on Judaism, and a vocabulary for comprehending how a world can end. After the Persian king Cyrus the Great defeated the Babylonians, the ruler allowed the Jewish remnant to return to Jerusalem.[1] During this period it was the Zoroastrian faith of the Persians which was the most formative influence on Judaism in the development of the apocalyptic. What the Zoroastrians possessed was a comprehensive *eschatology*, that is, a complete understanding of what the apocalypse entailed.

Whether out of gratitude to Cyrus's decree or as a result of the horrors of their treatment by the Babylonians, apocalyptic thinking became an important current of Jewish thought. Culture is anathema to a vacuum; all beliefs, values, sentiments, thoughts, philosophies, ideologies, and religions are born first from experience, so that though apocalypse provides a language that billions of people have applied to their own faith, the concept itself came from this history before the Common Era. During the generations when the Israelites ruled over their own kingdom in the Levant, which due to political turmoil later split into two separate states—Judea with its capital Jerusalem in the south and Israel with a capital of Samaria in the north—the religious conception of the end of days was largely undefined and inchoate. Eschatology is a way of thinking that doesn't make sense if there isn't yet a conception that reality itself can come to an end.

Among the rulers of Jerusalem, including kings like Solomon and David, as well as the priestly caste who performed rites within the massive limestone temple upon the Holy City's tallest mount, this was a land overflowing with milk and honey that was promised to the Hebrews if they upheld their covenant with the Lord. A conception of all of that coming to an end arguably relies on a tangible tragic experience, an intimation of apocalypse before there is the ability to speak of such a thing for the entire universe. The northern successor state of the once unified kingdom of Israel was the first to collapse, when 720 years before the Common Era the Neo-Assyrian ruler Sargon II invaded and deported thousands of women and men. Refugees streamed south to Judea to live among their coreligionists. In accounts of murder and pillaging, rape and destruction, the Israelites and their cousins had both experienced narratives of unfettered horror.

The unified book called the Bible is a historical fiction, the Hebrew Scriptures composed of some twenty-four individual books, written across a multitude of genres from epic to legal code, erotic poetry to philosophical dialogue, in the hands of thousands of different scribes, redacted together over the course of centuries into a quasi-cohesive whole.[2] There has been disagreement since the nineteenth century—when contemporary secular biblical scholarship was first established—on the exact contours and chronology by which this happened, but that scripture is a multi-threaded tapestry woven by many hands is beyond disagreement. Part of this process of composition began after the Neo-Assyrian destruction of Israel, as those survivors in Judea became involved in a project whereby their nations' respective foundational epics would be synthesized together into a revised work that would express the aspirations and beliefs of this newly combined people.[3]

Whoever was the actual Israelite author of certain portions from Genesis and Exodus, he (or she) has been designated by philologists and biblical scholars as the "Elohist" for their preferred name of God—"Elohim"—a plural word that roughly translates to "God" (or more accurately "gods"). Their Judean colleague, author of the oldest portions of Genesis and Exodus, is often known as the Yahwist, for her (or his) preferred name for the Lord being the unutterable tetragrammaton of Yahweh. Though some scholars would disagree with the description, the resultant books bear similarity to the poetic genre of epic, with David Alter in *The Art of Biblical Poetry* describing those features as including "an interplay of narration and dialogue, [where] the formal burden of the poetry is the telling of a traditional tale; and the narrative tempo is leisurely enough to allow for detailed descriptions of feasts, of hand-to-hand combat, even to some degree of the physical appearance of the actors, human and (for the most part) divine."[4] These two separate strains would be edited together into the version read today; contradictions (such as the two separate accounts of creation) were less important than the project of making a cohesive epic to reflect a cohesive state.

To Genesis and Exodus would be added three more books—Leviticus, Deuteronomy, and Numbers—along with two more potential writers and a "redactor" who is sometimes identified with the biblical prophet Ezra, at least according to proponents of the "Documentary Hypothesis" formulated by nineteenth-century secular scholars.[5] These five books, a complex interweaving of various narratives, traditions, and texts, constitute the central scripture of Judaism which is known as the Torah. Alongside the Torah are the texts known as Nevi'im, or those books of the prophets, and Ketuvim or "writings," which includes works like Ecclesiastes, Song of Songs, and Job. This is the corpus of texts which Jews call the Tanach (the name is an acronym from those three constitutive divisions). The exact ordering of these books wasn't decided upon by rabbinical authorities until the first or possibly the second century after the Common Era, when the introduction of the codex—the bibliographical term for what we think of as a "book"—led to the replacement of papyrus scrolls as the primary literary technology.[6] Suddenly a strict order for this canon became an intellectual possibility, one which had important religious implications. The early Christians, for example, placed the prophets last, which suggested a direct line between those men and Christ in the New Testament (also why, despite having a similar listing of contents, the Hebrew Scriptures and the Christian Old Testament are not identical).

In the context of the Hebrew Scriptures, the preponderance of apocalyptic thinking comes from the writings of the prophets. James L. Kugel explains in *The Bible as It Was* that "For centuries before the Babylonian exile, prophets had acted as divine spokesmen. . . . They were seen, quite literally, as messengers of God, and the messages they brought—words of rebuke and announcements of divine judgment and punishment, as well as messages of hope and divine encouragement or simply divine directives and commandments—compelled the attention of kings and commoners alike."[7] Apocalyptic thinking most often occurs in the writings of Isaiah, Jeremiah, Ezekiel, and then Daniel, who is included by Jews in Ketuvim but by Christians among the prophets. Both Isaiah and Jeremiah wrote before the Babylonian captivity, though large portions of the book of Isaiah were composed by somebody else after the historical events of the exile (however, there is scholarly disagreement on the exact chronology).[8] Speaking of the captivity, Isaiah (or somebody writing under that persona) declared in Isaiah 5:12 that "hell hath enlarged herself, and opened her mouth without measure," an invocation of how the dragon of apocalypse disorders the regular harmony of our material world, of how it pulls perdition up into our reality.

Among the prophets who engaged in apocalyptic thinking before the destruction of Jerusalem, the woeful narrative of the Israelites being conquered by the Neo-Assyrians provided a potent example and warning for potential destruction wrought as an act of divine punishment. Jeremiah in particular, descended from Israelites himself, warned that inequity and a turning away from the laws of the Covenant would doom Judea to God's wrath, for he foretold the destruction of the land by the Babylonians, which he lived to see, finally dying in exile while living in Egypt. "And I will prepare destroyers against thee, everyone with his weapons," it reads in Jeremiah 22:7–9, "and they shall cut down thy choice cedars, and cast them into the fire. And many nations shall pass by this city, and they shall say every man to his neighbor, wherefore hath the Lord done thus unto this great city? Then they shall answer, because they have forsaken the covenant of the Lord their God, and worshiped other gods, and served them."

Prophets are popularly understood as a type of soothsayer, a figure who tells the future. This is a woefully incomplete understanding of what a prophet actually is, for their primary vocation is to speak a moral truth to those in power. Jeremiah was able to see into the future, but his reasons for doing so were to warn the people and their rulers what the punishments for transgression would be. The prophet has lent his name to a genre of sermonizing known as the "Jeremiad," in which a speaker reminds his audience of the nation's or faith's highest values, while demanding that they live up to those principles lest disaster befall them. In the context of the book of Jeremiah, the prophet had spoken out against the pagan backsliding of the Judeans who increasingly embraced any number of practices from unbiblical ritual sacrifice to the worship of foreign deities, all in conflict with the strict belief in the single God. Because reforms were not made and because Judea was not purged of these sins, the Babylonians and their mad king Nebuchadnezzar were used as a tool of the Lord to punish His chosen people.

Thus, another theme of apocalyptic thinking, where a decadent and degenerated society suffers as a result of its own sin—as indeed had happened in the Genesis story of Noah, or with the incineration of those wicked cities of Sodom and Gomorrah. Quoting the Lord, Ezekiel 38:14 says that "On that day when my people Israel are dwelling in security, will you not know it? You will come from your place, from the remotest parts of the north, you and many peoples with you, all of them riding on horses, a great assembly, a vast army. Like clouds covering the land, you will come against my people Israel." The dragon is thus used as a beast of unforgiving justice. Ezekiel lived in exile by the Chebar River in Mesopotamia, and though the Judeans had yet to return to Jerusalem, the prophet foretold not only their restoration but also future persecution against them during the last days of the world's existence. Ezekiel is an incantatory, hallucinatory, almost psychedelic book; the prophet has visions of angels that look like wheels rotating within wheels covered in eyes and of deserts of dead bones resurrecting themselves.

A hallmark of apocalyptic writing is often this fevered, disturbing, and surreal assortment of strange images which appear as if they should be symbolic, but for which each interpretation is often illusive. "Within . . . were what looked like four living creatures," writes Ezekiel, and the "appearance of each one was like that of a human. Each one had four faces and four wings. Their feet were straight, and the soles of their feet like those of a calf, and they were shining like the glow of burnished copper." In this regard, Ezekiel's language anticipates future prophets like Daniel or John of Patmos. As Kugel notes, prophets like Ezekiel "were an intermediary in communications between God and humanity."[9] As the Lord is so totally alien, foreign, and other from our own experience, the sacred a vast gulf of distance away from the profane, there is a certain cracked sense that such visions would be so bizarre. Both the horror and trauma of the Neo-Assyrian destruction of Israel and the Babylonian conquering of Judea and the subsequent exile inculcated a certain experiential wisdom about destruction which was invaluable to the development of apocalyptic thinking, but it was from the Zoroastrianism of the liberating Persians that much of the subsequent cosmology would be adapted, perhaps as a mark of gratitude. Like almost all ancient peoples, the Jews believed in malevolent and demonic spirits who could affect and hurt people. The idea came from the Zoroastrians that there was a singular absolute evil responsible for all misfortune in the world, and that some future battle would have to be waged against that force.[10] Derived from the teachings of an enigmatic Persian prophet named Zarathustra, who most likely lived no later than a millennium before the Common Era, the ancient religion is arguably the origin of the most important tropes in the apocalyptic narrative, with scholar Mary Boyce arguing in *Zoroastrians: Their Religious Beliefs and Practices* that these doctrines have "probably had more influence on mankind, directly and indirectly, than any other single faith."[11] The Zoroastrians were cosmological dualists—they believed in two equally powerful gods—which clearly contradicted the strict monotheism of Judaism. In an important sense those who returned to Jerusalem were far more monotheistic than they had been before the exile, taking heed of Jeremiah's warning about backsliding. Reconciling evil with a monotheistic God has always been a difficult proposition, not just in Judaism, but for Christians and Muslims as well. Though the Jews didn't adopt the dualism of Zoroastrianism, some of the literary sense of that eternal conflict between good and evil found its way into Judaism, even if it was difficult to ever fully make consistent with belief in a singular omniscient, omnipotent, omnipresent, and omnibenevolent deity. Yet from Zarathustra—the most important historical figure of which the vast majority of people living today are unaware—came the basic script of good and evil confronting each other in a future world-ending battle.

The first time that Satan is referred to with the singular grammatical article is in the biblical book of Job, a sophisticated meditation on the subject of why evil things happen to good people, most likely composed after the end of the

Babylonian captivity.[12] Recounting a divine bet made between God and the devil as to whether the latter can tempt the righteous Job to curse the former if enough misfortune should befall him, the author refers to that wicked supernatural entity as *ha-Shaitan*—"the Adversary." Satan, however, is not yet the almost-deified being he'd appear as in works such as Revelation (indeed many references that were written earlier than Job, such as the serpent in Genesis, were retroactively interpreted as concerning him). By contrast, the Zoroastrians had long believed in a purely evil being that existed in tension with an entirely benevolent god. In temples where Zoroastrians practiced their rites, a holy fire would be tended which represented the benevolence of Ahura Mazda, the "Wise Lord" who creates and maintains existence.

Since the beginning of the universe, Ahura Mazda exists in conflict with Angra Mainyu, a destructive and evil force that's nearly the equal in power of the righteous god. "In the beginning there were two primal spirits," reads the Zoroastrian sacred text *Ahunavaiti Gatha*, "Twins spontaneously active, / These are the Good and the Evil, in thought, and in word, and in deed."[13] Such a dualism was anathema to the strictly monotheistic Jews adhering to the *Shema*, the credo that the "Lord is our God, the Lord is one," yet as belief in Satan evolved, especially within Christianity, it clearly owed something to the totalism of Angra Mainyu. Even while apocalyptic thinking was already in evidence in scriptures written before the exile, the Persian religion offered a fully detailed model of an epic future confrontation between the powers of good and evil, where, regardless of the suffering of the innocent and wicked alike, the final victory of righteousness was still assured. Known as *Frashokereti* by Zoroastrians, this purging at the end of the world signals a return to the purified state of nature before creation; it is a resetting of the proper equilibrium of existence—of the descent of the dove after the dragon has finished its task. The period of Frashokereti sees a battle between two respective representatives of Ahura Mazda and Angra Mainyu; the latter's son Azi Dahaka, associated with serpents and dragons, will be defeated by a figure known as the Saoshyant, "the one who brings benefit."[14]

Boyce describes Zoroastrianism's innovations as such—that there is a belief in a "supreme God who is the Creator; that an evil power exists which is opposed to him . . . that in its present state [the world] will have an end; that this end will be heralded by a cosmic Savior, who will help to bring it about . . . that at the end of time there will be a resurrection of the dead and a Last judgment . . . and that thereafter the kingdom of God will come upon earth."[15] Stripped of detail in this manner, the similarities to Judaism are remarkable; meanwhile the congruencies with Christianity are almost exact. Significant in the Jewish incorporation of Zoroastrian beliefs is Cyrus the Great, a figure that is spoken of as a redemptive liberator, a great advocate for the Jewish people despite his not being of the faith.

Within the Hebrew Scriptures, a certain title is used to honor him which translates to the "anointed one." That designation is applied to several biblical figures, including Solomon and David, but Cyrus is the only instance in which it is used to describe a gentile. Upon the end of the Babylonian captivity, the Jews would begin to develop a systemized understanding of the implications of this title, as would the Christians later on. As a concept, it would be intertwined with belief in the apocalypse. Before any of that, however, the anointed one who was Cyrus was simply called a "messiah" by the Jews.

There Shall Be a Time of Trouble

Ancient Jewish Apocalypticism

The Judean Desert is an alien landscape, other-worldly and desolate, punctuated with steep hills and deep valleys, honeycombed throughout with caves, the whole vista seemingly blasted of any vegetation, its sand the color of the sun at a summer day's height, when temperatures rise well above a hundred degrees. Even the water in the Dead Sea is salted. As Jewish and Christian conceptions of punishment developed over time—whether in the afterlife or at the end of time—they understandably drew upon the imagery of burning and brimstone, fire and heat which the Judean Desert inspires. Near the Qumran caves on the north shore of the Dead Sea, in what is today the Palestinian West Bank, such nightmares of perdition and apocalypse come easily. Winter is a more forgiving season, if no less forlorn, so late November of 1946 afforded a fifteen-year-old Bedouin shepherd named Muhammed edh-Dhib—affectionately nicknamed "The Wolf"—the opportunity to explore the caves which sat along the cliff faces of the desert. While herding goats through Qumran, the Wolf was joined by his cousin and a friend; along the sandy rock faces, the three observed a small entrance that appeared human-made. A rock was thrown inside; there was an echo. The cave of a dragon.

Inside, the boys found seven rough-hewn earthenware pots, each of which contained parchment fragments. Brittle, delicate, and fragile, the scrolls had characteristic, though illegible, Hebrew letters on them. Careful not to damage what they'd discovered, the Bedouins brought both the jars and their contents back to the encampment. After much debate on what to do with the scrolls, they decided to look for an antiquities trader in Bethlehem who might be interested in them. After finally finding a buyer, the shepherds sold the first fragments of the Dead Sea Scrolls for the equivalent of $325.[16]

The enormity of what had been discovered at Qumran would not be understood by the wider world for more than two years, when a biblical scholar working at the American Schools of Oriental Research became aware of their existence. Millar Burrows, a minister and scholar, released a press statement in

1948 informing the public of the "discovery in Palestine of the earliest known manuscript of the Book of Isaiah," as well as several other texts, including many from "some comparatively little-known sect or monastic order, possibly the Essenes."[17] Archeologists and Bedouin traders descended on the Qumran caves; over the next several years (and decades) twelve separate sites would be discovered that contained thousands of scroll fragments, largely written on goat vellum, but also on parchment and papyrus, which included not only portions of the earliest manuscripts from several books of the Hebrew Scriptures, but also apocryphal religious writings. The corpus was mostly in Hebrew and Aramaic, though some were in Greek, as well as a few Latin texts and a handful in an obscure Akkadian language called Nabatean. Many of these were totally unknown to scholars, including several ritual and theological texts by the mysterious Essenes.

After their return from exile, the Jews would develop among themselves a startling degree of intellectual diversity, what Melvin Konner describes in *Unsettled: An Anthropology of the Jews* as "a time of intense religious ferment."[18] As Solomon's Temple (now the largest building in the ancient Mediterranean) was rebuilt, a group named the Sadducees represented the interests and beliefs of the conservative elite responsible for the maintenance of the site. Drawing mostly from the priestly castes who were tasked with fulfilling Temple rituals, the Sadducees held to a straightforward interpretation of the Torah and had little interest in metaphysical speculation, including questions about the afterlife or the end of the world. By contrast, the Pharisees formulated a rich and democratic method of scriptural interpretation, as they began to develop the exegetical tools that would lead to the compilation of the Palestinian and Babylonian Talmuds, comprehensive collections of oral law that would become a central pillar of Judaism.

Despite how they're erroneously depicted by the authors of the New Testament, the Pharisees countenanced an open and non-dogmatic understanding of religious law that emphasized ethics as much as ritual. With the Pharisees, the center of Jewish life began to shift from the Temple to decentralized synagogues so that rabbis as teachers replaced the priests as authorities. The Essenes were radically different from the other two, neither elite nor democratic, but rather otherworldly and secretive, a monastic and ascetic community of contemplatives and mystics who were apocalyptic-minded and may have made their home near Qumran.

What Muhammed edh-Dhib had accidentally found was an Essene *Genizah*, a repository of frayed and decaying Jewish religious texts that are buried after they are unable to be used anymore—the equivalent of a book cemetery. Baked in the desert heat and preserved by the absence of moisture, the Dead Sea Scrolls pushed back the earliest known copies of multiple books of the Bible by more than a millennium, demonstrating in part the remarkable degree of consistency regarding the content of Scripture as it has been transmitted over the centuries. At the same time, more than half of the fragments found were from scrolls that had extrabiblical material that has helped further illuminate the beliefs of the Essenes. As with any such discovery, there is much scholarly disagreement on who composed the texts and when they were written; radiocarbon-dating technology used on linens that were found with the texts puts the earliest year of composition sometimes in the second century before the Common Era, though they may have been placed for safekeeping in the caves during the first century of the Common Era.[19]

Most biblical scholars do agree that the provenance of the Dead Sea Scrolls is from the Essenes, but there is far from uniform consensus on that conclusion. The presence of ritual baths known as *mikvahs* and of several sets of the phylacteries called *tefillin* definitively confirms a Jewish origin. They also provide an unparalleled glimpse into the worldview of a sect living in the centuries around the Common Era, when apocalypse couldn't help but appear to be coming from everywhere—first from the Greek-speaking Seleucid Empire who had conquered Judea after the return of the Jews to the Holy Land and then from the Romans who'd been requested to assist in the expulsion of the Seleucids.

From the fourth cave found at Qumran, a reading on the 521st fragment: the "heavens and the earth will listen to His Messiah, and none therein will stray from the commandments of the holy ones. . . . And He will glorify the pious on the throne of the eternal Kingdom. . . He who liberates the captives, restores sight to the blind, straightens the bent. . . . And the Lord will accomplish glorious things which have never been."[20] The fragment "A Messianic Apocalypse" was unknown to scholars before its discovery at Qumran, canonical to neither Jews nor Christians, but evidencing the roots of a type of eschatological thinking shared by both. What the nameless scribe of this scroll expresses is an example of a characteristic element of apocalyptic thought, that a human figure charged with a divine purpose will bring upon the earth what's later called a "millennial age," when after the conflicts at the end of history there will be a period of perfection. Apocalypticism such as this is explicitly political, where rather than accepting inequity, injustice, and persecution as perennial aspects of the status quo, such rhetoric imagines the possibility of overturning that order and establishing something new. Apocalypse is the mother of revolution. At Qumran dozens of apocalyptic writings were uncovered, some canonical works such as Isaiah and Ezekiel, others newly found, like "A Messianic Apocalypse" or "The Renewed Earth," which promised the "earth so that there will be no more guilt in the land."[21]

What the Essenes yearned for—along with other Jews and eventually Christians—was the restoration of an imagined, perfect kingdom on earth after all evil had been burnt away by the Lord through the actions of his chosen messiah. In other words, an epoch of the dove. Anathea E. Portier-Young argues in

Apocalypse Against Empire: Theologies of Resistance in Early Judaism that "Empire claimed the power to order the world. It exercised this power through force, but also through propaganda and ideology. Empire manipulated and co-opted hegemonic social institutions to express and reinforce its values and cosmology."[22] Apocalypse's utility announced itself first when the Neo-Assyrians dispersed the Israelites; it matured with the Babylonian captivity of the Jews; and then with oppression from the Seleucids and later the Romans it reached a critical necessity. "Resisting imperial domination required challenging not only the physical means of coercion, but also empire's claims about knowledge and the world," Portier-Young writes, concluding that the "first Jewish apocalypses emerged as a literature of resistance."[23]

Depending on when the Dead Sea Scrolls were deposited in the Qumran caves, resistance may have been personally, tangibly, and physically on the minds of the Essenes. A large contingent of biblical scholars has argued that the texts were moved into the cave in the first century of the Common Era during the ill-fated First Jewish–Roman War of 66 CE, in which a radical political contingent known as the Zealots, among others, tried to expel the Romans who occupied Judea, but which resulted in almost the entire destruction of Jerusalem and of the Temple some four years after the war started. "Most of the victims were peaceful citizens, weak and unarmed, butchered whenever they were caught," writes Flavius Josephus, both a Jew and a Roman citizen, in his first-century *History of the Jewish War*. "Round the Altar the heaps of corpses grew higher and higher, while down the Sanctuary steps poured a river of blood and the bodies of those killed at the top slithered to the bottom."[24] Jerusalem had been defended by around 10,000 Zealots, but even after a valiant struggle, by July all hope perished as the future Roman emperor Titus breached the walls of the city with a much larger contingent of soldiers, taking fire to its walls and stealing the treasures of the Temple, including religious objects kept in the central room known as the Holy of Holies which was only in the purview of the priests. The Temple's massive menorah was paraded through the streets of triumphant Rome along with a thousand enslaved Jews, later memorialized on a still-extant monumental column built in honor of Titus. For the second time in their history the Jews had been expelled from Judea, and again the beginning of this diaspora necessitated adaptations in religious observance. The Sadducees' positions made little sense in a world without the Temple, which had been the focus of Jewish ritual observance in both of its manifestations, so as it developed, rabbinic Judaism replaced the geographical specificity of previous worship with a more abstract and universal faith based in the study of the Torah. The Bible effectively became the new Temple for these survivors of the war. Christians, by contrast, who during the earliest days of their sect had also worshiped in the Temple alongside their fellow Jews, more fully replaced the idea of the Temple with the idea of Christ himself. Though both Jews and Christians shared numerous religious texts, how they interpreted them was radically different. Central to the apocalyptic beliefs of both Jews and Christians—who'd undergone something that was very near to apocalypse in the first century during the First Jewish–Roman War—was the biblical book of Daniel, the oldest extant manuscript which was hidden in a Qumran cave. Daniel is arguably the most significant and influential of apocalyptic texts in the Hebrew Scriptures. Composed some two centuries before the Common Era, the narrative takes place during the Babylonian captivity and involves the strange visions of its titular prophet, visions that are pregnant with symbolic and allegorical import. Now that exile was once again the condition of the Jews, Daniel offered apocalyptic hope and warning about the new world to be reborn, a synthesis of both the dragon and the dove.

A divinator as much as a prophet, Daniel is gifted with the ability to interpret dreams, and is called upon by the Babylonian king Nebuchadnezzar who has been troubled by disturbing nightmares. Daniel's is a narrative-heavy book, with accounts of the prophet's persecution at the hands of Nebuchadnezzar as well as the favor which is granted to him because of his visionary gifts, but it's specifically his interpretation of the king's dreams as they relate to predictions about future history that is enduring. "There shall be a time of trouble," as the prophet explains. In the second chapter of Daniel, it is written how the king has rejected the counsel of his Chaldean advisers, the priests of Babylon, fearing that they will merely be obsequious.

As a test, Nebuchadnezzar explains to Daniel that he will only trust the prophet's interpretation if it can be offered without the dream first being recounted. God imparts to Daniel a description of the king's dream and its interpretation. "Thou . . . sawest, and behold a great image," Daniel says in 2:31–32, "This image's head was of fine gold, his breast and his arms of silver, his belly and thighs of brass, his legs of iron, his feet part of iron and part of clay." Drawing from Greek divisions of history, both Daniel and subsequent exegetes have understood each segment of this metal idol as a stand-in for a historical empire. Written long after the actual end of the Babylonian captivity during the oppressive reign of the Seleucids, it's been argued that the author of Daniel would have interpreted the golden head as signifying Babylon, the silver arms and chest the Medians, the belly of brass the Persians, and the iron and clay extremities the Seleucid Greeks.[25] Nebuchadnezzar's dream is of a monstrous statue dedicated to the glories of temporal magnificence and power, but then the king "sawest till that a stone was cut without hands, which smote the image upon his feet . . . and brake them to pieces." The ruins of the statue "became like the chaff of the summer threshing floors; and the wind carried them away, that no place was found for them: and the stone that smote the image because a great mountain and filled the whole earth."[26]

Both Nebuchadnezzar's dream and Daniel's reading are disquieting, but it's the enigmatic stone which is the hope, this divine pebble which crushes the vanities of man, a grace from God, the Messiah of Zion. As soon as the Romans supplanted the Seleucids the earliest interpretation of Daniel was immediately rendered moot, but a convenience of cryptic apocalyptic rhetoric is that it's endlessly variable in identifying who any of those four kingdoms could be—indeed the proper identity of the stone. Later, Daniel has his own dream to consider. "And four great beasts came up from the sea, diverse from one another," reads Daniel 7:3. The prophet has been imparted a terrifying visage, the "first was like a lion, and had eagle's wings," while the second was "like to a bear, and it raised up itself on one side, and it had three ribs in the mouth of it between the teeth of it: and they said thus unto it, Arise, devour much flesh." A third beast was "like a leopard, which had upon the back of it four wings of a fowl; the beast had also four heads; and dominion was given to it." Finally, after this "I saw in the night visions, and behold a fourth beast, dreadful and strong exceedingly; and it had great iron teeth: it devoured and brake in pieces and stamped the residue with the feet of it: and it was diverse from all the beasts that were before it."[27]

More visceral and upsetting than Nebuchadnezzar's dream, again each one of the four monsters was and has been interpreted as a historical and oppressive kingdom, with the final beast indicative of some future and uniquely terrible empire. Finally, as with the stone that smashes the idol, Daniel is given vision of the "Ancient of days . . . whose garment was white as snow, and the hair of his head like the pure wool: his throne was like the fiery flame, and his wheel as burning fire." After God's "judgment was set, and the book were opened . . . even till the beast was slain, and his body destroyed, and given to the burning flame."[28]

Daniel concludes by prophesizing about the coming rule of the "Son of man," of a liberatory figure endowed with divine sanction who overthrows the oppressive regimes of the world and institutes an earthly heaven based upon righteousness and justice. Like Ezekiel before him, Daniel's imagery is disturbing and hermetic, yet precisely because its symbolism can be yoked to any current events, it is scripture which has long endured in the wider culture. Who or what this final beast is supposed to be has historically been a question of grave importance. The author of Daniel may have thought that it represented the Seleucids, but later Jews and Christians alike saw it as the Romans, while during the Reformation Protestants thought that it was the Catholic Church and in the twentieth century some evangelicals variously associated it with Nazi Germany or the Soviet Union.[29]

Just as important is who the stone is supposed to be, this Son of Man. Messianic thinking is obviously present in Christianity, but it has had an importance in Judaism for two millennia as well, albeit the significance of such a figure differs widely. As Christianity developed following the destruction of the Temple, Christ as messiah was made equivalent with God through the complex Trinitarian theologies that developed over the first three centuries of the Common Era. Within Judaism, however, the messiah could never be elevated to that sort of primacy, for it would be a violation of the strict monotheism that defined the faith. Rather the Messiah—the "anointed one"—was effectively a political and military leader bringing liberation more than redemption, yet still imbued with a mystical sense of God's grandeur. Gershom Scholem writes in *The Messianic Idea in Judaism: And Other Essays on Jewish Spirituality* that "Judaism, in all of its forms and manifestations, has always maintained a concept of redemption as an event which takes place publicly, on the stage of history and within the community. It is an occurrence which takes place in the visible world and which cannot be conceived apart from such a visible appearance."[30] When the stone is thrown, all can see it.

Messianism has had a conflicted history within Judaism, not merely because of Christian persecution of Jews, but because there have been a multitude of figures who've emerged that such messianic hopes have been projected onto. Apocalypticism and messianism are both fonts of political and theological will; they inspire belief in emancipation, but they can also engender dangerous expectations (as well as zealotry). In the second century of the Common Era, the conquered Jews of what the Romans had renamed Palestine invested their aspiration for independence in a hot-headed general named Simon bar Kokhba, among one of the most popular messianic claimants to have emerged within Judaism. During the Third Jewish–Roman War, bar Kokhba led a brutal resistance campaign whereby an independent Judea was reestablished for four short years from 132 until 136.[31] So triumphant were bar Kokhba's successes that the famed Rabbi Akiva heralded him as the long-waited-for messiah, a stone thrown by God directly at the clay feet of Rome. His title of "bar Kokhba" was bestowed by Akiva—it means "Son of the Star."

In the new Judea, preparations were made to rebuild the Temple, a state was reestablished, currency was even minted. Rome poured so much blood and money into maintaining its foothold in the Levant that legions were pulled from the imperial periphery; the empire's over-extension allowed the Celtic chieftain Boudica her opportunity to burn down Londinium. But just as the revolt of the Britons would be squashed, so too would the rebellion of the Jews, at hideous cost. Emperor Hadrian expended all of his resources on reconquering Judea, so that by the end of the war the historian Cassius Dio records that 580,000 Jews had perished, one of whom was bar Kokhba himself, felled during a siege at Betar.[32] Within the Jerusalem Talmud, he would be renamed "bar Kusiba"—son of deception. At a cave in the Judean Desert not unlike those at Qumran, twentieth-century archeologists discovered the corpses of forty women, men, and children murdered by the Romans during the bar Kokhba rebellion. The archeologists would call this the "Cave of Horror."

CHAPTER TWO

Hell Followed with Him

Early Christianity and the Church Fathers

The Broken Seals

Early Christian Apocalypticism

A BREEZE OFF the Aegean, fragrant groves of lemon and olive trees, the gentle and warm currents between Patmos and the mainland of Asia Minor: Before the pagan oracles went mute, Patmos was believed to be a sunken island which was brought to the surface of the Aegean by the intercession of the goddess Artemis, who had convinced her father Zeus to perform such a feat.[1] By the last decade of the first century of the Common Era, Patmos was just another unimportant outcrop of the Roman Empire. An island of Mediterranean pleasure, this small and rocky outpost of Greece is separated by only a narrow band of sea from modern-day Turkey, yet before the first century came to an end this was where a pseudonymous Christian prophet named John had the most influential nightmares of apocalypse which have ever been rendered. Exiled to Patmos during the anti-Christian persecutions of the emperor Domitian, John had a vision of the end of days within one of the island's caves, later writing a letter to seven different communities of Christians in Asia Minor to inform them of the "Revelation of Jesus Christ, which God gave unto him, to shew unto his servants things which must shortly come to pass."

Revelation's composition is dated to around 95, so that John's visions happened twenty-five years after Vespasian and Trajan's destruction of Jerusalem's Temple, twenty-seven years after the suicide of the brutal Emperor Nero who had violently persecuted Christians, and some six decades following the crucifixion of this apocalyptic cult's messiah.[2] Since the days of Christ, his followers had assumed that the world's end was approaching quickly, so that whatever had compelled John into exile on Patmos seemed to confirm those beliefs. Had John been in Rome some thirty years before his visions, he may have been witness to Nero's brutality, when Tacitus records in his *Histories* that the faithful were "thrown to the beasts, crucified, and . . . burned alive."[3] The Sibylline Oracles had predicted that Nero had faked his death and that the emperor would return to Rome and rule with unimaginable cruelty.[4] John put great stock in the mystical significance of numbers, using the Jewish numerological tradition of gematria to parse congruencies and coincidences. For example, the name "Nero" appears nowhere in John's account, yet when each letter of the emperor's name in either Aramaic or Hebrew is converted into the proper corresponding number a rather auspicious result is rendered. "Let him that hath understanding count the number of the beast," as is written in Revelation 13:18, "for it is the number of a man; and his number is six hundred and sixty-six."[5] Born four years after Christ was crucified, Nero would model the template for a very different type of being—the antichrist.

Because the author of the New Testament's final book was named John, early Christian Church Fathers assumed that he was Christ's apostle and the man responsible for the fourth gospel. As a result, that incantatory and surreal book of Revelation was largely considered to be a canonical work of scripture. This was a seminal accident. Modern scholarship has reached consensus that John the gospel writer and John the revelator were entirely two different people, with neither of them being the same as the apostle.[6] As a result of this error, Revelation became the single most influential work of eschatological prophecy ever written, inspiring millennial movements and apocalyptic cults, inculcating both fear and desire, obsession and madness. As Elaine Pagels writes in *Revelations: Visions, Prophecy, and Politics in the Book of Revelation*, this text attributed to a man named John is the "strangest book in the Bible—and the most controversial," a set of passages rejecting both conventional narrative and even moral instruction in favor of "visions—dreams and nightmares."[7] That those involved in the process of deciding what would be canonical or not happened to include Revelation because of that error is, upon consideration, rather remarkable.

Consensus was hardly universal even during the period of Revelation's canonization; officials like Dionysius, bishop of Alexandria, the church fathers, Eusebius, and Cyril of Jerusalem, had varying degrees of certainty concerning the book's inspired nature.[8] Even for nonspecialists, a cursory reading of John's Gospel and the Book of Revelation will evidence just how different the narrative and rhetoric is between these texts. Where the gospel is erudite, philosophical, and elegant, Revelation is fevered, psychedelic, and hallucinatory. The author of the gospel was well versed in Neoplatonist philosophy, his Greek is subtle, nuanced, and complex. John the Revelator, by comparison, writes in a fiery pitch, his metaphors pushed to the extreme, his allusions unclear, his imagery frequently terrifying.

Revelation is the only work of apocalypse considered canonical in Christianity, and his forerunners of Isaiah, Ezekiel, Zechariah, and Daniel provide the narrative and rhetorical impetus for his poetic imagination, but he suggests the Hebrew Scriptures far more than he quotes them. The result is idiosyncratic, unique, and singular. Yet despite any misgivings those theologians involved with codifying the scripture of the faith might have had, it appears that by the ecclesiastical Council of Rome in 381, Revelation would be officially considered part of the New Testament. Ever since, it has had a complex and ambiguous relationship with Christianity.

John of Patmos's prose is obscure, hermetic, and occult, so that Christianity has long had an uncomfortable relationship to this final book of Scripture, even while it's also had a profound influence. As a representative example of John's rhetoric, consider Revelation 6:12–13 wherein "there was a great earthquake; and the sun became black as sackcloth of hair, and the moon became as blood; And the stars of heaven fell unto the earth, even as a fig tree casteth her untimely figs, when she is shaken of a mighty wind." Despite Revelation's often frenetic and wild tone, it would be wrong to dismiss the book as lacking complexity—quite the opposite. Where the Gospel of John might be erudite, Revelation is baroque to the point of incomprehension, a morass of complex interlocking plots, bizarre personages, events, and imagery which seems symbolic of some deeply personal inner language.

This subjective quality hasn't prevented divinators and would-be prophets from attempting to interpret contemporary events through Patmos's eccentric rhetoric. That "prophecy" is so often conflated with simply predicting the future, and apocalypse with the end of the world, is in large part due to Revelation, where both of those things happen to be what that book is concerned with. Apocalypse more broadly refers to any unveiling, any initiation into divine secrets—it just so happens that those divine secrets of John concerned the end of days, that "God had revealed . . . the future course of events, in which he was soon to overthrow the forces of evil and establish his Kingdom on earth," as Bart Ehrman writes in *Jesus: Apocalyptic Prophets of the New Millennium*.[9]

While the John who wrote Revelation is not the same person who wrote the gospel, it's fairly clear that, like all of the authors of the New Testament (with the exception of Luke), he was ethnically Jewish. Furthermore, the scribe of Patmos had a singularly Jewish religious conception that is relatively free of the influence of Greek philosophy. "Putting it bluntly," writes John W. Marshall in *Parables of War: Reading John's Jewish Apocalypse*, Revelation "is a Jewish and not a Christian document."[10] As radical as Marshall's interpretation might be, it does underscore the complexities of religious designation in the first century, where even the mention of "Christ" might not be a "sufficient criterion for positing a 'Christianity.'"[11] From Revelation's distinctly Jewish "throne mysticism" that perseverates on God's monarchical palace to the literal belief in the physical resurrection of the dead, John's apocalypse bears hallmarks of first-century Jewish thought. If not an adherent of what was developing into rabbinic Judaism, then it seems not unlikely that John may have been a member of an extinct sect called the Ebionites, Jews who recognized Christ as a distinctly Jewish messiah rather than the incarnated God and who rejected other Christians' abnegation of Levitical law. Regardless of the specificity of John's own religious commitments, his apocalypse is deeply involved with the Jewish tradition of eschatology, a work that though written in Greece owes far more to Jerusalem than Athens. Though in the tradition of Daniel and Ezekiel, *what* exactly the narrative of Revelation is can be difficult to ascertain. Within its pages the sun turns dark and the rivers become red, stars fall from the sky and fire rains down, but how we're supposed to understand these omens—whether they're real or not—is ambiguous. Following John's addresses to the seven churches in Asia Minor (all of which seem to recognize his authority), we're told of his encounter with God in the Lord's throne room, where seals are broken on seven different divine scrolls, each of which contains a prophecy regarding the apocalypse. A number of natural disasters are described, including earthquakes, eclipses, storms, pandemics, and something which sounds almost like an asteroid. We are told of a final confrontation between Christ and Satan, the latter of whom rules over the earth for a period of time through the power of his son the Beast, even while the ultimate defeat of evil is preordained.

John predicts a thousand-year period of earthly peace and perfection known as the millennium, but whether Christ returns to inaugurate that epoch or just arrives at its conclusion is a matter of theological disagreement that had a profound impact on later Christian history. The question of whether Revelation is to be read as allegorical or historical, as predicting an actual future or describing spiritual transformations, has been at the crux interpretations of the text for two millennia, and John himself isn't helpful in deciding how the book is supposed to be interpreted. "We might easily grasp a sign, a simile, or an allegory," writes David L. Barr in his contribution to *The Oxford Handbook of the Book of Revelation*, but "symbols and metaphors grasp us."[12] This is to say that Revelation is arguably still spoken of precisely *because* it's hard to interpret, *because* its symbols are ever shifting, and *because* John offers a nightmare panoply of invented archetypes that prove enduring twenty centuries later.

Drawing from Zechariah, John describes the infamous four horsemen of the apocalypse who bring with them war, pestilence, famine, and death. Then there is the enigmatic and alluring Whore of Babylon, a "woman drunken with the blood of the saints, and with the blood of the martyrs." Satan makes his appearance as the "great red dragon, having seven heads and ten horns, and seven crowns upon his heads," and in a text so overdetermined with numerology the repetition of these numbers has long held important if widely varying implications. Gog and Magog are mentioned, these eastern armies which clash at Armageddon during the apocalyptic conflagration leading up to millennium having been associated with widely varying militaries in history.

Such disparate images have proven to be enduring, in part, because their mysteriousness generates disquiet and terror as well as fascination. For being a book that has so often engendered literalist enthusiasms about being able to tell the future, few biblical texts are quite as symbolically obscure, with its descriptions of seven-eyed, seven-horned sheep and dragons arising out of the sea. Biblical inerrantists may hold that John's prophecies are binding, but only a madman would believe that these passages describe something literal. The book itself is an ever-shifting collection of obscure poetic tropes and images that can be ever fit to the circumstances in which the Scripture itself is being read. Depending on theological, hermeneutical, and exegetical inclinations, these images have been read as signifying historical personages in John's own era, as being obscure allegorical tropes for spiritual truths, or as encoded symbols predicting future events.

Consider the "antichrist," a term which appears nowhere in Revelation though he is very much alluded to, with that title being rather mentioned in the First and Second Epistle of John, another text misattributed to the gospel author. The transition from "antichrists" to "antichrist" was not dissimilar to the way "messiah" moved from being a designation for an exemplary leader touched by God, to a chief liberator, to God incarnate Himself. When used in earlier instances, the spirit of antichrist seems to be whatever or whoever stands in opposition to the church, but coming out of a reading of Revelation, the figure began to be understood as the polar opposite of the messiah, as he who shall oversee the tribulations of apocalypse, as the Son of Satan. The spirit of the dragon made incarnate. Shades of Zoroastrianism, since God must be balanced with the devil. As the Lord has a Son, so too must Lucifer—whatever the attributed monotheism of Christianity might technically countenance. Bernard McGinn, author of *Anti-Christ: Two Hundred Years of Human Fascination with Evil*, explains in an interview with *Cabinet* magazine how "Just as Christ is the savior and the ideal model for humanity, his last opponent will be a single figure in whom all evil becomes concentrated,"[13] so that the correct identification of just who this figure will be becomes important to those who believe Revelation describes events which have not yet happened.

Throughout the past two millennia any variety of people have been associated with the antichrist by their opponents. During the Reformation, Protestants made it a mainstay of their rhetoric to accuse whoever happened to be the pope as being the antichrist and the Vatican returned the favor, with Martin Luther, John Calvin, and Henry VIII occasionally being slandered as this manifestation of all evil. Approaching modernity, variously Robespierre and Napoleon, Bismarck and Kaiser Wilhelm have been fingered as such. Adolph Hitler, Joseph Stalin, Saddam Hussein, and Osama bin Ladin have all been feared as being the Beast of Revelation.[14] The role remains the same, but new actors are always auditioning for the part.

From Nero to Vladimir Putin, cruelty, terror, and evil have been persistent to the human narrative. So much of what John describes in Revelation doesn't need to wait for some distant future—it's already happened. It's already happening.

The four horsemen are harbingers of war, pestilence, famine, and death, but surely it must be observed that there has never been a period of complete peace in human history, that pandemic and plague have always taken lives, that bellies are always aching somewhere, and that death remains the only assured destination for all of us. Revelation isn't just about the future, it's also about the present; it isn't just abstract, it's also concrete; it's not just eccentric, but also individual; it's not just allegorical, but also autobiographical. Whoever John was, whatever traumas he'd experienced, his book was a reaction to the degradation, oppression, and persecution of those who worshiped like him. If Revelation is a book of poetry, it's specifically a volume of *political* poetry. Theologian Elisabeth Schüssler argues in *Revelation: Vision of a Just World* that John's scripture must be read in its "sociopolitical context as a canonical prototype and as a utopian language resource for illuminating present situations of suffering and injustice."[15] That is to say that Patmos wasn't just concerned with the dragon, but with the dove as well.

Indeed, part of the genius of Revelation is that it gives us a potent rhetoric for discussing inequity, injustice, and inhumanity in the form of the Beast, and the great red dragon, and the antichrist. John also gives us a vocabulary of redemptive hope, of the world made shining and new, of equity, justice, and humanity. The revelator has visions of the "New Jerusalem," this "bride, and wife of the lamb," a golden, crystalline, gleaming metropolis which descends from the heavens and where goodness and righteousness "shall reign forever and ever." To dismiss such language as a children's fable would be a perilous mistake, for we need not take Revelation literally to see the impact of such a narrative in a society which took hierarchy for granted, which assumed that wealth, and strength, and power were what defined right. As with the Hebrew prophets who came before, John of Patmos was integral in honing an understanding of the world which didn't only give injustice a name, but could conceive of it being defeated. The ability to imagine the defeat of injustice wasn't merely an abstraction for people, as the coming centuries of darkness would demonstrate.

The Eclipse of Antiquity

Apocalypticism at the End of the Classical World

In 410, the Visigoth commander Alaric breached the walls of the eternal city, Rome. Despite the capital of the western portion of the empire having been moved north to Ravenna years before, when the Visigoths laid siege to Rome it was still home to a little under a million people, by far the largest city in the world. Encircled by the wagons of the pagan king, the Romans slowly starved as disease ran rampant. All four of Revelation's horsemen were at their gates. So dire was the situation within what had once been the most powerful, the most feared, and the most honored city on earth, that the pope countenanced the resumption of pagan rituals to placate the Visigoths, such practices having dwindled after the unprecedented conversion of the empire to Christianity in 325 during the rule of the emperor Constantine. If such a conversion was to show God's favor upon the empire that had once so fully persecuted those who were faithful to Him, it wasn't in evidence as Alaric battered at Rome's walls. As the Visigoths sacked Rome, they indulged in a frenzy of pillaging, vandalism, rape, and murder. Thousands of Romans were kidnapped and sold into slavery, including the sister of the emperor. Churches and mausoleums were profaned, while treasures and relics were stolen by the marauding army.[16]

Three years later, the church father St. Jerome, translating the Hebrew, Aramaic, and Greek of the Bible into the Latin of his Vulgate from the safety of his perch in that auspicious city of Bethlehem, would remark of Alaric's sack that the "world sinks into ruin.... The renowned city, the capital of the Roman Empire, is swallowed up in one tremendous fire."[17] For those awaiting the apocalypse, it must have often seemed as if it had already arrived.

Rome wouldn't fall for another sixty-six years, when the final emperor, Romulus Augustulus, was deposed by the Germanic conqueror Odoacer who refashioned himself as the King of Italy. All of this is a bit simplistic, obviously, for the eastern portion of the empire credibly endured for another millennium in the form of the Byzantines, who rightly thought of themselves as a continuation of Rome, and even on the Italian Peninsula there were shifting power allegiances that placed regions under the jurisdiction of Constantinople.

Arguments that Rome never fell, however, can be overly precious, for it's true that during the fifth and sixth centuries Europe experienced profound changes that resulted in mass death, disease, and poverty, as well as the breakdown of basic services that had defined the relatively high standard of living within the empire. John Kelly gives an overview of these shocking demographic shifts as late antiquity transitioned into the early Middle Ages in his book *The Great Mortality*, explaining that "In the second and third centuries, Roman Europe had 50 to 70 million people; by 700, Europe had 25 to 26 million people."[18] The population of the eternal city itself fell from over a million people at its height to under 20,000 by the year 800. He explains that, by the ninth century, dense woodland had reclaimed almost 80 percent of Europe, and connections to much of the wider world in Africa and Asia were effectively closed off. Even the still-powerful, sophisticated, and cosmopolitan Byzantines didn't survive unscathed, with possibly half of the capital of Constantinople perishing in the sixth century from what is remembered as "Justinian's Plague."

Prior to the most catastrophic stigmata of collapse, a fifth-century chronicler named Orosius would note that, in the "middle of the debris of great cities, only scattered groups of wretched peoples, witnesses to past calamities, still attest to the names of earlier ages."[19] Debates about the causes of this decline are legion, though few today subscribe to the eighteenth-century historian Edward Gibbon's contention that the adoption of Christianity was responsible. Imperial overextension, political and cultural disunity, government corruption, disease and ecological calamity, or some combination of all of these features, surely played a part.

As regards Christianity, if anything, the enduring social, political, and cultural networks of the church helped preserve classical literature, philosophy, and science as the empire began its eclipse. A historiographical emphasis on all that's different between the ancient world and the medieval serves to obscure the deep continuities which thread between these arbitrarily designated eras. Yet it's hard not to believe that the shrinking of Rome's borders, the removal of imperial legions from the periphery of the empire, and the sheer population drop in cities like Rome must have clearly felt to many like the end of the world, because in an obvious sense it was.

If apocalypticism became an enduring feature of medieval thought, it comes out of the experience of those who actually lived through a fall and decline. During the first few centuries of the Common Era, when theologians and church fathers, bishops and popes, disputed over the parameters of Christian theology, a fully-fledged eschatology emerged with answers to what the day of judgment would be like, but in many ways this sense of the apocalyptic is bookended by two catastrophic events that haunted the emotional register of Western apocalypticism. The first event was the responsibility of Rome and the latter event was what happened to Rome. The empire's fall, at some diffuse point in the late fifth and into the sixth century, was the concluding touchstone to Christendom's development of eschatology, but the spark for apocalypticism in both Christianity and Judaism happened some four centuries earlier with the Roman destruction of the Temple. From that horror would come an intimation of apocalypse on earth, the flames from Solomon's temple provided visions to Christian priests and Jewish rabbis alike, as those religions evolved in response to that conflagration while fully developing a number of interpretations of the world's end. Before the Temple would be destroyed, however, Christianity was already based in the profoundly apocalyptic preaching of the man from whom the faith derives its very name. Jesus Christ's primary concern was apocalypse. His followers expected the world's end to come while Christ was alive, then they expected it after his crucifixion and supposed resurrection. All of them anticipated that the apocalypse would happen within their own lifetimes. Ehrman writes that "Jesus is best understood as a first-century Jewish apocalypticist . . . [who] fully expected that the history of world as we know it . . . was going to come to a screeching halt, that God was soon going to intervene in the affairs of the world, overthrow the forces of evil in a cosmic act of judgement, destroy huge masses of humanity, and abolish existing human political and religious institutions."[20] Deeply conversant in the Hebrew Scriptures and fully and completely a first-century Jew, Christ's own storehouse of poetry and imagery was derived from the apocalyptic traditions of the prophets. "Think not that I am come to send peace on earth," Christ says in Matthew 10:34, "I came not to send peace, but a sword." Christ understood himself as both dove and dragon.

During his own ministry Christ made repeated declarations that the apocalypse was approaching. Foreseeing a time when "Nation shall rise against nation, and kingdom against kingdom," Christ looks upon the mighty walls of Jerusalem's Temple and in Luke 21:6 predicts that "days will come, in the which there shall not be left one stone upon another, that shall not be thrown down," though of course the fact that such an account was written after the Temple itself had been razed should be considered in any judicious accounting. Even more terrifying, recalling both Isaiah and prefiguring Revelation, is the so-called "Olivet Discourse" (because it was delivered on the Mount of Olives) which appears in the three synoptic gospels of Mark, Matthew, and Luke. Christ warns of pestilence, plague, and war, of persecution and false prophets, of forthcoming days of unthinkable tribulation. He intones in Mark 13:24–30 that the "sun shall be darkened, and the moon shall not give her light, and the stars of heaven shall fall, and the powers that are in heaven shall be shaken. . . . Verily I say unto you, that this generation shall not pass, till all these things be done. Heaven and earth shall pass away: but my words shall not pass away." Read literally, Christ seems to be saying that those gathered around him on the Mount of Olives will actually see these things, but as the world did not end in the first century, Christianity had to adapt the official interpretation, in the same way that it had to grapple with the reality of a crucified messiah.

Christian eschatology, in all of its variation and complexity, is an attempt to answer that conundrum, the question of whether Christ was speaking of something that was to literally occur in the future or rather of an invisible and spiritual unveiling. The church fathers, that assortment of theologians who established Christian theology in the first half of the first millennium, had a multitude of approaches when confronting this issue. Tertullian, for example, understands Revelation's promise as being literal, writing in *Against Marcion* that a "kingdom is promised to us on the earth . . . a thousand years in the divinely built city of Jerusalem."[21] By contrast, the seminal North African theologian Augustine rejected the idea that apocalypse was imminent or that Christ's preaching or John's vision refer to a physical transformation, rather arguing that Revelation was an allegory concerning the redemptive sacrifice of Christ, the passing of the old covenant into the new. Such a position is known as *amillennialism* and is historically the dominant eschatology in the Roman Catholic Church, as well as the Orthodox Church and among most Magisterial Protestants, but it's not the only view concerning the apocalypse.

Still another variation is seen in Origen, a theologian who also read Revelation as allegorical, affirming that the apocalypse would herald the redemption of every soul—including Satan—in a final event known as the apocatastasis.[22] There are premillennial adherents, who hold that Christ will return to inaugurate a period of perfection on earth, postmillennialists who maintain that Christ will arrive after that period of perfection, and amillennialists such as Augustine's who understand Revelation as referring to a spiritual transformation, with numerous gradations to all of these perspectives. In addition, there are preterists who believe that Revelation depicts things which have already happened, futurists who understand it to be a work foretelling that which is to come, and idealists who read the text as entirely symbolic. All of these approaches, whether explicitly stated or not, demand that the Christian reconcile Christ's promise of an incipient apocalypse with the visible reality that the world is still here two thousand years later.

Both Christianity and Judaism had to grapple with the destruction of the Temple. Christians repositioned Christ as a divine replacement for that sacred site in Jerusalem, while rabbinic Judaism transformed the Torah into a textual Temple. Between the sack of Jerusalem and then the sack of Rome a veritable science of apocalypse would develop. Historically, a shameful position of supersessionism has underscored Christianity, the position that the church has replaced the Jews in their covenant with God.[23] Even while liberalizing reforms have officially eliminated that line of thinking in many denominations, the popular fallacy which configures the relationship between the two faiths as being a simple issue of Judaism being "older" and Christianity being "newer" still endures. While such a reduction both flatters and denigrates those religions in some measure—Judaism can be understood either as the more authentic position or an archaism, Christianity as progressive or as a neophyte upstart—the reality is far more complicated and interesting.

There is an undeniable historical connection between rabbinic Judaism and the priestly faith of the Temple, but both Judaism and Christianity developed through the aftereffects of Jerusalem's destruction at the same historical juncture. Judaism and Christianity are religions of the post-Temple; they evolved because of the impact of that apocalyptic event, existing in a mutually reciprocal relationship that responded to many of the same issues. Chief among the similar processes these religions underwent during the first few centuries of the Common Era was deciding what scripture was official and what the correct order of organizing the individual books of Scripture should be. This development was a function of bibliographical technology, for the Romans had introduced the codex—basically our modern form of the book—as a convenient replacement for unwieldy scrolls. For the Romans this was an issue of convenience in their own governmental, military, and financial recordkeeping, but for Jews and Christians it soon became a way of structuring holy text into something more cohesive.

Suddenly, the individual scrolls of each book of what would be organized into the Bible required authorities to impose a coherence onto the unruly books of Scripture. There are wide divergences on lists of "official" Scripture as compiled by various church fathers in the earliest centuries of Christianity, with some later canonical books left off and some now heterodox texts included; a similar phenomenon is noted in Judaism. By the late first century, however, a gathering of rabbis at the Council of Jamnia largely confirmed tradition regarding canonical texts, deciding on the proper order of these works in the Hebrew Scriptures; in 382, the Council of Rome convened by Pope Damasus established the Christian ordering and canonicity for the books of the Old Testament and of the New.

Arguments would continue to define differences between individual sects and denominations, but the overall narrative of these two respective versions of the Bible were largely complete by the time Alaric called on Rome. Within the Hebrew Scriptures, apocalypse would have a central presence in prophetic works like Daniel, Isaiah, and Ezekiel, while in the New Testament Revelation just barely found acceptance, despite Christ's own eschatological perspective. What's clear is that however they developed in subsequent centuries, both faiths were heavily influenced by an apocalypticism that has lurked in the margins of these religions, sometimes appearing in dramatic ways. "What this meant," writes Diarmaid MacCulloch, "was that from now on there was a large literature of books excluded from the mainstream, both Jewish and Christian in origin, taking the form of 'Gospels,' 'Apocalypses,' 'Acts' and the like."[24]

Many of these apocryphal texts received quasi-official sanction as supplementary material to the Bible, but of the hundreds of works of unofficial scripture, some of the most engaging are those deemed heretical and suppressed. Early Christianity was a profoundly diverse and at times anarchic assemblage of beliefs, many of which bear little similarity to the faith as it later developed. Chief among these competing groups are the evocative and mysterious Gnostics, who themselves weren't a unified group belonging to a single denomination so much as an assemblage of complicated and contradictory sects. As a contested umbrella term, "Gnosticism" includes a variety of exotic groups such as the Valentinians, Marcionites, Sethite-Barbeloites, and so on. What all of these various Gnostics emphasized, regardless of which individual cult is being considered, was a belief that the fallen world was the creation of a lesser god known as the Demiurge (who was given various proper names) and that the real God was transcendent of this universe and didn't intercede in its affairs. Coupled with this cosmology was a conception of the material world itself as being an evil product of the Demiurge.[25]

Unlike orthodox Christianity, Gnosticism was a mystery cult that emphasized hidden knowledge available only to its initiates, so that hermetic and occult wisdom was integral to the soul's ascension. Explicitly mystical, the Gnostics were obsessed with the visions and unveilings that define the genre of apocalyptic writing. While no scholar would argue that Revelation was a Gnostic text—it's written too early for one thing—the symbolism, the confusing imagery, and the emphasis on mystical vision are reminiscent of latter apocryphal scripture. Walter Schmithals writes in *The Apocalyptic Movement* that in both orthodox apocalyptic thinking and Gnosticism "salvation lies outside the world . . . outside the course of the world."[26] What any apocalyptic thinking shares is a preference for secret knowledge, an attraction toward encoded predictions, complex metaphors, baroque symbolism.

Consider *The Apocalypse of Adam*, just one of the numerous apocryphal Gnostic scriptures discovered at Nag Hamadi in Egypt in 1945, a few years before the uncovering of the Dead Sea Scrolls and arguably the more important of these two events. The anonymous author of the text, who purports to be the first man, recounts the story of creation to his son Seth some seven centuries after Eden, yet this Adam's story bears little similarity to the account in Genesis. In the Gnostic version, the name of the Demiurge who created the first couple was Yaldabaoth, a malevolent being who imprisoned human souls in matter and was long identified and worshiped as the God of the Jews and orthodox Christians.

Yet Adam prophesizes that an "illuminator of knowledge" shall arrive in the future to liberate the children of man from the machinations of Yaldabaoth, not through faith, grace, or works, but by recourse to secret mystical knowledge that shall bind the Demiurge. "Then the peoples will cry out with a great voice, saying, 'Blessed is the soul of those men because they have known God with a knowledge of the truth! They shall live forever, because they have not been corrupted . . . but they have stood in his presence in a knowledge of God like light that has come forth from fire and blood," says the author of *The Apocalypse of Adam*.[27] Not much will be familiar in Gnosticism to the conventional Christian, and yet, like a countermelody, both heresy and orthodoxy desire that that which is hidden shall one day be revealed, that the secrets of millennium will become apparent at the end of the world as the dragon makes way for the dove. For both the Gnostic and the Christian, "apocalypse" remains an unveiling.

CHAPTER THREE

The First Millennium Approaches

Islam and Christianity in the Early Middle Ages

Awaiting the Mahdi

Apocalypticism in Islam

FOR THE UNBELIEVER, there are a variety of hypotheses as to the origins of the *al-Hajaru al-Aswad*, the irregularly shaped Black Stone of about six inches in length that has been set and reset into concrete and silver over the centuries. With its flecks of red and yellow and white, it has been conjectured that the Black Stone is a volcanic agate, an assemblage of various minerals compressed by heat and time into this object held in reverence today by nearly two billion people. Others have proffered that the Black Stone is some kind of natural glass, formed elsewhere and brought to the city of Mecca millennia ago, when this distant desert trading post at the eastern corner of Arabia was famed for the trade in leather and camel butter as much as for holiness.[1]

By far the most commonly attributed theory of the Black Stone's origins, at least among those that don't hold it as sacred, is that it's a remnant of celestial detritus that remained after the formation of the solar system billions of years ago, a rocky meteorite that fell to earth and has been winnowed down into the small object set into a corner of the canvas-covered sanctuary of the Kaaba within Mecca's Grand Mosque, the location to which Muslims direct their prayers five times a day, the most sacred point of geography in the universe.[2] This last theory, whatever its merits may be (there have been increasing doubts), bears the most similarity to a popular belief in Islam, which holds that the Black Stone crashed from the sky so as to demonstrate for Adam and Eve where Allah wanted his first and greatest temple to be constructed.

Regardless of where the Black Stone came from—heaven or the heavens—it was a focus of worship before the prophet Muhammad instructed the first Muslims to pray in its direction, long held in regard by the Arab pagans who gathered in Mecca to venerate their gods and to purchase and sell the goods which made the city wealthy. "Black stones that descended from heaven were not restricted to Mecca," writes Aziz Al-Azmeh in *The Emergence of Islam in Late Antiquity: Allah and His People*. He continues, "The Greeks, classical and late antique, knew and venerated these celestial aerolites, as did the Phrygians, the Phoenicians and the Emessians."[3]

Just as Judaism and Christianity grew from the rich soil of Levantine paganism, so too was Islam born out of the context of Arab polytheism, though Muhammad claimed that his purging of the Kaaba of any relationship to gods other than Allah was restoration rather than revolution. "The Meccan Black Stone was clearly inhabited by a preternatural power, and still is," writes Al-Azmeh.[4] There is something appropriately apocalyptic in the idea that the Black Stone is either a fragment of an asteroid or a sign sent to the first couple, since, whether natural or supernatural, the relic is nonetheless associated with the disruption of the normal order, with signs and portents that are the vernacular of what Muslims call *Qiyamah*, or judgment day. The Black Stone is thus a connection between the transcendent and the immanent, a portal between the sacred and the profane, where Allah's divinity is inscribed into the quotidian materiality of a rock. Apocalypse is written in the poetry of the heavens, but experienced in the prose of lived reality, where something as normal as a stone is enchanted with the magnificence and terror of God. There is an allegorical *hadith*, the genre of narratives about Muhammad collected by his followers after the prophet's death, which holds that the "al-Hajaru al-Aswad will appear at the Qiyamah with eyes to see and a tongue to speak, and give evidence in favor of all who kissed it in true devotion, but speak out against whoever indulged in gossip or profane conversations."[5]

Just as Islam shares Judaism and Christianity's monotheism, so too is it also an apocalyptic religion, the first Quranic Surah of Muhammad's revelation as translated by Yusef Ali reading "In the name of Allah, Most Gracious, Most Merciful. Praise be to Allah, the Cherisher and Sustainer of the worlds; Most Gracious, Most Merciful; Master of the Day of Judgement." According to the Qur'an, the holy scripture of Islam that was divinely imparted over several years to the prophet as he held vigil in a cave outside of Mecca, the first appearance of the Archangel Jibril (or Gabriel as he is known in the West) came to Muhammad in the year 610. As a profoundly textual faith, it was the delivery of the Qur'an itself which is understood as the most awesome of Allah's miracles. Such immaculate Arabic poetry recited by the illiterate Muhammad was lyrical evidence of divinity. Where both the Hebrew Scriptures and the Christian Bible were written and edited by dozens of authors over the course of centuries, the Qur'an was compiled by a single man over the course of a few years.

In a manner far more similar to the Jews' relationship to the Torah than the Christians' relationship to Christ, the Qur'an was understood as the mystical basis for reality itself, with the translator M. A. S. Abdel Haleem writing in the introduction to his English version that the "entire religious life of the Muslim world is built around the text of the Qur'an." Another aspect of what's striking about Muhammad's tenure—indeed part of what feels so miraculous about his life—is the sheer *rapidity* of Islam's stunning success. The time between

Muhammad's initial revelation to the prophets conquering of the entire Arabian Peninsula was only a mere twenty-two years. The first major political manifestation of the *ummah*, the universal community of Muslims established by Muhammad, was the Rashidun caliphate, and by the end of the seventh century it stretched from Morocco to India. In Muhammad there is a figure who, with his combination of the timeless and the temporal, is as if Jesus Christ and Emperor Constantine were combined into one. For Christians, Islamic victories were interpreted not as evidence of God's favor, but of something else, and this understanding of the new faith would have apocalyptic consequences in the subsequent millennium.

A bit more than a century after the toppling of Romulus Augustulus in far-off Rome, the dawn of Islam provides a convenient break between late antiquity and the very beginnings of the Middle Ages, though such periodization is always arbitrary. Still, it's hard not to see in Muhammad's example a decisive rupture with what came before; this prophet who must be listed alongside Abraham, Moses, and the pharaoh Akhenaten as among the most radical and successful of monotheists to ever promulgate his creed. Karen Armstrong writes in *Muhammad: A Prophet for Our Time* that he "was not trying to impose religious orthodoxy—he was not much interested in metaphysics—but to change people's hearts and minds," waging a "tireless campaign against greed, injustice, and arrogance,"[6] particularly against the avarice of the Meccan ruling class within his own Quraysh tribe.

Fundamentally a moral reformer, Muhammad's revelation of the Qur'an was clearly both inspired by the example of Jewish and Christian communities who had settled in the Arabian Desert, as well as internal changes within Arabic polytheism which had increasingly gravitated toward a religious understanding of one God being primary above the rest, a similar course of evolution that had taken place within Canaanite Judaism thousands of years before. In its earliest history, the Kaaba was consecrated for the veneration of 360 gods worshiped by the nomadic Nabateans, a deity for each day of the lunar calendar. By the time of Muhammad's youth, the Kaaba was reserved for a primary deity known as "Allah," whose name simply translates to "God." There had been suspicion among many of the Arabs even before the revelation of Islam that this Allah was the same God worshiped by the Jews and Christians, and indeed the history of the Kaaba couldn't be disentangled from those faiths, tradition having associated the temple's construction with the patriarch Abraham and his son Ishmael, the latter long considered the father of the Arabs.[7] Upon Muhammad's triumphant yet peaceful reentry into the city of his youth in 630, a little less than a decade after having been exiled from Mecca due to his judgment of the ruling classes, the prophet purged the Kaaba of all of its idols, transforming it as a temple for Allah, preserving only images of Maryam and Isa—the Virgin Mary and Jesus. At the core of Muhammad's teaching was the elegant and parsimonious *Shahada*, the creed which holds that there is no god but Allah. Similar to the Jewish statement of faith known as the *Shema*, Muhammad's declaration of the singularity and oneness of God is referred to as *tawhid*, an unsparing and consistent dogma of absolute monotheism that broaches no division in Allah. To the *Shahada* can be added four other pillars of Islam, including *Salah*, or the proscribed five daily prayers; *Zakat*, or almsgiving to the poor; *Sawm*, or the daytime fasting during the holy month of Ramadan; and *Hajj*, or the pilgrimage to the Kaaba during the final month of the lunar calendar, required of all Muslims at least once in their life. Initially Muhammad had required the direction of *Salah* to be toward Jerusalem, but following the defeat of Mecca, the prophet required Muslims to redirect their supplications toward the Kaaba, thus simultaneously solidifying Islam as a faith with an Arabic origin, as well as avoiding undue deference toward the Byzantine Empire, which governed that Levantine city.

Like rabbinic Judaism, Islam was a religion concerned more with questions of behavior than belief, so that at the same time that church councils were parsing the finer points of Christ's relationship to the Holy Spirit or the nature of the Second Person of the Trinity's dual human–divine natures, Muslims were establishing a complex legal framework that extended to the social and political spheres. Despite metaphysics being of less interest to Muhammad than ethics, the Qur'an was still enmeshed in apocalyptic thought, and indeed it had been eschatological passages in the holy book that had occasioned the early Muslims' flight from Mecca to Medina, after the ruling Quraysh grew impatient at the prophet's denunciations of their immorality.

"When the sky bursts open, obeying its Lord as it must, and when the earth is flattened out, and ejects all its contents and becomes empty, obeying its Lord as it must, surely you will all be judged," reads the qur'anic chapter which is known as *Al-Inshiqaq* or "The Sundering," Muhammad in the guise of both the dragon and the dove, just like Christ. Fully a third of the Qur'an is apocalyptic in nature, or apocalyptic-adjacent, and it was the so-called Meccan Surahs such as *Al-Inshiqaq* that were responsible for Muhammad's running afoul of the ruling elites in his home city.[8] Organized roughly from the longest to the shortest, the Surahs of the Qur'an are divided between the Meccan chapters and the Medinan chapters based on where Muhammad received his revelation, the later Surahs dated from the time after the prophet and his earliest followers were forced into exile from Mecca, before their triumphant return and establishment of a government in what would become Islam's holiest city. "And as for those who are given their record 'in their left hand' from behind their backs," reads Mustafa Khattab's translation of *Al-Inshiqaq*, "they will cry for instant destruction, and will burn in the blazing Fire. For they used to be prideful among their people, thinking they would never return to Allah."

Muhammad's apocalypticism is in part the result of his uncompromising monotheism; denouncing anyone who values wealth, or prestige, or power higher than Allah as being guilty of *Shirk* or idolatry. Just as the Hebrew prophets and Christ used apocalypticism as a means of denouncing injustice and envisioning a more perfect world, so too did Muhammad. Todd Lawson in *The Quran, Epic and Apocalypse* describes Muhammad's dogma as "more than mere theology, but a 'modernity' that challenged the entrenched social and cultural mores of his time and place."[9] And just as the prophets from Ezekiel to Elijah recorded that the experience of theophany, of being visited by an angel as a manifestation of the Lord, was a terrifying experience, so too were Muhammad's revelations painful and disquieting. Blinding headaches and uncontrollable nausea, epileptic fits and quivering shakes, the appearance of Gabriel to Muhammad was entirely commensurate with the sublimity of being in the presence of the divine, that unveiling of those things which are ultimate and final.

Those details of Muhammad's biography are largely drawn from the Hadith, the collection of methodically sourced accounts of his life gathered in the two centuries after his death, intended to supply a deeper understanding of both the prophet and his prophecy. "There are striking similarities between the Christian and Quranic descriptions of the Apocalypse, the Last Judgement, and the paradise awaiting those who have been saved," writes Reza Aslan in *No God But God: The Origins, Evolution and Future of Islam*. "These similarities do not necessarily contradict the Muslim belief that the Quran was divinely revealed," argues Aslan, "but they do indicate that the Quranic vision of the Last Days may have been revealed to the pagan Arabs through a set of symbols and metaphors with which they were already familiar, thanks in some part to the wide spread of Christianity in the region."[10] Most of these eschatological details are found in the Hadith, which offers an extensive account of the day of judgment and elaborates on those Surahs of the Qur'an which are concerned with the apocalypse.[11]

True to the radical upending of political, economic, social, cultural, and religious hierarchies which the apocalypse has promised since the days of the Hebrew prophets, one of the six volumes of Hadith entitled *Sahih al-Bukhari* records that "On the Day of Resurrection Allah will hold the whole earth and fold the heaven with His right hand and say, 'I am the King: where are the kings of the earth?'" Similar to the chronology offered in Revelation, the Hadith maintains that the *Qiyamah* will be preceded by a great battle known as *Al-Malhama Al-Kubra* in which, after facing a common foe, Islamic and Christian armies will clash, with the victorious Muslims conquering Constantinople (an event which happened in the fifteenth century). After this victory, there shall be a Great Tribulation, a time of apostasy, heresy, and blasphemy. Into this godless epoch shall emerge a figure known as the Mahdi, a direct descendant of Muhammad who is a paragon of holiness and piety, occupying a position not unlike that of the messiah in Judaism. First establishing dominion over the earth, the Mahdi suffers military losses whereby he and the Muslims who have sworn allegiance to his rule must retreat back to only Mecca and Medina.[12]

During this period, the Mahdi is opposed by an infernal figure known as Al-Masih ad-Dajjal. Roughly similar to the antichrist, the Dajjal will be a miracle-working false prophet commandeering the impious as his followers, a one-eyed apostate from the east whose head is marked with the Arabic letters that spell out *"Kafir"*—"Unbeliever."[13] The Dajjal will be defeated by Isa, the second most important prophet of Islam who is better known in the West as Jesus. Following Jesus's vanquishing of the Dajjal, he will pray alongside the Mahdi who will restore Allah's dominion over the earth, with the *Qiyamah* following.

Muhammad's followers didn't conceive of the apocalypse as some distant, abstract concept, but rather as a narrative which described their own experiences in a tumultuous age. "The Qur'an is eschatology in action, not in the future," writes Stephen J. Shoemaker in *The Apocalypse of Empire: Imperial Eschatology in Late Antiquity and Early Islam*, "the Hour was already arriving even as the community was expanding."[14] Perhaps to Muhammad and the generation which followed, their astounding military victories appeared providential, as a portent that this was indeed the last and greatest of prophecies that subsumed and explicated all of that which came before. Shoemaker writes that "there was no need to explain how the world would come to an end when one was living out the Hour's arrival on a daily basis, expecting the conclusion of history at any moment."[15]

No religion has ever been so successful that quickly, as Islam propagated not just monotheism but also that prophetic sense of the apocalyptic. Like all other major world religions, Islam would experience convulsions and division, notably between the Shia and Sunni branches as they emerged shortly after the prophet's death. In addition to schism, however, Islam would also see the caliphates of the Umayyads and the Abbasids, of Cordova and the Ottomans, as well as of a Golden Age that would ensure the survival of much of the classical learning that had disappeared in Europe's late antiquity. As Islam moved across Arabia into Northern Africa and the Iberian Peninsula, Central Asia and the Indian Subcontinent, then ultimately downward through Southeast Asia and Indonesia, belief in monotheism spread further than it ever had before. Varieties of what's known as Oriental Christianity had long proliferated in many of those regions, as well as the now extinct but once widespread Neo-Zoroastrian faith known as Manicheanism, which perhaps ensured that qur'anic teachings about the apocalypse were more acceptable to the inhabitants of those regions.

But as Islam spread further than either of those religions by the end of the millennium, the faith was arguably even more responsible for introducing large portions of the globe to that irresistible belief which holds that history has a preordained shape, a narrative with a beginning, middle, and end, with prescribed characters who will act out a divine plan before the world itself is ruptured by an event that upends all of that which came before. Apocalypse was arguably as radical and innovative a belief as monotheism, both allowing us to measure our hope for the future and our pain in the present, but a combustible faith either way, a doctrine of both dove and dragon—equally gift and curse.

Anticipating the Year 1000

Millennialism at the Turn of the Millennium

Deep in chill Northumbria, not far from that wall of granite that centuries before had delineated the northernmost boundary of the Roman Empire that was built by the order of Hadrian, a monk named Bede at the Monastery of St. Peter put quill to vellum and forever changed the very years by which we mark our calendar. Descendant of the only recently Christianized Angles, Saxons, Jutes, and Frisians who had sometimes migrated and sometimes violently invaded the former colony of Britannia, Bede recounted his ancestors' stories in *An Ecclesiastical History of the English People*. Tonsured and berobed, Bede would have spent hours in the dim candlelight of St. Peter's scriptorium scratching away at tanned and stretched goat hide, providing his account of the once pagan tribes that had come to supplant the Romanized Celts. "The present life of man," Bede wrote, "seems to me, in comparison of that time which us unknown to us, like to the swift flight of a sparrow through the room. . . . So this life of man appears for a short space, but of what went before, or what is to follow, we are utterly ignorant."[16]

Arguably the most learned cleric in what was becoming England (the only native Anglo-Saxon to be declared a "Doctor of the Church"), Bede made it his religious vocation to illuminate a bit of that unknown time, of the epochs that both preceded him and which would stretch out until Doomsday. An expert in not just history, but also pedagogy and tidal variation, astronomy and Latin poetry, hagiography and calendrical calculation, Bede was deeply involved with the Synod of Whitby in which the English church was reconciled to the Roman Catholic Church over issues of the proper calculation of Easter's annual date, no small issue.[17] E. G. Richards writes in *Mapping Time: The Calendar and Its History* that Bede's "apparently pedantic attitude . . . stemmed from his belief that the terrible pillaging and massacres instigated by bloodthirsty tribal kings, which had become endemic in England after the last Roman legions had left, could be curbed only by uniting all men behind a common set of Christian beliefs."[18] Bede completed his history in the year 446 after the reign of the emperor Diocletian, or the Third Regnal Year of the reign of the Northumbrian King Ceolwulf, but as the monk rather reimagined it, 731 Anno Domini. That is, some seven centuries, three decades, and a year after Christ's incarnation.

If Bede began work on his history in the fifth century, then by the vagaries and contingencies of the calendar he ended it in the eighth, dispatching of that hodgepodge of calendars that dated from this or that Roman consul or tribal chieftain in favor of reorienting time itself around the Son of God. So influential was this reordering of the cosmos that by the ninth century (AD) a Swiss monk with the fantastic name Notker the Stammerer would say that "God, the orderer of natures, who raised the Sun from the East on the fourth day of Creation, in the sixth day of the world has made Bede rise from the West as a new Sun to illuminate the whole Earth."[19] Bede didn't invent Anno Domini, but he's crucial in its final proliferation.

The innovation of marking the twelve months of each year in the Julian Calendar from a first year set at the Nativity of Christ can be traced back to a Scythian monk named Dionysius Exigus who lived in a corner of the Byzantine Empire that today is in Romania. While working on the Paschal calculations that properly decided when Easter would be celebrated, Dionysius rejected the convention of dating years from the rule of Diocletian, an emperor notorious for his persecutions of Christians. Dionysius reset the beginning of the solar twelve-month Julian calendar to the year of Christ's birth, naming his system the Latin for "Year of the Lord," so that if the monk started this task in 240, he ended it in 525.[20] Bede was so taken with this innovation that he posthumously gave Dionysius the honorific of "Abbot," despite the monk having never led a monastery. Through a circuitous network of teacher to student, Anno Domini migrated from *An Ecclesiastical History of the English People* into actual calendars. David Ewing Duncan writes in *Calendar: Humanity's Epic Struggle to Determine a True and Accurate Year* that Bede's book was "found in over a hundred libraries and collections of medieval manuscripts across Europe, attesting to its popularity. No comparable scientific work was written about time and the calendar in the Latin world until . . . almost five centuries later."[21] Otherwise, the biggest shift in calendars would be the halting replacement of the Julian Calendar with the Gregorian from the sixteenth through the twentieth century, where the difference is some thirteen days accounting for slight astronomical errors, but the axis of the whole system remained Anno Domini.

Bede's student Ecgbert would become the archbishop of York and the latter's student Alcuin moved to the Kingdom of the Franks, where he would become a favored scholar in the court of Charlemagne, who then oversaw a respite in the early Middle Ages which would be memorialized as the Carolingian Renaissance. Within that heady environment, Alcuin introduced the Anno Domini system into official court documents, though even the papacy didn't universally avail themselves of it until the eleventh century, meaning that for large portions of the populace approaching the year 1000—which before the common use of Arabic numerals would have been the year M—there would be no awareness that the millennium was ending at all.[22]

Apocalypticism doesn't require calendars, but calendars imply apocalypticism. Finality is built into the mathematical progression of the calendar, as years end, decades end, centuries end, so that it suggests time itself shall end. Though New Year's Day is an arbitrary construction denoting the shift from one calendar year to another, there is a bit of the apocalyptic in the connotations of change and transformation that attend the human-measured progression of time. Though Revelation specifies periods of time, from hours to months, there are no exact dates anywhere in the text, which is also true for the writings of the Hebrew prophets and the Qur'an. Vagueness serves the allegorical and the strategic; the first because it elevates the eschatological from the unseemly realm of mere prediction and the latter because when the world inevitably doesn't end, scripture itself isn't doomed to obsolescence. Cycles within epicycles, orbs within orbs, the progression of seconds into minutes, hours into days, weeks into months, years into decades, centuries into millennia—all have a clockwork precision in which certain dates are charged with numerological significance.

Drawn from rigorous astronomical observations, the science of calendrical calculation serves estimably practical concerns—agricultural tables for planting and harvesting, governmental and ecclesiastical recordkeeping—as well as situating these profane affairs within a realm transcendent and sacred, making individual human stories mere chapters in an epic of eternity as the years accumulate on toward either infinity or finality. "Our obsession with measuring time is itself timeless," writes Duncan. "After self-awareness, it may be our most distinctive trait as a species, since undoubtedly one of the first things we became self-aware about was our own mortality—the fact that we live and die in a set period of time."[23]

Zoroastrian apocalypticism, as filtered first through Judaism, Christianity, and Islam, rejected the cyclical models of time that had predominated in the pagan world. As a result, so did the Jewish and Islamic lunar calendars, dated as they are from respectively the creation of the world and Muhammad's flight from Mecca. Though neither the Hebrew Scriptures, the New Testament, nor the Qur'an are ever specific with the dates for judgment day, that hasn't stopped theologians and magicians, saints and mystics, from drawing upon the skeleton evidence in Scripture to try and pinpoint the date of apocalypse with some accuracy. Often the reasoning itself is implicit within the favored calendars used by these respective faiths. Revelation makes clear that Christ will rule for a millennium, a period of a thousand years, and this has sometimes been proffered as an explanation as to the eschatological mania that consumed Europe in the year 1000 (which is more urban legend than fact), but the New Testament is never clear on *which* millennium marks Christ's return, or that it should correspond to the calendar's millennium.

Within Christian history there was perhaps some fear surrounding the year 1000; there's a bit more evidence for mania in anticipation of the year 1500 in a

Europe right at the verge of Reformation; there was trepidation surrounding the ominous date of 1666; and as many may recall the year 2000 was met in some quarters with an impending feeling of the apocalyptic.[24] The Jewish calendar is based on an *Anno Mundi* convention, marking years off from the supposed creation of the earth, and because of the Kabbalistic tradition which holds that a single day of God's life is as if a thousand years to us, some have reasoned that the year 6000 will signal the end of the Lord's week of creation, with the seventh millennium ushering in a paradisical era (in the Gregorian Calendar this will commence in 2240).[25]

Central to apocalypticism, in all of its varieties, are theories of time. Duncan describes that much of how we describe time—its beginnings and ends, or by contrast its cyclicalism—draws upon spatial metaphors. A clock goes round and round in a circle, and indeed tomorrow's 3 p.m. will by definition always be twenty-four hours after today's, *ad Infinium*. Dates are more singular; even though it will never again be April 25, 2022, it will be April 25 again and again, even after the earth has stopped spinning and the sun has engulfed our orbit, for it's a simple matter of mechanical precision in terms of how calendars march forward on a never-ending line. In their mathematical regularity, calendars naturally attract a desire for many to try and calculate last things, to predict what day the world will end. These calendars are born from cultural models of time, but understandings of time also generate calendars. If Western eschatology has generally hewed toward a model of linear narrative from creation unto apocalypse, with the details to be sorted out by the various scriptures, religions, theologies, and denominations, then other cosmologies have differing conceptions of how past, present, and future operate, though often conflagrations that appear very similar to Armageddon are featured in these mythologies.

The complex Hindu Yuga cycle, for example, posits a series of four ages—each an astounding 4,320,000 years in length—which repeat over and over throughout the infinite age of the universe. Beginning with the Krita Yuga, a paradisical time of enchantment and connection with the gods, the cycle moves through the Treta and Dvapara Yugas, both progressively degenerated, until culminating in our current epoch of the Kali Yuga, when humanity is most distant from our divine origins, and iniquity and wickedness reach their fullest power and extent.[26] "Covetousness and avarice will overwhelm them all," reads the Hindu holy text the Mahabharata, and "wedded to avarice and wrath and ignorance and lust men will entertain animosities towards one another."[27] Our corrupted age will finally be brought to a termination by Kalki, the tenth incarnation of the god Vishnu, a messianic figure who abolishes the Kali Yuga and inaugurates a new Krita Yuga, thus beginning the entire cosmic rotation again, though we're still more than 400,000 years away from that predicted event according to most accounts. As the Mahabharata promises, the "destruction and re-birth of all things at the end of the Yuga, is, indeed, fully of wonder!"[28]

With antecedents that most likely go back much further, the Mahabharata's final form was completed around the fourth century, the same era in which both Judaism and Christianity were finalizing their canons and their apocalyptic scriptures, an eschatological congruence stretching from the Indus River to the Tiber.[29] The apocalypse spoken of in Revelation is a unique event, but despite its singularity it lacks the sheer scope of Hindu eschatology, where even within cycles the years which are dealt with aren't mere millennia, but millennia upon millennia, with the Yuga cycle inserted into even more baroque systems of millions of reoccurring years. Wendy Doniger writes in *The Hindus: An Alternative History* that the Yugas allow for the "idea that time is both linear and cyclical,"[30] a model of how history operates that conforms to our own experience, the continual movement of seasons overlaid on the inevitable birth, growth, and decline of a human life.

Another non-Western cyclical calendar is the Mesoamerican Long Count Calendar, which shared a similarly epic scope to the Yugas, and whose earliest antecedents go back to five centuries before the Common Era. Both complex and ingenious in its accuracy, this pre-Columbian calendar was mathematically a combination of both a base-twenty and a base-eighteen system that merged two annual calendars known as the 260-day Tzolk'in and the 365-day Haab.[31] By synthesizing the Tzolk'in and the Haab, the Long Count Calendar was intended to have a cosmic scale in charting the passage of particular eras, for, as F. Kent Reilly III writes in his contribution to Deborah L. Nicholes and Christopher Poole's collection *The Oxford Handbook of Mesoamerican Archeology*, there was an "importance of a complex religious calendar to these state cults . . . both historical and mythic . . . to specific cycles of time."[32]

Structured around thirteen long periods of time known as *b'ak'tuns*, the Long Count Calendar, invented by the Olmecs though primarily associated with the Mayans, charted the cycle of these periods from the creation of the world, which they believed occurred on the equivalent of August 11, 3114 BCE. Affirming that this process is ever-cyclical, the Mayans maintained that we were in the fourth turning of this particular iteration of the Long Count Calendar, with the thirteenth and final *b'ak'tun* ending on the Gregorian equivalent of December 21, 2012. Rather predictably, a panoply of occultists, spiritualists, and other New Age enthusiasts interpreted the ending of the thirteenth *b'ak'tun* as apocalyptic, even while scholars of Mesoamerican antiquity emphasized that it was fallacious to project onto Mayan belief something which so clearly mimicked Christian theology. While it's arguable whether or not the Mayans invested the completion of this cycle with anything that could be understood as cataclysmic in the same manner as the day of judgment, they clearly didn't interpret it as being a finality either way, rather seeing in the endless turning of this wheel something that mirrors creation itself, what their holy text of the Popol Vuh describes as "when all is silent and placid. All is silent and calm. Hushed and empty is the womb of the sky." A millennial promise, a kingdom of the dove.

Archetypal narratives about a once-Edenic past degenerating into our current, fallen epoch were also common in the literature of ancient Greece and Rome. From the Greek poet Hesiod's mythological compendium of the seventh-century BCE *Works and Days* is derived the schema known as the "Ages of Man." Hesiod describes civilization's movement through five successive eras; a Golden Age, a Silver Age, a Bronze Age, a Heroic Age, and his own final Iron Age. Tim Whitmarsh explains in *Ancient Greek Literature* that the purpose of Hesiod's story is to "express humanity's descent from its former state of godlike happiness to the suffering and immorality of the present."[33] In a manner evocative of the four Yugas, Hesiod writes of this primogeniture epoch whereby people "lived like gods without sorrow of heart, remote and free from toil and grief."[34] Following that was the Silver Age, inhabited by a degenerated race who, though still living in what we'd consider to be a utopian environment, had declined from their ancestors in the previous generation. The Bronze Age was defined by humans who were "terrible and strong," who loved the "lamentable works of... violence."[35] With the Heroic Age, Hesiod imagines an improvement from the subsequent era, this being the period in which much of the Greek myths are set, populated by a "god-like race of hero-men who are called demi-gods, the race before our own, throughout the boundless earth." Finally, Hesiod placed himself in the fallen Iron Age, which like the Kali Yuga or the thirteenth *b'ak'tun* is the most degenerated of epochs, when "men never rest from labor and sorrow by day, and from perishing by night; and the gods shall lay sore trouble upon them."[36]

Works and Days may bear some similarity in its "Ages of Man" to the four Yugas of the Mahabharata, but it even more clearly seems to map onto Daniel's prophetic dream from the Hebrew Scriptures, particularly in the conflation of ages and empires with particular metals. *Works and Days'* "eschatology," if it can be called that, isn't necessarily meant to be taken literally, but as Whitmarsh notes the "relationship between past and present is complex: the two are linked in terms of cultural continuity, and severed in terms of quality."[37] Hesiod writes not in *logos*, but *mythos*, arguably true of the Mahabharata and Daniel as well. Whether or not there is an influence between two or all three of these different visions, or if they're indicative of something deep and primordial in the universal human psyche, is impossible to know. Nevertheless, this master cosmic narrative of a pristine and perfected past that slowly descends into our own unpleasant present is a plot with an enduring popularity, a convenient mythopoeic telling of why our world happens to be the way that it is.

It would be reductive to claim that the ancient Greek readers of Hesiod understood *Works and Days* to be metaphorical while readers of Revelation interpreted it to be making actual predictions about the future. There were and are partisans of both allegory and literalism in every culture, religion, faith, and tradition. A utility to apocalyptic language, such as Hesiod's account of decline and fall, is that it provides a potent rhetoric of our experience, it elevates the profane realm of life into an eternal domain of the sacred. Just as Dionysus and Bede reoriented all of history around the seminal metaphysical event of the incarnation, so too do the varied systems of the Hindus, the Mayans, or the Greeks do something similar. Calendars are often central in this process, the mathematical precision and rigor of these complex systems yoked to a lyrical concern with ultimate things. In our own calendar, with its months named after Roman emperors and our days of the week after Germanic gods, there is a liturgy of regularity, a counting of the weeks like beads on a rosary.

Systematizing time lends itself to mythologizing, where the most eager of adherents can veer into the didactic certainty of this or that date, signaling the time when things shall be no more. Basing their calculations on a combination of scriptural, personal, and sometimes unclear logic, men like Pope Innocent III thought the world would end in 1284, the radical anabaptist Thomas Müntzer saw 1525 as the beginning of the end, and the father of modern physics Isaac Newton figured that it would be on a date no later than 2060 (he still has room to be correct).[38] Strung between the poetry of allegory and the certainty of mathematics, apocalypticism can swing between lyrical descriptions of decline and fall that are pertinent to any individual spiritual experience, though it can also welcome the vulgar literalism which tries to provide a date for the undatable. Ironically, it seems that the year 1000 wasn't one of those times of prevalent millennial mania, for though a vague trepidation is indicated in some quarters, life largely went on without much interruption, no doubt in part due to the relative novelty of the Anno Domini system. Arguably the turn of the last millennium saw more widespread anxiety than a thousand years earlier, though in the inevitable forward movement of the calendar, at the very least there was some numerical connection to those who came before us, that long filament of years branching the dead to the living and the earth to the heavens.

CHAPTER FOUR

The Broken Seal

Mystical Millenarians of the Middle Ages

Onward to New Jerusalem

Imagining the End During the Middle Ages

DEEP WITHIN THE leather-bound, vellum-paged voluminous medieval town records of the charming German town of Hamelin, a city of handsome half-timbered homes and cobble-stone streets, there is a cryptic entry from 1384 that in a single unelaborated-upon sentence reads "It is 100 years since our children left."[1] This is one of the earliest references to whatever occurred in Lower Saxony which was the inspiration for the folktale "The Pied Piper of Hamelin," that disquieting story about a mysterious stranger in mottled pants and a jester's cap who was paid by the town fathers to exterminate the city's rats, and when stiffed for that service retaliated by playing a magic flute which lured all of their children into the countryside, where they then disappeared.

This is the version of the story as it appeared in the fifteenth-century Lüneburg manuscript, where an anonymous hand recounted how some two hundred years before a stranger had "began to play all through the town a silver pipe of the most magnificent sort. All the children who heard his pipe, in the number of 130, following him to the East Gate and out of the town to the so-called execution place or Calvary. There they proceeded to vanish, so that no trace of them could be found."[2] Various hypotheses have been proffered; that the children migrated to eastern Europe as part of a settlement campaign, that they were victims of the so-called "dancing plagues" which afflicted peasants during the Middle Ages, even that they were sacrificial victims of residual Teutonic pagans. Another theory was that they were "lured away by someone who wanted them to take part in the Children's Crusade," as Wolfgang Mieder writes in *Tradition and Innovation in Folk Literature*.[3] Whatever happened in Hamelin occurred a good seventy-two years after the Children's Crusade, yet it's easy to see the thematic correspondences.

If the Pied Piper's origins are obscure, that of the Children's Crusade are slightly less so, even if no less disturbing. In 1212, a young German shepherd named Nicholas of Cologne, said to have miraculous powers, gathered an "army" of some seven thousand children from throughout the Rhineland to march toward Italian ports, claiming that the Mediterranean would part and they would go onto the Holy Land whereby the example of their piety, innocence, and devotion would convince the Muslims to convert.[4] Simultaneously, during Pope Innocent III's campaign against the Cathars, in northern France a twelve-year-old shepherd named Étienne of Cloyes had a series of millennial visions whereby Christ told him that he must assemble a group of children who would depart for the Levant to win the Saracens for Christ. Étienne is believed to have raised as many as thirty thousand children for this purpose.

There are disagreements as to whether these campaigns were as large as has been depicted, or if their "soldiers" were as young, but what's incontrovertible is that the sea didn't part for Nicholas of Cologne's crusade, and that the children assembled by Étienne of Cloyes never made it to the Levant. "As innocents," writes Thomas Asbridge in *The Crusades: The Authoritative History of the War for the Holy Land*, "they claimed, children would be able to fulfil God's divine purpose in a manner impossible for adults sullied by the taint of sin."[5] Of those who did embark onto ships in French and Italian ports, traditionally it's been maintained that the bulk of them were sold into slavery. Parallels to the Pied Piper, whatever the historical connections, are clear: An account of an enigmatic but charismatic stranger, whether Nicholas, Étienne, or the Piper, who drives otherwise normal people into madness and doom, all for a pointless cause. Such a tale is an apt metaphor for the Crusades as well, which had many pied pipers, from Peter the Hermit to Pope Urban II. When Urban II delivered a homily in 1095 at the Frankish town of Clermont, the idea of a Christian Holy War against the Muslims was novel. Further solidifying the authority of the papacy, Urban thundered to the assembled prelates how the "Holy Sepulcher of the Savior and the Holy Places, [are] ravaged and profaned by an impure race. Valiant soldiers, descendants of those who never know defeat, make your way to the Holy Sepulcher and tear the Holy Land from the grasp of this abominable nation."[6] Despite Urban's rancor, Western Christians had until this point been largely indifferent to four hundred years of Islamic rule over Jerusalem, as their pilgrims were largely able to travel to the Holy City unmolested. "Eras of coexistence and commingling . . . make up another facet of Islamic and Christian contact in the Middle Ages," writes Stephen O'Shea in *Sea of Faith: Islam and Christianity in the Medieval Mediterranean World*. Describing what in Islamic al-Andalus was understood as the attitude of *convivencia*, O'Shea explains that from Constantinople to Cordoba there "would be more to the relationship between Christian and Muslim than merely the sword."[7]

Of course Muslims and Christians had waged war against each other before, especially on the Iberian Peninsula, where a caliphate was established that would endure until the fifteenth century, as well as at the borderlands of the Byzantine Empire, but Urban's innovation was to emphasize that such fighting wasn't simply territorial, economic, or political, but explicitly religious, granting dispensation for any crusader who should fight in such a campaign. The immediate occasion for this call to arms was a request from the Byzantine emperor Alexios I Kommenos for assistance against the Seljuk Turks, and yet that alone seems insufficient to explain the following two centuries, which saw eight Crusades to the Holy Land, not including campaigns that weren't sanctioned by the papacy (such as those of Nicholas and Étienne), the development of widespread and unprecedented anti-Jewish violence, the establishment of four separate Crusader kingdoms in the Middle East, and even the sacking of Constantinople during the Fourth Crusade. Estimates of the number of people who perished during these two centuries are hard to accurately calculate, but range from one to nine million dead. A stunning example of how the apocalyptic dragon can move from the realm of metaphor into actual repercussions.

By the time that Urban made his exhortation, Christendom had developed the apocalyptic fervor that was ironically missing a century before. The eleventh century had been a difficult one for the faithful; East and West, Constantinople and Rome, Orthodoxy and Catholicism, had finally suffered schism in 1054, perhaps a trauma that was inevitable considering the theological (and more importantly ecclesiastical) differences between them, hence a particular irony in a Byzantine emperor being the catalyst for the Crusades. There were also economic concerns, as always, since the population of Europe was beginning to grow following the demographic catastrophes that marked the collapse of the Roman Empire, so that potential knights who would commit to holy war had a way of making their fortune in the Levant that they wouldn't have in France, Germany, or England.

To understand the Crusades as only a nascent colonial enterprise is anachronistic however, as it is also reductionist to dismiss the feelings of those engaged in such campaigns as being purely material, however malignant the wars themselves may have been. The faith which pushed men into ports at Marseille and Genoa and to disembark on the Palestinian coast was genuine, however violent it may have been. Furthermore, Urban's declaration was unmistakably apocalyptic, and a millennial piety—particularly in the various unsanctioned Peoples' Crusades—demonstrated a growing eschatological anxiety among Christians. Jay Rubenstein argues in *Nebuchadnezzar's Dream: The Crusades, Apocalyptic Prophecy, and the End of History* that "In its initial conception, the First Crusade was understood and interpreted in biblical, prophetic language," and that theologians and religious authorities believed that by "taking Jerusalem, the crusaders had fulfilled the book of Daniel."[8]

The fervency of this apocalypticism is clearly seen in the various Peoples' Crusades which accompanied those officially sanctioned by the church, events punctuated by outbursts of all-consuming emotional zealotry which motivated the peasantry into volunteering alongside nobles. Peter the Hermit, a French priest who was most responsible for raising such a campaign during the First Crusade, is a particularly damning example of the dangers of unmitigated apocalypticism. Claiming to receive instruction from Christ, Peter assembled a massive force of peasants, who rather than fighting for their own economic liberation (as was not unknown during the Middle Ages) enlisted to travel to Jerusalem and kill Muslims.[9]

Many of Peter's fighting force observed "enemies of Christ" far closer to home in the form of the small Jewish communities that had proliferated throughout Europe, and so it was that the Peoples' Crusade enacted what could be considered the first widespread pogroms during the Rhineland massacres. Thousands of Jews would be slaughtered, synagogues destroyed, and women and men forced to convert to Catholicism or risk being murdered.[10] The church's official position regarding the Jews was that while deprived of certain rights, they should be allowed to largely practice their faith, drawing from the explicitly anti-Jewish reasoning of the fourth-century theologian Augustine who argued that the community should be preserved as a means of demonstrating religious error to faithful Christians.[11] Even that damning "tolerance" was too much for those men who joined Peter the Hermit, and while the response of the church was largely to protect the Jews within their bishoprics, the Rhineland massacres still saw thousands of innocent people murdered.

For many who enlisted with the Peoples' Crusade, there was undoubtedly a cynical opportunism, the promise of pillaging and rape, but these atrocities were also justified by an appeal to a noxious apocalyptic expectation. These unprecedented massacres also inadvertently encouraged a new messianism among the Jews of Europe. Historian Israel Jacob Yuval explains in his monograph *Two Nations in Your Womb: Perceptions of Jews and Christians in Late Antiquity and the Middle Ages* how the martyrdom of Jews during the Rhineland massacres contributed to a growing sense of unity among Sephardic Jews in al-Andalus, Byzantine Jews, and the German-speaking Ashkenazic Jews who were the targets of the Peoples' Crusade.[12] This was combined with a burgeoning eschatological interpretation of mass death, whereby Jews as the descendants of Jacob were understood as being persecuted by the inheritors of Esau, the patriarch's wild brother, who were called "Edomites" and were associated with the Christians.[13] As Yuval writes, the "religious ideology underlying the sacrificial ritual cannot be understood without noting its relation to the vengeful messianic position. According to this view, the shed blood of the martyrs reaches the very Throne of God and arouses God to set out on his great campaign of retribution, on a messianic holy war," so that for the Christians apocalypticism offered the promise of glory and for the Jews of liberation, but such emotions were complex, genuine, and burnt with a gemlike intensity.[14]

It is hard to quite understand the previous scholarly reasoning which diminished the religious impulse as a cause for the Crusades in favor of interpreting it only through a mercantile or nascent colonial lens, and yet as Rubenstein makes clear, those who both justified and engaged in military missions to the Levant increasingly understood the apocalypse as a "drama in which Christians would play important roles, many of them heroic . . . a call to arms, an exciting tale, and adventure,"[15] and of course also a moral travesty. What resulted from Urban's call was a militant political theology, a dangerous conception of being able to enact apocalypse through temporal means, and if not the origin of armed eschatology at least among the earliest examples of it within Christianity. With the push into the Middle East, the crusaders interpreted the allegorical New Jerusalem of millennium as the actual Jerusalem ruled over by the Fatimids and the Seljuks. Many Islamic chroniclers from the time period didn't even seem to acknowledge the motivations of the Christians as being religious per se, since Muslims had long clashed with the Byzantines over territorial ambitions. "The crusaders, of course, represented a fusion of secular and spiritual interests and therein lay one of their great strengths," writes Jonathan Phillips in *Holy Warriors: A Modern History of the Crusades*. "But in the Islamic world it took decades for this combination to form a shared agenda that would inspire Muslims to cohere in sufficient numbers to expel the Christians."[16] Muslims were fighting for land, but Christians believed themselves to be fighting for heaven.

While Muhammad himself was a military commander, battles for territorial expansion weren't necessarily interpreted as religious (as indeed conversion of those conquered wasn't a requirement), and the concept of jihad was frequently understood as referring to internal struggle as much as it was temporal military engagement. When it came to the Crusades themselves, writes Richard Fletcher in *The Cross and the Crescent: Christianity and Islam from Muhammed to the Reformation*, there was an "interesting contrast here with medieval Islam. . . . For contemporary Islamic narrators the Crusades were not much more than skirmishes which inflicted pinpricks upon the fringes of the Islamic world."[17] Ironically, however, over time, as the Crusades became a touchstone in both the West and the East, this militant apocalypticism in Christianity was directly responsible for a defensive theology, whereby "jihad became the driving force of Islam's response to the events of 1099," as Phillips notes.[18] Ten years after Urban had challenged Catholics into crusade, an Islamic legalist named al-Sulami preached in a Damascus mosque that "the Franks acted as they did because of the Muslim's blame of God. . . . He warned you with a punishment the like of which He did not warn you with before. . . . If only you would desist from sin! Otherwise He will make you fall into the hands of your enemy. . . . May God hasten your waking up from the sleep of neglect." Al-Sulami organized his thoughts into a tract entitled *Kitab-al-Jihad—The Book of Holy War*.[19] Christian crusade would be answered by jihad.

Challenges of the Demiurge

The Cathar Heresy

Most likely beginning his encyclopedic task around 1235, Vincent of Beauvois, the Dominican friar of the Cistercian monastery in Royaumont Abbey north of Paris, spent almost three decades compiling an entire history of the world—divided into volumes devoted to the natural, historical, and doctrinal—his magisterial *Speculum Mais*, or *Great Mirror*. From Creation to Caesar, Constantine to Charlamagne, Vincent of Beauvois attempted to capture as much of history as was possible in the thirteenth century, to give an accounting of the providential ways in which God acted through the affairs of men, of what was worthy of "contemplation . . . admiration or imitation."[20] The founder of Vincent's order, the titular Spanish monk St. Dominic de Guzman, had died only fourteen years before the friar began work on the *Great Mirror*, but that saint's task of identifying heresy had continued and was well attested to in this history of the world.

Long associated with the Inquisition, though that institution was founded after Dominic's death (even while many Dominicans long staffed its offices), the monk's reputation is less than saintly today. He was a fanatical, zealous, and extreme defender of orthodoxy willing to consign thousands to the punishments of secular authority after he'd made his ecclesiastical rendering of their guilt.[21] While Vincent worked on his massive compendium, the southern French region of Languedoc was still in the midst of a hideous crusade, the Roman Catholic Church persecuting a heterodox Christian faith known as Catharism, which the papacy had long associated with heresy as the minority religion spread throughout Provence and into northern Italy. Calling themselves simply "Good Christians," the Cathars (whose name translates to the "Pious Ones" in Greek) were the first major challenge to medieval religious uniformity in Western Europe.[22]

Following the seven ecumenical church councils which defined proper Christian doctrine during late antiquity, the several centuries erroneously called the "Dark Ages" were marked by, if not tolerance of "heretics," then at least indifference to everyone other than the leaders of those occasional renegade movements, partially because issues of decentralized authority and geographic distance made enforcement of uniformity difficult.[23] As the second millennium began, religious consensus hardened, not least of all because the 1054 split between the Orthodox East and the Catholic West demonstrated that fractures could exist within Christendom. Also, it must be said that, even if from the sixth until the tenth century there wasn't much in the way of widespread persecution of heretics, the turn of the millennium saw a flowering of apocalyptic, millennial, messianic, and prophetic sentiments which threatened the church's hegemony. "By the end of the eleventh century," writes Norman Cohn in his classic study *The Pursuit of the Millennium*, "newly awakened religious energies were beginning to escape from ecclesiastical control and to turn against the Church,"[24] so groups like the Cathars emerged who often preached and lived a radically different version of the faith than the official one, where the popular enthusiasms of apocalypticism (or a variety of it at least) were on ample display. Vincent refers to the schismatics as "Albigensians," a not uncommon term for them, based on the preponderance of Cathars around the southern French bishopric of Albi, which was where Dominic himself was embroiled in disputation with the Cathars, part of the church's new and brutal push to exorcize heresy from Christendom.

Andrew McCall writes in *The Medieval Underworld* how this renaissance in heretical thinking was indirectly promulgated by ecclesiastical authority itself; how Pope Gregory VII's call for church reform awakened "in the hearts of many Christians, expectations which the Church proved quite incapable of fulfilling," in part generated by "widespread dissatisfaction of both poor and rich alike with the lack of piety or enthusiasm for pastoral duties among the regular Catholic clergy."[25] Even among those who remained Catholic, most likely the majority of Languedoc's residents, the Cathars provided a model of a consistent, humane, tolerant, and generous Christianity. In response, Dominic said of the famously pious Cathars that "Zeal must be met by zeal, humility by humility, false sanctity by real sanctity, preaching falsehood by preaching truth."[26]

An anonymous artist from the Low Countries depicts the most fabled moment of Dominic's ministry to the Cathars in an illuminated manuscript version of the *Great Mirror* made sometime in the 1470s, now housed in the British Library. The scene in the manuscript illustrates events which are supposed to have happened in the Provencal town of Fanjeaux in 1204. On the left is seated a secular ruler clothed in a blue smock; on the right is St. Dominic in the characteristic black cowl and white vestments of the order which he founded. Several men are assembled as Dominic preaches, some seem to be wearing turbans, another a yellow "Jew's hat" which the church forced on members of that persecuted faith. The saint, we are to understand, is in the presence of the church's enemies. Between these two gatherings of men is the red conflagration of an *auto-da-fé*, a heap of books used as kindling. A pile of Cathar holy texts are being immolated, along with a manuscript of the gospels, the latter of which levitates miraculously unscathed from the flames, complete and unburnt: Dominic's dramatic demonstration of Catholicism's truth over the errors of Catharism. A certain romance has always been associated with the doomed Albigensians of Languedoc, spurious connections made between the "Good Christians" and the Knights Templar or the Holy Grail, even while the particulars of their faith are still debated, so thorough was the church's genocidal war of extermination. Initially having pursued a policy of missionary work, Pope Innocent III declared a "crusade" against the Cathars following the 1208 murder of a papal legate in Occitan, war breaking out between northern French nobles on the side of orthodoxy and Languedoc nobles who, though largely not Albigensians themselves, were associated with their defense. Stephen O'Shea describes in *The Perfect Heresy: The Revolutionary Life and Death of the Medieval Cathars* how the horror of the crusade involved "mass burnings, blindings, and hangings, the catapulting of body parts over castle walls, the rapine, the looting, the chanting of monks behind battering rams, the secret trials, the exhuming of corpses, the creakings of the rack."[27]

Contemporary disagreements are to be had about how unified Cathar thought was, the expanse of their influence, even if they were a real or imagined threat to the church's hegemony. Similarities between Catharism and Gnosticism, at least in the doctrine of a dualism between matter and spirit, as well as the belief that the God of Scripture was actually a fallen demiurge, are obvious. Tracing any uninterrupted chain between the ancient Gnostics and the medieval Cathars is difficult, however. There are also parallels between Catharism and the ancient Persian religion of Manicheanism, which combined elements of Neo-Zoroastrianism, Christianity, and Buddhism and that once had followers stretching from the English Channel to the Sea of Japan, but was extinct everywhere but China by the fourteenth century.

Like the Zoroastrians, Manicheans, and Gnostics, Cathar theology was dualist, as they believed that the universe is split between a righteous spiritual realm and an evil material world which was the creation of a demonic demiurge. This latter being was associated with the deity of the Old Testament, with the Cathars believing that the God of both Judaism and Catholicism was equivalent with the devil, while the New Testament God was the Lord of light and goodness.[28] Everyone's soul was angelic, according to the Albigensians, but had become captured in the material prisons of our bodies, with every soul involved in a cycle of reincarnation until the Cathar ritual of *Consolamentum*, almost a combination of baptism and communion and their only recognized sacrament, could free the suffering individual from this otherwise endless process of metempsychosis.[29] As such, Cathars eschewed anything which could increase the devil's share of this world, which often meant a rejection of procreation, as well as an ascetic lifestyle which included poverty, pacifism, and pescatarianism, a millennialism of the dove far more than that of the dragon. Their antimaterialism was absolute, with the thirteenth-century Dominican inquisitor Bernardo Gui complaining that the Cathars held that the Catholic Eucharist "comes from straw . . . that, moreover, it passes through the body and comes to a vile end, which, they say, could not happen if God were in it."[30]

By the sixteenth century Reformation polemicists like the Englishmen John Foxe in his *Acts and Monuments*, frequently known as the "Book of Martyrs," were ignoring or denying Cathar dualism in an attempt to enlist the extinct religion in the ranks of proto-Protestants. Foxe and those in his stead were almost certainly wrong about that interpretation, but it is true that the Cathars were antisacramental and anticlerical in a manner that would seem familiar to reformers. Effectively without organized clergy (though ironically they recognized bishops, of a sort), the Cathars respected a category of women and men called *Perfecti*, those initiates who before death had undergone *Consolamentum*, and thus could be guaranteed liberation from the cycle of rebirth, then helping others in that task.[31] Indeed the Cathars were notable in accepting and encouraging women *Perfecti*, such as the celebrated Esclaramonde of Foxe, who championed almshouses and hospitals throughout Occitan (while demonstrating the frequently elite position of some Albigensians).[32] Far more Buddhist than Protestant, the Perfects were a type of Western Boddhisatva, for in some accounts a segment of the Cathars believed that the good and evil gods were respectively the archangel Michael and Satan, and that the former incarnated as Jesus Christ to teach the methods by which humanity could be redeemed from the continual cycle of rebirth.

In ninth-century Bulgaria, Macedonia, and the Balkans a similar creed was promulgated by a preacher named Bogomil, whose name means "Beloved of God," perhaps the first of the true great medieval heretics. If the connections between Catharism and Gnosticism or Manicheanism are tenuous, they're far clearer to Bogomilism. At an 1167 conclave held by the Cathars at Saint-Félix-Lauragais, the Bogomil bishop of Constantinople Nicetas was in attendance; scholars also know that despite the vast preponderance of unique Albigensian scripture being destroyed in the subsequent crusade, they did hold sacred the Bogomil apocryphal text *Book of the Secret Supper*. Other than the accounts made by inquisitors like Dominic, Gui, and Jaques Fournier, who would be the future Pope Benedict XII, scholars have perilously little to draw on from the Cathars themselves, though knowing that they held the explicitly apocalyptic *Book of the Secret Supper* in reverence is important. "Apocalyptic and prophetic sentiments were very important in the development of medieval religious beliefs, both orthodox and heterodox," writes Michael Frassetto in *Heretic Lives: Medieval Heresy from Bogomil and the Cathars to Wyclif and Hus*.[33]

Revelation was held in esteem by the Cathars, but they interpreted Patmos's words as allegorical and referring to spiritual transformation—which was everything. Furthermore, the Cathars maintained what could be called a "postmillennial" eschatology, effectively believing that the redemption of the world and the second coming of Christ was the responsibility of humanity, that it was in the performance of the *Consolamentum* that women and men battled against Satan, a position which by the schema delineated is clearly a variety of the dove's apocalypticism. Andrew Philip Smith writes in *The Lost Teachings of the Cathars: Their Beliefs and Practices* how their mythology was "not just a static piece of scripture handed down from the Bogomils. It was a living and essential part of the lives of Cathars . . . used in all contexts of Cathar life. The strictures and disciplines of the perfects were not merely considered good practice in themselves, they were essential to the Cathars [sic] ongoing involvement in the cosmic drama."[34] "When the number of the just shall equal the number of the fallen angels," explains the *Book of the Secret Supper*, then "shall Satan, raging mightily, be 'loosed out of his prison'" at the day of judgment. The *Book of the Secret Supper* provides a radically alternative reading of Christianity; structured as a conversation in heaven between the evangelist John and Christ, the Bogomils provided a completely different imagining of Scripture. Christ explains how the material universe—all the work of Genesis—was actually created by Satan, with the first pure intrusion of the spiritual realm being the nativity. Contrary to orthodox Christianity, the Bogomils and Cathars maintained that Christ's "physical" body was an illusion, and the purpose of his arrival on earth was to liberate the spiritual angels trapped by our materiality. "Glory and boundless honor shall be the reward of those who have cherished the angelic life; while the portion of the servants of iniquity shall be wrath, fury, distress, and displeasure," reads the *Book of the Secret Supper*, recounting how during the apocalypse the "Son of man shall separate His just from the company of sinners and shall say to them, echoing Matthew, 'Come, ye blessed of my Father, possess you the kingdom' . . . while to the sinful He shall say, 'Depart from me, you cursed, into everlasting fire, which was prepared for the devil."[35]

For the Cathars, the Catholic Church was an institution devoted to the satanic, concluding at their 1167 council that it was the "harlot of the Apocalypse," maintaining that "Since the fruit of the Roman Church is evil, its faith is evil," a sentiment recorded in the thirteenth century from the interrogations of the inquisitor Moneta of Cremona.[36] The church interpreted the Cathars in a similarly derogatory light, of course, often understanding the Albigensian church as a sign of incipient apocalypse.

With the launching of a crusade against the Cathars, the Catholic Church eradicated a rival religious claimant, an event that was both based in apocalyptic belief while also being literally apocalyptic. Perfects, such as Peire Autier and Guillaume Bélibaste, were executed, with over two hundred alone burnt at the stake near Montsegur in 1244. Provencal nobles who were viewed as not enthusiastic enough in their persecutions were stripped of landholdings, enriching northern French aristocrats like the notorious Simon de Montfort. Lay Cathars who were interrogated by the Dominicans might keep their lives, but in a foreshadowing of our own age, they were forced to wear a yellow cross on their clothing to indicate that they were heretics. "They were simply ordinary people following their instincts to protect their loved ones," writes Rene Weis in *The Yellow Cross: The Story of the Last Cathars' Rebellion Against the Inquisition, 1290–1329*, "and it was their misfortune that their tiny part of the country fell under the scrutiny of a vindictive established church."[37]

By the middle of the fourteenth century there would no Cathars left, anywhere. Representative of the brutality of the church's campaign is the infamous account of the crusader Arnaud Amalric, who in 1209 besieged the Cathar fortress at Béziers, with the commander bragging in a letter to the pope that "Our men spared no one, irrespective of rank, sex or age, and put to the sword almost 20,000 people." Within Beziers the Cathars were joined by a multitude of their Catholic neighbors, who, inspired by the piety and faith of the Albigensians, joined them in the defense of the fortress. After the garrison fell, a lieutenant of Amalric asked him how to distinguish between Catholic and Cathar, to which the crusader responded "Kill them all. God will know His own."[38]

The Age of the Spirit

Medieval Spiritual Anarchism

During the midst of the Fifth Crusade in 1218, the fourth Ayyubid sultan of Egypt, al-Malik al-Kamil Naser ad-Din Abu al-Ma'ali Muhammad, who was known in Western sources as "Meledin," had an unusual meeting in his encampment with the privileged son of an Italian silk merchant from Assisi. Al-Kamil was a nephew of the feared and respected Islamic commander Saladin, who had defeated the kingdom of Jerusalem in the Second Crusade and sparred with the English king Richard the Lionheart and Philip II of France in the Third, but despite such victories was still regarded by Christians as an honorable opponent. That sultan was even placed in the pleasant environs of Limbo by the great Catholic poet Dante Alighieri in his 1320 epic *The Divine Comedy*.

On the field of battle alongside the Nile, where Muslims and Christians had been meeting for two centuries in a conflict fit for Armageddon, al-Kamil paused to meet with St. Francis of Assisi, an idiosyncratic Catholic miracle-worker who would be canonized and remembered as one of the most influential spiritual thinkers of the Middle Ages. "Francis's mission to Egypt is . . . neither an aberration nor a simple footnote to the history of the fifth crusade," writes John V. Tolan in *Saint Francis and the Sultan: The Curious History of a Christian–Muslim Encounter*, "It is a key moment in his life, essential for those who wish to understand Francis and the attitude of his new medicant order towards Islam,"[39] indeed to comprehend the stunning complexities of medieval faith as well. The saint had come to convert the sultan, and in this he failed. But Francis was welcomed generously into the encampment, and al-Kamil listened patiently and respectfully to the friar, who was received warmly and left the Muslims in peace, gifted an ivory trumpet before his departure.

This was an undeniably remarkable and dramatic interaction, an intimation of heaven in the midst of hell, or millennium during an ongoing apocalypse, of the dove arising out of the flames of the dragon: A communion of shared divinity between brothers in Abraham. "Where there is charity and wisdom, there is neither fear nor ignorance," reads the 27th admonition in *The Counsels of the Holy Father St. Francis*, for "Where there is patience and humility, there is neither anger nor vexation." This is a meeting that it's impossible to imagine St. Dominic making, yet it speaks to the radicalism of Francis, a figure who shared much with the assortment of heterodox mendicant friars and heretical preachers who proliferated during the Middle Ages, and yet not only escaped censure but was canonized by the Catholic Church.

Far from the only popular misconception about the Middle Ages, but a common one, is the fallacy that this was an era marked by religious uniformity. If anything, the theological possibilities during the period were incredibly vibrant and diverse. Cohn explains that these centuries were marked not just by authority, but by a "tradition of religious dissent which persisted throughout the Middle Ages."[40] Every single position that would be put forward during the Reformation was considered by some thinker or some sect prior to the early modern era, and while it's true that the multitude of these groups were persecuted for heresy, much that was heterodox was able to be explored within the confines of the church, from mystics like Meister Eckhardt and Hildegard von Bingen to Julian of Norwich and Thomas à Kempis. Francis is perhaps one of the most remarkable of these figures, for he became so intrinsic and iconic within Catholicism, but he and the order which he founded narrowly escaped being banned (part of the eternal friction between Franciscans and Dominicans), while many of those influenced by him were prohibited.[41]

Francis would be canonized in 1228, only two years after his death, a reflection of not only his tremendous popularity throughout the Catholic world, but also of the ways in which lay energy which was so prominent in groups that normally didn't receive official sanction from the church could be harnessed for the purposes of religious authority. Rhetorically, though not necessarily doctrinally, Francis's adoration of the natural world had qualities which were borderline pantheistic, the ethos expressed in his celebrated *Canticle of the Sun* with its evocation of "Sister Moon and the stars" and of "Brother Fire." The Franciscan brothers took a complete and total vow of poverty in emulation of the communal living of the apostles in the book of Acts, so that Francis's political theology was effectively a form of ecological communism.

Alongside groups like the Beghards, the Beguines, and the Brethren of the Free Spirit, all of whom would ultimately be labeled heretical, the Franciscans had an anarchic approach to the idea of material wealth, owning all things in common as a reflection of millennial possibility. This approach toward possessions was ultimately a more difficult transgression for Rome—a temporal as well as a religious power after all—to countenance. Being a saint is one thing, but actually administering any sort of organization is entirely another, so the papacy created a legal fiction whereby all of the wealth required to run the order would be owned by the church but leased free of charge to the Franciscans.

By the last decades of the thirteenth century there emerged a radical segment of the order known as the "Spiritual Franciscans," or the "Fraticelli" (for "Little Brothers"), who believed that the arrangement with the church was a profound dishonor to the intentions of their founder. Deemed heretical by Rome in 1296, the Fraticelli returned the favor, as numerous divisions and sects that splintered off from the order engaged in polemic against the papacy.[42] Describing a related group from the same period in northern Italy known as the Apostolic Brethren, Frassetto writes that they believed that the "Church of Rome . . . was the whore of Babylon . . . it had turned away from the faith of Christ,"[43] now that responsibility and power had been transferred to these new orders. A surprising aspect of medieval diatribe is just how common anticlericalism was, along with accusing whoever happened to currently occupy the Throne of St. Peter as being the antichrist, yet for believers who affirmed an unfractured Christendom there was no inconsistency between such rhetoric and being a pious Catholic, as indeed the Fraticelli's conduct unassailably demonstrates. Decima L. Douie argues in *The Nature and Effect of the Heresy of the Fraticelli* that their devotion wasn't the "result of a fanatical and misplaced enthusiasm for minor and insignificant details in the teaching of St. Francis, but had as its basis a conception of the meaning of the Christian revelation and of the ultimate regeneration of mankind."[44]

As with the Apostolic Brethren, founded by a layman named Gerard Segarelli who'd been rejected for membership in the Franciscans, such enthusiasms were congruent with fervent apocalypticism, which the Fraticelli embraced as their veritable birthright. Peter John Olivi, a Franciscan and fellow-traveler to the Fraticelli who was raised in Béziers, France, which only a few decades before his birth in 1248 had been a den of Catharism, provided eschatological gloss to these questions about poverty.[45] Producing idiosyncratic readings of both Daniel and Revelation, Olivi divided history into a succession of seven ages, with the final epoch a millennial period which he thought was rapidly approaching. Conflating the church with Satan, Olivi believed that Francis was "after Christ and under Christ, the first and principal founder and initiator and exemplar of the sixth period and its evangelical rule," as close to a messianic figure as he could imagine in his *Commentary on Revelation*.[46]

More than a century after Francis's death, another member of the Fraticelli, the pseudonymous Telesphorus of Cosenza, wrote one of the most popular prophetic treatises of the Middle Ages, entitled *A Book of Great Tribulations* and completed in 1386. Telesphorus supplies a number of predictions with specific dates, including a 1393 end of the Western Schism, when there were competing claimants to the papacy in Avignon and Rome; the ascension of an "Angelic Pastor" to the papacy who will enact the Rule of Francis throughout the entire church; and a final holy crusade to Jerusalem which will convert all Jews and Muslims, among other prophecies. Even the first of those predictions was off by twenty-four years, and it was the closest that he got to being accurate.

If anything united Spiritual Franciscans like Olivi and Telesphorus, it was an extreme veneration of the Holy Spirt, and a zealous millennial expectation that the third person of the Trinity was about to radically transform the universe. This emphasis on the Holy Spirit comes less from the influence of Francis than it does from a figure who was actually far more central to the apocalyptic thinking of the Fraticelli, and that was an eccentric twelfth-century Calabrian named Joachim of Fiore, who is undoubtedly the single most influential eschatological writer of the Middle Ages, arguably the most important since John of Patmos.

According to Joachim's *Exposition of the Book of Revelation*, all of human history can be divided into three sections which each correspond to a person of the Trinity. The first of these periods is associated with the Jews' covenant with God the Father, when the dictates of the Old Testament reigned supreme, and the operative rule was the Law, all of which ended with the incarnation of Christ. The second period is associated with the Son and the new universal covenant of Christianity, when the dictates of the gospels reign supreme, and the operative rule was of grace. This period, Joachim believed, would end in 1260, when a third and final period would begin, associated with the Holy Spirit, where the operative rule would be freedom. Joachim claimed that with the coming of this perfection all humans would be capable of understanding divine language, that we'd speak in perfect allegory and no longer have any need for law, that even redemption would be subsumed into the greater, more glorious, and wholly beautiful realm of pure unfettered freedom. What awaits us is "perfection of the spiritual order which he will see to be one spirit with his God and walking according to his doctrine in the paths of his commandments."[47] An age of the Spirit is, quite naturally, an epoch of the dove. Bernard McGinn writes in *Visions of the End: Apocalyptic Traditions in the Middle Ages* that more than simply another iteration of millennialism, Joachim's thought represented a "distinctive form of utopianism that sought not only to give ultimate historical validation to the institutions to which Joachim was most devoted, especially monasticism, but which [were] also . . . conceived of as a new divine irruption into history rather than a return to the past."[48]

This was a "New Order," and in this way Joachim conceived of a powerful form of millennialism that was amenable to a secular understanding of progress. His great innovation was understanding history as operating in a tripartite structure, as involving a certain dialectical process. While Joachim himself was never excommunicated or deemed heretical per se (though some of his writings were), those who followed in his stead, such as the Fraticelli, certainly were. His conception of a "New Order" was a dangerous one, especially since his Third

Age of the Holy Spirit seemed to promise millennial change without Christ, an amendment to Christian apocalypticism that would mutate into a number of secular utopian ideologies in the ensuing millennium. Because of the influence of Christianity on secular thinking, McGinn argues that Joachim is among the "most significant theorists of history in the Western tradition," a figure who advocated for an "organic and melioristic vision of history [which] was to have many heirs in the West, even if few of them were in any sense direct . . . a new stage in the history of the apocalyptic tradition and in European philosophy and theology of history."[49]

As hermetic and occult as Joachim may seem to us today, it could be argued that he fundamentally invented the idea of *progress*, interpreting history not just as a long and decadent degeneration from the halcyon days of Eden, but that through successive epochs there could actually be improvement. Not just improvement it should be said, but of differing ways of understanding the world, of changing perspectives and evolving consciousness. For all of their sophistication, people in the Middle Ages had trouble conceiving of a better future per se, as the Golden Age was always in the past, and yet as Joachim's message proliferated, by the thirteenth and fourteenth centuries some in his native Italy began to conceive of rebirth—of a New Order—of renaissance. Joachim, Olivi, and Telesphorus were firm believers that before millennium or judgment or the Third Age there would still be great tribulation. And so it was that in the 1240s there would be a red horse ridden by Mongols from the far east; and in 1315 there would be a black horse that would spread famine throughout the entirety of Europe; and related to those two events there would be a pale horse that would come in 1346, and that final black horse would see almost a third of the continent dead from the pestilence. Apocalypse had migrated from prophetic scripture and theological tractates into life. Apocalypse itself came to Europe not as metaphor or allegory, poetry or rhetoric, but as bacterial reality.

A White Horse

Pestilence Comes to Europe

Perhaps only a few of the English sailors who loaded their cargo onto a ship in the early autumn Norfolk sun in September 1349 felt sick. Strapping young men fixing bundles of wool in the belly of a small skipper, Norway bound, whistling hymns as they worked on the swaying ship held to dock with heavy rope as they prepared to ship off. Maybe some of the workers felt a strange, uncharacteristic chill despite the high golden autumnal light; maybe as they made their easterly trip a couple of the men developed fevers. Sailors would have started to get fatigued not far after their leaving; somewhere in the midst of the North

Sea would be when the diarrhea started, weak ale and hard tack defecated into buckets until the crew became too weak to even dump the refuse into the sea. Perhaps by the time they were off the coast of the Low Countries, north of what would be Germany, or near Denmark, the men would have begun hemorrhaging sticky black blood, from their mouths, from their noses, from their rectums. By the time they were almost in view of the rocky beaches of Norway, with lines of tall, spindly green-fingered pines above the black shores, they'd have developed the characteristic gangrenous buboes, swollen black sacs hanging from armpit and groin. When their ship crashed into the harbor of Bergen, Norway, every single man aboard was dead.[50] Such calamity in those dark years from 1347 to 1353, when upwards of two hundred million people would die in the same grotesque manner.

The bubonic plague remains the most devastating pandemic in Western cultural memory, even while the Plague of Justinian a century earlier may have killed a higher percentage of people. Striking as it did in the middle of the fourteenth century, the Black Death devastated a continent that had fully recovered from the demographic declines of the Roman Empire's collapse, at a time when political, economic, and social connections had improved to a remarkable degree. Ironically, Europe was in the midst of a veritable cultural renaissance when the plague spread, but the result would be an irrevocably altered continent. "The plague was interpreted, in normal medieval fashion, as a divine chastisement for the transgressions of a sinful world," writes Cohn,[51] and predictably a heightened apocalypticism emerged along with the rats. Popular religious enthusiasms outside of the stricture of the church had already proliferated during these centuries, but as the death toll rose, borderline heretical groups such as the flagellants emerged.

Marching through towns first in Italy, but then through France, Spain, Germany, and England, the flagellants would excoriate their naked flesh with whips and leather scourges, an act of corporeal mortification intended to placate the angry God whom they assumed was punishing Christendom. Ironically these implements would often open the pus-filled buboes, further spreading the disease. "The flagellants were regarded as they regarded themselves," writes Cohn, "not simply as penitents who were atoning for their own sins but as martyrs who were taking upon themselves the sins of the world and thereby averting the plague and, indeed, the annihilation of mankind."[52] During this period apocalypse moved from being a conjecture of theological tracts and into the experience of actual people; eschatology was encouraged not by arid syllogism and hermeneutics, but by *Yersinia pestis*–infected fleas clinging to the fur of rats, a demonstration that material concerns can never be occluded in a proper understanding of the nightmares which a culture dreams about itself.

From the Tartar Steppes the bubonic plague would make its way westward, first to the Genoese colony of Kaffa on the Black Sea, where Italian merchants had been besieged by Mongolian invaders for months. The latter, in a pique of martial frustration, catapulted the most fetid of the rotting bodies over the heavy stones of the city walls.[53] A few years earlier, the Moroccan traveler Ibn Battuta wrote that Kaffa was "one of the world's celebrated ports," with a "wonderful harbor with . . . [hundreds] of vessels in it, both ships of war and trading vessels, small and large."[54] Wealth and pedigree can't stave off death however, for in 1346 Jani Beg Khan of the Golden Horde made the fateful order that marks the first recorded instance of biological warfare. In the harbor were galleys filled with Chinese oranges and lemons, Indian curries and Indonesian peppers, but on the cobblestoned streets of Kaffa, with her Venetian and Genoese merchants, there was now the stick of burst bodies, dead Mongolian soldiers propelled through the Crimean air and exploding like bags of viscous blood- and bile-filled refuse. Such an order was indicative of Jani Beg's desperation, and indeed the siege of Kaffa failed, but it was the sailors of that metropolitan city who now hosted the living fleas from dead bodies. A Genoese lawyer named Gabriel De' Mussi, who was witness to the siege, notes that when the survivors left for Venice and Genoa, Palermo and Florence, "it was as if they had brought evil spirits with them."[55] Only three years after Kaffa, and in distant Wales a poet would write "Death comes into our midst like black smoke."[56]

John Kelly writes in *The Great Mortality: An Intimate History of the Black Death, the Most Devastating Plague of All Time* that "Seven hundred years after the fact, what we call the Black Death—and what medieval Europeans called the Great Mortality, and medieval Muslims, the Year of Annihilation—remains the greatest natural disaster in human history."[57] Such a pandemic is as if a null point in human history, all of our theological and ethical theses about meaning approaching a type of absolute zero. In the fickle unpredictability of who will be struck down by the disease, simple religious moralizing about God punishing the wicked and rewarding the pious is given demonstrable falsification as some of the good die and some of the evil flourish. Such horror acts as a test of human intention, as both wickedness and compassion are born from the fetid rot of a dying populace; some eager to exploit, some eager to console.

Likewise, social stratification and culture mean little as pestilence turned Fortune's wheel, crushing the noblemen and their peasants alike under its rotation. A man of great erudition and learning like the Florentine Giovani Boccaccio could be effected by the plague, writing in *The Decameron* (the Black Death's greatest literary work) that "hardly any neighbor troubled about others, relatives never or hardly visited each other . . . such terror was struck into the hearts of men and women by this calamity, that brother abandoned brother, and the uncle his nephew, and the sister her brother, and very often the wife her husband . . . fathers and mothers refused to see and tend their children, as if they had not been theirs."[58] For all of his eloquence, learning, and power of description, Boccaccio didn't necessarily experience the plague any more deeply than simpler people did, for what a Sienese cobbler named Anglo di Tura lacked in poetry, he made up for in brevity, simply writing in a letter that "This is the end of the world."[59] In such an environment—the stench of pus-filled buboes permeating the fetid air, the piles of cadavers left in town squares and in front of cathedrals, grim Death's vacant eye-sockets staring out over mocking, toothless grin—cultural shifts would be inevitable. Kelly writes that the Black Death "cast a deep shadow across the centuries that followed, and it remains part of the collective memory of the West."[60] Apocalypticism, or at least an obsession with death, became omnipresent in Western art. Such is the trope of the *Danse Macabre,* which depicts prelate and priest, bishop and bureaucrat, all united in their station of death. Popular in the fifteenth century, the earliest example of the form dates from 1425 and can be found in Paris's Holy Infants Cemetery, only seven decades after the plague had moved across Europe, leaving untended fields and empty houses:[61] Some grandchild of a survivor saw fit to memorialize when the infected had wandered across the continent, crowds of zealous flagellants prostrating themselves before a God who brokered no release.

A typical example of *Danse Macabre* might depict a darkened horizon, as dusk sets her spindly fingers across the severe terrain, where shadowy figures hold hands and kick up feet, performing their dreadful, beautiful dance on the scarred earth. In ruins lie great Gothic cathedrals, their sanctuaries emptied out and their roofs caved in, and crumbling Roman walls and moss-covered aqueducts. In front dance the dead, the dying, the momentarily alive. Decomposing stump to decomposing stump, flesh hanging in tatters from bone-exposed limbs, mushy gums with teeth falling out and wisps of hair clinging to sandy pates. They kick up their heels in dusty exuberance, dancing to some unheard music. There is a bishop, the pope himself, his miter covering a caved-in skull, rotted eye-sockets now blind to piety and sinfulness alike, a stole slick with accumulated adipocere. Next to him is an emperor, cleaved beard clinging to a chin rotted away and speckled with mold, his crown having sunk to where eyes once looked out. Over to the right, holding up both pope and king, is the merchant, his bag of wares now composed of pulpy, rotting fruit, half a leg stumping him along in their infernal circle, a bevy of walking skeletons linking arms with the trio to the edge of this vision.

The *Danse Macabre* existed for a pedagogical reason, reminding the viewer that they had no choice but to go through death. Good death or bad, the result will be the same, as the ironically joyful dancers remind you. From Paris to Basel, London to Krakow, the *Danse Macabre* became a mainstay of medieval funeral art, just another way to keep the mind focused on the inevitability of such final things.

The most famous example of the art form dates from slightly after the Reformation, when the German engraver Hans Holbein the Younger made a series of block prints in 1538 to illustrate the theme. Protestant children were no less fixated on mortality than were their Catholic parents, and Holbein's series was ecumenically popular, a means for everyone to try and conceive of that radical equality promised by the reaper. The earliest edition promises "Images and Illustrated facets of Death, as elegantly depicted as they are artfully conceived," and it's true to its word.[62] Holbein presents the pope, being met by the college of cardinals, not noticing that one red-clad gentleman wearing his ecclesiastical galero is a disguised, slyly smiling skeleton. In the following print, there is a haughty emperor sitting confidently upon a resplendent throne; he looks distractedly to his right, mouth open as if he were speaking (or ordering) something of the numerous attendants who surround him, unaware that behind him a skeleton is slinking off with his crown. Death isn't a snob, however; another illustration in the book includes a peasant in tattered clothes plowing his fields, weary as he walks behind a pack of mules tilling the soil, not noticing the rag-draped corpse who walks alongside him. Between here and Armageddon it's impossible to know what history will do to us, but one unequivocal verity is that death shall, in one way or another, lay low all. There is no bribing the reaper, and no threatening him either. A generation after the plague, the children of those who survived the Black Death made their own failed attempt to try and threaten the princes of this world. On July 13, 1381, a garrison of rebelling peasants from Norfolk, Essex, and Kent marched into London, the gates of the city left open either out of sympathy for the cause of this army or out of fear regarding their strength. Many of the rebels had a bit of land to their names, but were still constrained by the strictures of an increasingly draconian feudalism. At the same time, these workers had ironically found themselves increasingly able to move between social classes and professions in a manner that would have been impossible only a few decades before. The dissatisfaction of the leaders of the Peasant's Revolt, men with names like Wat Tyler, Jack Straw, and the radical priest John Ball, was in part gestated within that incongruous space between new possibilities and restricted rights.

The striking and marching workers demanded a new covenant with both church and state, God and king.[63] What could have theoretically begun as a relatively moderate call to overturn decades-old legislation instead took on more revolutionary and millennial aims, an attempt to summon Joachim's New Order, an alliance of the dove and the dragon, whether they would have thought of it in those terms or not. As the Peasant's Revolt built toward the crescendo of marching on London, Ball would preach an open-air sermon south of Greenwich wherein he did "exhort you to consider that now the time is come, appointed to us by God, in which ye may cast off the yoke of bondage, and recover liberty."[64]

An important biographical fact to know about a man like Ball, and there is a dearth of facts about the men who led the rebellion, is that he was around ten years old when the Black Death swept through England in 1347. Many of the peasants had living memory of those dark years when perhaps 50 percent or more of their fellow subjects perished from the bubonic plague, or they at least knew people who had survived those years. Being able to draw direct correlations between that pandemic and subsequent social, cultural, and religious changes is difficult. But in a direct manner, it's fair to say that the Peasant's Revolt was shaped by the death and destruction from a few decades before, as well as from the more abstract apocalyptic writings of religious thinkers. Samuel K. Cohn Jr. and Douglas Aiton note in *Popular Protest in Late Medieval English Towns* that, as concerns insurrections, "nothing of note appears in the English chronicles until after the Black Death."[65] The Parliamentary legislation which was the locus of the revolt's anger—laws which fixed wages and made it impossible to strike—was passed because of the plague's reduction of the workforce. Concurrently, in a perhaps more intangible manner, the indiscriminate horror of the plague had upended the religious and political expectations of the medieval world, inculcating new doubts as well as new possibilities.

From pandemic then grew rebellion. An outcome of the plague in England was the proliferation of new theologies, such as that of Lollardy associated with the Oxford professor John Wycliff, who condemned ecclesiastical excess and promoted more egalitarian social arrangements. "Wyclif's impact was felt well beyond his original Oxford circle and the lesser clergy that taught variations of his propositions and reached all levels of the laity," explains Frassetto. "His strident denunciations of the clergy and of their worldliness and wealth certainly resonated with the laity responsible for paying tithes and taxes to support the Church."[66] It was Wycliff who, in the prologue to his vernacular Bible translation, envisioned a reordering of the English state on behalf "of the People, by the People, and for the People."[67] Lollardy in some ways anticipated the Reformation which was still more than a century off, but its concerns were very much with the economic and social situation of the Middle Ages, and it was in part a direct outgrowth of the radical changes that had been ushered in by the Black Death. The plague made all unexamined truths dissipate, challenging the authority of both monarchy and church. As a warning, there is something to keep in mind from the Peasant's Revolt, despite its initial promise—Tyler, Straw, and Ball failed in their march on London, and were captured and publicly decapitated in that orchard of heretics and traitors at Smithfield, their heads placed on pikes throughout the capital. There was a brief moment in 1381 when millennium struggled to be born, but the promise of that moment was deferred. Millennium remains deferred.

CHAPTER FIVE

Rebirthing the End

Renaissance Humanism and Reformation Apocalypticism

An Occult Apocalypse

Magic in the Renaissance

UNBEKNOWNST TO THE other participants in the council, Georgios Gemistos Plethon arrived in Florence during the autumn of 1431 not merely to assist in suturing the divisions between the Catholic West and the Orthodox East that had festered for nearly five centuries, but also with a far more idiosyncratic intent in mind. Plethon was also in attendance to work toward the reintroduction of the worship of Apollo and Dionysius, Zeus and Athena, for the Byzantine philosopher's greatest desire was to resurrect classical paganism while abandoning the faith of the Resurrected. "Apollo, lord, you patron and guide," Plethon wrote in a hymn to that god, included in his *Treatise About Laws*, only discovered upon his death in either 1452 or 1454, with contemporary translation by Manuela Simeoni.[1] The philosopher describes the deity as being "of everything in nature, you who trace back everything / to one, and submit the whole itself. . . . Inspire the desire of divine beauties, / lord, to our souls." For the Greek thinker, a renewed paganism was the only manner of promulgating the Platonism which had been preserved in the Byzantine Empire, but for Cosimo de' Medici, the powerful head of the notorious banking family that dominated Florentine politics and society, Plethon was merely one of the most notable philosophers of the east, and he would be intrinsic in the reconciliation of the church's two halves.

Several times between 1431 and 1449, hundreds of clerics and theologians gathered in Tuscany in this grand ecumenical attempt, with the conclave nearly successful, releasing a bull of union with the vast majority of attendees agreeing on the particulars.[2] Despite having the fervent heart of a pagan, Plethon did the work of an ambivalent Christian. Niketas Siniossoglou explains in his *Radical Platonism in Byzantium: Illumination and Utopia in Gemistos Plethon* that the philosopher's "support for Roman Orthodoxy . . . was not the product of Christian sympathies but of intellectual expediency. Plethon opted for the Greek Church because of an inner persuasion that the pagan reform . . . was possible only within the intellectual context of the East."[3] Plethon failed on both accounts; while the ecumenical Council of Florence made great theological, doctrinal, and ecclesiastical strides in healing the schism that had split Christendom since 1054, that goal wouldn't come to fruition as a result of these meetings. Regarding the philosopher's more esoteric intent, there would be no formal reintroduction of the Olympian Pantheon either through the work of the council or through Plethon's own efforts, but an unintentional result of the Greek theologian's Italian sojourn may have been the Renaissance, or at least a particularly occult-minded iteration of it.

As a committed Neoplatonist and classical pagan, Plethon didn't believe in the end of days, rather adhering to the creed that our reality is sustained by an unchanging world of transcendent forms. Regardless of his own dogma, apocalypse is what Plethon very well may have experienced, however. Tradition has often dated Plethon's death to 1452, as if to spare the philosopher having to witness the Ottoman Turks' final conquering of his beloved Constantinople, though evidence suggests that he did indeed survive a year longer than Byzantium did. The reverberations of Constantinople's fall were cacophonous through Christendom, a seeming harbinger of the apocalypse which Plethon didn't believe in. Constantinople had long configured itself as a New Rome, if not a New Jerusalem, a resplendent, glorious, and sacred city dominated by the massive dome of the Hagia Sophia, its interior inlaid with mosaics of celestial blue and shimmering gold, but with Sultan Mehmet II's siege and toppling of the empire, those who survived turned toward apocalyptic explanation.[4] "Why didn't everything shake? Why didn't the sky fall in? Why didn't the earth quake? Why didn't the stones shatter into pieces?" asked the scholar Ioannes Eugenikos, confused that the world itself should still stand even after the city has fallen.[5] Within Europe itself, there was lamentation about how far Mehmed, configured as an antichrist, would march. "Now, the Italians will lament, the Celt will cry, as will the Galatians, the British, the Germans, the Illyrians, the Thracians, and the Paeonicians," wrote Andronikos Kallistos, "now the Iberians will sob; now the Indians will grow sullen."[6] Any hope from the conclave's goal for ecumenical rapprochement was disrupted by the Turks; Christian unity would be permanently deferred, with Mehmed conquering Constantinople only a few months after the Byzantine leadership had agreed to the theological terms of the Council of Florence.

Despite repeated incursions to the West, the Ottomans didn't bring about the apocalypse, even while such "eschatological scenarios . . . effectively marked the end of a world and the birth of another," as Siniossoglou argues.[7] If the story of the Cinquecento is of an Eastern dusk and a Western dawn, then it's a narrative about two cities. Rather than being beneath the limestone dome of the Hagia Sophia, the intellectual center of Christendom would now be beneath the crimson tiles of terracotta which adorned the magnificent dome of the Cathedral of Santa Maria del Fiore, the Bosporus would be traded for the Arno, and Byzantium's Messe with its tents of merchants would be replaced by Florence's sublime bridge of the Ponte Vecchio. Between Florence and her sometime adversary of Venice on the Adriatic, the Italian Peninsula had been a center for learning and literature, art and engineering for generations by the time Plethon visited there in the fifteenth century. Florence was already the city of that immaculate writer Giovani Boccaccio and of the heavenly poet Dante Alighieri, even while artists like Leonardo DaVinci, Sandro Botticelli, and Michelangelo either had yet to begin applying paint to plaster or were still at the very beginning of their careers.

The nineteenth-century Swiss historian Jakob Burkhardt, who inaugurated the study of this period, famously wrote in *The Civilization of the Renaissance in Italy* that this age was marked by the "spirit of mankind recovering consciousness and the power of self-determination, recognizing the beauty of the outer world and of the body through art, liberating the reason in science and the conscience in religion, restoring culture to the intelligence, and establishing the principle of political freedom."[8] Such a conclusion is hopelessly reductionist, as historians today understand both the Renaissance and the periods which preceded it in a less halcyon light, but the romance which Burkhardt presents is undeniable, and not without its own truth. Nobody used the word "Renaissance" until historians like Burkhardt, yet for those in the Medicis' Florence, there was an undeniable sense of rebirth afoot at the very moment that the last of the Roman Empire collapsed in the East.

All of which is to say that had Plethon not arrived in Florence, the "Renaissance" would still have happened—indeed it was already beginning—for history doesn't operate by the discovery of secret manuscripts or buried treasure changing the course of human affairs. Rather, history is a messy process of mutually dependent social, cultural, and economic forces operating together and against one another. As early as the thirteenth century a variation of the philosophical, cultural, artistic, and literary, but most of all pedagogical, movement known as *humanism* was already in evidence throughout Italy. Much is attributed to humanism, but fundamentally it was a program of educational reform concerned with the engaged study of classical texts that were being rediscovered throughout Europe, a phenomenon that would only increase with the multitude of Byzantine refugees who would arrive in Italy after 1453, bringing with them copies of Greek and Latin works that hadn't been read west of the Adriatic for a millennium. Anthony Gottlieb in *The Dream of Reason: A History of Western Philosophy from the Greeks to the Renaissance* describes humanism as "a new model of intellectual excellence" which "emphasized literary studies, philology, oratory, poetry, and history"[9] that would have resounding influence not just within the cloistered universities, but among the secular and even ecclesiastical rulers of the continent. Central to humanism was the reinvigoration of

Platonism and its replacement of the turgid, arid, and labyrinthine complexities of Aristotelian medieval Scholastic philosophy with something more elegant. In this respect, Plethon was instrumental, for as the leading Neoplatonist philosopher in the Byzantine Empire he would introduce a particular version of that metaphysics—to which his paganism was crucial—that would alter the development of humanism in Florence, initiating a golden age of occult, hermetic, astrological, and magical writing which had important influences on apocalypticism.

Less than a decade after Plethon's death, in a Florence flush with recently arrived Byzantine scholars who had fled what was now Istanbul with their copies of Plato and Plotinus, Marsilio Ficino, a keen reader and student of the late-Byzantine philosopher, received the deed to a Tuscan villa named Montevecchio in 1462—established by Cosimo de' Medici himself—for the purposes of restoring the ancient Platonic Academy of Athens.[10] Ficino was attracted to Plethon's thinking, drawing upon the Greek's work in creating his own comprehensive systematization of Neoplatonism. Along with his most brilliant student, Giovani Pico della Mirandola, Ficino redefined Platonism as a humanist philosophy of supernatural striving, breaking down the hierarchies in beliefs surrounding the "Great Chain of Being" which had held sway during the Middle Ages in favor of an antinomian creed of mobility which imagined that people would be able to transform themselves through contemplation of the transcendent Forms. "The rational soul in a certain manner possesses the excellence of infinity and eternity," wrote Ficino in his 1495 *Five Questions Concerning the Mind*. "If this were not the case, it would never characteristically incline toward the infinite."[11]

Naturally, the Florentine Academy was drawn to questions of ultimate significance, of hidden things and veiled secrets, and, even if not borrowing all of Plethon's paganism, they were attracted toward esoteric systems of thought. From Ficino and Mirandola's stead there would develop a renaissance of occultism; the Jewish mystical system of kabbalah would be adapted for Christianity, as Hebrew became a popular subject throughout Europe, and the collection of ancient writings known as the Hermetic Corpus was instrumental in the emergence of a distinctly occult sensibility during the sixteenth century, which understood the manipulation of letter and number as having profound powers. Thus rises the Age of the Magician, the Epoch of the Wizard.

Dame Frances Yates, in her classic *Giordano Bruno and the Hermetic Tradition*, explains how the "genealogy of ancient wisdom, which Ficino did so much to propagate, was also favourable to a revival of magic."[12] If someone is unfamiliar with the vagaries of the Renaissance, it can seem strange to consider that the fifteenth through the seventeenth centuries were an age of magic par excellence, but the reality is that the rejection of syllogistic Scholasticism meant an emergence of an intellectually sophisticated body of magical writing. "The ban of the mediaeval Church on magic had forced it into dark holes and corners," writes Yates, but by the Renaissance scholars like Ficino "could no longer regard magic as the trade of ignorant and inferior persons,"[13] in part because of the respectability of philosophers like Plethon. Folk magic—the tasks of cunning women and men related to simple spells or potions—did and does have a role in everyday life, but Renaissance hermeticism elevated Neoplatonist magic into the realm of respectability. As a result, subjects like divination, alchemy, and astrology took on an invigorated significance, and figures like Paracelsus, Cornelius Agrippa, Johann Weyer, and Johann Reuchlin commanded tremendous respect, even though they are studied today more for cultural context than intellectual fortification. Divination in particular has a natural relationship to the broader religious subject of the apocalypse, for the moment anyone claims that they can predict the future, it's inevitable that they will wonder when humanity will run out of days left to predict. All manner of divination was explored by Renaissance mages, from bibliomancy (the use of randomly selected book passages to predict the future, usually from the Bible or Virgil's *Aeneid*) to scrying (entering a trance state through the contemplation of polished mirrors or stones).[14] No method, however, was as popular as astrology. The complex calculation of star charts and the position of planets in the solar system—especially during a century when there were fierce debates over the new Copernican model—made astrology both fascinating and attractive. In the sixteenth century there was a veritable pantheon of Renaissance astrologers, in part influenced by the Neoplatonist principle which reasons that as is the case in heaven, so it must be on earth. Hermetic figures like Elizabeth I's court astrologer John Dee and the infamous Italian heretic Giordano Bruno tried their hand at casting horoscopes, making complex calculations based on the position of stars and planets so as to predict the future. More conventionally scientific figures were also proficient in astrology; both Johannes Kepler and Galileo were involved in the vocation, though it seems as if the latter's enthusiasms were more financial than genuine.

Astrology doesn't necessarily demand apocalypticism, but during the religious tumult of the sixteenth century these two ways of understanding the universe were certainly connected. Keith Thomas observes, in *Religion and the Decline of Magic: Studies in Popular Beliefs in Sixteenth and Seventeenth Century England*, that "astrological interests were not confined to court circles, or to the entourage of the great . . . but were widely disseminated throughout the people. For this the invention of printing was chiefly responsible."[15] As the sixteenth century began—a numerologically auspicious year in its own right—the most popular astrological text was *Mirabilis Liber*, an anonymously redacted compendium of prophecies from a variety of figures, including the Roman Sibylline Oracles, St. Augustine, Hildegard von Bingen, and Joachim of Fiore, as well as somebody listed as "Merlin," the fictional wizard of Arthurian romance. "The wicked shall descend into hell with the beast," notes the redactor of the collection, the "righteous shall live in eternity, and shall be endlessly glorified with the King of Heaven."[16] A union of both the dove and the dragon.

What *Mirabilis Liber* lacks in originality it maintains in tradition. The earliest manuscript copies of the collection can be traced back to the eleventh century, and it wouldn't be printed until 1524 in France, but quickly the variety of vague and flexible predictions that tended to focus on natural disasters became popular for an anxious populace wearily eyeing events on the eastern edge of Europe.[17] *Mirabilis Liber*, among other texts, would be cannibalized and repurposed into what has proven to be a far more enduring work of astrological prediction, a book published in 1555 entitled *The Prophecies*, and written by a Provençal apothecary and grandson of Jewish *conversos* named Michel de Nostredame, but whom posterity recalls as Nostradamus. Born in 1503, four years after Ficino's death, Nostradamus inhabited the same Neoplatonic worldview as the Florentine philosopher, albeit operating at an intellectually less sophisticated level. Regardless, both had powerful patrons, with the French seer supported in part by Queen Catharine de' Medici of France, the great-great granddaughter of the same Cosimo who reestablished Plato's academy. Yet the popularity of *The Prophecies*, which has proven far more enduring than the ambivalent reception he received in his own century, demonstrates the democratic universalism of astrological thinking during the Renaissance, even while, or maybe especially if, the psychic plagiarized several complex Neoplatonist thinkers of the first few centuries of the Common Era. "If I have eschewed the word prophet," Nostradamus writes in the preface to *The Prophecies*, "I do not wish to attribute to myself such lofty title at the present time."[18] If clairvoyance was his actual talent, then such a protestation as that in the beginning of his book must be interpreted as false humility, otherwise it's simply a paradoxically failed prophecy—for being a prophet is precisely what Nostradamus has been understood as over the last five centuries.

Nostradamian rhetoric is marked by vagueness, inscrutableness, and flexibility of language which retroactively makes it seem as if the seer had foretold any number of future events. Attributed to *The Prophecies* are any number of clairvoyant passages, ranging from Napoleon's invasion of Russia to the German crossing of the Maginot Line, the Apollo Moon landing to the terrorist attacks of September 11. Nostradamus's ambiguities have elevated him from his immediate historical context into a figure bestride history, at least in the collective eyes of popular culture. Indeterminacy is to the great benefit of the psychic's posterity. Written in verse across a mélange of language including Latin, Greek, Occitan, and French, *The Prophecies* is composed of quatrains that are then organized into "Centuries." Predictions are not in chronological order, they are perhaps purposefully ambiguous, which has again contributed to Nostradamus's volume being continually in print for almost five hundred years. "The great man will be struck down in the day by a thunderbolt," Nostradamus writes, an "evil deed foretold by the bearer of a petition," so that after November 22, 1963, occultists made the connection to the assassination of John F. Kennedy, but you'll note that nothing in that quatrain was specific enough to keep the president from going to Dallas that day. Of course, there is the paradox of prognostication whereby if such quatrains were clear—definite dates, locations, and names—then people could simply avoid unpleasant futures, rendering the predictions now incorrect.

Reading *The Prophecies* through the lens of the cryptographer trying to find clues for events that happened between that book's publication and our present day is an exercise in fallacious reasoning. However, Nostradamus's unusual prosody deserves closer attention, with his modern translator Richard Sieburth hailing the prophet's "poetics of futurity," categorizing him properly as a kind of Renaissance avant-garde versifier who deserves to be included among other prophetic-poets including "Virgil, Dante, . . . Du Bartas, Milton and Blake."[19] Indeed, one sees a bit of what the translator means as Sieburth renders some lines of Nostradamus as "Sudden fall: news, news shall rise / Fields divided: new beginnings / Obstinate mockery: confusion, evil, raving," which if not read for prognostication does begin to take on the tenor of modernist poetry. Something else which connects Nostradamus to Dante, Milton, and Blake is that, like all of them, it's not easy to extricate the poet's own vision of himself as a prophet from his poetry, albeit the Frenchman was more enmeshed in astrology than anything else. *The Prophecies*, at least in this regard, is representative of its author's model of the universe. "Perfect knowledge of such things cannot be acquired without divine inspiration," he writes, "given that all prophetic inspiration derives its initial origin from God Almighty," and indeed the author's theology is in many ways equivalent with astrology.[20]

A profound apocalyptic anxiety marks both *The Prophecies* and *Mirabilis Liber*; for all of the mistiness when it comes to exact predictions in both volumes, there is a shared sense of the shape which Doomsday will take. For Nostradamus and the compiler of *Mirabilis Liber*, there is an expectation that an Islamic antichrist beckons at the door of Europe, that a Saracen Gog and Magog will march into Christendom, will destroy Rome and depose the pope—the arrival of a dragon in a turban. A little more than a century after the fall of Constantinople, with the sultan often configured as an antichrist, the faithful examined the heavens for signs of judgment and relied on experts like Nostradamus to do so for them. "When 1999 is seven months over," reads one quatrain, "Shall heaven's great king—albeit a dread host, / Restore the King."[21] Many read that as a prophecy of apocalypse, though as this book's copyright date will indicate it would seem that either Nostradamus was wrong in his prediction or his readers were wrong in their interpretations.

During the sixteenth century there were a number of other proffered dates for the end of the world, which the prophets who made them rather audaciously often placed only a few short years into the future, the easier for their own inaccuracy to be confirmed. The German astronomer Johannes Stoffler thought Doomsday would come in 1524, later updating it to 1528 when the world was still there. The Spanish theologian Michael Servestus predicted an end date of 1585, though he wouldn't live to see it, as the Socinian would be burnt at the stake for heresy in Geneva some three decades before the imagined judgment day.[22] For Botticelli, the great Florentine painter who had once rendered scenes of pagan sumptuary so gorgeous that they would have stirred Plethon's soul, the apocalypse would commence in 1504.

Botticelli's painting *The Mystical Nativity*, composed in 1500, demonstrated his conversion to a particularly apocalyptic form of Christianity, and away from the classical themes that had been his previous mainstay, such as the birth of Venus and the springtime dancing of nymphs. Of the painter's entire oeuvre, *The Mystical Nativity* is the only composition which Botticelli signed, alongside a Greek inscription explaining that the work had been finished "at the end of the year 1500, in the troubles of Italy . . . in the second woe of the Apocalypse, during the release of the devil for three and a half years."[23] Rendered in the unmistakable High Renaissance style that marked Botticelli's secular and classical paintings, with his startling application of reds, blues, yellows, and greens that in their vibrancy seem almost more real than the prosaic hues of everyday life, *The Mystical Nativity* depicts the birth of Christ in the center of the canvas, alongside the expected retinue of the Holy Family, the magi, and assorted shepherds, while above that tableaux is a rotating chorus of twelve angels and beneath them are demons fleeing into the underworld. With the satanic assemblage and the celestial visions, there is an uneasiness to the composition, despite its Christmas imagery. Importantly, the vision was not Botticelli's, it rather originated with a fanatical and authoritarian Dominican monk named Girolamo Savonarola, whom the artist, and much of the rest of Florence, had fallen under the sway of during the four-year period starting in 1494, after which the monk ruled as a de facto theocratic dictator in what had been the most cosmopolitan city in Christendom.[24] Prone to visions and prophecies, Savonarola saw apocalypse as much as Neoplatonist astrologers did, but he was steadfastly against occultism, consigning the works of Ficino and Mirandola to the flames, inaugurating what's best understood as a veritable Counter-Renaissance in the heart of Renaissance Italy, a terrifying enactment of apocalypticisms' dangerous powers when unleashed, especially when it comes in the form of the dragon. Almost twenty years before Savonarola rose to power and deposed the Medici family, the friar wrote to his father explaining why he joined the Order of St. Dominic: "because I could not stand the great wickedness of the blind people of Italy, especially when I saw that virtue had been completely cast down and vice raised up."[25] Savonarola—ascetic and diabolically ferocious in his religious enthusiasms—had lived a mendicant life after joining the Dominicans in Bologna, fulminating against what he viewed as a softening of their vows, preferring to travel through northern Italy where he attracted large crowds of the poor who were enervated by his apocalyptic preaching. With the Chair of St. Peter occupied by the licentious, powerful, and greedy Roderigo Borgia, who reigned as Alexander VI, lay Catholics were enraptured by Savonarola's anticlericalism, denunciations of church corruption and excess, and his agitation for the poor, as well as his more puritanical positions regarding Renaissance learning.

Judgment day focused Savonarola's thoughts, writing as early as 1475 in a poem about how Rome "is crawling on the ground, / And never will return to its great office. / Those times once chaste and pious are long past."[26] Apocalypticism was examined by the Neoplatonists, but it was lived by Savonarola, who gravitated toward the darker aspects of millennium, seeing in the auspicious approaching year of 1500 the possibility of all sin, inequity, and wickedness being destroyed in a cleansing fire. David Weinstein argues in *Savonarola: The Rise and Fall of a Renaissance Prophet* that the "Apocalypse sermons were unequivocally new: he delivered them with a conviction and an authority he had previously hesitated to claim, drawing upon the capital accumulated in years of studying and teaching Scripture and poring over the commentaries and glosses of the masters."[27] By 1489, the friar's preaching took on a markedly eschatological tone, thundering in Brescia about how they "would see rivers of blood in the streets; wives would be torn from their husbands, virgins ravished, children murdered before their mothers' eyes; all would be terror, fire, and bloodshed."[28] From his readings, the monk developed a violent political theology which threatened all that the humanists had constructed in Tuscany.

Ironically Savonarola was invited back to his native Florence by Mirandola who appreciated the friar's keen mind and perhaps shared a sense of the heretical, although, as the philosopher would learn, they were divergent heresies. Even more ironically, the monk would be given an official ecclesiastical position in the government of Florence by appointment of Lorenzo de' Medici, even though it would be Savonarola who would see to it that the family was forced into exile. Quickly the ecstatic preaching of the monk attracted followers who organized into a potent political party known as the Frateschi, having acquired real civil power, while young partisans loyal to Savonarola assembled into roving gangs known as the Piagnoni, the "Weepers," who were the puritanical shock troops of this new revolutionary vanguard. Florence may have been the glittering city of the Renaissance, but the cleric understood all of that to be only so much worldly dross, decadence, and degeneracy committed by an elite; he claimed that the church was in bondage, the papacy corrupted, and that a "New Cyrus" would act as a messiah to liberate the holy from the clutches of servitude.

Florence was to have a central role in this eschatology as a veritable New Jerusalem, "more glorious, richer, more powerful than she has ever been," though not through the financial speculation of the Medici, but rather "in the sight of God," for the city "will be the reformation of all Italy, and from here the renewal will begin and spread everywhere."[29] Savonarola's renewals seemed possible after the French invaded Italy in 1494, so that the cleric cannily negotiated a reprieve for Florence that spared it a long siege or a violent occupation. The Medici family fled the city and the monk became the absolute ruler of the republic. Alexander VI denounced Savonarola, to which the monk responded that "Whoever excommunicates me, excommunicates God." Apocalypse had come to Florence and the friar wanted all to know that the "sword of the Lord will descend suddenly and quickly upon the earth."[30]

A sense of Savonarola's Luciferian intensity is imparted in the famous portrait of the monk rendered by Fra Bartolomeo, an artist who became a Dominican because of the preacher's influence and who depicted the cleric in profile, his corpuscular face emerging from the darkness of his monastic cowl, a beak-like protuberance of a nose underneath eyes vital in their complete certainty. These were the eyes which looked out upon the infamous Bonfire of the Vanities, held periodically during his reign, but with the largest conflagration ignited on Shrove Tuesday underneath the staid clocktower of the Piazza della Signoria in 1497. Copies of Boccaccio's *The Decameron* and Petrarch's *Canzoniere*, rich tapestries of red, blue, and green depicting Apollo and Bacchus, immaculately carved violins and mandolins, cosmetics, jewelry, and fine clothes, and presumably any number of Renaissance masters' works, all piled into the pyre of an *auto-da-fé* and sacrificed to the dark lords of apocalypticism.

Strangely, a number of the intelligentsia had at first been attracted to the preacher for the same reason that Mirandola was; his apocalypticism seemed a cipher for a radical politics which denounced avarice and exploitation. Botticelli became a zealous member the Piagnoni, even consigning some of his own paintings to the Bonfire of the Vanities, that heaping of "lascivious, vain and detestable objects" as described by the Neoplatonist poet Girolamo Benivieni in his *Canzoni*,[31] giving a firsthand account of the immolations. Even Ficino first hailed the arrival of the monk, but Savonarola's positions were substantially darker than they may have realized. The philosopher "later rejected Savonarola," writes Alison McQueen in *Political Realism in Apocalyptic Times*, while explaining that "he did so within the apocalyptic imaginary—denouncing the friar as the antichrist who had led Florence astray."[32]

Like a bonfire, apocalypticism freely stoked with the oxygen of prophecy can quickly go out of control, and Savonarola would himself be singed, metaphorically and literally. By 1498, Florentines grew weary of the Piagnoni and Savonarola's authoritarian rule and in the ever-combustible world of Tuscan republicanism the Frateschi began to lose influence. The Dominican was challenged by a rival Franciscan leader over claims that he was a visionary prophet able to command miracles; Savonarola said that he would walk through fire to prove his own favor from the Lord, but blanched as the event approached, having been granted a reprieve by a downpour. The Florentines who began to suspect that his ministry was a charade had their suspicions confirmed. Finally, in the spring of that year Savonarola, who'd both lost the narrative and the trust of his fellow citizens, was arrested alongside two of his compatriots. While imprisoned, he variously claimed that his visions had been a hoax and then recanted those recantations. A sentiment arose among the denizens of the city that, far from being a holy man, Savonarola was a false prophet, the sort warned against in the gospels, and a harbinger of apocalypse rather than a saint who would institute millennium. On May 23, 1498, after having already been hung, Savonarola was placed upon the kindling in the Piazza della Signoria, the same square where a year earlier he'd presided over the Bonfire of the Vanities. He was finally committed to the test of those flames, though God's mercy was to be found wanting.

After his execution, civil authorities gathered the ashes and distributed them at several undisclosed places on the Arno, to prevent a martyrology accruing around the monk and his schismatic heresies of disunion. The year of the Dominican's execution, far to the north in Eisenach, Germany, a fifteen-year-old boy would begin his religious studies, later writing "Christ canonizes Savonarola through us even though popes and papists burst to pieces over it."[33] By 1512 the Medici had returned to Florence, aided by papal troops who occupied the rebellious city. Five years after that, the same young man studying in Eisenach who'd adored the model of Savonarola was now an Augustinian monk himself and in October of 1517 he would nail a protestation to the church door in Wittenberg, threatening not just apocalyptic disunion in a single principality as the Dominican had done, but indeed through all of Christendom.

The Ends of the Earth

The Age of Exploration

Having received his royal commission to embark from Palos de la Frontera on the southwest coast of the Iberian Peninsula on August 2, 1492, the Genoese navigator Cristoforo Colombo had to delay setting sail by one day, as his original departure date coincided with the Jewish holiday of Tish'a B'Av which commemorated the destruction of the Temple in Jerusalem and now also happened to be the date set by the decree of the dual monarchs of newly unified Spain as the deadline by which all unconverted Jews and Muslims must leave the kingdom.[34] Palos de la Frontera itself had been part of the Almohad caliphate in just the previous century, but now with the completion of what King Ferdinand and Queen Isabella—the funders of Columbus's expedition—called *Reconquista*, the various Christian kingdoms of Castille and Aragon, Navarre and Catalonia had unified over time and pushed the Muslims out of southern Spain, the final Islamic stronghold of Granada having fallen only eight months before Columbus's departure, bringing to a close the dream of al-Andalus, that nearly eight-centuries-old civilization of creative firmament now reduced in its own apocalypse.

This was a realm where "Muslims, Christians, and Jews lived here in concord, turning al-Andalus into a cosmopolitan Arabo-Islamic society, and making Cordoba, 'the ornament of the world,' a magnet for scholars and scientists and a model of cosmopolitan enlightenment," as Brian A. Catlos writes in *Kingdoms of Faith: A New History of Islamic Spain*.[35] In the place of al-Andalus would be the zealous monarchy of Spain, whose rulers not only demanded the conversion or exile of Jews and Muslims (with many *conversos* being outwardly Catholic while adhering to their original faith), but who steadfastly charted the genealogical background of even pious new Christians, thus introducing a new bigotry into the world which obsessed over the myth of blood.[36] While the sailor Colombo, better known by his Latinized name Columbus, waited to leave port, Palos de la Frontera was crowded with some of the 800,000 Jewish refugees forced by the Catholic sovereigns to flee a realm that had been their home for centuries. On ships bound for Italy and Morocco, Greece and the Levant, Jews bundled Torah scrolls and menorahs, copies of the Zohar and mezuzahs pried from doorposts as they fled the only homes they'd ever known. Among the crowded docks of Palos de la Frontera, the expedition of the Santa Maria, the Pinta, and the Nina would have scarcely registered among the anxious multitude.

"My heart is in the east, and I in the uttermost west," wrote the greatest Sephardic poet, the Toledo-born bard Judah Halevi, pining for the Jews' return to Jerusalem. Columbus dreamt of that Holy City as well, but his plan to return to the east required him to first go west. Granada may have become part of Spain, and the great minarets of the Alhambra Mosque were now of a cathedral, but Jerusalem was still Islamic, and Columbus hoped to find a revenue stream to fund an apocalyptic final crusade which the captain believed would see the city of Jesus Christ's crucifixion in the hands of the church once again.[37] As a means of gathering such capital, while avoiding the perilous navigation around the African Cape of Good Hope, Columbus imagined an easier access to the lucrative Asian spice trade, across the Atlantic. The day after Christmas in 1492, when Columbus had already crossed ocean and come upon some unexpected lands which he was unaware of, and he noted in his diary that his desire was to amass wealth that could be put toward the preparation "to go conquer the Holy Sepulcher . . . to spend all the profits of this my enterprise on the conquest of Jerusalem."[38]

This proposal had been put to John II of Portugal and Henry VII of England, both of whom rejected it, finally receiving a modest sum from the unified Spanish crown after he had an audience with Ferdinand in January of the year he departed, held in the encampment outside of Grenada itself. Ahistorical nineteenth-century affectations have had many erroneous legends accrue about the character of Columbus; that he proved the globe was round and that he was a man of science in a world of superstition. Both of these contentions are steadfastly false; that the world was spherical was widely known and accepted among all authorities since before the Common Era, and far from being a secular, democratic, empirical figure, Columbus possessed a firmly medieval mind. "Columbus believes not only in Christian dogma," writes Tzvetan Todorov in *The Conquest of America: The Question of the Other*, "but also (and he is not alone at the time) in Cyclopes and mermaids, in Amazons and men with tails, and his belief, as strong as Saint Peter's, therefore permits him to find them."[39] In contrast to the Columbian hagiography which dominates our culture, the navigator's landfall in the Caribbean some two months after his departure was based on error and luck. Regarding error, Columbus had severely misjudged the size of the planet, the standard calculation of the earth's circumference in the 1490s surprisingly close to accurate. Had two large continents not been in the way of Asia, Columbus would have never reached land—but as regards luck, there did happen to be an entirely new part of the world in the western hemisphere.

This was a man who affirmed that Eden still existed on earth and that he could travel to it, the shape of the world not actually being round but more akin to that of a woman's breast, with paradise located at the nipple, which he assumed was perhaps in the temperate climes that he eventually landed in. Fundamentally, Columbus functioned from an eschatological and occult perspective extreme even by the standards of the late fifteenth century, which included penning his own *Book of Prophecies*. Carol Delaney writes in the journal *Comparative Studies in Society and History* that according to Columbus, the "conversion of all peoples to Christianity and the re-conquest of Jerusalem are necessary preconditions for the 'Second Coming' when Christ will return before the 'End of Days.' Columbus felt strongly the imminence of this event; he also came to feel that he had a providential role to play in the drama."[40] The explorer had intended for Chinese, Indian, and Japanese treasures to help fund the ushering in of an apocalypse, but the discovery of an unknown fourth part of the world would arguably have an eschatological significance broader than even Columbus could have even envisioned, especially as he noted in the *Book of Prophecies* that "for the execution of the journey to the Indies I was not aided by intelligence, by mathematics or by maps. It was simply the fulfillment of what Isaiah had promised."[41] From the moment that Columbus's slipper sank into the white sand of the Bahamas, buffeted on his journey by warm trade winds, America was already an apocalyptic place.

Much debate has been had about how aware Columbus was or wasn't about the actual location of his landings across four separate voyages. Columbus had maintained in his letters to the Spanish crown that Puerto Rico, Cuba, Hispaniola, Trinidad, and the coasts of Central and South America were all islands off the coast of Asia, even while he admitted that these were realms that were unknown to Christendom, as were the Carib, Arawak, and Taino people whom he mislabeled collectively as "Indians." By changing perspective, however, what are North and South America but literally islands "off the coast of Asia," albeit massive ones that happen to be very far from that other continent? Historian Edmundo O'Gorman argues in his work *The Invention of America* that the "great American historical problem" is to "explain how the idea of America arose in the consciousness of Western culture," claiming that the shift in the decade after Columbus acknowledged that he'd found lands that Christendom was unaware of to the more epoch-shattering contention that an entire "New World" had been found was an audacious act of cultural metaphysical engineering.[42] "This new concept," O'Gorman notes, "is that of America not discovered but invented."[43] This act of reclassifying these unknown lands as an entirely new part of the world was, furthermore, a prophetic act; it was and remains an attribute of the apocalyptic imagination.

By 1552, the Spanish notary Francisco López de Gómera would write in his *General History of the Indies* that the discovery of America was the "greatest event since the creation of the world, save the incarnation and death of Him who created it."[44] During that five-decade interlude between Columbus's arrival and Gómera's pronouncement, the Spanish had waged a series of wars of colonial conquest across the Caribbean, Central and South America, and Mexico, growing fat with filched gold and making the Hapsburg Dynasty by far the wealthiest power on earth. These conquistadors, who established New Spain upon the ruins of the Aztec Empire which had been decimated by smallpox, unleashed upon the Americas an actual apocalypse which would be compounded as the other European powers—Portugal and England, France, and Holland—established their own colonies in the New World. For many of those colonizers the discovery of America was a providential act, an opportunity to spread the gospel and increase the share of the Lord's people on earth, as well as to expand royal coffers.

As the early seventeenth-century English advocate for American colonization Robert Johnson wrote, "we may verily believe, that God hath reserved in this last age of the world, an infinite number of those lost and scattered sheep, to be won and recovered by our means."[45] The more immediate result of this Colombian exchange, which saw potatoes and tomatoes, chocolate and corn imported into the rest of the world, propelling growth and catapulting Europe out of its relative economic, social, and political backwardness, was also interpreted as the mark of beneficent providence. More than any of those material justifications, the discovery of America had an apocalyptic significance not because of any of the events which followed Columbus's arrival, but because of the mere existence of these continents, once they were understood not just as newly discovered lands but indeed an entirely "New World." This had profound prophetic implications, a disruption in the medieval perspective of reality, arguably an event even more jarring than Copernicus's heliocentric model of the universe. With the invention of America came the demolishment of an entire worldview, the so-called "discovery" of these continents like a comet in the sky or blood in the water, an omen of the last days which are to come.

Among medieval geographers, a tripartite model of the earth, heavily mediated in a spatial mythopoeic language, dominated understandings of what the world was actually like. With its unmistakable Trinitarian associations, the world was envisioned as "equally" split between the continents of Europe, Asia, and Africa, with Jerusalem as the connective navel of all three.[46] In the "T-O maps" produced during the Middle Ages, so called because in their abstraction they resembled a letter "T" inscribed within a letter "O," there was a harmony and balance between the lands of humanity. Other maps sometimes depicted the continents as being like a three-leaf clover, which shouldn't be mistaken as an understanding of what the "actual" world was like. Merchants and navigators, diplomats and pilgrims, understood that coasts are craggy, rivers are crooked, and the earth is curved, *but on an allegorical level, on a lyrical and poetic level, on a metaphysical and mystical level*, the division of the world into threes reflected a Christian cosmology. What then is the disorder caused by the discovery of a fourth part of the world? For that matter, among historians who believed that the three sons of Noah populated each of these continents—Shem into Asia, Ham into Africa, and Japheth into Europe—how did you explain the existence of the "Indians," a people mentioned nowhere in Scripture?

But to envision the Americas as a *separate* and *entirely new* part of the globe wouldn't happen until 1507, in a volume entitled *Introduction to Cosmography* by the Alsatian cartographers Mathias Ringmann and Martin Waldseemuller, within a short paragraph where they describe post-Columbian expeditions to the western hemisphere, whereby "a fourth part has been discovered by Amerigo Vespucci. . . . Since both Asia and Africa received their names from women, I do not see why anyone should rightly prevent this from being called Amerigen—the land of Amerigo, as it were—or America, after its discoverer, Americus, a man of perceptive character."[47] In the book's attendant map of the world, the first instance of the word "America" is inscribed in small letters next to the thin ribbon of the east coast of South America running north to south, all which had so far been explored.

Both Columbus and Vespucci had charted the same shores, but only the latter—at least according to Waldseemuller and Ringmann—had conceived of it as a New World, which made all the difference. The revelation of a hitherto unknown segment of Creation (or its "invention," as O'Gorman would emphasize) seemed so freighted with providential significance that Christian expectations about space and time were completely upended. That the Reformation begins in earnest only a decade after the christening of America is not mere coincidence. Furthermore, America's western directionality from Europe had apocalyptic and millennial associations as well, the land of the sun's dusk inevitably connected to endings and finality. This is what the Dutch historian Jan Willem Schulte Nordholt calls the "heliotropic mythos" in *The Myth of the West: America as the Last Empire*, or as I've termed it in my contribution to *Prophecy and Eschatology in the Trans-Atlantic World, 1550–1800* as "directional poetics," the sense that the West has an overwhelming apocalyptic significance that was important throughout colonialism.[48] Because America was to the west, it would be understood as Hesperus, Paradise, Utopia, Atlantis, Eden.

In his study, Nordholt examines hundreds of incidences of Western directionality as being imbued with implications of apocalypticism. There are several English-language examples, as that nation belatedly began to colonize the east coast of North America (perhaps there being a sense of national regret regarding Henry VII's rejection of Columbus's proposal). The Scottish speculator and poet William Alexander enthuses about American colonization in his epic *A Doomes-Day, or the Great Day of the Last Judgement*, describing the continent in millennial terms as a "second Eden's gardens of delight" proclaiming how "Christ a Church over all the Earth may have, / His righteousness shall barbarous realms array / if their first love more civil lands will leave, / To Europe may America succeed, / God may of stone raise up to Abram seed." In this schema, Alexander typifies Europe as a place of decline and degeneracy, the wheel ever turning as that civilization falls into decay, but America offers opportunity for a final godly realm before millennium. America's relative location toward the direction of the setting sun and thus of the miniature apocalypse which occurs every day was typological in predicting where the final millennial monarchy would be situated before Christ's return. Richard Sibbes, a late sixteenth-century English Calvinist theologian, reasoned that the "Gospels course hath hitherto been as that of the sun, from east to west, and so in God's time may proceed yet further west. No creature can hinder the course of the sun, nor stop the influence of heaven, until Christ hath brought all under one head" while his contemporary, the missionary John White, rhetorically opined that "our Savior choose to name the Lightning that shines out of the East into the West unless it to be to expresses not only the sudden shining out of the Gospel, but withal the way, and passage, by which to proceeds from one end of the world to the other, that is, from East to West."[49]

Here the direction of providence is clearly stated, the light of divinity emerging in the east but bestowing its glow upon the west.

More than just an esoteric concern, the idea that Western colonization had apocalyptic import encouraged European powers to better to position themselves as the last and greatest kingdom before judgment day. England in particular had an acute eschatological anxiety related both to its increasingly radical Protestantism and its belatedness in colonialism, especially when compared to the hated Spanish. Questions of which European power would have a role in providential history as related to their Western colonialism was specifically tied to a concept known as *translatio studii et imperii*, that is the "translation," as in "transference," of knowledge and power from one temporal kingdom to the next. In such a schema, history always operates by the rise and decline of respective empires which carry the mantle of knowledge, power, and, in some cases, righteousness, until decadence causes their inevitable dissolution.[50] Often there was an understanding of the identity of these various empires as moving specifically east to west, so that the most ancient imperium was oriental Babylon, whose decline saw the rise of Alexander's Greece, followed by Rome, and then, depending on who was doing the calculations, variously Hapsburg Spain, England, or some other European power.

Though *translatio* was a concept that derived from classical sources, it was often combined with the prophetic language of the Book of Daniel, where history was divided into four different empires, with the fifth monarchy being associated with Christ. Among advocates for New World colonization, a prophetic rhetoric of *translatio* was instrumental in yoking theological concerns to those of contemporary geopolitics, so that England, for example, could be imagined as the fifth monarchy, the stone which shatters the clay feet of the godless idol that represents those previous kingdoms; the shock troops for Christ's millennial return. "World history would therefore be at last completed in England, in the West. It would be the last empire," explains Nordholt.[51] Such a manner of thinking, that a contemporary state can act as a "redeemer" in some sense for the world, would have profound implications in the coming five centuries.

An irony in all of the European considerations about the eschatological import of America—whether it heralded the coming of the millennium, the dawn of judgment day, or an opportunity to build God's kingdom in a New World—was that Columbus's arrival signified the beginning of a very real series of apocalypses for the possibly hundred million people who already occupied these two massive continents. "Throughout the sixteenth and seventeenth centuries novel microorganisms spread across the Americas, ricocheting from victim to victim, killing three-quarters or more of the people in the hemisphere," explains science journalist Charles C. Mann in *1493: Uncovering the New World Columbus Created*.[52]

First the Spanish, then the Portuguese, the English, the French, and so on, engaged in conquest, ethnic cleansing, and genocide against the Indigenous peoples of the Americas, but it was the unseen spirochetes and bacterium brought by the Christians that devastated the New World, in a pandemic which dwarfed the Black Death, a trail of disease and horror that is almost inconceivable. Listing the viruses and bacteria which Europeans introduced, and which Indigenous peoples had no natural immunity against, Mann tabulates "smallpox, influenza, hepatitis, measles, encephalitis, and viral pneumonia . . . tuberculosis, diphtheria, cholera, typhus, scarlet fever, and bacterial meningitis."[53] Because deadly disease often preceded the colonists themselves, transferred on goods traded between tribes, two erroneous beliefs took hold—that this was a virginal and Edenic land largely devoid of people and free to become a utopian commons and that God had cleared the land of Indigenous people for the benefit of Europeans. More than an Eden, America was a graveyard of blanched skulls, a place of horror in the howling wilderness where, if there was a "fall," it was brought by Lucifer on boats. "In the annals of human history there is no comparable demographic catastrophe," writes Mann.[54] Supernatural explanations—apocalypticism—became a means by which the Indigenous peoples interpreted the colonial situation, and more importantly, a way in which they resisted European brutality. "The old notion that native peoples were a docile, conservative population, traumatized into political impotency by the shock of the conquest and lulled into passivity by the paternalistic regime of the hacienda has fallen by the wayside," writes Kevin Gosner in *Soldiers of the Virgin: The Moral Economy of a Colonial Maya Rebellion*. "We now recognize that Indians often responded in kind to the violence and brutality of colonial life."[55] Among the second generation of Andean Incas living thirty years after the brutal Spanish invasion of Peru led by the conquistador Francisco Pizarro, there developed a mystical millennial faith known as Taki Unquy. Around 1562, the Incas were afflicted with something they called the "dancing sickness," a type of ecstatic, visionary state whereby it was believed that women and men were possessed by the indigenous spirits of the Andes who were offended by the presence of the Spanish (interestingly, similar bouts of "dancing plague" were occurring contemporaneously in Europe). For the authorities, Taki Unquy was something to be feared, and the movement was quickly put down, but other indigenous apocalyptic movements had a greater impact.

A curious syncretic example happened in 1772 in Chiapas, then part of New Spain and today in Mexico. Among the indigenous Tzeltal people emerged an apocalyptic faith which was a fusion of indigenous beliefs and devotion to the Virgin Mary, whereby the Spanish were interpreted as irrevocable enemies of Christ, and it was believed that the Mother of God would assist the Tzeltal people in their anticolonial rebellion against the colonial authorities.

This movement was inaugurated after an indigenous prophetess named Maria de la Candelaria was visited by Mary, who requested that the woman build a chapel in her honor.[56] Rejected both by her Spanish parish priest and the local bishop, who accused Candelaria of lying, the Tzeltal grew increasingly angry at the occupation. They overthrew civil and ecclesiastical authority in Chiapas over the course of the following year, until the revolt was violently suppressed. Even more enduring is the faith of Inkarri, based on a prophecy of messianic return from Atahualpa, the final king of the Incas who, before he was executed by the Spanish, vowed that he would return to expel them from the land. Such beliefs were promulgated during the rebellion of Tupac Amaru against Spanish rule in Lima, and Inkarri endures even today as a means of anticolonial resistance.[57]

Perhaps the most striking apocalyptic narrative from the conquest of the Americas involves the dramatic, epic, and horrific war of conquest which the conquistador Hernán Cortés waged across the deserts and rainforest of Mexico in 1519, as the Spanish first sailed along the coast and then marched toward the capital of the Aztec Empire. Tenochtitlan was a city of wide canals and splendid aqueducts, ball courts and palaces, temples and pyramids, a desert metropolis built within a lake, surrounded by blooming prickly pear cactus and maguey. At the time when Emperor Moctezuma II first heard reports concerning the strangely dressed men speaking an unknown language who'd been making inroads along the Gulf Coast, the population of Tenochtitlan was 400,000—more than eight times the size of Constantinople when it had fallen sixty-six years before. The Aztec city was twice the size of Europe's largest cities of Paris and Naples, and nearly four times the size of Florence. Recalling the entry of the Spanish into Tenochtitlan, the conquistador Bernal Díaz del Castillo said, "We were astounded. These great towns and buildings made of stone, rising from the water, seemed like an enchanted vision . . . it was all so marvelous that I do not know how to tell it: things never seen, heard of, or even dreamed of before," though as he says, "But now all is overthrow and lost; nothing is left standing."[58]

Initially there had been an uneasy coexistence between Cortés and Moctezuma, but the former was never going to accept the status quo when gold, glory, and God—in that order—remained his priorities. Tenochtitlan would be besieged for several months in 1521 by the small core of Spanish conquistadors and their Indigenous allies, leaving the Aztecs to suffer first from famine, then plague, then collapse, and finally occupation. From the stones of the Aztec temples the Dominicans would build the cathedral of Mexico City.

"The fall of Tenochtitlan has become less a fixed event than an emblematic point of origin that generates multiple fables: of betrayal and treachery, hubris and retribution, unthinkable violence and prolonged mourning," writes Kirsten Silva Gruesz in her contribution *A New Literary History of America*.[59] Because such an overwhelmingly powerful military force as the Aztecs fell relatively quickly to the Spanish, many of these explanatory fables which Gruesz mentions have taken on an eschatological tenor. Originating with Cortés himself is the possibly mythic claim that the Aztecs regarded the conquistador as a manifestation of the feather-plumed serpent god Quetzalcoatl, whom prophecy had said would arrive from the east as the Spanish indeed had. According to this conjecture, the Aztecs had been made soft by their millennial expectation that this deity would return to earth, and Cortés very cagily used that conflation to his advantage.

Most likely this tale is completely false, flattering as it does Cortés's own pretensions regarding his importance, and yet it's true that as the Spanish made their way toward Tenochtitlan, emissaries of Moctezuma presented the Spaniard with treasures, many of them gold, which was perhaps interpreted by the invaders as an act of religious fealty as opposed to the demonstration of power which was the emperor's intent. Regardless, the generation of those who survived the conquest, the first of those who lived an existence that merged Spanish and Aztec cultures, were tasked with recording what their parents and grandparents remembered of Cortés's invasion. Compiled by the Franciscan scholar Bernardino de Sahagún, numerous Aztec authors recounted those years in their native language of Nahuatl, illustrating the manuscript with the colorful art of Mesoamerica. By 1575, Sahagún's manuscript had returned to Spain; shortly afterward it was forgotten until rediscovered centuries later by scholars, the last echo of a culture destroyed. In the interim, it would sit on a shelf in the Laurentian Library, founded in 1523 in the shadow of the great dome of the Cathedral of Santa Maria del Fiore, the Nahuatl manuscript making its circuitous way to the city of Plethon and Ficino, Mirandola and Savonarola, and forever after known as the Florentine Codex.

In the translation rendered by Miguel Leon-Portilla in *Broken Spears: The Aztec Account of the Conquest of Mexico*, we are told that when Moctezuma first heard of Cortés, "what he felt in his heart" was that the "new arrival was our prince Quetzalcoatl."[60] The authors explain how Moctezuma gathered a contingent of his jaguar-warriors to travel to the Spaniards with presents, to welcome Quetzalcoatl here at the ends of the world. Such offerings included "a serpent mask inlaid with turquoise, a decoration for the breast made of quetzal feather . . . a helmet in the shape of a cone, yellow with gold and set with many stars, a number of earrings adorned with little gold bells . . . a collar of fine shells," and so on.[61] When the jaguar-warriors made contact with the Spanish, after having done "reverence to Cortes by touching the ground before him with their lips," they outfitted the Christian with their finery. Cortés with his sparse black beard, a barrel-chested conquistador with his crucifix and rosaries, was fastened by the jaguar-warriors in the "divine finery." The authors record that Cortés asked the Aztecs, after having been dressed in the serpent mask and the helmet, the woven vest and the collar, "And is this all?"

Wittenberg's Church Door

The Reformation Arrives

All of the intellectual currents which dominated the conversations of the Reformation—doctrines of salvation through faith alone, reliance on scriptural inerrancy, the denial of the real presence of the Lord in the Eucharist, iconoclastic fury directed at religious imagery, vernacular translation of the Bible, anticlericalism and the condemnation of ecclesiastical excess, avarice, and hypocrisy—all of those trends predate the sixteenth century. If looking for a beginning to the Reformation, a cognizant case could be made that it "began" in 1412 when the Bohemian theologian Jan Hus declared Christ and not the pope the ultimate head of the church, while condemning the selling of indulgences and the waging of religious war; or, it could be said that the movement started with the English Peasant's Rebellion's prophet John Wycliffe and his vernacular translation of the Bible in 1382; or perhaps even as far back as 1179 when the Lombard preacher Peter Waldo was excommunicated for denouncing belief in transubstantiation and purgatory, among other tenets of the Catholic faith. As it is, most people date the beginnings of Protestantism to when a fiery, brilliant, pugilistic, earthy, and complicated theology professor and Augustinian monk named Martin Luther nailed his *Ninety-Five Theses* to the church door in the sleepy, scholarly Saxon city of Wittenberg on October 31, 1517. Rather than an arcane academic debate, what resulted were a series of schisms, movements, and denominations that would rend apart Western Christianity.

"On the eve of Reformation," writes Brad S. Gregory in *The Unintended Reformation: How a Religious Revolution Secularized Society*, "Latin Christianity comprised . . . the far from homogenous yet institutionalized worldview within which the overwhelming majority of Europeans lived and made sense of their lives," while by contrast today "Westerners live in and think with and even feel through the historical results of its variegated rejections and appropriations."[62] From Luther's pounding of his mallet on the heavy oak doors of Wittenberg would come Protestantism, but also, as has been argued, capitalism, positivism, and secularism. None of this was his intent, for despite Luther's protestations in 1517, he considered himself a good Catholic. Luther's way of understanding the world was firmly of his time and in his choice of monastic vocation is evidenced just how much of the theological discourse of the time was fundamentally a matter of differing interpretations of Augustine's legacy.

By far the most important theological figure in Western Christianity, Augustine's thinking included both an emphasis on the papacy's legitimacy through apostolic succession and a strong current of believing that only faith, or grace, and not "good works," merit salvation, as well as having a strong streak of affirming some variation on predestination, with all the attendant implications for free will. The Catholic Church obviously affirmed the fourth-century theologian's strong commitment to the support of the papacy, while they consistently rejected the privileging of faith over works. Luther rather reversed these positions, with Diarmaid MacCulloch writing in *All Things Made New: The Reformation and Its Legacy* that this "is the basis of the Protestant Reformation. It was saying loud and clear what Augustine had said long before."[63]

Teutonic Catholicism was austere, stern, sin-obsessed, and apocalyptic. Even after taking monastic orders in 1507, Luther was haunted by scrupulosity, the obsessive-compulsive need to fulfill the minutiae of sanctifying ritual so as to ensure that one merited salvation through such works. Not enough rosaries could be prayed, not enough confessions could be offered, not enough contrition could be presented for Luther to be certain that he wasn't damned. *Sola fidei*, the doctrine that it's through faith and not good works that the Christian merits salvation, with the latter merely evidence of the former, wasn't novel to Luther's theology, but in the life of the monk himself this discovery was a tremendous consolation.

In a document from 1519, Luther reflected on his previous anxieties and the conversion experience which banished his intrusive feelings of guilt; he writes, "I, blameless monk that I was, felt that before God I was a sinner with an extremely troubled conscience. I couldn't be sure that God was appeased by my satisfaction."[64] Such inadequacies kindled a blasphemous heart within the Augustinian, but when reflecting on Paul's Epistle to the Romans, Luther "began to understand that in this verse the justice of God is that by which the just person lives by a gift of God, that is by faith."[65] In other words, there is no number of good deeds we can do, blessed thoughts that we may have, rituals that we can perform—or indulgences that we can pay to the church—which will come close to meriting our salvation. Rather it is only the beneficent gift of faith from God which can do this. A great burden was lifted from Luther, this realization "was for me the very gate of paradise." Luther's theology didn't arrive fully formed as his conversion did, it developed over the course of his life both before and after 1517, but often the core of his faith is reduced to the so-called "five solas," the basic principles of the earliest Reformation as expressed by the theologian. Absolutely none of them are novel to Luther or to early modern Protestantism. *Sola fidei* is the doctrine that humans achieve salvation through faith alone—Waldo, among others, preached something similar in the twelfth century. *Sola gratia* is the doctrine that grace is the unmerited gift of the Lord—strains of such thinking existed in the premodern Orthodox and Catholic churches (and arguably still do). *Solus Christus* is the doctrine that only Christ is the mechanism for salvation and that there is no need for the intercessory system of priests and bishops, saints and angels—Waldo and Wycliffe would have agreed. *Soli Deo gloria* is the doctrine that all glory must be afforded to God alone, rather than for the works of man—St. Francis would have concurred. And concerning Luther's least Catholic of principles, *Sola scriptura*, which maintains that all doctrine must ultimately derive from the Bible alone—any number of thinkers before the German monk, including Waldo, Wycliffe, and Hus, would have been in consensus on that score. "Like many turning points in history, the controversy sparked by this monk was long in coming," writes Carlos Eire in *The Reformation: The Early Modern World, 1450–1650*. "Only an obtuse observer could have failed to notice their presence, for discontent and cries for reform were endemic. What no one could tell at the time, not even Luther, was how much of a punch those explosive elements really packed."[66] What then makes Luther different from Waldo, Wycliffe, or Hus (though there are denominations which credibly trace their origins back to all three)?

Fundamentally, Luther's success comes down to four separate elements. The first, and it has been often overstated in triumphalist historiography, was the innovation of the printing press allowing for wider distribution of Reformation tracts. The second is the exemplary rhetorical genius of Luther himself, for what he lacked in originality he made up for in prodigious verbal panache, a writer who was simultaneously learned and earthy, polemical and funny, erudite and human; the sort of raconteur who could quip in his 1520 pamphlet *To the Christian Nobility of the German States* that "If it were art to overcome heresy with fire, the executioners would be the most learned doctors on earth." A prolific writer of veritable logorrhea, Luther in some ways simply turned a phrase better than his antecedents—his German translation of the Bible to his language is what Shakespeare is to English. The third explanation for Luther's success was the protection offered by some nobles in the Holy Roman Empire, such as Prince Frederick III, elector of Saxony. This support was indispensable in helping the theologian evade the punishment of ecclesiastical authorities, even after his excommunication. It was in Frederick's Wartburg Castle that Luther was allowed to write and publish unhampered; "my Patmos," as he explicitly connected himself to that prophet of apocalypse.

For a period, there was a genuine possibility of Luther and his nascent movement being reconciled to the church, as past schismatic groups had been, especially since certain currents within Catholicism, such as the *spirituali* in Spain, were in agreement with the monk on the majority of his positions.[67] This was not to be, however, and it is the fourth and final reason for Luther's tremendous influence. At the Diet of Worms in 1521, where the cleric was famously asked to recant, and he instead declared, "Here I stand. I can do no other," the placement of Luther outside of the church was clear.

What made the Reformation unique, and successful, was more an issue of bureaucratic wrangling, a twist of diplomatic language, and something almost incidental. By the 1529 Diet of Speyer, when an assemblage of Catholic leaders and those sympathetic to Luther (or "evangelicals") had gathered, the inadvertent result was the first appearance of a term for a new category of believer. Initially meant to refer to a political designation, "Protestant" (for those who "protest") became something singular in Christian history, indeed that which fully differentiated Luther from those who preceded him. This or that doctrine was perhaps an issue for disputation, but the division between Catholics and Protestants meant that somebody could consider themselves to be a Christian outside of the confines of the church. Not even the schism of 1054 did that, as both the Catholics and Orthodox still considered themselves part of one holy and apostolic Church, as rent as it may have been. Now the very concept of Christendom itself had lost meaning.

This was, in both the sense of an unveiling and of the world being turned upside down, genuinely apocalyptic. Marc Greengrass in *Christendom Destroyed: Europe 1517–1648* opines that the "Protestant Reformation, [was] a rift in Roman Christianity" that was "spectacular and . . . permanent."[68] Luther's desire to return to the root of the gospels, his disavowal of papal authority, and his stark reliance on faith and Scripture led to an "irrecoverable breach with the Roman Church and a monumental Protestant division of theological opinion," as now "Christendom" could no longer be conflated with Rome, as the "true Church had no external forms, no vestments, special prayers, bishops or buildings."[69] Conservatives viewed this as an assault on the very idea of the sacred, of the experience of the divine, and Luther was labeled accordingly—a serpent in the garden, a demonic whisper in the ear of German princes, perhaps the antichrist.

The reformer more than happily returned the compliment, writing in tracts with titles like *Against the Roman Papacy, An Institution of the Devil* that "I myself, in Rome, heard it said openly in the streets, 'If there is a hell, then Rome is built on it,'" or in his posthumous collection of recorded conversations charmingly titled *Table Talk* that "I am entirely of the opinion that the papacy is the Antichrist . . . if anyone wants to add the Turk, then the Pope is the spirit of the Antichrist, and the Turk is the flesh. . . . They help each other in their murderous work."[70] True to the melancholic religiosity of his native Germany in the early sixteenth century, Luther was an eschatologically obsessed man, even while doubting the authority of Revelation and arguing that it should perhaps not be considered canonical. Despite his misgivings about John of Patmos, Luther fully expected that his was the end of days, imagining that Christ's return wouldn't be after 1600.[71]

Apocalypticism flourished in the sixteenth century because of the Reformation; such a historic rupture altered how eschatological anxiety manifested itself within Christianity. While the papacy was content to label Luther an antichrist, such rhetoric—which had always had a home within the church, even if on the fringe—began to siphon off from Catholicism. This is not to say that Catholicism abandoned apocalypticism per se; varieties of eschatological belief were and are present within the church. But the sheer intensity and fervency of groups like the medieval flagellants, Beguines, Beghards, Joachimites, and so on, who, even if heretical, still considered themselves to be within the church, found more amenable spiritual homes separate from Rome, so that this variety of apocalypticism transferred to become a largely Protestant phenomenon.

The Reformation was arguably a pressure valve within the church, as more extreme apocalyptic sentiments departed and Rome largely embraced the version of allegorical amillennialism which predominates today. None of that means that this century was less apocalyptic in perspective—the opposite is true, as during the sixteenth century the Reformation would be the catalyst for horrific religious wars fought in central, eastern, and western Europe, particularly in France, with hundreds of thousands of deaths resulting. If anything, the seventeenth century would prove to be an even more horrific era for religious war. Doomsday's trumpet echoed throughout early modern Europe, and apocalyptic nightmares were on full display in treatises, tracts, and pamphlets, the dragon's very library. Consider the anonymously compiled 1550 German manuscript from the Lutheran stronghold of Augsburg entitled *The Book of Miracles*, a title that's appropriate because of how beautiful its illustrations are.[72] In vibrant colors, the artist depicts a multitude of apocalyptic signs and prophecies, from comets and hailstones to floating golden orbs and eclipses. Sea monsters emerge to devour people, crowned dragons fly above Bohemia, a grotesque chimera with a donkey head, a bird leg, and a goat leg, crowned with a human torso, is announced as the "Tiber monster," which is to say the papal antichrist. The Great Dragon of Revelation itself emerges from the ocean.

Central to Luther's rejection of clericalism, of the papacy, of the Latin Vulgate, was a firm belief in a "priesthood of all believers," but whether it was arrogance or naivety that led him to conclude that a reading of Scripture alone would result in the multitude coming to the same interpretation is another question. "If Satan can turn God's Word upside down and pervert the Scriptures," Luther pensively worried in *Confession Concerning Christ's Supper*, "what will he do with my words—or the words of others?" Luther's worst fears were verified in that *Sola scriptura* combined with the priesthood of all believers didn't naturally lead to a single clear doctrine, but rather the multitude of thousands of denominations that can in some sense be traced back to that October day in Wittenberg, each of which had and has varying relationships to apocalypticism, from the most staid and metaphorical interpretation of that future event to foaming, zealous, literal manifestations of shaking and quaking belief. As Greengrass summarizes the legacy of the Reformation, what "made it the more painfully complicated was that western Christianity splintered violently,"[73] both figuratively and literally.

In the decades after Luther many of the major theological currents of Protestantism arose. Broadly speaking, during the sixteenth century these could be divided between the Magisterial Reformation and the Radical Reformation, both of which had varied and sometimes contradictory approaches toward apocalypticism. Among the former were those theologians, and the sects and denominations which emerged in their stead, who emphasized a complementary position between civil and church authority. The Magisterial Reformation included thinkers like Luther, the French Huguenot theologian John Calvin, the Swiss theologian Ulrich Zwingli, and the complex case of the English Reformation which was pushed from the top down by monarchical authority, beginning with Henry VIII's schism from Rome, something unprecedented when compared to continental movements (and which had a tendency to shift back and forth between the Protestant and Catholic over the course of the century, as well as between different "settlements" of Protestantism).

Often, as with Luther, there was a strong ambivalence about apocalyptic thinking among the Magisterial Reformers, even while it had a rhetorical power. Calvin, who wrote extensive and complex commentaries on almost every book of the Bible, excluded just a single one—Revelation. Patmos's vision was also the only book of Scripture which Zwingli ignored. Staid, doctrinaire, extreme—Calvin has in many circumstances been rightly considered a puritan but, being even more indebted to Augustine than Luther was, the Huguenot took from the ancient theologian not just the unforgiving doctrine of predestination, but also an entirely more humane amillennialism. Writing in *The Institutes of Christian Religion* about various apocalyptic sects, he says with his characteristic pugilism that "their fiction is too childish either to need or to be worth a refutation."[74] The situation was entirely different as concerns the Radical Reformation, which true to its name rejected an interdependence between civil and church authority, seeing an irrevocable tension between the realms of Christ and Caesar, a position both generated by and encouraging an engaged as well as revolutionary apocalypticism. Perhaps the earliest moment at which Luther's fears about the direction the priesthood of all believers might go in were realized was with the emergence of radicals like the Saxon Zwickau Prophets who rejected all sacramental theology, whom the author of the *Ninety-Five Theses* dismissed as "fanatics," or the former Augustinian's one-time associate Andreas Karlstadt, who inaugurated the first iconoclastic furies throughout the Holy Roman Empire, when there was widespread destruction of liturgical statues and stained-glass windows, relics and altars, which were smashed as idols of superstitious popery.[75]

No figure is as associated with the earliest manifestation of the Radical Reformation more than the German preacher Thomas Müntzer. As with the others among the most radical contingent of the Reformation, Müntzer is often considered to be an Anabaptist, because of his rejection of infant baptism (the prefix in that position means "Again," a slur used by both Catholics and other Protestants). "Perhaps there is no group within Christian history that has been judged as unfairly as the Anabaptists," writes William R. Estep in *The Anabaptist Story*. "Theirs has been the lot of the widely misunderstood, deliberately misrepresented, or completely ignored."[76] Estep is correct in his appraisal, for despite the disdain in which Luther held the Anabaptists, they more fully intuited the radical implications of Protestantism than the man who supposedly initiated it, while simultaneously connecting the promise of that potentially liberatory creed to movements that sought to actually transform peoples' material lives.

In this regard, Müntzer was a figure more polemical, more zealous, and more urgent than Luther, and what he lacked in a similar erudition he made up for in his commitment to the prophetic mode, to actually enacting theory as praxis as a leader in a growing movement against aristocratic excess and economic inequity. By 1524, a mere seven years after the nailing of the *Ninety-Five Theses* to the Wittenberg church door, German-speaking lands were embroiled in the beginnings of what has been remembered as the Peasant's Revolt, the most widespread proletariat rebellion in Europe until the French Revolution of more than two centuries later.[77] Agitating against increasing privatization and enclosure by the aristocratic class in the Holy Roman Empire, as well as the material precarity among peasants who began to be reduced to the conditions of serfdom, the rebels considered themselves partisans for the protestations of the Reformation, seeing in Luther's theology a bold and defiant stand against injustice and untruth.

Relying heavily on those same nobles, Luther decried violence, while also advocating for moderate policies to ameliorate the conditions for the populace. On the eve of the rebellion, Luther would write a pamphlet in 1522 entitled *A Sincere Admonition to all Christians to Guard Against Insurrection and Rebellion*, condescendingly intoning that "We must calm the mind of the common man, and tell him to abstain from the words and even the passions which lead to insurrection."[78] Two years later, and Luther's position has obviously hardened in a more reactionary manner, as seen in the title of another tract, this one with the rather unsubtle title of *Against the Murderous, Thieving Hordes of Peasants*. Here the father of the Reformation fulminated against those who partially drew inspiration from his example, inveighing that the peasants "doubly deserved death in body and soul as highwaymen and murderers . . . they cloak this terrible and horrible sin with the gospel . . . thus they become the worst blasphemers of God and slanderers of his holy name."

While Luther's condemnation of the working class during the German Peasants' War certainly didn't help the cause, it's difficult to say that the revolution finally failed entirely because of the reformer. Whether or not Luther was hypocritical to his initial values or not is another question, for temperamentally he was always a figure who respected hierarchy, order, and authority. Because of this, we can't conclude whether or not Luther lacked courage in this regard, but we can certainly judge him as being on the wrong side of a conflict that saw the wholesale slaughter of over a hundred thousand peasants by a much smaller, much better trained, much better armed contingent of soldiers. For all that we can't say about Luther—whether he was a hypocrite or cowardly—we can authoritatively say that Müntzer suffered from no such deficiencies, even while the preacher was unequivocally a fire-breathing fanatic. "The people will be free and God alone will be their Lord," Müntzer thundered, and arguably he reached such a conclusion by consistently following all five of the *solas*, for from Scripture he understood how private property is fundamentally idolatrous, and from granting glory to God alone he knew that any reformation which eliminated bishops and priests but not kings and princes was no reformation at all.[79]

Alberto Toscano notes in his introduction to the works of Müntzer that his war "became a *locus classicus* for those who wished to meditate on the bonds between religious activism and social upheaval, and to explore the volatile combination of theological innovation and political strategy."[80] This then wasn't just a reformation, it was a revolution—arguably the first in European history—and one where Müntzer steadfastly held to a millennial yearning which believed that the kingdom of God would be founded on earth in anticipation of Christ, a commune and republic where all was in common and all were equal. Understanding the rebellion as being Armageddon, Müntzer declared himself an instrument of millennium, and to that end he helped raise armies, he assisted in training them, he preached to them, and he fought alongside them, writing in a missive to the peasants of Allstedt, "At them, at them, while the fire is hot! Do not let your sword get cold, do not let your arms go lame!," for, as he noted in a sermon of 1524, "God despises the powerful and the mighty, the likes of Herod, Caiaphas, and Annas, and he accepts for his service the small, like Mary, Zechariah, and Elizabeth." The German Peasants' War, Müntzer was clear, was a fight for the small.

After the defeat of the rebellion in 1525, with thousands of dead, peasants tortured, and farmsteads scorched, the German artist Albrecht Dürer sketched a preliminary design of an unbuilt *Monument to the Vanquished Peasants*. Dürer's own sectarian allegiances are ambiguous, though it seems that he had an affinity for Luther's theology in his private writings, which is what makes his monument design so fascinating. He imagined a ten-foot-tall polished black stone, surrounded by sculptures of domesticated farm animals such as cows, sheep, and pigs. At the corners of the pedestal, there are statues of "four baskets, filled with butter, eggs, onions, and herbs, or whatever you like," as Dürer explains in his notes. Piled atop the pedestal are other markers of the rural working class, assembled one on top of another, like a column; there's a chest, a kettle, a cheese bowel, a keg of butter, a milk jug, and hanging from those are "hoes, pitchforks, flails," all of which is to be "surmounted by a chicken basket, topped by a lard tub upon which sits an afflicted peasant with a sword stuck into his back." Stephen Greenblatt hypothesizes in *Learning to Curse: Essays in Early Modern Culture* that so "extreme a humiliation of a single, unarmed man is difficult to represent, however, without evoking Christ. . . . This aesthetic decision may signal a deep ambivalence on Dürer's part, a secret, subversive sympathy with the vanquished encoded at the very pinnacle of the victor's monument."[81] Besides, Dürer is unclear on who stabbed that peasant in the back, but as he was nearing the end of his life, he never took up a Lutheran theme in his work again.

Five years after the violent quashing of the rebellion, which saw men publicly mutilated and burnt to death, Dürer wrote in a letter to a friend that he did "confess that in the beginning I believed in Luther . . . but as anyone can see, the situation has become worse."[82] Some of that shared Teutonic melancholy and sense of the approach of Armageddon is on display in one of Dürer's masterpieces, an engraving done long before Wittenberg, made in 1498, the year that Savonarola was immolated in view of Florence's red-tiled dome. Entitled *The Horseman of the Apocalypse*, Dürer imagined those four apocalyptic riders bringing with them famine, plague, war, and death, the scene crowded with women and men alike trampled by the hooves of the infernal beasts. One horseman holds aloft a sword, the other a bow and arrow, while an angel of death flies overhead. With that auspicious date of 1500 approaching, Dürer provided artistic intimation of the bloody century which lay ahead. In the two centuries after Dürer made his engraving, the four horsemen seemed to run rampant through shattered Christendom, though war was the one who rode the longest and hardest.

Millions of Europeans would die in the sectarian conflicts of the sixteenth and seventeenth centuries, far overtaking the casualties of the Crusades. Apocalypticism was often the gasoline on the fire of these battles, while also providing a means of resistance and rebellion for those who'd been oppressed, proving that the flaming sword wielded by the horseman was double-edged. The German Peasants' War was the first example of proletarian revolution motivated by the millennial belief that the status quo doesn't need to be maintained, that hierarchies can be upended and injustices rectified, but it wouldn't be the last. As Cohn explains, "It was not only that the Anabaptists were confirmed in their hostility to the state and the established order—they interpreted their sufferings in apocalyptic terms as the last great onslaught of Satan and Antichrist against the Saints, as those 'messianic woes' were to usher in the Millennium."[83] The ethos of the peasants' rebellion spreading throughout Germany, moving northwards from Thuringia to Westphalia, was summarized by the humanist Sebastian Franck in 1531, for whom millennium would overthrow this practice of "dividing the world up and squabbling over property," of the creed of "Mine and Thine," but rather a republican commune would be instated, for "God had made all things in common, as today still we can enjoy air, fire, rain and sun in common."[84] Less than a decade after the conclusion of the German Peasants' War, a bit north of where that insurrection happened, there was another rebellion in the city of Münster, the leaders of which were so radical that they almost made Müntzer seem moderate by comparison.

Inspired by the same eschatological Anabaptist theology, the city of Münster was ruled as a communist theocracy from the beginning of 1534 until the summer of 1535, the example of which would reverberate through Europe and terrify both Catholics and Protestants. Here in the Westphalian city, a trio of three revolutionaries would come to power: a former Lutheran minister turned Anabaptist preacher named Bernhard Rothmann, along with two men with steadfastly working-class vocations, a baker and a tailor respectively named Jan Matthys and Jan Bockelson, the latter of whom was more often known as John of Leiden. Along with the wool merchant Bernhard Knipperdolling, who was elected mayor of the free city, Rothmann, Matthys, and Leiden would ascend to positions in the magistracy, easily buoyed by the growing Anabaptist community, which only increased as radicals from throughout Germany and the Low Countries made pilgrimage to Münster, which was imagined as a New Jerusalem. Residents had visions and prophecies, fits of ecstatic convulsing and dancing. Cohn writes that the doctrine that this was the end of days spread throughout the region: "The rest of the earth, it was announced, was doomed to be destroyed before Easter; but Münster would be saved and would become the New Jerusalem. Food, clothes, money and accommodation would be ready for the immigrants on their arrival, but they were to bring arms."[85] Rising as if it was the stabbed peasant from the top of Dürer's monument, the resurrected corpse of the proletarian Christ returning to upend the world, for eighteen months Münster was among the most revolutionary of states in world history.

Private property was completely abolished, in imitation of the early apostles, so that Münster enacted that paradise from Acts 4:32–35, whereby "neither said of them that ought of the things which he possessed was his own; but they had all things common . . . and distribution was made unto every man according as he had need." Darker currents were also in evidence among the partisans, as reformations have a way of devouring themselves every bit as much as revolutions do. Outside elements made the maintenance of government difficult; the previous Catholic bishop of Münster Franz van Waldeck laid siege to the city for months—assisted by Lutheran troops in an early act of ecumenical rapprochement. Starvation began to set in among the populace, and the four men leading the revolution fell to internecine division. Matthys would be murdered, decapitated, and castrated, his penis nailed to the city door of Münster.

Leiden, under the sway of an increasing apocalyptic paranoia, had decided that the Westphalian city was Zion, and that he was the resurrected David, an anointed one, a messiah, and he successfully declared himself king of Münster.

Styling himself as the last monarch before Christ's return, Leiden "did everything possible to emphasize the unique significance of his accession," writes Cohn. "The streets and gates in the town were given new names, Sundays and feast days were abolished and the days of the week were renamed on an alphabetical system; even the names of new-born children were chosen by the king according to a special system."[86] For all of the utopian promise of communal living, Leiden ruled the theocracy as a tyrant, instituting a program of iconoclasm, forced baptism, book banning, and polygamy, as well as public execution. His motto, minted on coins in the city, was "One King over all, One God, one Faith, one Baptism."[87] Eventually the fortifications of the city wavered, and van Waldeck took the city.

Throughout Europe, Münster became a byword for the extremity that unchecked religious enthusiasm could reach, and Anabaptism became a marginalized Protestant position, the most enduring influence of the violence in Westphalia being an embrace of pacifism among those who grew out of that moment, such as Menno Simons from whom the Mennonites would be formed. Six decades later, the English playwright Thomas Nashe would fictionalize the siege in *The Unfortunate Traveller; or, the Life of Jack Wilton*, arguably the first novel written in English, wherein he described how the army of Münster was composed of "Very devout asses" wearing old boots as helmets and brewer's aprons as armor, who maintained that "there was not a pea's difference betwixt them and the apostles: they were as poor as they, of as base trades as they, and no more inspired than they."[88] Foolish though the Anabaptists were in Nashe's estimation, the scene of their slaughter at the hands of Catholic and Lutheran alike is harrowing, as "their swords, their pikes, their bills, their bows, their calivers slew, empierced, knocked down, shot through and overthrew as many men every minute of the battle as there falls ears of corn before the scythe."[89] High Church Anglican and respecter of authority that Nashe was, he might mourn for Münster, but he makes clear that this tragedy was their own fault.

The experience at Münster is a reminder that the status quo concedes rarely and is more than willing to present for all a warning of the wages of trying to reform things too much, of trying to tip the world over at an angle which is too steep. Following the collapse of Münster, Leiden and Knipperdolling were publicly tortured and gruesomely executed, with their corpses placed within iron cages which hung from the steeple of St. Lambert's Church. Ten years before, during the German Peasants' War, following his defeat at the battle of Frankenhausen, Müntzer had been captured, tortured, and executed, his head placed on a pike overlooking the Thuringian countryside. By comparison, Luther lived until 1546, dying quietly of a stroke in bed, comforted by family members and servants applying hot towels to his face. As Nashe rhapsodized, "The ignorant snatch the kingdom of heaven to themselves with greediness, when we with all our learning sink into hell."[90]

CHAPTER SIX

The Whores of Babylon

Apocalypse in the Early Modern Period

A Window in Prague

Religious Violence in Early Modern Europe

FIRST EXHIBITED AT London's Royal Academy of Art in 1852, the Pre-Raphaelite painter John Everett Millais's *A Huguenot on St. Bartholomew's Day* was a triumph of maudlin sentimentality. In the imagination of the painter, two young lovers from across the sectarian divide meet in Paris on the eve of St. Bartholomew's Day, 1572,[1] a day that among the evangelicals of early modern Europe would represent Catholic perfidy, but in the rendering of Millais provides a moment to contemplate the intensity of innocent love. The young woman—a Catholic—is embraced by her lover—a Protestant. She wears a ruffled and heavy black dress, as if already preparing for mourning, while he is in a purple jacket, wearing the flat cap favored by many of the Reformers. Staring intently at each other, the lovers appear to be in some kind of garden, the bucolic pastoralism of their surroundings belying the violence which the viewer knows is coming. Beneath Millais's composition was a caption which explained "When the clock of the Palais de Justice shall sound upon the great bell, at daybreak, then each good Catholic must bind a strip of white linen round the arm," so that it would be possible for Catholic zealots to separate papist from Protestant. With one hand around his back and the other reaching up to his arm, the young woman valiantly attempts to tie a white ribbon to her lover, but without breaking their gaze the pious Protestant surreptitiously pulls the ribbon loose, content to die for his faith as a truthful adherent of the Reformation cause.

Millais's vision is of velvet and lace, ruffled collars and white ribbons. *A Huguenot on St. Bartholomew's Day* is a masterpiece of Victorian romance and pathos, a mawkish composition that would have only been possible to paint some three centuries after the horror of the anti-Protestant massacres which occurred in the French capital on August 24, 1572. By the time of his painting, the distance of history had obscured the blood of that day, when the desire for Christian to murder Christian had momentarily stalled through the benefits of modernity and secularism. During the sixteenth century, the Seine was still too red to tell fairy tales. More true to that abyss than any romances of Millais was the witness account of the historian De Thou, who recounts how the decapitated body of the Huguenot admiral and nobleman Gaspard II de Coligny—whose assassination initiated the massacres—was "placed upon the gibbet of Montfaucon, where it hung by the feet in chains of iron; and then they built a fire beneath, but which he was burned without being consumed; so he was, so to speak, tortured with all the elements, since he was killed upon the earth, thrown in the water, placed upon the fire, and finally put to hang in the air."[2]

Disagreement reigned from the moment the killing stopped as to who exactly was responsible and just how many people had been murdered, with Mack Holt forlornly writing in *The French Wars of Religion, 1562–1629* that the "St. Bartholomew's massacres have generated much controversy ever since they occurred, and the historical debate does not appear to be letting up."[3] The particulars of the event are that thousands of Huguenots—the powerful Calvinist minority in France who may have constituted as much of 10 percent of the population at the time—had descended on the overwhelmingly Catholic capital to celebrate the marriage of their coreligionist Henri de Navarre to the Catholic princess Margaret de Valois. According to a common view, the Queen Mother and still-powerful regent Catharine de' Medici, enthralled to a pernicious philosophical Machiavellianism, used this opportunity to eliminate the majority of powerful Huguenot aristocrats, with fanatical Parisians taking that as permission to kill as many Protestants as they could. Which they did.

Estimates for the lower end of the death toll on that single day are around 5,000 dead; guesses at the higher end are over 30,000.[4] Regardless of which accounting is accurate, that bloody event was the most violent single day during Europe's early modern sectarian conflicts. It constitutes a miniscule percentage of the overall number of women, children, and men who would be killed. During the conflicts which raged across Europe from the start of the Reformation until the middle of the seventeenth century that have been loosely called the "Wars of Religion," the St. Bartholomew's Day Massacre was the most representative event in the minds of Protestants, who saw themselves embroiled in an apocalyptic conflict against the Catholic Church. Adrianne Streete explains in *Apocalypse and Anti-Catholicism in Seventeenth-Century Drama* that among Protestant polemicists, the massacre was evidence that the church was an "anti-Christian counterfeit, a spiritual front for temporal ambition," noting that the Whore of Babylon from Revelation became a symbol of Rome among evangelicals, and that to "drink from her cup is to experience religious and affective disorientation."[5]

It was an error, however, to think that Catholics had a monopoly on atrocity, for the Wars of Religion were defined on all sides by a common inhumanity, with the decades marked in murder, rape, assassination, pillaging, and destruction, a commitment to the sense that all factions could assist in bringing about the end of days. The seventeenth-century Dutch historian Pieter Corneliszoon Hooft recounts many horrors in his *Netherlands History*, with John Lothrop Motley's writing in *The Rise of the Dutch Republic* that during the Eighty Years' War, many Calvinists took "fierce pleasure in . . . acts of cruelty. A Spaniard had ceased to be human in their eyes. On one occasion a surgeon at Veer had cut the heart from a Spanish prisoner, nailed it on a vessel's prow, and invited the townsmen to come and fasten their teeth in it, which many did with savage satisfaction."[6] During the Wars of Religion, there were many antichrists and many whores of Babylon, for apocalypse never ceased.

Apocalypticism raged from the moment Luther's hammer hit that Wittenberg nail in 1517, and it would burn a course across the continent until 1648, when the pens of Europe's ministers finalized the Peace of Westphalia. Thereby a tepid toleration of religious difference became de facto international policy, albeit more from exhaustion than principle. In the intervening century-and-a-half, millions of Christians on the continent, from the Pyrenees to the Carpathians, from the Alps to the North Sea, would die. Scores more Catholics, Lutherans, Calvinists, and Anabaptists would murder each other in the name of Christ; more than Christians had killed Muslims during the Crusades.

Encompassing dozens of different conflicts across Europe, the Wars of Religion arguably include the German Peasants' War and the Münster Rebellion, the French Wars of Religion and the Eighty Years' War between the Dutch and the Spanish, and any number of other conflagrations from the Schmalkaldic War in the Holy Roman Empire to the Prayer Book Rebellion in England. As if a horrific coda to the entire period was the Thirty Years' War, which saw millions dead, fully a third of the German population perishing. Peter H. Wilson writes in *The Thirty Years War: Europe's Tragedy* that, by the seventeenth century, while the Counter-Reformation papacy and even Lutherans had officially distanced themselves from apocalypticism, the "ideas nonetheless gained ground from the 1580s," particularly among "ordinary Calvinists" and other Christians as well.[7] There is the theology of seminaries and then there is popular faith; in an understanding of what motivates the passions of people in a period, it's crucial to never confuse these two things with one another.

Signs and portents of judgment day were catalogued, while broadsheets and pamphlets reported astronomical phenomena like Halley's Comet in 1618, and deformed births and crop blight as indications that the apocalypse was approaching. "The increased frequency of hailstorms and other natural phenomena caused by climate change during this period, known now as the Little Ice Age, encouraged the view that the world was approaching its end. Witch-and-demon crazes appeared further manifestations of this," so that "radical Protestant leaders . . . commanded the resources to initiate Armageddon," writes Wilson.[8] In part, the very convulsions of modernity—increased urbanization, population growth, and the changing scientific understanding of the world—inculcated apocalypticism. During the centuries of religious wars, there was a mutually reinforcing and reciprocal relationship between political events and religious interpretations, a feedback loop of apocalypticism whereby the nightmare of violence encouraged a sense of the world's ending, which in turn initiated more violence. Religious toleration was an enigma to Christians, who since Constantine had associated personal faith with civilization; to broach any schism within the church—on any side of those sectarian divides—would seem an abandonment of faith itself, so that even the most grotesque of war crimes was justified as righteous.

The Peace of Augsburg, established in 1555, was only ever partial and incomplete, establishing a principle of *Cuius regio, eius religio*, or "whose realm, his religion," whereby the patchwork of semi-independent principalities which constituted the Holy Roman Empire would have their populace's faith decided by their rulers, whether Catholic or Lutheran. But the agreement did nothing to situate Calvinists or Anabaptists and the failure of imagination that made a full-throated secularism as yet impossible meant that a century of religious strife was unavoidable. The result was apocalypse, until the populace and their princes grew tired of that, with MacCulloch writing that the "fear of the Last Days only began to fade in the last years of the seventeenth century,"[9] though there would inevitably be resurgences afterwards. A broad and deep chasm separates De Thou's horrific account from Millais's gauzy and romantic fantasy, the intervening period containing the story of how Europe became modern. France's Wars of Religion, which included as many as eight civil conflicts in a few short decades, demonstrate just how much the seventeenth century altered the course of religious history in Europe. Huguenots—the name for this group remains of unclear etymology—contributed as much to the Reformation project as any other sect. Despite being popularly viewed as a firmly Catholic nation today (at least culturally), France was instrumental in the Reformation, along with many other surprising regions, from Poland to Hungary, where Protestants constituted a sizable percentage of the populace, in some areas the majority. By the conclusion of the European Wars of Religion, the Catholic Counter-Reformation had been successful in retaking much of the territory that had been lost during the sixteenth century, even while Protestantism became firmly ensconced in many both militarily and economically powerful nations, including Britain and Holland. MacCulloch emphasizes environmental influences on the tenor of the age, writing that the "appalling weather conditions of the 1590s, triggering the worst harvest in living memory and probably for some centuries, were an extra incentive to belief. . . . So, of the Four Horsemen of the Apocalypse, famine and war had both entered and taken their bow on the stage."[10]

During the Wars of Religion, apocalypticism was a major motivating factor in both interpreting and encouraging violence, particularly among Protestants who rather understandably identified the perpetrators of crimes such as those on St. Bartholomew's Day as the result of the antichrist. Catharine de' Medici—who prior to the massacres charted a moderate course of religious toleration and whose responsibility for the violence may have been grossly overstated—was often at the center of such discourse, due to her gender, her nationality, and her association with occultism (such as her support of Nostradamus). Rumors of witchcraft inevitably accrued to powerful women, none more so than Medici. In England, propaganda about the Catholic antichrist was particularly virulent, in part due to Queen Elizabeth I's adept information campaign, as well as the large number of Huguenot refugees who settled in London. When the dramatist Christopher Marlowe wrote the prologue to his play *The Jew of Malta*, he depicted the soul of the malevolent Italian political philosopher Nicolo Machiavelli as possessing the body of the Catholic Duke of Guise, who had been responsible for much of the violence that August. For Marlowe, who had his own occult associations, the duke is a nihilist, with the character Machiavel intoning that "I count religion but a childish toy, / And hold there is no sin but ignorance,"[11] the threat from the papacy not a religious one, but rather an antireligious one.

Fears of witchcraft, such as the slander leveled against Medici, are not synonymous with apocalyptic paranoia, but are still certainly connected to it. John Demos writes in *The Enemy Within: 2,000 Years of Witch-Hunting in the Western World* that the fear of witchcraft manifested as a conspiracy, "dark and dire, and hidden behind a veil of secrecy; vast in scope . . . with a fundamental aim to undermine—or even to reverse, in direct counterpoint—all that right-thinking folk would regard as true; proceeding through nefarious, covert methods, and thus liable to become a kind of unwitting contagion; creating high stakes around the outcome, if not a threat of apocalypse."[12] The sixteenth century, and especially the following century, saw a rapid increase in the widespread belief in the existence of witches. During the Middle Ages, belief in witchcraft's existence was considered heretical, so that a period often marked as synonymous with superstition hewed toward a more rational position in this particular case. By contrast, the early modern period was replete with hideous violence against those suspected of witchcraft or any kind of relationship with the demonic, the vast majority of those who were persecuted and executed being women of marginalized status, particularly the elderly.

Lurid and fevered fantasies about the machinations of witches centered on the Black Mass, a type of inverted Christian sacrament, which was capable of conjuring Satan and the antichrist. Witchcraft paranoia can be somewhat dated to the publication of the Dominican priests Heinrich Kramer and Jacob Sprenger's *Malleus Maleficarum* in 1487, a virulently misogynistic guide to accusing witches which became the single most popular source in the ensuing gynocide of the subsequent centuries. For the Dominicans, apocalypse was ensured from the moment of the fall itself and the responsibility for that transgression was entirely the fault of a woman, so that "He that pleaseth God shall escape from her; but he that is a sinner shall be causeth by her," for the union of Satan and the feminine is more "bitter than death."[13] The *Malleus Maleficarum*—whose title translates to *Hammer of the Witches*—may have been written by two Catholic priests in the waning days of the Middle Ages, but it became most popular among Protestant ministers, as the persecution of suspected witches was most virulent in northern Europe, particularly in war-ravaged Germany and the British Isles, with Scotland notably extreme in the number of people put to the stake. Within England, apocalyptic rhetoric was instrumental in the building of an explicitly Protestant state. Only matched by the numerous English-language translations of the Gospels, and which promoted the evangelical cause within the kingdom, was the anthology *Acts and Monuments* by the Protestant propagandist John Foxe, which is more popularly remembered as *The Book of Martyrs*. Printed in 1563, shortly after Elizabeth's coronation, the door stopper of a folio detailed the persecutions of Protestants and those whom Foxe viewed as antecedents to the Reformation, with a particular focus on the indignities suffered under the queen's Catholic sister Mary I.

The tome is over 2,000 pages long, with some 150 oftentimes gruesome woodcuts depicting the torture and execution of those whom the author regarded as martyrs of faith. Foxe details such barbarities as William Tyndale, who translated the Gospels into English, being burnt at the stake in the Low Countries in 1536 because of the intervention of a still-Catholic Henry VIII; Anne Askew, immolated a decade later because of her Anabaptist positions, lecturing the priest for his scriptural errors as she slowly burnt; and the three Oxford Martyrs, mutilated and executed by Mary I in 1555, including the archbishop of Canterbury, Thomas Cranmer, London's bishop Nicholas Ridley, and Worcester's bishop Hugh Latimer, who upon the pyre said to the former, "Be of good comfort, and play the man, Master Ridley; we shall this day light such a candle, by God's grace, in England, as I trust shall never be put out," at least according to Foxe.[14]

The Book of Martyrs fulfilled an important function in Protestant England, replacing all of the saints' hagiographies that had instilled religious values in medieval Catholic readers by giving them new and approved evangelical models. Mary's reign was the time of tribulation and Elizabeth's pointed toward the possibility of millennium (that the latter actually executed more people is of no accounting). This was the great Protestant hope of a nation purged through suffering to become a light unto the nations, a chosen and covenantal kingdom of Christ.

Religious violence was the currency of early modern Europe, so in an important regard there was nothing particularly surprising about the event of May 23, 1618, which has been remembered as the Defenestration of Prague, beyond the outsized importance given to its significance. A window some seventy feet above the ground along the wall of the ivy-covered Karlštejn Castle, almost twenty miles outside of the Bohemian capital, is where the Thirty Years' War supposedly began. It was there that four Catholic Lord Regents of the newly elected Holy Roman Emperor Ferdinand of Styria arrived to placate Protestant nobles who were disturbed by the reversal of toleration policies that had thrived under the previous emperor, Rudolf II. After the crowning of Ferdinand, a fervent proponent of Counter-Reformation with a Jesuit confessor, the building of Protestant chapels was stalled, and certain rights were revoked. The meeting between the emperor's representatives and his Protestant subjects grew contentious, so that Count Jindřich Matyáš Thurn-Valsassina declared to the Lord Regents that "You are enemies of us and of our religion . . . [you] have horribly plagued your Protestant subjects . . . and have tried to force them to adopt your religion against their wills or have had them expelled for this reason."[15]

Then the assembled Bohemian noblemen hoisted each of the Lord Regents one after the other—Count Jaroslav Borita of Martince, Count Vilem Slavata of Chlum, Adam II von Sternberg, and Matthew Leopold Popel Lobkowitz—and expelled them through the window of the castle to the cheers of the Protestant crowd assembled below. Miraculously, all four men survived. Catholic propagandists attributed their survival to the intervention of the Virgin Mary; Protestants rather supposed that their fall was broken by the prodigious pile of horse manure at the base of the tower. Regardless, the events which followed this defenestration were as clear as they are dizzying in their complexity. Ferdinand would be deposed as emperor, replaced by the Calvinist Frederick V, and war began in earnest, fighting that continued for the following three decades, subsuming virtually every European power other than England, an orgy of bloodletting that saw the population of some European corners reduced by double-digit percentages. Commoners suffered from war, pandemic, and famine in a manner that had been unthinkable in previous epochs, and the devastation would be unmatched until the twentieth century: An apocalyptic war—with as many as eight million people dead—triggered by a fall out of a Prague window into some horseshit.[16]

Examining that window today, a handsome if undistinguished aperture in the dark granite of the Gothic castle, one can be misled into believing that history ever operates in such obvious causal ways as is implied by the anecdote. The memorials, the plaques, the tour guides—all conspire to give an origin story that never actually exists. Because if it wasn't this window, it would have been another one; had those nobles not been tossed, different ones would have fallen. Religious war of the scope of the Thirty Years' War was a foregone conclusion; such apocalyptic conflict was inevitable the moment that schism occurred and was successful. Historians have rightly examined the political and economic justifications for warfare during this period—Catholic France's allying with the Protestant League during the Thirty Years' War, at the urging of Cardinal Richelieu, a literal prince of the church no less, is representative of the complexities of the seventeenth century—but such a conflict remains inextricably connected to the fervency of apocalyptic impulse. "If ever there was a moment when the ravages of the apocalyptic horsemen war, famine, plague, and death were evident," writes John Theibault in *The Journal of Social History*, "it was during the war."[17]

Portents and prophecies marked the Thirty Years' War more than any other stretch of the early modern period, a culmination of all of the eschatological anticipation that had preceded it. "Anno 1642, all the misery continued just as bad as in the previous year, so that the despair pressed all the harder . . . whoever has not himself seen and lived through such circumstances cannot believe what I note here," wrote Lorenz Ludolf, a pastor of Reichensachsen.[18] Christians of the period, whether Catholic or Protestant, had implicit within them the ability to heal these wounds, to alter the perspective which totalized religious truth. Only exhaustion had the honor of being that teacher. Describing the sheer alterity of religious war for those inculcated in the ideology of secular republicanism, Mark Lila in *The Stillborn God: Religion, Politics, and the Modern West* writes that "Western liberal democracies have succeeded in creating an environment where public conflict over competing revelations is virtually unthinkable today. . . . Yet here is a deeper reason why we in the West find it difficult to understand the enduring attraction of political theology. . . . We live, so to speak, on the other shore."[19] By 1648, with farmland destroyed, cities leveled, and millions dead, a truce could be made, so that out of the Peace of Westphalia, perhaps beyond even the understanding of the men who signed the treaty, emerged the modern political order.

A result of the Thirty Years' War's conclusion was the implementation of the one inviolate rule of contemporary international relations—the ultimate sovereignty of the nation-state. A legacy of Westphalian sovereignty was the acknowledgment of religious toleration, which, while in and of itself is far from modern secularism, is at least a prerequisite to it. It would be a grievous error to assume that Westphalia marked the eclipse of apocalypticism, however. First, 1648 hardly signaled the end of religious politics, that being the year before Puritan revolutionaries in England would behead their king and establish a theocratic Commonwealth. Nor did religious politics end when millennial expectations were migrating westward from Europe toward the English colonies of North America, where an apocalyptic nation-state would eventually be established, based on sublimated doctrinal values. Second, the concept of the nation-state, or secularism for that matter, is not evidence of the absence of theology; it is simply justified by theologies which differ from orthodox Christianity and is just as prone to apocalypticism as is any other Abrahamic faith. Rather, what

Westphalia represented was an alteration in religious politics, and thus in apocalypticism. The world didn't end in 1648, though in an intrinsic way it would continue to end many times over in the coming centuries. Apocalypticism is a sentiment that can't be easily repressed.

The Fifth Monarchy

Radical Religion in Early Modernity

If tradition has held that the Thirty Years' War started with a kick out a window, than it's also maintained that the English civil wars, or the Wars of the Three Kingdoms, which raged across England, Scotland, and Ireland, were initiated when an angry parishioner of Edinburgh's St. Giles Cathedral named Jenny Geddes beamed a stool toward the minister as he read from the Episcopal *Book of Common Prayer* in 1637 and a riot ensued. Just as we're to believe that the shoving of some counselors from an open window resulted in eight million deaths, so is the English Revolution, the execution of King Charles I, and the ensuing Puritan Commonwealth supposedly the responsibility of angry Geddes and her flung chair within the dark, Gothic sanctuary of a Scottish cathedral.

Scotland had experienced a particular doctrinaire Reformation, with many of that country's ministers trained in Calvin's Geneva during the period of the Marian persecutions. With the establishment of a Presbyterian system, Scotland's religious authority was governed by councils of elders on an individual church basis rather than through the hierarchical episcopal structure of bishops still maintained in the Protestant Church of England. There was an irony to this, as, after the death of Elizabeth I, the Scottish Stuarts were enthroned as monarchs overseeing a dual kingdom from London and Edinburgh, but it was Charles I, the second in this line, and his archbishop of Canterbury, William Laud, who began to reintroduce ritual and liturgy which, to more fanatical Protestants, had the stink of Catholicism about it. Being king of England and his native country to the north, Charles I sought to harmonize the conventions of the national churches in both realms, among his first of many errors. And so, when those Scottish worshippers who were used to Presbyterianism and Calvinism were confronted with the *Book of Common Prayer*, penned by the steadfast reformer and martyr Thomas Cranmer nearly a century before, it sounded as if Catholic pipe organs and bells rang in their ears. "Devil cause you colic in your stomach, false thief," Geddes is supposed to have said as she lifted her folding stool toward the dean of the cathedral, "dare you say the Mass in my ear?"[20] Then she threw it.

The king's head would be laid on the block on a cold January 30, 1649, morning, meaning that there were some twelve years for hooliganism to transmute into regicide; but the course of events is never so linear. Geddes did heave a chair during the riot which marks the start of what's known as the Bishops' War, when the Scottish political contingent known as the Covenanters resisted the imposition of increasingly baroque rituals which the staunch Presbyterians associated with popery. That a stool converted into a projectile should initiate such a conflict is not historiography, but myth. And yet myth has its own uses, for in Geddes's example we see the division, the sectarian strife, and the rage which motivated the decade-long conflict between Puritan supporters of Parliament and the High Church Anglican partisans of the Royalist cause. Three centuries later, the idea of a civil war starting over disagreements surrounding the use of a prayer book can seem absurd, but as Michael Braddick writes in *God's Fury, England's Fire: A New History of the English Civil War* "conflict over religion had profound political implications," even in the long after-effect of those events, for "Out of a chaos of opinion and anxiety, and of the catastrophe and trauma of civil war, had come ideas about freedom and citizenship, religious toleration and the exclusion of secular power from matters of conscience,"[21] principles that we rightly associate with liberal democracy and republicanism, but which were forged in the theological cauldron of the seventeenth century. The Peace of Westphalia may have signaled the beginning of one version of modernity, but so did the English civil wars, seeing the rise of a contemporary state army, the idea of a nation-state with an ideological mission, and the execution of a king at the hands of commoners.

Even by the standards of an apocalyptic century, the English civil wars were charged with millennial expectation. A sense of providential mission among the Puritans endured, a common belief that the kingdom of man was being overthrown for the coming kingdom of Christ. To properly situate the events of the 1640s, it is necessary to return to more than a century earlier, when England underwent its own fitful, contentious, and singular Reformation. England, due to the unique way in which the Reformation unfolded in that country over the course of the sixteenth century, also had a unique relationship to apocalypticism, arguably understanding its own national role in a providential manner that was different from continental perspectives regarding the relationship between church and state. Because the Reformation was initially a top-down affair, mandated by Henry VIII for largely political reasons, and enforced on a population that was steadfastly Catholic and resistant to Lutheran innovations from the continent, England underwent a tumultuous cycle of religious settlements throughout the sixteenth century that rather predictably resulted in widespread civil war by the middle of the following century.

Henry's justifications for separating from Rome have been widely debated, with consensus often being that the king was largely a religious conservative who separated from the Catholic Church for reasons of *realpolitik* rather than religious conscience, but the fact that the English Reformation was initiated by the monarch himself meant that the course of religious history in the British Isles would have a unique tenor. Ironically, Henry started his reign as a steadfast Catholic, even granted the title "Defender of the Faith" by the pope for anti-Lutheran tracts printed under his name, and probably penned by his counselor Thomas More. Henry's trusted adviser, later infamously beheaded by his king, understood the Roman Church as a means to fight the demonic power that was Luther, a position to which the Tudor ruler assented when it aided him.

Henry was not an intellectual man, but he was a man who understood the value of intellectuals. The Tudor court was filled with brilliant and competing personages, from the arch-Catholic More to the great engine of the early English Reformation Thomas Cromwell, the poets Thomas Wyatt and Henry Howard, Earl of Surrey, and Cranmer, a crucial importer of Lutheran ideas from Germany. Following the imbroglio with the Catholic Church regarding the annulment of the king's first marriage, figures like Cromwell and Cranmer saw the opportunity to combine civil and ecclesiastical authority into one, and to impose Reformation on a country in a manner that had been largely untried on the continent, reaching a head with the 1534 Act of Supremacy, which recognized the king as the rightful head of the church.

Cromwell was a leading proponent of the dissolution of the monasteries, the forcible confiscation of Catholic monastic houses and the transfer of their wealth to the state, from which it was then doled out to aristocratic supporters of the regime, a policy which began in 1536 and continued for five years. In the process, walls were whitewashed, relics destroyed, statues smashed, stained-glass windows shattered, and books ripped apart, an incalculable loss of England's cultural treasures going back into the Middle Ages. Radical in the truest senses of that term, Cromwell was adamant about restructuring the English church and society completely, using Henry as the regal means by which to accomplish this task. Such reforms were unpopular, especially in rural areas, where the populace held steadfastly to medieval Catholicism and where there were several significant uprisings, though these always adhered to the idea that they were rebelling in support of a king led astray by counselors. "For townsmen and countrymen alike," writes Eamon Duffy in *The Stripping of the Altars: Traditional Religion in England, 1400–1580*, the "rhythms of the liturgy on the eve of the Reformation remained the rhythms of life itself."[22] Among many of the English, particularly in the north and in the western Celtic fringe, Catholicism was in no need of reform, and the influence of advisers like Cromwell (who would ultimately, like so many others, be executed by Henry) was anti-Christian in its perniciousness.

That Henry was fundamentally Catholic in his theology shouldn't be doubted; his *Six Articles*, written in 1539, were steadfastly orthodox in all matters but papal supremacy. The Henrician religious settlement, despite the influence of religious radicals who were often trained on the continent, was ultimately of a traditional nature, and the king's role in persecuting Protestants continued even after the establishment of the Church of England, with numerous executions recounted by Foxe. When Henry was the hammer of the pope, having More denounce Protestantism in tracts, Luther responded in a fevered 1522 pamphlet that called the king a "disciple of idle monsters," a font of "poisonous blasphemies," and a tool of the Roman "scarlet woman."[23] Ironically, only twelve years later it would be Henry himself who expelled papal authority from England, making the king the exemplary Renaissance figure who could be accused of being an antichrist by both Protestant and Catholic.

While Cromwell established a fearsome propaganda operation that made use of both theater and printed broadsheets to denounce the church as the inheritors of pagan Babylon, the average English believer largely still held conventional opinions on the true presence of the Eucharist, the reality of purgatory, and the power of saints. Pious Catholics, content to remain respectful of kingly authority nevertheless saw the scheming of the antichrist in the form of his Protestant advisers, as evidenced in the form of a 1540 satirical letter which claimed to be a missive from the demon Balthasar to Henry. In the missive, Balthasar describes himself as "King of Babylon," "Steward of Hell," and the "Anti-Christ," offering the hand of his daughter in marriage to the famously profligate Henry, as it's never been said that apocalyptic rhetoric need not be funny.

The death of Henry occasioned the possibility of a far more radical Reformation in England, which the king's surviving counselors heartily embraced upon the ascension of his ten-year-old son Edward in 1547. In his 1545 pamphlet *The Image of Both Churches*, polemicists like the Protestant John Bale would interpret the events of Christian history through the opening of the seals in Patmos's Revelation, seeing the Henrician Reformation as the sixth seal before the coming millennium. Paul Kenneth Christianson notes in *Reformers and Babylon: English Apocalyptic Visions from the Reformation to the Eve of Civil War* that men like Bale and his compatriots awaited "that time when the elect would glory in the fall of Babylon and the erection of a New Jerusalem," with the pamphleteer goading the revanchist bishop Hugh Gardiner that "You shall be overcome . . . at the latter day . . . which is not far off."[24] That Bale was correct—Gardiner would ironically be executed by the Catholic Queen Mary I for his Protestantism—but that he was wrong on the who and the why, speaks to the religious complexities of this century. With Edward's accession, figures like Cranmer could briefly imagine a true and thorough purging of all of the popery which had remained in the English church, with Edward VI configured as a Protestant heir to the ancient Judean king Josiah, who in the Bible had similarly expelled any vestiges of paganism from Temple Judaism. The remainder of the sixteenth century is a narrative of ecclesiastical uncertainty and theological contradiction within the English church, all of which is necessary to keep in mind in order to understand the disunity that would inevitably rupture into bloody conflict during the following century.

Edwardian Reformation was as complete and iconoclastic as anything on the continent—the establishment of a genuine state church in the manner which Cromwell had dreamt of. The young king's tenure was short, however, the sickly boy dying only six years after his coronation, and with the reign of his half-sister Mary I, a vociferous Counter-Reformation Catholic who ruled alongside her husband King Philip II of Spain for five years starting in 1553, the Protestants who'd been so influential only a few years before either saw themselves silenced, in exile, or upon the scaffold and pyre. Marian persecutions became a touchstone for Protestants, the narrative heart of Foxe's *Book of Martyrs*. With many of the most prominent Reformation theologians fleeing to Calvin's Geneva, it became a finishing school for religious radicalization. "Bloody Mary," butcher of the sanctified Protestant martyrs executed at Tyburn field, was a proponent of the Inquisition and viewed by some as an emissary of the antichrist, perhaps the Whore of Babylon herself. Mary was a figure against whom the Scottish Presbyterian minister John Knox would write in his unsubtle 1558 tract *First Blast of the Trumpet Against the Monstrous Regiment of Women*, thinking of both her and her coreligionist Mary Queen of Scots when he explicitly tied women's rule to the antichrist, fulminating that to "promote a woman to bear rule, superiority, dominion or empire above any realm, nation or city, is repugnant to nature, contemptuous to God, a thing most contrary to his revealed will and approved ordinance, and finally, it is the subversion of good order, of all equity and justice."[25]

Such misogyny didn't impress Elizabeth I, the most successful of Henry's children in establishing a Protestant religious settlement that granted relative private independence to recusant Catholics and preserved a degree of grandeur both ritually and liturgically, even while bishops in the church became ever more Calvinist in their own theological positions. While remembered by Puritans in the next century as the great Protestant hope of England, especially when compared to the Stuart monarchs who followed her, Elizabeth was criticized by that same contingent during her actual reign, the *via media* or "middle way" that she charted for the church seen as conciliatory to Romish beliefs.

A cult of monarchy dominated during the Elizabethan period, a brilliantly executed policy of pronouncement and propaganda which helped maintain civil peace in a divided country, where much of the repressed desire for liturgical complexity was projected onto the queen herself, who in some ways replaced the Virgin Mary as a Catholic icon. "Most Protestant writers saw Elizabeth as having a major, distinctive, or even unique position in the Church's history," writes Bernard Capp in his contribution to the collection *The Apocalypse in English Renaissance Thought and Literature: Patterns, Antecedents, and Repercussions*, "though they stopped short of ascribing a messianic role to her."[26] Theologians like Thomas Becon described Elizabeth as "noble conqueror of Antichrist," while James Sandford gushed that there was "some diviner thing in her Majesty, than in the Kings and Queens of other countries."

The antichrist also stalked Europe, as he had for centuries, with Catholics on the continent—both in the Spanish court and the Vatican—seeing Elizabeth as an agent of apocalypse, while the pope and Philip II were similarly slandered by Protestants in England. As the locus of both trepidation and expectation, Capp writes that the "role of the godly prince in protecting religious truth was central to Elizabethan thought . . . the idea of England as God's elect nation, guided by Elizabeth towards a millennial golden age."[27] For an exemplary forty-five years, Elizabeth held the religious conviction of her schismatic church in check, even while she was excommunicated by the pope and she faced disunity from both foreign Catholic meddling and Puritans within England. The result was a national church that was in some ways refreshingly diverse in opinion, but which also bore the weight of its own contradictions.

When the second Stuart monarch, Charles I, took the throne in 1625, he inherited a church that was a chimera of Catholic and Protestant. Charles himself hewed toward much more traditional religious lines, a source of anxiety for the growing contingent of Puritans in his kingdom who wished to "purify" the English church of any taint of Catholicism, but who sensed the smells and bells of Romish superstition in the king's enthusiasm for more formal liturgy and ritual. "Puritans thought the whole government of the church antichristian," writes Christopher Hill in *The Antichrist in Seventeenth-Century England*, "that 'Antichrist reigneth amongst us.'"[28] Such fears were directed primarily toward two members of the king's retinue. The first was his French-born queen, Henrietta Maria, who actually was Catholic and was permitted to observe Mass with her confessors in a private chapel. Puritans suspected that the queen was influencing Charles to direct the Church of England into a more Catholic direction, to possibly even consider rapprochement with Rome.

Even more threatening than Henrietta Maria, however, was Charles's archbishop of Canterbury, William Laud, who took office in 1633. While the archbishop would have considered himself to be a staunch Protestant, Laud was also an adherent of the Dutch theologian Jacob Arminius, who, contrary to Calvin, softened many of the most extreme beliefs of Reformed thought, particularly in his abandonment of a belief in predestination. Along with a moderated theology, Laud reintroduced a variety of High Church worship that had been absent for decades. Where altars had been demolished, Laud had them reinstated; naked pews were outfitted with kneelers; and plain-dressed ministers were bedecked in the vestments of priests. According to Puritans, such novelties were the dross of Satan.

As with any event of such magnitude, the causes leading up to armed hostility between Parliamentarians and Royalists in 1642 were varied. There were economic, political, and social reasons for the eruption of war, and while none of those categories is reducible to religion, neither are they inextricable from it. Charles's own personal failings as a leader were manifest as well—his fickleness and overreaching with the many parliaments he called and his mismanagement of the state's convoluted national finances. In the leadup to war, the primary and overwhelming reason for conflict was religious, and apocalyptic at that. Hill explains that for the Puritans, the "orders and ceremonies of the church were antichristian, the non-preaching clergy were servants of the Romish Antichrist, wearing his liveries. In an age when every Englishmen was automatically a member of the state church, when uniformity in religion was regarded as essential to the unity of the state, it was thus no laughing matter to see Antichrist not safely distant in Rome, but in Canterbury and indeed in every parish in the country."[29] What this meant is that the radical Protestants of Europe didn't see the threat as being extrinsic to their nation; to the contrary, Catholicism threatened to infect the official Protestant church at home.

The English revolution began in fits and starts due to the miscalculations of Royalists, who could have never anticipated the execution of both Laud and Charles. At the outset of fighting none of those responsible for the regicide could have necessarily imagined such a radical result either, and yet apocalypticism was capable of carrying a movement further than its partisans understood. Far more disciplined and rigorous in their thinking and organization than had been the peasants during their various German rebellions, following the bloodshed of the civil wars, the Puritans were able to establish their "Godly" Commonwealth during more than a decade of Interregnum following Charles's execution, arguably the first modern revolution in European history. During that time a potent political theology developed which understood the English Republic as a millennial power, a means of hastening Christ's arrival. Such was the position of the influential radical contingent within the Parliamentarian New Model Army, who were known as the Fifth Monarchy Men, who were avowed chiliasts who recognized no king but Christ, and in the Republic saw indications that this was the final kingdom of the Lord as prophesized by Daniel. This was a moment of profound millennial promise and utopian potentiality. The Republicans who won the revolution were far from uniform in their opinions, and the collapse of royal prerogative and authority allowed for a flowering of political and theological thought that had been repressed for centuries. The repeal of printing licensing laws meant a cavalcade of pamphlets advocating for a stunning array of positions. Andrew Bradstock explains in *Radical Religion in Cromwell's England: A Concise History form the English Civil War to the End of the Commonwealth* that these "most traumatic and turbulent" years in English history were responsible for creating a "breakdown in censorship which allowed ideas hitherto considered heretical and kept underground to surface in print and in word,"[30] the ultimate resurrection of the peasant rebels defeated in the fourteenth century. Comparing 1640 and 1642, Bradstock notes that the earlier year saw twenty-two religious tracts printed and the latter year saw two thousand. A variety of heterodox religious and political groups with exotic names like the Levellers, the True Levellers or Diggers, the Muggletonians, the Brownists, the Familiasts, and so on, as well as more familiar denominations such as the Quakers and Baptists, emerged out of the excitement of the age. Such groups, Bradstock writes, "represent a wide range of theological, not to say eschatological, positions, and differ vastly in terms of their aims and visions, and their attitudes to politics and morality."[31]

At events like the 1647 Putney Debates held by the New Model Army, a variety of political arrangements were discussed which anticipated the coming Enlightenment. There, Colonel Thomas Rainsborough could intone that the poorest that is in "England hath a life to live, as the greatest . . . every man that is to live under a government ought at first by his own consent to put himself under that government; and I do think that the poorest man in England is not at all bound in a strict sense to that government that he hath not had a voice to put himself under," while the general Henry Ireton claimed that "no man hath a right to an interest or share in the disposing of the affairs of the kingdom . . . that hath not a permanent fixed interest in this kingdom."[32]

Radical ideas that would successfully manifest more than a century later in the secular and anticlerical revolutions of the eighteenth century are first evidenced in the English civil wars, but the rhetoric and reasoning was firmly millennial, the religious justifications only shorn off in the coming age while still present underneath. Rainsborough, Ireton, and those in their stead, radical though they may have seemed, were still bourgeois revolutionaries, and, as Bradstock notes, there were "groups who wanted much deeper political, economic, social and religious change than what was actually happening, if not the overthrow of the status quo to create the possibility of building something new":[33] Not just to await for Christ to come and impose millennium, but to build it for Him.

Following the king's execution in 1649, Gerrard Winstanley would write in "The True Levellers Standard Advanced" that the "old world . . . is running up like parchment in fire, and wearing away,"[34] the injustices and inequities of Babylon overthrown. Winstanley was the leader and theorist of one of the revolution's most radical contingents, the so-called "Diggers" or "True Levellers" (the latter to differentiate them from a more moderate camp), who agitated for a form of millennial anarcho-communism. They were known as the Diggers for their demolishing of the hedges which separated enclosed, privately owned estates, and Winstanley echoed the exact same argument made by the Lollards three centuries before, that "Those that buy and sell land, and are landlords, have got it either by oppression, or murder, or theft; and all landlords lives in the breach of the Seventh and Eighth Commandments."[35] Revolution is millennium—Winstanley simply lived in a century that was honest about those theological and political commitments. Writing in another tract, "A Declaration from the Poor Oppressed People of England," Winstanley promises that "we expect this to be the last tyrannical power that shall reign; and that people shall live freely in the enjoyment of the earth, without bringing the mark of the Beast in their hands or in their promise; and that they shall buy wine and milk without money or without price, as Isaiah speaks."[36]

Winstanley was of course wrong about this; Charles and Laud were far from the last tyrannical power. Rising from the ranks of the New Model Army itself was the Puritan general Oliver Cromwell (a distant relation of Thomas), who would become the ultimate personal benefactor of the civil wars, being declared Lord Protector of England in 1653. Though Cromwell wore plain black at his swearing in rather than royal regalia, the monarchical associations were obvious. The Commonwealth government was increasingly draconian, despised by traditionalists for banning Sabbath sports, the theater, and the celebration of popish holidays such as Christmas. Those who'd fought for the Parliamentarian side became increasingly disenchanted with a revolution that had seemed to devour itself, and with a Cromwell who had become the model of authoritarianism. Not just the Irish Catholics, who suffered under Cromwell's genocidal campaign, but even Protestants suspected something of the antichrist about the stern, doctrinaire, pious soldier who positioned himself as "God's Englishman." This was the Luciferian commander who, after he massacred 3,500 Irish at the Siege of Drogheda, could write "I am persuaded that this is a righteous judgement of God upon these barbarous wretches."[37]

Broadsheets and anonymous tracts appeared accusing the Puritan who had waged war against antichrist as himself being the antichrist; an enthusiasm for prophetic pronouncements grew, with visionary preachers—many of them women—denouncing the Lord Protector as an emissary of Satan. Representative was Abraham Nelson's unequivocal 1654 pamphlet "A Perfect Description of Antichrist, and his False Prophet: Wherein is Plainly Shewed that Oliver Cromwell was Antichrist"—revised and published six years later upon the Restoration of the monarchy—which was blunt on this score. "You shall find upon serious consideration . . . that the transaction that hath past since the year 1639 until the year 1660 to be the time of Antichrist, his false Prophet, their increase and reign, and their particular actions," writes Nelson.[38] A 1657 broadsheet entitled "The True Emblem of antichrist: Or Schism Display'd," hawked in newsstands and posted on tavern walls, announces that Cromwell is guilty of "Blasphemies, Antichristian Heresies, Bloody and Unnatural Rebellions, and utter Subversions of all Method, Peace, Order and Prosperity in a Christian Kingdom," depicting the warty Lord Protector in his martial armor and ringed by devils.[39]

Whether or not Cromwell was the antichrist, it's certainly true that his personal victory meant his revolution's defeat, as the initial promise of the war gave way to its subversion at the hands of a draconian and authoritarian order. The potential of groups like the Levellers and the Diggers was undermined, when not openly persecuted, and the potential of a very different Reformation was precluded. Hill writes in *The World Turned Upside Down: Radical Ideas During the English Revolution* that there had been "moments when it seemed as though from the ferment of radical ideas a culture might emerge which might be different from the traditional aristocratic culture and from the bourgeois culture of the Protestant ethic which replaced it. We can discern shadows of what this counter culture might have been like, rejecting private property for communism, religion for rationalistic and materialistic pantheism, the mechanical philosophy for dialectical science, asceticism for the unashamed enjoyment of the good things of the flesh."[40] As it was, that millennium wasn't in the future, though the Restoration of King Charles II was. With the crowning of Charles II in 1660, English millennialism—of either the dove or the dragon—would never reach such heights as it did during those heady days of revolution, those beliefs rather migrating elsewhere, away from that profoundly conservative island named Britain. Dissenters and nonconformists would endure even while groups like the Diggers disappeared, with Baptists and Quakers granted some religious toleration with the king's return, allowing them to preserve a bit of the apocalyptic enthusiasms that had burnt through England a generation before.

Many of those idealists who had sacrificed their safety and livelihood for the revolutionary cause understood how it had been betrayed, that Cromwell's hubris had ensured monarchical restoration. A member of the Council of State and of Parliament named Henry Vane, who had left political life in 1653 after Cromwell dissolved those bodies, reflected two years later on the failures of the revolution in *The Retired Man's Meditations, or, the Mystery and Power of Godliness*. Liberal, humane, and tolerant, Vane had perfectly embodied the synthesis of Protestantism and humanism, and had prayed that the Commonwealth would express such views, but he concluded rather that "Oliver was so drunk with the philtre of his power; he had grown corrupt,"[41] that Cromwell just might in fact actually be the antichrist. This must have been a crushing disillusionment, as Vane had given up substantial success and power abroad to return to his home country and assist in its redemption. Now, rather, many wondered if millennium would arrive in a land other than England. Vane considered that it could happen in a place that he had briefly been governor of, perhaps the true location of a millennial kingdom, a godly republic, a providential nation, a city on a hill. A land called Massachusetts.

Gathering the Kernels

Early Modern Jewish Apocalypticism

During that ominously numbered year of 1666, a Jewish prophet named Sabbatai Zevi, whom millions followed as the long-promised and awaited-for messiah, the living embodiment of God, was imprisoned by an Ottoman vizier on the orders of Sultan Mehmed IV in a dank and dark dungeon in Istanbul. Zevi had declared himself to be the messiah only a year before. His ministry had brought him through Jerusalem, Gaza, Cairo, and Istanbul. The charismatic rabbi's movement spread far beyond the Middle East, and is described by Gershom Scholem in *Sabbatai Sevi: The Mystical Messiah, 1626–1676* as the "most important messianic movement in Judaism since the destruction of the Second Temple."[42] Despite an imposition of *cherem*—similar to excommunication—by a Turkish rabbinical council, synagogues in Warsaw and Vilnius, Amsterdam and Venice displayed engravings of Zevi alongside pictures of King David, while his birthday—which fell on Tisha B'Av, a traditional day of mourning—was converted into an ecstatic and joyful celebration. Europe's Jews had suffered incalculably during the seventeenth century. The Cossack Bohdan Khmelnitsky led a series of pogroms during which as many as a hundred thousand Jews were murdered in the 1650s, possibly a third of all adherents in the world, and from this holocaust Zevi's message of freedom and salvation promised the possibility of this fallen world being born anew. Hopes were to be momentary, however. To secure his release, the Jewish messiah converted to Islam. As Scholem argued, a converted messiah is even more disturbing than a crucified one, though Zevi's apostasy ironically didn't completely signal the end of the belief in his providential role to bring about the redemption of the Jewish people and the nations of the world.

Raised in the Greek-speaking city of Smyrna, Zevi's father had worked for a time in the household of English merchants, and imbibed much of that country's Protestant millennialism, especially its enthusiastic Hebraism that often declared belief in the reemergence of the Ten Lost Tribes of Israel as part of the millennial moment. Indifferent to the Torah, Zevi was proficient in Talmudic learning, but what he truly excelled at was kabbalah, visionary and creative in his interpretations of the Zohar. Drawn particularly to the school of Lurianic Kabbalah, Zevi's mission was dedicated to the idea of restoring the universe, of reconciling the divisions that had cleaved the Godhead at the moment of creation, which were socially most fully manifest in the Jewish condition of diaspora. As with the dissenters of the English Civil War who relished turning the world upside down, Zevi offered a prayer of benediction to "God who hath restored again that which was forbidden."[43] A staunch adherent to the mystical belief that the messianic age meant abolishing the prohibitions of the Jewish law known as *mitzvoth*, Zevi reveled in uttering the forbidden Tetragrammaton and consuming *treyf*, while considering making Yom Kippur a festival day.

Zevi's idiosyncratic theology was developed during his sojourns throughout the eastern Mediterranean and the Levant, where he acquired powerful supporters within Jewish communities even while most orthodox rabbis disparaged his mission. Scholem explains that Sabbateanism was a "movement which shook the House of Israel to its very foundations and has revealed not only the vitality of the Jewish people but also the deep, dangerous, and destructive dialectics inherent in the messianic idea."[44] For a year, Zevi's example had a profound pull on the imagination of oppressed Jews throughout the Christian and Islamic worlds. Yet, as with many apocalyptic movements across the Abrahamic faiths, there was a paradoxical relationship of this messiah to his own faith.

Among his most important supporters was a learned and enigmatic rabbi named Nathan of Gaza, a Levantine scholar of Ashkenazic background who positioned himself as Zevi's greatest exegete and champion, a combination of John the Baptist and St. Paul. Envisioning himself as the second coming of the prophet Elijah to Zevi's messiah, Nathan of Gaza was an adept proponent of the new movement, and largely responsible for its spread beyond its central figure's immediate circle.[45] As with Zevi, Nathan's religious vocation was transformed by his discovery of Lurianic Kabbalah, writing in 1673 how years before "the spirit came over me, my hair stood on end and my knees shook and I beheld the divine throne, and I saw visions of God all day long and all night." Such a vision was to be the prelude to his meeting the messiah from Turkey.

By the time Nathan and Zevi had their first encounter, the messiah had already built up a sizable following through the Levant, during which time he had taken as a wife a woman named Sarah, a Polish refugee from the Khmelnitsky pogroms who'd been forced into prostitution in Amsterdam. In marrying Sarah, who is described as equally charismatic as her husband, as well as being beautiful, Zevi made tangible his expressions about the subversion of constrictive morality, announcing the messianic age as being one where transgressions are forgiven.[46]

With regard to Zevi's marriage, his transgressions, and his blasphemies, Matt Goldish explains in *The Sabbatean Prophets* that "Nathan and other theologians of the movement successfully cast these bizarre episodes in a positive light, explaining that they were necessary mystical exercises by which the messiah would redeem the world."[47] According to Nathan, Zevi would bloodlessly overthrow the oppressive strictures of the world, including temporal powers both Christian and Islamic, and he would conquer the Holy Land "riding on a lion with a seven-headed dragon in its jaws."[48] By the time Zevi arrived in Gaza, a settlement which he would declare as the new Holy City due to the resistance of Jewish religious authorities in Jerusalem, Nathan had gathered a contingent to welcome him with a cacophony of shofar blows on Rosh Hashana. Here, at last, was the prophesized messiah.

According to Nathan's own reading of Lurianic Kabbalah, it was Zevi's solemn task and responsibility to gather up all of the sacred kernels hidden within a pained world marked by suffering, to elevate creation back to its original form. As the novelist Isaac Bashevis Singer writes in his twentieth-century fictionalization *Satan in Goray*, "the ritual ceremonies would no longer hold. Bodies would become pure spirit . . . new souls would descend. There would be no more eating and drinking. Instead of being fruitful and multiplying, being would unite in combination of holy letters. The Talmud wouldn't be studied. Of the Bible only the secret essence would remain."[49] Lurianic Kabbalah, and the special messianic message which it had to convey, was particularly important in the seventeenth century when trauma and atrocity marked the Jewish experience from the Straits of Gibraltar to the Bosporus. The founder of that mystical discipline never claimed to be the messiah himself, but Isaac Luria's teachings are appropriately otherworldly in their response to the particularly Jewish state of exile. Born in Jerusalem a century before Zevi and Nathan, Luria proposed some of the most influential and radical Kabbalistic amendments in the tradition's millennia-long history.

Affectionately known as "The Ari," or the Lion, by his followers, Luria established a kabbalistic academy in 1570 among the olive groves of Safed in the Galilee, where both mystical contemplation and poetry were emphasized. Scholem explains that the "principal founders of the new center were Spanish exiles, but they were soon joined by enthusiasts from other communities, until Safed became a kind of miniature distillation of the whole Jewish Diaspora."[50] The Ari's father was Ashkenazic and his mother Sephardic, so that Luria was inheritor of both branches of European Jewry, as well as of the full gamut of persecution which his coreligionists faced during the Renaissance.

At Safed, Luria hosted Sephardic refugees whose families had left Spain and Portugal only a generation before, so that those experiences of dispossession and diaspora became intrinsic to his revision of kabbalah. According to Luria, God himself had gone into exile at the moment of creation, shattering his divine sparks throughout all of fallen reality, meaning that the task of faith and piety is to gather together these kernels of holiness and to caste off the husks of profane, material reality. As Luria wrote in one of his few surviving lyrics, the bulk of his teachings recorded only by disciples, "I hereby call / to the Ancient of Days / to summon His will / to drive them away— / for when his favor / in this room is shown, / the husks are rendered / null and void."[51] This was the process written of earlier, where the divine Ein Sof contracts through *tzimtzum*, so that the redemption known as *tikkun olam* involves recognizing and elevating those shards of sacredness.

For Luria and his followers, ritual, contemplation, and ethics were means of restoring the universe; to perform the mitzvoth of the law, to meditate on divinity, to enact a *mitzvah* or a good deed were each a small stich in the overall tapestry of a cosmos that was being collectively restored. It is hard to overemphasize just how potent such a doctrine was for Jews experiencing the worst persecution since the Rhineland massacres of the Crusades. The expulsion of Sephardic Jews from the Iberian Peninsula had manifested a new form of anti-Jewish rhetoric and violence in the form of antisemitism, the difference being that now conversion to Christianity no longer assured acceptance, as a pseudoscientific discourse of race began to define Jews in terms of not just belief, but ancestry as well. The Reformation, which was initially welcomed by some rabbis as a potential means of being more fully accepted by the authorities, had generated its own antisemitic backlash, in part encouraged by Luther when the Jews did not collectively convert to Protestantism.

On Europe's eastern periphery, the horror of the Khmelnitsky massacres in a region where the Jews had heretofore had a degree of independence and security only underscored the dangerous position of diaspora. In this context, Sabbateanism is made a rather obvious means of mental resistance against both the oppressiveness of European authorities, but also of the God who seemed to barely uphold the covenant. "Traditional popular messianism was characterized by catastrophe and utopianism, and both elements play an important role in the dynamics of the messianic faith," writes Scholem.[52] These legends indulge in "uninhibited fantasies about the catastrophic aspects of redemption . . . a picture of violent upheaval, wars, plague, famine . . . redemption arises on the ruins of history, which collapses amid the 'birth pangs' of the messianic age."[53] In Zevi, many of the Jews of Europe saw a sanctification of their pain, an impartation of meaning onto something which would otherwise be inchoate and chaotic. Persecution of the Jews wasn't novel in the seventeenth century, but what Zevi had, which neither Christ nor bar Kokhba could have availed themselves of, was the printing press. Even while his ministry had rapidly spread through the Ottoman lands of the eastern Mediterranean, it was Nathan's declaration of Zevi's identity as the messiah in 1665 and his promise of the world's redemption a year later—the Christian numerological significance of that year duly noted by the rabbi—that proliferated over the following months. Even Christians cautiously paid attention to the growing movement; rumors of providential signs included a supposed ship composed of sailors from the Ten Lost Tribes of Israel spotted off the coast of Scotland and headed toward Istanbul to challenge the sultan.[54] Among Protestants there was a fascination with Sabbateanism, with some seeing Zevi as a precursor to Christ's Second Coming.

The Reformation had long had an ambivalent relationship with Judaism, in some cases arguably embracing a variety of double-edged philo-semitic Hebraism that in some circumstances granted more rights to Jews, while also continuing the supersessionist dogmas of the Catholic Church which claimed that the

Gospels of Christianity had replaced the original covenant of the Torah. Despite that, many Protestant nations exhibited a theological enthusiasm for the Jews, especially as regards eschatology, with a firm belief that either the dispersal of the Hebrew peoples around the earth, or paradoxically their migration to their ancestral land in the Levant, would be necessary before Christ could return. Such was the logic which justified Cromwell's readmittance of the Jews to England in 1656 at the urging of the prominent Dutch rabbi Menasseh ben Israel, after almost four centuries of official expulsion from that realm.[55] According to various Protestant eschatologies, the lead-up to Christ's return would see the reappearance of all of the Lost Tribes of Israel—many writers argued that the American Indigenous peoples were remnants of this group—and that these martial Hebrews would assist in battling the forces of the antichrist before the Jews finally converted to Christianity.

Strange as such prophecies might seem to us, these beliefs were encouraged by the increasing globalization of the world during this period, with Zvi Ben-Dor Benite writing in *The Ten Lost Tribes: A World History* that the "coming of the Messiah, the second coming of Jesus—apocalyptic events—were brought, through the search for the ten lost tribes, into a spatial as well as a temporal domain," what he terms "geographical theology."[56] This speaks to the surprising interconnectedness of this moment, when a Jewish messiah claimant could synthesize kabbalah, Christianity, and occultism while living in Gaza, and because of that Scottish sailors thought that they heard Hebrew being chanted in the distance through the Hebridean fog—a time when everybody expected the end of the world to be approaching.

Whatever believers expected that autumn of 1666, Zevi's conversion to Islam was not widely entertained as a possibility. And yet the "Sabbatean movement did not end at this juncture, as one might expect," Goldish writes, "but continued in various forms up until the present day."[57] Disillusionment was swift for the majority of those who held the faith, yet apologists like Nathan of Gaza argued that Zevi's apostasy was in keeping with his theology, that by embracing Islam, Zevi was paradoxically fulfilling his own teaching. For Nathan and for others who maintained faith in Zevi even after he himself seemed to lose it, his conversion was part of the process of *tikkun olam*, whereby sparks of creation were spread as widely as possible in order to redeem our fallen world. For the majority of Jews, even those who had once had fervent expectations for this "messiah," this explanation was unconvincing. The Sabbateans endured as an offshoot of Judaism which is still practiced today by a Turkish group called the Dönmeh.

In a more general sense, the apocalyptic enthusiasms of Zevi became sublimated within normative faith, a similar process to what occurred within many of the more fervent denominations of Christianity in the same time period. Just as the radical Anabaptists of Münster inspired the pacifistic Mennonites and Amish, or the dissenting nonconformists of the English seventeenth century only endured in the form of Quakers and Baptists, so too did the millennial expectations of Sabbateanism manifest in a variety of ecstatic movements that emphasized personal transformation more than they did imminent cosmic transformation.

Chief among these pietistic figures was the Polish rabbi known as the Baal Shem Tov, born at the end of the century, in 1698, some twenty-two years after Zevi died in exile in Macedonia. The Baal Shem Tov, known by the acronym of the Besht, taught an ecstatic and mystical version of Judaism heavily influenced by Lurianic Kabbalah, and though millennial elements were obviously present, he made no claim to being a messiah. Furthermore, the Baal Shem Tov was unassailably orthodox in his theological positions, rejecting the antinomianism of the Sabbateans, but preserving the sense of joy in the face of despair which animated the messianic movement.

Holding to the Lurianic belief that sparks of divinity existed in even the darkest place, that kernels of holiness could take root on the stoniest of ground, the Besht is recorded in the posthumous collection of accounts regarding him that is entitled *Tzavaat HaRivash* as saying that "Prayer with much joy is certainly better received . . . than prayer with sorrow and tears."[58] Sabbateanism is virtually extinct today, while the Hasidic Judaism inspired by the Besht is among the fastest-growing sects within the faith, a demonstration that the control of millennial fervency can be more enduring than that which quickly flames out like a brushfire that is quick to burn and equally quick to be quenched. *Tzavaat HaRivash* recounts that the Baal Shem Tov had become so holy that he'd developed the ability to spiritually ascend to heaven and to converse with any soul who resided there. In paradise, it's said that the Besht was able to speak to the awaited messiah, asking him "When will you come?" The answer—"When your wellsprings shall spread to the outside."[59]

A City on a Hill

America as Providential Nation

By the time Tisquantum returned to his native village of Patuxet in 1619, along the cold shoals of the North Atlantic and at the eastern edge of the massive North American continent, he discovered that there was now a kingdom of bare bones and bleached skulls. Virtually all of the natives of Patuxet had died from the mysterious pox that had spread northward from the English settlers in Virginia, who had infected the Algonquin-speaking peoples. Having survived slavery in first Spain and then England, Tisquantum came back to a home that was now but a graveyard, his family victim to the most virulent pestilence which has ever spread on earth.

Little endures of first-person accounts from those spared the worst of the spirochete invasion, from the ghosts of the Algonquins and Iroquoians who were felled in the thousands, if not the millions, by the mysterious illness which rapidly spread from the English and French. Bernard Bailyn writes in *The Barbarous Years—The Peopling of British North America: The Conflict of Civilizations, 1600–1675* that in "the years just preceding the first English settlements, measles, smallpox, and other virulent diseases were beginning to sweep through the most exposed groups and were carried by them into the interior."[60] The Wampanoag, Narraganset, and Patuxet in many cases had no direct contact with Europeans, rather they became sick through the trade of goods with other Indigenous intermediaries. Regardless, the effects were horrific; in Massachusetts, the native population was reduced by 90 percent. A sense of this tragedy is conveyed by Roger Williams, the nonconformist founder of Rhode Island, who compiled a list of common Narragansett phrases in his 1643 *Key into the Language of America*, reading as if apocalyptic verse—"I have a swelling / He is swelled / All his body is swelled / He hath the pox / The pox / The last pox / He hath the plague / The plague / The great plague."[61]

Living now among the surviving Wampanoag, Tisquantum returned to the ruins of Patuxet a year after his arrival, as another English boat had docked in Cape Cod Bay. Unlike their countrymen hundreds of miles south around the Chesapeake, the passengers on the *Mayflower* weren't soldiers or traders, but families. "New England attracted an unusual set of emigrants," writes Alan Taylor in *American Colonies: The Settling of North America*, "prosperous people who ordinarily stayed at home rather than risk the . . . uncertainties of colonial life."[62] Fluent in English, Tishquantum—whom the settlers quickly renamed an easier for them to pronounce "Squanto"—would have learned that these women and men viewed themselves as in exile from Babylon, as having fled from what they viewed as an oppressive Church of England and who now deigned in the Massachusetts wilderness to found a godly commonwealth. William Bradford, the first governor of the colony, writes in *Of Plymouth Plantation* that "Squanto stayed with them and was their interpreter and was a special instrument sent of God for their good beyond their expectation. He showed them how to plant corn . . . and guided them to unknown places, and never left them till he died."[63]

Rather than being a complex and multifaceted human being in his own right, Tisquantum became part of American mythology, reduced to a helpful guide to the pilgrims' odyssey in becoming American. Central to American myth-making as it relates to Plymouth—from its titular rock to the first Thanksgiving—was "Squanto's" role in helpfully assisting the English in agriculture, teaching them proper land stewardship based on indigenous wisdom. Ironically, the practice which he is most associated with—recycling fish heads with planted seeds so as to create a fertilizer for crops—wasn't actually an indigenous method, rather it was associated with medieval Europeans. Most likely Tisquantum learned it during his English bondage, and here in Massachusetts he taught it to the bookish clergy and academics who constituted the first wave of the great migration of pilgrims and Puritans to the New World, these men and women so ignorant in the basic work of agriculture that when Tisquantum gave them tutelage in farming techniques, they assumed it was something native to the Wampanoag.[64] What is true is that this colony would have most likely collapsed after a winter had it not been for Tisquantum's intercession; whatever the origin of his husbandry and planting knowledge, it was an awareness which the English lacked, and his mentorship was instrumental in assuring that they'd be able to survive that first season. Then, in most accounts, Tisquantum simply seems to fade away, having fulfilled his role in the providential fable of English Christian expansion westward.

"New World" was a most convenient appellation, for it was a way of erasing how America was in fact a very old place, with cultures that had developed in this landscape for millennia, a way of ignoring that a very real apocalypse had occurred here in only a few short years, a whole civilization collapsing from the invisible bacteria and viruses clinging to European people and goods, and with it, an entire way of understanding reality. "Shamans, medicine men, witch doctors were brought in to cure the sick and protect the tribes against further illness," writes Bailyn, "but the traditional remedies proved futile, and the authority of those leaders . . . was alarmingly and increasingly undermined."[65] Epidemic meant epistemic collapse, as the old ways of doing things, the previous folkways and faith ways no longer worked for the Algonquin of New England. This devastation was most convenient for the colonists, for not only did the inadvertent biological warfare seemingly "clear" the land for the English, but they believed that the mass death of women, children, and men signaled the superiority of Christianity. Bradford writes that "it pleased God to visit these Indians with a great sickness . . . the smallpox, and died most miserably."[66] Such was the beginning of the fallacy that America was ever a New World, ever a blank canvas on which the colonists could imagine their own dreams, written over the nightmares of the people who actually possessed this land.

For the initial stream of arrivals who came in 1620 aboard the *Mayflower*, their purposes were millennial inasmuch as the broader Calvinist program in England was millennial, but in a more pragmatic sense they were separating from a Church of England under the governance of Archbishop Laud, whom they believed was increasingly amenable to satanic Catholicism. Their primary interest was being able to establish their own system of authority, and America was important only in that it was sufficiently far from England. Where they differed from their countrymen who'd been settling in Virginia for more than a decade was that their purposes were not mercantile but religious, and the pilgrims arrived not as contingent of single men, but as whole families desiring to eke out an existence in the frigid northern wilderness. Eventually they and other Calvinists who arrived in New England would also begin to think of themselves as distinctly different from the other English, as "Americans"—a term that in British, French, and Spanish North America was almost always only applied to Indigenous peoples. That process of etymological shift would take decades, however.[67]

Schismatics to their core, the Pilgrims no longer considered themselves to be part of the Church of England; they were a root of international Calvinism which spread from Geneva to Edinburgh, and now Plymouth. A decade later, a second major wave of English colonists came on an armada led by the ship *Arbela*. This contingent, though almost theologically identical to their predecessors, did still consider themselves within the communion of the Church of England, however they desired to "purify" it of superstitious beliefs and practices, hence their designation as Puritans. Effectively this difference in the long run was a middling one, and Plymouth Plantation and the Massachusetts Bay Colony founded by the Puritans would merge, though the erasure of difference had generated the tendency to anachronistically read millennial purposes in New England colonization back to the moment the *Mayflower* landed.

"For we must consider that we shall be a city upon a hill," reads the most famous sentence in all of seventeenth-century American literature, written by John Winthrop, the first governor of the Massachusetts Bay Colony, traditionally said, in his *A Model of Christian Charity*, to have been delivered aboard the *Arbela* somewhere in the middle of the North Atlantic. In this sermon upon the book of Matthew, Winthrop tells his audience that the "eyes of all people are upon us, so that if we shall deal falsely with our God in this work we have undertaken, and so cause Him to withdraw His present help from us, we shall be made a story and a byword through the world."[68] Only rediscovered as a manuscript at the New-York Historical Society in 1830—exactly two centuries after it was supposedly delivered—*A Model of Christian Charity* seems to have had little contemporary impact on its listeners even while it has since become synonymous with the Puritan sense of providential mission in the New World, an explicitly millennial call to their exceptional purpose. Like Tishquantum, Winthrop's sermon has become part of the liturgy of American civil religion, a bit of patriotic flotsam interpreted in light of later events.

A Model of Christian Charity does express something of the Puritan belief in covenant, even while that metastasized in the American imagination from being "a city upon a hill" into *"The City Upon a Hill."* Even while the generation of the great migration may not yet have seen themselves as a redeemer nation with a role to play in the grand eschatological drama that had been initiated by Reformation, events in their native England—particularly Restoration—conferred upon them a sense of their singular destiny, and a conviction that the New Jerusalem would be a city in Massachusetts. "New Jerusalem" was after all Boston's original name. Even more crucially was the way in which Winthrop's call was repurposed in later American mythology. Abram C. van Engen writes in *City on a Hill: A History of American Exceptionalism* that it became a matter of faith that Winthrop had "called on us to serve as a beacon of liberty, chosen by God to spread the benefits of self-government, toleration, and free enterprise to the entire watching world."[69] Suddenly the relatively humble declaration of Winthrop became the dogma of American exceptionalism. A utopian vision—but a specifically millennial one as well. One capable of shifting between the dove and the dragon as needs must. Even more specifically, this was a postmillennial vision, which is to say that as New England became more certain of its providential role in God's vision for the world, this group of Puritans more closely hewed to the latter misinterpretation of what Winthrop actually meant in his sermon. A belief had developed that *human* beings through *human* actions and in *human* history could make the world more and more perfect in anticipation of Christ's return. In other words, paradise awaited not Christ, but we prepared paradise for Him. Ambivalence always threaded through the New England project, in part because even while the New World had been imagined as Edenic, paradisical, and unfallen, the tough reality of life in a Massachusetts buffered by blizzards and Nor'easters was much different, this howling wilderness where the Puritan divine Cotton Mather believed Satan had constructed his throne. Few societies have ever been quite as spiritually enmeshed with apocalypticism as was colonial New England; little surprise that among the most popular books printed during the period, just after the Bible itself, was poet Michal Wigglesworth's 1662 rhyming doggerel *The Day of Doom*, with his description of Christ's incipient return whereby at "midnight broke forth a light, / which turn'd the night to day: / And speedily an hideous cry / did all the world dismay."[70]

This sense of exulted mission combined with the difficulty of material circumstance led to a number of idiosyncratic aspects to Puritan psychology. In the subsequent generations following the great migration there was a continual anxiety that the English had fallen short of their purpose, that they had in Winthrop's fears become a byword for their inequities and transgressions. Thus resulted the emergence of the most popular rhetorical form in American literature and politics—the jeremiad. Drawing its name from the scriptural prophet, the jeremiad as a form demands that a people hold true to an explicit creed lest tragedy befall those who have betrayed the national promise, and by the late seventeenth century, as many New Englanders modified the stern strictures of Calvinism, it became an increasingly a popular form. Sacvan Bercovitch explains in *The American Jeremiad* how this genre that "originated in the European pulpit, was transformed in both form and content by the New England Puritans, persisted through the eighteenth century, and helped sustain a national dream through two hundred years of turbulence and change."[71] No literary genre has ever been as connected with the American project as the jeremiad, evident in both political pontification and literature. Jeremiad as a form promises entry to a millennium that's just upon the horizon, as long as the creed is fully believed and lived by the people—yet that's a task that is forever impossible. A tremendously useful form of rhetoric.

Taking the pulpit at the First Church of Roxbury, Massachusetts, in 1670, after five decades of settlement in the New World had already preceded, the Reverend Samuel Danforth worried that they had "forgotten our Errand into the Wilderness."[72] Danforth spoke rhetorically to his ancestors, describing how they had "cause of your leaving your country, kindred and father's houses and transporting your selves with your wives, little ones, and substance over the vast ocean into this waste and howling wilderness." From Columbus's discovery onward European chroniclers had often described America in Edenic terms, as a place of copious fruit and vegetation, and seemingly prelapsarian people existing in a state of innocence. It was described as a land of temperate climes and easy days. This was a mainstay of Spanish accounts of the western hemisphere, but also English accounts in royal colonies such as Virginia. However, the reality of New England intervened for the pilgrims and Puritans, and while they were if anything far more certain of their own chosenness in enacting millennium, they understood this as paradoxically having to take place in a hard and terrifying country. "What went ye out into the wilderness to see?," Danforth rhetorically asked his congregation. Was any of this worth it, describing this land as metaphorically "overgrown with thorns, and nettles," where the "stone-wall thereof is broken down," a place where the Christians had grown "careless, remiss, flat, dry, cold, dead frame of spirit."[73] If the American Puritans understood themselves as being at the center of things, then they also understood that New Jerusalem would be built from the stones of hell.

Hence another curious aspect of their psychology—a commitment to this project, but an ambivalence upon the stage in which they must act, a frustration in trying to find paradise in perdition. At the Roxbury Church, Danforth ministered alongside another preacher named John Eliot, among the most committed of missionaries to the local Indigenous peoples, who played a role in the eschatological perspective which the English held concerning the American continent. As with the Spanish, there was a theological concern regarding the origin of the Indigenous peoples, so a solution was to argue that they were actually the Ten Lost Tribes of Israel, and thus descendants of Noah's son Shem.[74] In this role, the conversion of the Indigenous peoples became instrumental to the work of millennium, but many Puritans also dismissed the natives as being vestiges of the natural world, a mentally convenient way of justifying atrocity. Richard Drinnon in *Facing West: The Metaphysics of Indian Hating* explains how the English often described the Algonquin as "natural man," writing that "those deadly subtleties of white hostility that reduced native people to the level of fauna and flora . . . reduced all the diverse Native Americans to a single . . . nonwhite group," while Daniel K. Richter notes in *Facing East from Indian Country: A Native History of Early America* that "stereotyped Indians . . . became central to the American story, but flesh-and-blood Indian people and the histories they made for themselves could not."[75]

Much of this hardening of heart and diminishing of spirit can be connected to a hideous war that started only five years after Danforth's sermon, when the howling wilderness was specifically equated with the chants of undifferentiated Indigenous peoples in the Puritan imagination. During the fiery haze of the 1675 King Philip's War—still per capita the most violent conflict in American history—a union of Wampanoags, Nipmucks, Podunks, Narragansetts, Nashaway, and Abenaki unsuccessfully attempted to dislodge the English and their Indigenous allies from New England. Out of the forge of that conflict would come two new aspects of the Puritan worldview—a hardened identity of being specifically "American" and a sense that to be among that sacred group meant that you were a soldier in the millennial kingdom. It is crucial to not underestimate the impact of King Philip's War, a brutal frontier conflict that seemed quite literally apocalyptic to the Puritans, on the American psyche. Even the English name which the settlers gave to the Indigenous sachem Metacomet—Philip—was meant to evoke the Spanish adversary of Elizabeth, to place this new war in a similar eschatological lineage.

Battle reduced Massachusetts into a "landscape of ashes, of farms laid waste, of corpses without heads," as historian Jill Lepore writes in *The Name of War: King Philip's War and the Origins of American Identity*.[76] Edward Wharton, a Puritan witness to the war, wrote home to England that "a most bitter spirit is entered the English, and Indians; in which they greatly endeavor the utter destruction one of another," a crusade of mutual extermination after coexistence had failed. Half of New England's settlements were destroyed in a year, and the inevitability of English victory was far from certain. Fighting was close, intimate, and horrific; a war of mutilation, rape, torture, and scalping. By 1676, a year after the English victory, the versifier Benjamin Tompson would print one of the most popular poems in the colonies, an epic about the war entitled *New-England's Crisis* that recasts the conflict into a millennial narrative of resurrection, where "Out of her ashes let a Phoenix rise / That may outshine the first and be more wise."[77]

As hopeful as that message may seem, *New-England's Crisis* is permeated with a gothic, apocalyptic sense, descriptions of demonic Indigenous peoples "besmeared with Christian blood & oiled / With fat out of human bodies boiled," while he gleefully describes the immolation of native women and children, the "hideous Indian cry / Of wounded ones who in the Wigwams fry."[78] Nothing about colonization—as can be expected—softened the English as they transformed themselves into Americans. In a 1676 sermon preached by the Puritan divine Increase Mather, on the subject of the biblical Amalekites whom the Lord commands the Hebrews to slaughter, he thundered that "Heathen people amongst whom we live, and whose land the Lord God of our Fathers hath given to us for a rightful possession" shall be eliminated, for a "Sword, a sword is sharpened . . . to make a sore slaughter,"[79] the genocidal logic of apocalypses purifying through fire and blood.

Nor were the Puritans of New England the only people in seventeenth-century America to connect the land itself, and the struggle over it, with apocalyptic and millennial connotations. Proprietary colonies such as Pennsylvania established a government based on complete religious toleration, in keeping with the Quaker principles of its founder William Penn. As such, a variety of migrants settled in the colony, particularly German Anabaptists who still adhered to the millennial convictions of the sixteenth century, albeit in pacifistic form. Pennsylvania became a haven for nonconformist thinkers, often drawn to specifically utopian or millennial causes, such as the idiosyncratic occultist and alchemist Johannes Kelpius who arrived in Philadelphia in 1694, interpreting the city of that same name in John of Patmos's Revelation as not being the one in Asia Minor, but rather the new town on the Schuylkill, believing that the dawn of the new order would be here in the American wilderness.[80] Millennial groups in Kelpius's stead—including the Society of the Woman in the Wilderness, the Ephrata Commune, and the community of Economy—all thrived in the liberal colony.

Indigenous peoples also embraced eschatological perspectives as they faced an existential threat in the form of the English along the Atlantic Coast, drawing from their own traditions and in some cases merging them with Christian forms. As an example, consider the traditional Seven Fires Prophecy of the Anishinaabe people who reside around the Great Lakes region, who, though they weren't participants in King Philip's War, would have encountered French and then later English settlers, and were engaged in defensive fighting against colonials into the eighteenth century. The prophecy, composed of several different "fires" which iterate subsequent history, includes predictions such as "Beware if the light skinned race comes wearing the face of death," for the "Anishinaabe will find the path to . . . a land in the west to which they must move their families," an eerily accurate accounting of settler colonialism and Manifest Destiny.[81]

Indigenous eschatology would further proliferate in the nineteenth century, in the form of syncretic religious faiths such as the Code of Handsome Lake among the Iroquois, or the Ghost Dance tradition in the American Southwest. As a counter to Winthrop's triumphalist vision of an American city on a hill, the

Seven Fires Prophecy rather warned of the hubris which interprets this "howling wilderness" as a means unto an end and not as something deserving of stewardship in its own right. The Anishinaabe apocalypse warns that centuries after the arrival of the Europeans, the "light skinned race will be given a choice between two roads. One road will be green and lush, and very inviting. The other road will be black and charred, and walking it will cut their feet." The choice will be between "an eternal fire of peace, love, brotherhood and sisterhood," and, if rejected, the "destruction which they brought with them in coming to this country will come back at them and cause much suffering and death to all the Earth's people."

CHAPTER SEVEN

Visions of the Last Judgment

Rationalizing the Apocalypse

Novus Ordo Seclorum

The United States as Providential Nation

ARRIVING IN THAT red-bricked, church-steepled metropolis along the Schuylkill in 1774, the English journalist Thomas Paine had come to a society on the verge of revolution. The colony's most illustrious and wealthy inhabitant—the publisher, diplomat, inventor, and scientist Benjamin Franklin—had invited Paine so that the young writer would avoid London's notorious debtors' prisons, but the democratic enthusiasms in America were more in keeping with his radical political allegiances anyhow. Nonconformism was patrilinear for Paine—his working-class father was a Quaker, though the son had largely eschewed organized religion, rather embracing Deism, which posited a distant, rational, impersonal God who treated the universe as if a clockmaker winding a timepiece, though critics saw little difference between that theology and rank atheism.[1]

Such a reputation has dogged Paine, the propagandist for revolution who had little room for God, and less for churches, writing in the second volume of his 1795 *The Age of Reason* that the "most detestable wickedness, the most horrid cruelties, and the greatest miseries that have afflicted the human race, have had their origin in this thing called revelation, or revealed religion," concluding that of "all the systems of religion that ever were invented, there is none more derogatory... more unedifying... more repugnant... and more contradictory in itself than this thing called Christianity."[2] While the latitudinarian settlements of the Church of England could countenance quite a wide range of theological positions, even they had difficulty with the sheer ferocity of Paine's impiety.

While his neighbors in Philadelphia wouldn't have completely taken to Paine's church of one, Franklin wasn't wrong that Pennsylvania supplied more possibility for free discourse. Paine now lived in the future capital of a nation that would enshrine religious disestablishment as part of its national creed, having drawn upon the example of theorists like William Penn and Roger Williams, and which, despite being a nation that in G. K. Chesterton's memorable phrase had the "soul of a church," was the earliest and most enduring officially secular country. Certainly much had changed across the colonies in the half-century after

King Philip's War. For one, the population of the colonies had greatly increased, and geopolitically America had become integral in the quarrelling between the great powers of Europe, particularly during the Seven Years' War between Great Britain and France. A relative high standard of living when compared to Europe also encouraged a variety of settlers from throughout Europe to emigrate, so that America possessed a startlingly high degree of ethnic and religious diversity. "The American experiment was frequently shaped by a rejection of old ways and openness to the new," writes Peter Manseau in *One Nation, Under Gods: A New American History*. "In religious terms, this rejection created over time a nation unique in its ability to absorb and be built by those of different beliefs; people who believed there were many gods, or none at all."[3]

Religious pluralism long preceded constitutional disestablishment of a national church, which, depending on how the history is interpreted, can lend itself to understanding colonial America as either God-obsessed or shockingly indifferent to sectarian questions. In part, this is because of the reality that the area which would become the United States was colonized by multiple European powers of various sectarian allegiances, including the Catholic Spanish and French and the Protestant English and Dutch, among others, as well as the population including both Indigenous peoples and Africans. Within the cauldron of America, not just in the mid-Atlantic, but from New England down to Georgia, there were English and Spanish, Dutch and Germans, French and Swedes; there were the Congregationalist Puritans of Massachusetts, the Dutch Reformed of New York, the Quakers of Pennsylvania, the Catholics of Maryland, and the High Church Anglicans of Virginia and the Carolinas, alongside a surprising diversity of people who held non-Christian beliefs, including Jews and Muslims, as well as the faith of the Abenaki and the Iroquois, and the Wolof and the Ibo. As a result, much debate has centered on just how traditionally religious Americans happened to be in the last quarter of the eighteenth century, and what role that played in the coming revolution.

The First Great Awakening of the 1740s burnt a circuit from Boston to Savannah; evangelical preachers like the Wesleyan minister George Whitfield introduced an ecstatic, fervent variety of worship to America heavily indebted to the Pietism of Lutheran Germany (of the same historical moment as Hasidic Judaism). Such revivals were both a rejection of High Church ritual and liturgy as well as Puritan staidness, and they did much to influence American religion, though it's questionable what role they played in American politics. It's been argued that the First Great Awakening was instrumental in forging a separate American identity, especially as separate from the Church of England, while others such as Jon Butler in *Awash in a Sea of Faith: Christianizing the American People* argued that the significance of the revivals was "invented," saying that a perseveration on the Great Awakening "may say more about subsequent times than about its own. The term was not contemporary, nor was it known to the historians of the revolutionary and early national periods," concluding that its "long-term effects have been greatly exaggerated."[4]

Indeed, by the time Paine would have strolled down Market Street, ostensibly only a few decades after preachers like Whitfield and Jonathan Edwards had packed fields and churches with moaning, convulsing, ecstatic crowds of worshipers, religious identification in the country would be at the lowest in its national history, far less than the decades and centuries following independence. Leonard Woolsey Bacon, writing in his 1897 *A History of American Christianity* opines that the "closing years of the eighteenth century show the lowest low-water mark of the lowest ebb-tide of spiritual life in the history of the American church," blaming the pernicious influence of European philosophies like Deism, as well as the new science.[5] Lest Bacon's contention be interpreted as mere Victorian emotionalism, the sociologist Rodney Stark confirms in his book *The Churching of America, 1776–2005: Winners and Losers in Our Religious Economy* that on the "eve of Revolution only about 17 percent of Americans were churched,"[6] which is to say a baptized member of a religious community—the lowest level it has ever been, certainly much lower than it is today.

Bacon's impulse may have been to hold responsible the exact sort of emerging, secular philosophies that Paine was so enthused by, but we must interpret data such as Starke's with both an awareness of the material circumstances and of the subtlety of belief itself. Concerning the first issue, the popularity of the revivals of the middle of the century speaks to both peoples' interest in religion and also the relative dearth of opportunities to express it in sparsely populated, frontier communities. In other words, church membership was low because there weren't as many churches in some places. There is also, certainly in the case of New England, the reality that stern, doctrinaire, unforgiving, and impossible-to-live-up-to Calvinism made joining the church far less appealing to many, so that people left organized religion entirely, the ministers more than happy to have halfway enthusiasts out of their congregations. Regarding the second issue is the reality that much of what Bacon may have interpreted as being areligious, or even antireligious, was simply faith by another name; where despite somebody like Paine's avowed impieties, the old Quaker was in many ways blissfully divine and crucially *millennial* in his orientation.

Born less than a century after the English Civil War and raised among the religious dissenters who flourished during those years, Paine's theories may have been secular, but his rhetoric betrayed the millennial and apocalyptic impulses which permeated even a society supposedly uninterested in faith, a staunch adherent of both the dragon and the dove. The conscious absence of religion always contains traces of faith; the negation of belief simply belief turned upside down. Nowhere is the millennial nature of Paine's project more apparent than in his most celebrated and influential book, the forty-seven-page pamphlet *Common Sense* which rolled off the printing presses in 1776, just in time for the Declaration of Independence. Read in the churches of Boston and the coffee houses of New York, the pubs of Philadelphia and the taverns of Jamestown, *Common Sense* has been rightly valorized as among the most successful and unifying of ideological efforts to define the coming conflict with Great Britain not as a civil war between anglophone cousins—mere squabbles over taxation and licensing—but rather an epoch-defining Revolution which would completely reshape the world.

If Wigglesworth's *Day of Doom* was seventeenth-century America's most-read book, *Common Sense* was the eighteenth-century republican equivalent, and arguably just as eschatological. Describing the spiritual liberals and freethinkers who followed from Paine's example in the subsequent centuries, Lehigh Eric Schmidt in *The Church of Saint Thomas Paine: A Religious History of American Secularism* explains how they often described themselves as "agnostic moralists, free religionists, ethical culturists, religious positivists, moral philanthropists . . . they might espouse the religion of humanity, the religion of this world, the religion of Thomas Paine, the religion of deeds, the religion of life, or the religion of the future."[7] What's notable is that the preponderance of these examples are of people—Deists, pantheists, agnostics, even atheists—describing theirs as a "*religion*." More than that, American progressivism was often a variety of sublimated postmillennial yearning, of the dove's faith with its sense that a perfected society could be built on earth (whether or not Christ would return at the consummation of that project); a belief that the political project embodied by the American Revolution could bring an ever-more perfect heaven down to earth, that the arc of history would bend toward justice. The parallels with several of the factions in the English Civil War are obvious, albeit in the American examples Christ was often obscured, secularism becoming the Protestant faith without a messiah. Certainly this was the case with Paine, even with his fervent heresies, blasphemies, and impieties (or maybe even especially because of them).

Was ever there so obviously a millennial tract like *Common Sense*? "The cause of America is in great measure the cause of all mankind," writes Paine, a conflation of the provincial country with the universal imperium, the election of the nation to the status of a Fifth Monarchy (or republic rather).[8] "The sun never shined on a cause of greater worth. 'Tis not the affair of a city, a country, a province, or a kingdom, but of a continent," the pamphleteer again underscoring that America's purpose is liberty and liberty's purpose is for all humanity. "In the early ages of the world, according to the Scripture chronology there were no kings," where despite the journalist's avowed secularism he not only appeals to the Bible but interprets it as a manual for a prelapsarian future. "But where, say some, is the King of America? . . . so far as we approve of monarchy, that in America the law is king," replacing the temporal sovereign with an abstraction, just as the English revolutionaries deposed a king and elevated Christ and the gospel upon the throne (or at least claimed to). "A situation, similar to the present, hath not happened since the days of Noah until now," writes Paine. "The birthday of a new world is at hand, and a race of men, perhaps as numerous as all Europe contains, are to receive their portion of freedom from the event of a few months."

Remarkable rhetoric, for if Paine had a consummate talent it was to turn a phrase with a fierce and perceptive urgency. So millennial is his vision—so apocalyptic—that to even analyze such passages closely is a redundancy. In only a few dozen pages, Paine cast what was essentially an argument about taxation and representation into a universal battle for redemption, a crusade for freedom, and a war to usher in an entirely *Novus ordo seclorum* as the heraldry of that young republic would soon proclaim—a "New Order of the Ages."[9] Thus the American Revolution as invented by Paine wasn't simply an issue of American representatives to Parliament being able to sit in Westminster, or of Massachusetts, Pennsylvania, and Virginia having more independence or being able to settle beyond the Ohio River Valley, but rather this was the cause of mankind; there was now the intention to forge an entirely new race, a new type of human. "We have it in our power to begin the world over again," writes Paine, the "atheist" who fervently believed that the kingdom of God—even if not called such—was the cause of this revolution. As for what to name this new nation, Paine suggested something for the first time in *Common Sense* which ultimately gained some traction—*The United States of America*.[10] The American project was arguably the most successful millennial project of the post-Christian era, the Enlightenment consummation of recasting the world, which paradoxically could only reach its apex within a secular order. Paine's role in this can't be minimized, even while his genius was arguably to synthesize many of the currents that already existed at the popular level. *Common Sense* was instrumental in giving the revolutionary cause a zeal which would have otherwise been lacking; not only did it encourage more colonial Americans to enlist, it sutured together a common identity among thirteen colonies that were profoundly different. They were in need of one. "During the very long period from 1629 to 1775," writes David Hackett Fischer in *Albion's Seed: Four British Folkways in America*, "the present area of the United States was settled by at least four large waves of English-speaking immigrants."[11]

Fischer divides these migrations between the Puritans of New England, the Royalist Anglicans and a scattering of Catholics around the Chesapeake, North Midlands English and Welsh with a predilection for nonconformism in the Delaware Valley, and finally Scots-Irish Presbyterians on the western Appalachian frontier. Despite all being anglophone, mostly Protestant, and considering themselves to be British subjects, Fisher writes that they "differed from one another . . . in their religious denominations, social ranks, historical generations," down to the ways in which they built their homes and the dialects they spoke. There had been a desire for greater cohesion among the colonies for decades—as with Franklin's failed 1754 Albany Plan of Union—but fundamentally these settlements were in many ways different nations. For an Anglican in Georgetown, Maryland, it would be hard to see why a Boston Congregationalist's anger at Westminster would necessarily be pertinent. That ultimately such a hypothetical gentleman did understand that, especially a century after the Southern colonies had largely sided with the Royalist cause in the English Civil War, is remarkable, and due in no small part to the powerful writing of Paine.

What *Common Sense* presupposed was a transcendent and unifying identity beyond the insular ethnic and religious categories that so often defined the colonies; an identity which would be fundamentally creedal. At its core, the new order of the revolutionary cause established a covenantal nation, a polity which like ancient Judea and Israel was built around a commitment to an idea, in this case not that of the God of Abraham but rather of universal democratic and republican values. "If England had thirty different religions," writes Gordon Wood in *The Radicalism of the American Revolution*, "then America had hundreds, and none of them was traditionally organized."[12] This is literally accurate, but arguably America in the years after the Revolution would really only have one religion—that of Americanism itself.

This was, it must be emphasized, a faith that was congruent with the principles of the European Enlightenment, clothed in the mantle of reason and logic, science and democracy. Even the traditional faiths would be interpreted in this manner, explains Wood, writing that "God could no longer be absolute or arbitrary. Religion, some now said, had to rest not only on faith and revelation but also on nature and reason."[13] Yet even those surrogate secular religions imported from the intelligentsia of Europe, from Freemasonry to Rosicrucianism, evidenced those traces of liturgical faith and ritual, and what so often marks the rhetoric which surrounds the American Revolution is this sense that the new country is in many ways the last country—which is to say that the United States is responsible for the perfectibility of the world in terms of liberty and freedom. By the time the Treaty of Paris baptized America as an independent nation, "most Protestants believed that the United States had a divine, and perhaps millennial, purpose, advanced by the revolution," writes Alan Taylor in *American Revolution: A Continental History, 1750–1804*.[14] That much of this language of millennium came from Paine speaks to the complexities of belief and disbelief during the end of days.

Nor was millennialism filtered through the American grain exclusive to Protestants or settlers of English extraction. A most remarkable book of the eighteenth-century colonies was the Frenchman J. Hector St. John de Crèvecœur's surprisingly engaging 1782 *Letters from an American Farmer*. A hybrid work of both fiction and nonfiction, Crèvecœur's account was a series of lyrical, essayistic observations from a gentleman farmer living at the very edge of the frontier in Carlisle, Pennsylvania. Crèvecœur, born in Normandy and a veteran of the Seven Years' War who fought against the British in the western Pennsylvania wilderness, settled in upstate New York, where he would reflect on the flora and fauna, culture and mores of the New World. The Old World was overpopulated, polluted, and hierarchical, but here in America there were "fair cities, substantial villages, extensive fields . . . decent houses, good roads, orchards, meadows, and bridges, where an hundred years ago all was wild, woody, and uncultivated."[15]

Europe was haunted by the enclosure of the commons, yet it was said that there had been a paradisical age before the establishment of feudalism wherein each peasant was their own king, and in America these utopian yearnings could be projected onto a landscape they misapprehended as "empty." Across the Atlantic, *Letters from an American Farmer* was by far the most popular book from an American's pen, a work which questioned even the conventional wisdom of *who* could be an American. French and Catholic—indeed educated by Jesuits—Crèvecœur emphasized that "Americanness" was an assent to a creed, a covenant, rather than an ethnicity. "What, then, is this new man, the American?," asks Crèvecœur, a question as Edenic as it is millennial. "They are a mixture of English, Scotch, Irish, French, Dutch, Germans, and Swedes. From this promiscuous breed, that race, now called Americans, have arisen."[16] For Crèvecœur, the exact same qualities that made American identity porous and inchoate—its diversity and the massive expanse of the land itself—were the basis of American identity. Furthermore, this was the cauldron in which would be formed a "new man," an unescapably millennial project.

Crèvecœur wasn't the primogeniture of the "American Dream," nor of the creedal belief that previous identities could be subsumed within being a new type of man, but he did handily express these sentiments as they were funneled into the revolution and then outward into the Republic itself. The Frenchman actually returned to his home country upon the outbreak of hostilities between America and Great Britain, jailed briefly in Loyalist New York under the suspicion of being a spy for the revolutionaries. He wasn't, and in fact had mixed opinions of the revolutionary cause himself, but like many Americans, Crèvecœur saw something providential in the nation's geography, demography, and history—all the more remarkable because *Letters from an American Farmer* expresses none of these beliefs in a conventionally Christian manner. In keeping with Stark's observation about the relative agnosticism of colonial Americans, Crèvecœur often times denigrates traditional belief, while also valorizing the toleration which predominates in his adopted country, contrasting it to the factionalism and strife which marks Europe.

Religious toleration is intrinsic to understanding not just the development of American religion, but in many ways how America itself *became a religion—specifically a millennial and an apocalyptic religion at that.* Emergent national polities in the eighteenth century had to define themselves into existence, as Benedict Anderson claimed in *Imagined Communities: Reflections on the Origin and Spread of Nationalism*, arguing that "Communities are to be distinguished . . . by the style in which they are imagined."[17] Unlike European powers, with their myths of blood and soil, the United States of America was believed by its faithful to be the apex of history, a font of universal liberty, the new order of which Paine prophesized. Less than a century after American independence, at the conclusion of the apocalyptic war which threatened to rip the entire nation asunder, and underneath the wrought-iron, white-painted dome of the United States Capitol Building in the federal district named after the first president, the Greco-Italian painter Constantino Brumidi rendered a remarkable fresco entitled *The Apotheosis of Washington*. Here, the revolutionary war general and mythic father of his nation is represented as an Olympian deity, bedecked in the blue uniform of the Continental Army but with a purple robe over his knees, a chorus of various celestial beings about the president, representing commerce and agriculture, military prowess and science. Nearest to him is Columbia, the goddess Liberty, manifestation of American freedom in Phrygian cap.

To divinize a man such as Washington—who evidenced no particular millennial affectations himself, and was a largely stalwart if disinterested Episcopalian—demonstrates how increasingly "America" itself came to be understood as a sacred object, especially in the century following the Revolution. "In the beginning," writes Robert N. Bellah in *The Broken Covenant: American Religion in Time of Trial*, "and to some extent ever since, Americans have interpreted their history as having religious meaning"—crucially, *even when individually they might not be traditionally religious.*[18] According to Bellah, the United States developed a unique ideological formulation of a "civil religion," that is something which in many ways appears to be a religion in that it has sacred scripture—as in the Declaration of Independence and the Constitution; sacred sites—such as the National Mall in Washington, DC; sacred liturgy—the Pledge of Allegiance and the "Star Spangled Banner"; sacred objects—the Liberty Bell and the Statue of Liberty; sacred holidays—Thanksgiving and the Fourth of July; and a sacred origin myth in the worship of the so-called "Founding Fathers."

In an essay for *Dædalus: Journal of the American Academy of Arts and Sciences*, Bellah writes that the "American civil religion was never anticlerical . . . it borrowed selectively from the religious tradition in such a way that the average American saw no conflict. . . . In this way, the civil religion was able to build up without any bitter struggle with the church powerful symbols of national solidarity and to mobilize deep levels of personal motivations for the attainment of national goals."[19] And so a politician could be imagined as a god without the stench of idolatry accruing. Among Americans, civil religion takes a variety of forms, from the more explicitly theological to the superficially secular, but at its core is the same decree of Paine that the nation itself was capable of making the world anew. While the level of hagiography concerning the founders hasn't necessarily been consistent over the centuries, the origins of such thinking can be traced back to that generation itself, even while acting as if the radically different and often personally antagonistic coterie of men like Washington, Franklin, Thomas Jefferson, and John Adams were divine prophets is particularly virulent in our own day.

As an example of how such valorization was common even when these men were alive, consider the still-extant *Great Seal of the United States*, placed into commission in 1782 with its hermetic symbol of an incomplete pyramid topped by the omniscient eye of providence, declaring the nation to be *Novus ordo seclorum*—a "New Order of the Ages." Not even the monarchies of old, where the divine right of kings was an article of fideism, were quite as brave as the designers of America's official heraldry. Even more adamant was a proposed design which Franklin had a part in designing, a depiction of the Israelites led by Moses leaving Egypt and entering the Holy Land. That Franklin himself had little use for organized religion only speaks to the attraction of this new American faith. Writing in *Redeemer Nation: The Idea of America's Millennial Role*, Ernest Tuveson defines the American self-conception as of being a "Chosen race, chosen nation; millennial-utopian destiny for mankind; a continuing war between good (progress) and evil (reaction) in which the United States is to play a starring role as world redeemer."[20] Such are the vagaries and dangers of this religion, as it both inspired the cursed religion of Manifest Destiny and the blessed one of the abolitionists.

In the belly of the beast itself, the great British poet William Blake—a political and religious radical and the direct inheritor of those millennial and apocalyptic yearnings which burnt through his own nation a century before—looked admiringly across the Atlantic. His 1793 epic *America: A Prophecy* was to be Blake's scripture for this new order, an evocation of the ways in which the entire world was being born anew in the revolution. "The Guardian Prince of Albion burns in his nightly tent," writes Blake, "Sullen fires across the Atlantic glow to America's shore. / Piercing the souls of warlike men who rise in silent night. / Washington, Franklin, Paine. . . . Meet on the coast glowing with blood from Albion's fiery Prince."[21] If Paine believed that the Revolution had the ability to make the world anew, so would Blake depict that through myth and poetry. Occult and obscure, Blake's prosody is that of Patmos, where a "dragon form, clashing his scales: at midnight he arose, / And flam'd red meteors round the land of Albion beneath: / His voice, his locks, his awful shoulders, and his glowing eyes / Appear to the Americans upon the cloudy night." And yet the colonies, protected by thirteen celestial angels, harrow the halls of hell. "The King of England looking westward trembles at the vision."[22] Blake would not remain enthused about *America: A Prophecy* over the course of his life, not because he lost faith in the Revolution, but he began to intuit that the Revolution never had the same faith as him.[23]

By 1788, much of the initial antinomian promise of the Revolution was constrained by the federal agreement which led to the ratification of the Constitution. That document enshrined the power and rights of slave owners, with fully 18 percent of Americans in bondage. For Blake, who detested any form of manacles over the body or mind, such a reality was worse than hypocrisy—it was betrayal. It was a sin. Religious dissenters in the new Republic—nonconformists to both faith and politics—similarly detested the slavocracy that grew south of the Mason–Dixon Line even as the institution faded in the north. Herman Husband, a backwoods prophet who was involved in the Whiskey Rebellion in western Pennsylvania, the first serious political threat to the new Constitutional order, dreamt of the abolition of slavery and the descent of a gleaming New Jerusalem from the heavens which would alight somewhere in his beloved Allegheny Mountains.[24] By the end of the century, there began to be convulsions of revival again, ironically encouraged by the government's official disestablishment of religion, leading into a Second Great Awakening. Like Husband, many of these groups embraced fervent abolitionism and rejected the American civil religion, apostates to a faith which in its official documents countenanced such an immorality.

Naturally, in a nation that had replaced politics with faith while pretending that that isn't exactly what had been done, to stand athwart the official church of American exceptionalism was to be a type of heretic, but such dissension also found natural home within that civil religion. Even Paine—always an abolitionist—lost faith with the United States, rather seeing a mystic cause for "America" wherever tyranny needed to be fought. By the middle of the nineteenth century, there were glaring fissures between the ideals of the Declaration of Independence and the reality of the Constitution. Thundering in an apocalyptic tone in 1854 while before the Massachusetts Anti-Slavery Society, the abolitionist William Lloyd Garrison would declare the Constitution to be a "covenant with death . . . an agreement with hell," before setting fire to a copy of that document, iconoclasm always an act which simultaneously endows and disparages a sense of the sacred.[25] As the rising power in the west increasingly took to the millennial role which its founders envisioned for it, a question remained among many—both inside and outside of the new country—whether America was Israel or was it Babylon, of the dove or of the dragon?

Liberty, Equality, Prophecy

France's Apocalyptic Revolution

On a brisk 20th of Brumaire during Year II—at least according to the new revolutionary calendar, but outside of Republican France it would have still been November 10, 1793—Antoine-François Momoro, a former bookseller who was now a powerful member of the populist Society of the Friends of the Rights of Man and of the Citizen, as well as a leader in the radical Hébertists faction, saw the culmination of months of organizing when across the nation his new religion named the Cult of Reason reached fruition, the inaugurating ritual held in the Temple of Reason, repurposed from Paris's former Cathedral de Notre Dame.[26]

All across France and crucifixes were torn down with more enthusiasm than they ever had been by the Huguenots, altars were demolished and religious inscriptions replaced with paeons to enlightenment and rationality. "For many of the revolutionary militants," writes Jeremy D. Popkin in *New World Begins: A History of the French Revolution*, "this de-Christianization campaign was the logical culmination of the Enlightenment critique of revealed religion and the revolutionary program of insisting on exclusive loyalty to the nation,"[27] though as the form and script of the new rituals perhaps evidenced, such sentiments could only be converted or sublimated, not eliminated.

Gates in front of graveyards had affixed above them reliefs which declared that "Death is an Eternal Sleep," while the Temple of Reason, which had previously observed the Catholic Mass since its cornerstone was laid in the twelfth century, now had carved above its entrance "To Philosophy." At the Brumaire Festival of Reason, Momoro's wife came dressed as the goddess Reason, an avatar of Liberty and the Revolution itself. The *Pere Duchene* newspaper reported that in "place of that altar or really of that stage for charlatans, a throne had been constructed for liberty. In place of a dead statue, there was a living image of that divinity, a masterpiece of nature . . . a charming woman, beautiful like the goddess she represented."[28] A phalanx of Phrygian-capped youth bedecked in the tricolor of red, blue, and white, sang hymns to rationality before the goddess while *La Marseillaise* played, celebrating the dechristianization of France and the elevation of this new, atheistic, logical faith. By the time Momoro's cult was unveiled, the *ancien régime* had crumbled and King Louis XVI had already faced the guillotine alongside thousands of aristocrats and reactionaries, while France was already at the beginning of the Reign of Terror. Soon the Revolution would begin to consume even itself, as more blood pooled among the cobblestones of Paris.

Momoro wouldn't even survive for another four months. Having orchestrated the downfall of the moderate Girondists, Momoro challenged the powerful Committee on Public Safety, particularly its leaders George Danton and, most ambitious of all, Maximillian Robespierre. The former bookseller would be decapitated on the 4th of Germinal, still Year II of the revolutionary calendar, though by this point it was 1794 everywhere else in the world. A committed Deist, Robespierre was disgusted by the Cult of Reason, but he was no partisan of the Catholicism which had dominated France since the church's victories over the Huguenots, and instead of either he introduced his own novel faith in the form of the Cult of the Supreme Being.

Robespierre, most infamous of the Jacobins, understood the Cult of the Supreme Being to be a theistic religion, and most of all a *rational* religion, based not in prophecy and revelation, but on the sober, judicious, and philosophical consideration of first principles.[29] This was to be the theology of revolution and democracy, with Robespierre describing his political goals in a 1794 speech as wanting to "fulfil nature's wishes, to further the destines of humanity, to keep the promises of philosophy, to absolve providence of the long reign of crime and tyranny. So that France . . . may become the model for all nations, the terror of oppressors, the consolations of the oppressed. . . . That is our ambition, that is our goal."[30] Thus a second redeemer nation arose from the tumult of the Enlightenment, where the Jacobins had more ambitious aspirations than even the Americans did, their central document championing not just political independence, but indeed titled the Declaration of the Rights of Man and of the Citizen, a dictate for the whole of humanity.

The Cult of the Supreme Being, enforced by the Committee on Public Safety as a replacement for both Momoro's short-lived sect as well as for Catholicism, was meticulously planned by Robespierre. The details of its liturgy and its celebrations were carefully informed by his ideals; a massive holiday was planned for the 20th of Prairial in the Year II, and under the structure of the new calendar supplications were to be offered every tenth day of the decimal week. New symbols, new faiths, even a new sense of time—nothing attempted before was as radical as the French Revolution, but like every passing into a new world the traces of the old were still evident.[31] Messianism was central to the French Revolution, sometimes figurative, though not infrequently literal as well, as Robespierre's words concerning the French national destiny in the salvation of humanity surely evidences. Dechristianization as a policy of the Hébertists, Girondists, and Jacobins was not antireligious; to the contrary, it was the final conflation of politics with religion, the only question is what new faith would constitute the latter.

Among the urban working class known as the Sans Culottes and the rural poor, certain enthusiasms began to emerge. Simon Schama in *Citizens: A Chronicle of the French Revolution* writes of how some "proclaimed Robespierre to be the herald of the Last Days, the prophet of the New Dawn."[32] An attitude that Robespierre, who styled himself the "messianic schoolmaster," didn't dissuade, and perhaps even believed, the famously stern and puritanical revolutionary living a rather monastic life, even as, especially as, he sent innocent and guilty, friends and enemies, to the Place de la Concorde where they faced the guillotine's blade. Robespierre got his own chance to travel to that stage, less than six months after he declared the Republic's millennial ambitions during what is named—after one of the new months—as the Thermidorian Reaction. Here now was the decapitation of a man welcomed by some as the messiah and by others as the antichrist.

In theology, according to the political theorist Eric Voeglin in *The New Science of Politics*, to "immanentize the eschaton" means to compel the end of days through direct action, to bring about millennium on earth (or to attempt it).[33] American secularism involved a careful and nuanced détente between church and state, whereas the French—who suffered more under a centralized church than the Americans ever did—were rabidly opposed to the established religion. This meant not the halfway measures of American civil religion, but an entirely new faith. Thus a type of eschaton was immanentized on July 14, 1789, the first day of the new era, the inauguration of a millennium, when a few dozen mangy prisoners were liberated from the royal Bastille Prison in Paris.

Because of its anticlericalism—the seemingly vociferous secularism of the French Republic, especially when compared to the lackadaisical disestablishmentarianism of the United States—the eschatological nature of the Hébertists, Girondists, and Jacobins can be obscured; an error, for the French Revolutionaries fully intended to not just to compel a new epoch, but they desired to abolish the ancient ways of existing within time entirely. Witness the infamous and aforementioned metric calendar, which set the origin of the new universe with the establishment of the Republic itself. That the French Revolutionaries, particularly the most radical contingent of Jacobins, understood themselves as remaking the world, as establishing a type of millennial Republic, is obvious from the ways in which the old order was so thoroughly demolished. The names of all months were purged of any religious association and the Revolution aimed to remake time itself—the very currency of apocalypse.[34]

In conventional understandings, the French Revolution has often been framed as both the consummation of the Enlightenment and its negation; Enlightenment, that multifaceted and often contradictory international movement of intellectuals across a Republic of Letters in Paris and London, Edinburgh and Philadelphia, whose advocates believed in the possibility of human knowledge in the arts and sciences as improving the predicament of mankind, where toleration, democracy, openness, and rationality would ever progress. "All that is required for this enlightenment is *freedom*," enthused the Prussian philosopher Immanuel Kant in his 1784 essay "What Is Enlightenment?," "namely, the freedom for man to make public use of his reason in all matters."[35]

Figures like Kant and Franklin, Voltaire and Denis Diderot, David Hume and John Locke, as varied as they were, as much as they may have disagreed, were exemplars of the supposed openness of the Enlightenment. Consummately curious, the coolly logical tenor of the Enlightenment, and its glowing optimism, might make it seem the very opposite of apocalypticism, and yet the eschatological is inevitably thread through a movement that assumes the perfectibility of humanity, an ideology that presupposes a coming millennium, even if brought by science rather than Christ. That Enlightenment millennialism is steadfastly of the dove rather than a dragon is no reason to discount its status as millennialism.

Events in America like the First Great Awakening didn't happen in opposition to the Enlightenment, or even in spite of it, but in some ways *because* of it. Susan Juster suggests in *Doomsayers: Anglo-American Prophecy in the Age of Revolution* that "we stop seeing the enlightenment and religious enthusiasm as distinct and antagonistic forces."[36] Puritan Divines and Wesleyan ministers alike were enthused partisans of the new science; those who founded contemporary physics, like Isaac Newton, were frequently purveyors of prophecy with their own profoundly millennial expectations. The Enlightenment, it has to be emphasized, was also an obvious reaction to the religious bloodshed of the seventeenth century, the calm, ordered, judicious, and skeptical personality crafted by the leading philosophers of the age an attempt to moderate the passions which had led to such horrors. "Whatever you do, crush the infamous thing," Voltaire wrote of superstition and the church in a 1762 letter, for organized religion had been the obvious cause of so much misfortune, because "anyone who has the power to make you believe absurdities has the power to make you commit injustices."[37] The irony of the Revolution, of course, was that the belief in human progress might have been one of the most pernicious of absurdities.

Implicit within any eschatology are those twinned pairs of millennialism and apocalypse, of the dove and the dragon, and insomuch as the French Revolution was both fulfillment and negation of the Enlightenment, it was because the enthusiasm of the uprising shifted from millennialism into apocalypse. If the American revolutionary saw a postmillennial future, then the radical and anticlerical French revolutionary thought that judgment day and apocalypse would have to precede millennium. Since Christ himself was a myth, this purging and purification relied not upon the supernatural, but rather the people themselves, who would free the country from the machinations of bishops and kings. By resetting the calendar to Year I, there was something of Joachimitism about the Jacobins, this sentiment that an Age of the Spirit was upon the earth, an antinomian rebellion of liberty and equality. "Modern revolutionaries such as the French Jacobins . . . detested traditional religion," writes philosopher John Gray in *Black Mass: Apocalyptic Religion and the Death of Utopia*, "but their conviction that the crimes and follies of the past could be left behind in an all-encompassing transformation of human life was a secular reincarnation of early Christian beliefs."[38] The French Revolution birthed a prophetic faith, one that was vociferously apocalyptic in orientation, for its sectarians adhered to a belief that the entire world could be turned upside down and made over, that liberty, equality, and fraternity could be willed onto an unjust order, and most importantly that a curative violence would be necessary to do so. As Gray notes, "Modern revolutionary movements are a continuation of religion by other means."[39]

While historians have debated as to which revolution—the American or French—was more "radical," the example out of Paris was far more earth-shattering in the moment, the rebellion of bourgeois merchants and gentleman farmers a hemisphere away positively conservative when compared to the events within the heart of Europe. That this would be read through the lens of Revelation was inevitable. Juster explains that the "heady events of the French Revolution had . . . provided a welcome opportunity for millenarians to recapture the political high ground they had vacated after the Restoration."[40] France's tumult redeemed the lost promise of more than a century before, when the English had briefly seemed capable of birthing the world anew. In some ways this heralded the origin of contemporary politics, left and right in part literally defined by the relative seating arrangements of partisan factions in the French National Assembly, but in Britain conservatism also emerged against the possibility of immanentizing the eschaton, a relative and fundamentally anti-utopian position. An anti-millennial position.

As the political theorist Edmund Burke would write in *Reflections on the Revolution in France*, "men of intemperate minds cannot be free. Their passions forge their fetters."[41] Perhaps 1789 is the birthdate of contemporary politics, left and right merely reactions to a revolution at the dawn of modernity, but there is something arbitrary about this, for why not push the birth back to the English Civil War, or the German Peasants' War, or the English Peasants' Rebellion? What makes the French Revolution unique is the mask of secularism, but the face underneath remains that of religion. Nor should it be assumed that those who are millennial are on the left and those who reject such perfectibility are on the right; that's not how those orientations need be categorized, for there is every possible arrangement of millennial enthusiasm across the ideological spectrum. While no doubt many revanchists understood somebody like Robespierre as being an antichrist, a conservative philosopher like Burke doubted that there was such a thing, even while he readily assented to the revolutionary as being a tyrant. At the same time, a revolutionary thinker like Voltaire could embrace the estimably nonutopian, nonmillennial dictate to "tend your own gardens," as he advises in his satirical novel *Candide*.

Arguably, the scale of violence during the Reign of Terror has been overstated, even while it was no doubt horrific, barbarous, and often indiscriminate and paranoia was understandably rife as various factions turned on each other.

Regardless of the horror of the guillotine, philosopher Slavoj Žižek, writing *In Defense of Lost Causes*, argues that critics of the Jacobins want a "'revolution without a revolution': they want a revolution deprived of the excess in which democracy and terror coincide, a revolution respecting social rules, subordinated to preexisting norms, a revolution in which violence is deprived of the 'divine' dimension."[42] A crucial point on what separates the moderate from the revolutionary: the latter is adamantly apocalyptic, in all connotations of that word. And, for some perspective, a single night during the St. Bartholomew's Day Massacre killed three times as many people as the ten months of the Reign of Terror.

Of course these human sacrifices at the Place de la Concorde, public executions both feverish in their blood lust and coolly rational in their detachments, must have seemed to many across the Pyrenees, across the English Channel, across the Atlantic Ocean, as if the world really was in disarray, as if some kind of divine consummation was at hand, where whether the Jacobins did God's will or that of the devil became a fundamental question. "France's nightmare was a dream come true for most millennialists," argues Juster, "a polarizing moment in millenarian politics—energizing those on the left and the right."[43] Juster gives examples of the range of eschatological interpretations of the Revolution among the English, from the Anglican divine George Stanley Faber who first saw Robespierre as a potential antichrist, and then passed that honor onto Napoleon, to the Baptist minister James Bicheno who saw democratic revolution as establishing God's kingdom on earth. Joseph Priestly, the English chemist, discoverer of oxygen, and Unitarian who firmly assented to a postmillennial theology whereby scientific progress could hasten the coming of Christ, enthused often and publicly about the redemptive project of the Jacobins.

Christians and Europeans were not the only people to parse the significance of the Gallic immanentizing of the eschaton. A rebellion that had pushed God from His throne was bound to inflame millennial expectations wherever that event was heralded, both for partisans on behalf of the Revolution and against it. A particularly strange incident, for example, is the case of the Polish-Lithuanian Jew Jakob Lejbowicz, who changed his name to Jakob Frank and believed himself to be the reincarnation of Shabbatai Zevi.[44] As with his predecessor, Frank valorized kabbalah and the Zohar above all aspects of Judaism, going so far as to reject the Talmud entirely. And also like Zevi, Frank pursued a doctrine of "purification through transgression," advocating for the forced conversion of his followers to Catholicism so as to "liberate the sparks" hidden within gentile religions.[45] If Zevi was a man of the late Renaissance, then the eighteenth century was firmly Frank's era, an age of both liberty and libertinage where this messiah could embrace both antinomianism and revolutionary fervor. Frank himself died in 1791, the same year that the Republic was declared, though through all of his perambulations the prophet himself had never reached France, ultimately expiring in Offenbach am Main in the Holy Roman Empire.

His followers, however, greatly took to the French Revolutionary cause, in part because the Jacobins had taken to full emancipation of all Jewish citizens, as well as the granting of equal rights. Moses Dobruška, a cousin of Frank and an adherent of his sect, would travel to France in 1792, changing his name to Julius Frey and becoming a committed member of the Jacobins.[46] Later, while many on the continent reviled Emperor Napoleon I as either a traitor to the Revolution or its anti-Christian consummation, Frankists like Frey viewed him as the messiah. Like many who understood the revolution of liberty, equality, and fraternity as the beginning of millennium, the future would be "characterized by the downfall of all institutionalized religions," writes Pawel Maciejko in *The Mixed Multitude: Jacob Frank and the Frankist Movement, 1755–1866*, an expectation of the "imminent downfall of all political and religious structures."[47]

Frankism faded just as Sabbateanism did, having little influence on normative Judaism, but crucial as an example of how revolutionary politics and eschatology often coincided during the Enlightenment. A far more long-lasting, important, and for many shocking permutation of revolutionary enthusiasm which seemed to turn the world upside down can be traced to an uprising of the enslaved on the French colony of Saint-Domingue in the Caribbean. Beginning in 1791, some two years after the storming of the Bastille, what came to be known as the Haitian Revolution was the first and most successful uprising of the enslaved on the colonial periphery of empire. "Haitian and broader Caribbean history were founded on the apocalyptic meeting Europeans and Amerindians," writes Martin Munro in *Tropical Apocalypse: Haiti and the Caribbean End Times*, and then "shaped by the no less apocalyptic reality of plantation slavery and colonialism, and their enduring legacies."[48] A stark reminder that as theologians debated apocalypse, actual apocalypse was a reality for millions, from the Wampanoag and Abenaki of New England to the Aztec of Mexico and the Africans enslaved from San Domingo to South Carolina, Virginia to Jamaica. Partially inspired by the exact same values espoused in the Declaration of the Rights of Man and of the Citizen, and the Haitians as ultimately led by Toussaint Louverture demanded to hold France true to its own convictions.

Before the United States would abolish slavery, before Great Britain, before France, before several northern American states, the self-liberated Black women and men of Haiti rose up and emancipated themselves, an act so unprecedented and revolutionary in the minds of so-called defenders of liberty that it was spoken of in apocalyptic terms. Among many Americans, though certainly white slave owners, there were fevered nightmares of plantations in flames, and women, children, and men slaughtered by those held in bondage. "If something is not done, and soon done, we shall be the murderers of our own children," wrote

Jefferson, then the secretary of state, fearing that Louverture's example might inspire similarly violent uprisings throughout the southern United States.[49] While president, after Haiti's victory in 1805, Jefferson refused to acknowledge the nation's independence.

For critics, there was something satanic about the Haitian Revolution, but as Phillippe Girard writes in *Toussaint Louverture: A Revolutionary Life*, "To his admirers," the father of Haiti was the "George Washington of his race, the black Napoleon, the new Spartacus, or even the Messiah";[50] a title that Louverture, a dedicated Catholic who attended Mass every day, and studied with the Jesuits and Capuchins, would never have applied to himself. From San Dominque, whatever the religious intent of a man like Louverture, revolution still displayed its uncompromising and consistent logic. A millennium which is not redemptive for the entire world is hardly a millennium; a revolution which denies the universal scarcely deserves to be called as such. With the example of Haiti, revolution—and apocalypse—moved beyond the insular, the provincial, the limited, and fully embodied the implications of its own concept. If modernity meant anything, for both good and bad, it's the universalization of apocalypse and millennium across continents, colors, creeds.

CHAPTER EIGHT

A Terrible Swift Sword

Armageddon in the Nineteenth Century

The Burned-Over Country

America's First Great Awakening

FROM THE ORANGE-LEAFED Berkshires to the red-hued Adirondacks, the Poconos to the Catskills, amidst the Alleghenies and down the Appalachians, there was a great disappointment on a fine autumnal day on October 22, 1844, when the promised end of the world didn't occur. Reverend William Miller, a Baptist minister and sometimes elected official from Poultney, Vermont, had derived that particular year—the second predicted date for Armageddon after the first did not come to pass—based on his mathematical interpretation of the book of Daniel. Followers subsequently narrowed it down to the month, day, and even hour (4 p.m.). "The word *strange* appears frequently in discussions of William Miller and the Millerites," writes David L. Rowe in *God's Strange Work: William Miller and the End of the World*. "Strange were the ideas he promoted," but stranger still was the stunning long-term success that a movement based on a failed prediction would have, in the form of "several denominations, national and global," which would in turn "shape several others, and contribute to two of the most significant movements in American religious life, fundamentalism and Pentecostalism."[1] If Christianity could emerge from the example of a crucified messiah, then it's less difficult to see a movement derived from a merely inaccurate prophet.

Respectable, hard-working, patriotic, and self-taught, Miller was largely unremarkable, despite his eccentricities, which included a clipped manner of speaking and an introversion easily dismissed as Yankee idiosyncrasy. Raised a nonsectarian Deist, and attracted to the writings of Voltaire, Hume, and Paine, Miller's conversion was initiated during the War of 1812 at the battle of Plattsburgh, where a shell that exploded mere feet from him left the future preacher unharmed, despite killing several others.[2] Like many of the generation after the Revolution, in which his father had fought, Miller was initially convinced by the rational, logical, noninterventionist deity of Enlightenment philosophy, but in the rapidly changing new Republic, that distant God was arid and cold. Asked to address a Baptist congregation whose church he'd begun to informally attend, Miller recalls that "Suddenly the character of a Savior was vividly impressed upon my mind. It seemed that here might be a Being so good and compassionate as to Himself atone for our transgressions, and thereby save us from suffering the penalty of sin."[3] He was to reject both the stern Calvinist and the logical Newtonian Supreme Being (both of whom were shockingly similar anyhow) in favor of a personal, visceral, emotive God who desired of His followers that they freely be "born again."

Miller began a detailed reading of Scripture and in the process became convinced that the postmillennialism of the dove which had dominated the Congregationalist churches of New England and which had secularized into Enlightenment faith in progress, were unbiblical. Such postmillennialism had also marked the series of revivals which dominated the first half of the nineteenth century, which in many ways would be brought to a close by Miller's rejection of that eschatology in favor of a literalist premillennialism of the dragon. According to the minister, there was no way for humanity to bring about the perfectibility of institutions and morality that would usher in a new period of peace, harmony, and justice, but that rather great tribulation would precede Christ's return and His inauguration of the millennium. Believers wouldn't have to wait long, however. Basing his reasoning on the belief that a "day" in prophecy was equivalent to a calendar year, Miller understood Daniel 8:14's injunction that "Unto two thousand and three hundred days; then shall the sanctuary be cleansed" as referring to Christ's fiery return to earth exactly 2,300 years after the 457 BCE rededication of the Temple in Jerusalem, so that in the cracker-jack language of the American frontiersmen "I was thus brought . . . to the solemn conclusion, that in about twenty-five years from that time 1818 all the affairs of our present state would be wound up."[4]

Such literalism had preceded Miller, but his mathematical focus established an American tradition of apocalyptic arithmetic which has flared up in popularity over the past hundred and fifty years. Any number of preachers and ministers who claim this or that date is the day of judgment are working in Miller's stead. Silent with this discovery at first, by 1832 he would publish a series of articles enumerating his prediction, along with similar calendrical and numerological calculations, in the *Vermont Telegraph*, a popular Baptist newspaper, as well as in a short tract entitled *Scriptures and History of the Second Coming of Christ, about the Year 1844: Exhibited in a Course of Lectures*. Promulgated in print and preaching, as well as through the intervention of the Boston-based Baptist minister Joshua Himes, thousands of "Millerites" became convinced of the minister's calculation, to which a certain appreciation of his audacity must be granted. Rowe writes that in "his own day, popular commentators described him as demented, dishonest, and divisive, and that reputation lingers in the work of writers who have maintained and refined it,"[5] though nothing in Miller's own biography indicates that his was not a genuine faith, even if he was wrong. If anything, an argument could be made that his certainty and steadfastness were indications that he was not dishonest, for in a movement based on being able to "effectively market their vision," as Rowe writes, the possibility of failure couldn't be countenanced.[6] Where many prophets are content to shield their predictions in the insurance of ambiguity, Miller's confidence both measured the depth of his faith, as well as an unconcern with being inaccurate. Which, of course, he was.

"Our fondest hopes and expectations were blasted," remembered the Millerite leader Hiram Edson, "and such a spirit of weeping came over us as I never experienced before. . . . We wept, and wept, till the day dawn."[7] The movement was no small party; it's been estimated that as many as fully 50,000 women and men expected Christ's return in October of 1844, maybe more. "Some merely waited expectantly and passively, but many others uprooted themselves and their families, unsettling churches and neighborhoods to prepare for the great event."[8] As with Nathan of Gaza's solution to Zevi's conversion to Islam, so did men like Edson and Himes, and especially the prophet Ellen G. White, discover ways to interpret the seeming Great Disappointment, even while the father of the movement would never reach that promised land himself, expiring only five years after Christ failed to materialize. The events of 1844 were now understood in a different way, as having inaugurated a "spiritual transformation" with Christ's invisible Advent. Emerging from the Millerites would be a number of Christian denominations that adhered to this belief, most notably the Seventh-Day Adventists, who today have over twenty million members.

Adventism was one of a multitude of American sects and denominations which emerged during the nineteenth century, often with a strong millennial or apocalyptic disposition, and are an example of what was developing as a burgeoning national genius for novel theologies. Following in Adventism's stead, there were a tremendous number of new religious movements advocating for a stunning variety of beliefs, from Charles Taze Russell's Jehovah's Witnesses founded in 1870 to Mary Baker Eddy's Christian Science whose origins date from 1875. Such movements often constitute part of what's called the Third Great Awakening, but in many ways it's more accurate to see them as the afterheat of the Second Great Awakening, arguably the most fertile period for religious innovation and creativity in Christianity since the nonconformists of seventeenth-century England, or even the Gnostics at the beginning of the Common Era. Miller delineates the division between the interrelated Second and Third Great Awakenings, his own teachings, especially as regarding the millennium, differing substantially from the standard beliefs which marked the earlier series of revivals; yet the contours and borders of such movements are often arbitrary.

If historians have disagreed as to how influential the First Great Awakening was, there is far less reticence regarding its sequel, which ran from the end of the eighteenth century into the late Antebellum era. Ironically, faith proliferated in large part because of the new nation's officially secular designation. "Congress shall make no law respecting an establishment of religion," the First Amendment reads. But national piety was ensured by what follows that comma, for the state shall not prohibit "the free exercise thereof." Such latitudinarian tolerance in the establishment clause and the free exercise clause was responsible for transforming America into a veritable spiritual laboratory. The French historian Alexis de Tocqueville, in his 1835 *Democracy in America*, argues that the greatest aid for faith was removing it from its position of direct political power, noting that "religion cannot share the material strengths of the rulers without suffering some of those animosities which the latter arouse."[9]

During his travels, when Tocqueville would inquire as to the reasons for such spiritual vibrancy in the New World, Americans "mainly attributed the peaceful dominion of religion in their country to the separation of church and state." The establishment clause is America's unique and singular contribution to political theory. American soil would bear the fruits of new religions, more than almost any corner of the earth. Over the centuries, the United States has been the origin of the Longhouse Religion and the Ghost Dance, the African Methodist Episcopal Church and American Unitarianism, New Thought and Moorish Temple Science, Theosophy and Discordianism, all because the nation with a soul of a church had no official church.

The first great indication that America would be an ecclesiastical laboratory was during the Second Great Awakening. Centered in what would be remembered as the "burned-over district" of upstate New York, radiating upward into the backwoods of New England and downward through the Appalachians, the Second Great Awakening represented a Cambrian Explosion of American religiosity following the relative secularism of the revolutionary generation. Nathan O. Hatch explains in *The Democratization of American Christianity* that the "wave of popular religious movements that broke upon the United States in the half century after independence did more to Christianize American society than anything before or since."[10] Grown in the fertile soil of American disestablishmentarianism, women and men would be able to explore, innovate, and worship in a manner unprecedented in Christian history, and they did so. The Second Great Awakening would see the decline of Calvinist denominations in favor of more fervent and pietistic faiths such as the Baptists and Methodists, as well as the emergence of enduring heterodox religious movements. What many of these movements shared, Hatch writes, was an "ethic of unrelenting toil, a passion for expansion, a hostility to orthodox belief and style, a zeal for religious reconstruction, and a systematic plan to realize their ideals."[11]

If the First Amendment and Jacksonian Democracy were the superstructure, than the Second Great Awakening's material basis was the sheer geographic expansiveness of the frontier, which necessitated a manner of conducting worship differently than on the east coast, so that religious innovation was the inevitable result. The frontier was sparsely populated; settlements were often distant from one another, so that millions of Americans had no particular investment in organized religion. Quite literally, the back country lacked the infrastructure that supported congregations in Boston, New York, Philadelphia, Williamsburg, Charleston, and Savannah. Certain pragmatic tools of evangelism were needed to reach the largest possible number of converts. Circuit riders—itinerant preachers who went from community to community—were instrumental. Camp meetings—large open-air revivals which evolved from the Holiness Fairs of Scots-Irish Presbyterianism, and were easily replicated in the wilderness of Ohio, Indiana, and Kentucky—became frequent.

Throughout the Ohio and Indiana territories, the traveling revival circuit was often peoples' only sustained experience of worship. Commensurate with the entrepreneurial spirit, preachers knew how to keep their audience entertained. Revivals were known not just for emotional preaching and mass baptism, but also for drinking, gambling, and prostitution. Initially, camp meetings were often sponsored by Presbyterian ministers, historically the most popular denomination in the Appalachians, but the raucous nature of the revivals and the fervent ecstasy of the religious conversions was foreign to the infamously staid denomination. Into that void came the Methodists and Baptists, many of whom shared the Romantic turn toward Pietism, which emphasized emotion over doctrine, and arguably replaced the *sola Fidei* of the Reformation with what could be called *sola Motus*—salvation through feeling alone. Such was American evangelicalism's most enduring theological contribution, for both good but very often bad.

Brett Malcolm Grainger describes the traditional interpretation of these decades in *Church in the Wild: Evangelicals in Antebellum America*, regarding the "radical novelty of American revivalism, contrasting its rowdy energy and egalitarian spirit with the formal outposts of European religious establishment planted on the east coast."[12] Beyond tabulating which denominations increased their memberships or not, there were massive theological shifts within the culture as well. The Second Great Awakening signals the beginning of American Calvinism's long dusk, even in the northern Midwest which was often settled by New Englanders. Cold predestination was thawed by the hot enthusiasms of the revivalists, and in place of the Calvinist doctrine which held that salvation was entirely out of the hands of the justified sinner, most Methodist and Baptist preachers embraced a variant of Reformed teaching called Arminianism (after the seventeenth-century Dutch theologian Jacob Arminius). By the dictates of that tradition, salvation was a matter of the individual repentant sinner's choice to be saved. A result of this Arminian shift in American religious life was the liberation of the convert to more fully claim control over their own spiritual condition, to make something like a "relationship" with God possible.

As with Miller at the end of the Second Great Awakening, an individual believer could embrace being born again, making them partner in the grand act of redemption. Faith became not just an emotional expression, but an intensely personal experience as well, and in many ways both God and Christ became personified for each believer. Because, in some sense, the Second Great Awakening ushered in a widespread post-theological society, there was a liberation in each individual's ability to craft their own religion; a true priesthood of all believers finally, where every man (or woman) was a potential prophet, and everything they wrote possibly inspired scripture. "There are indeed millions of Christians in the United States, but most Americans who think they are Christians truly are something else," argues literary critic Harold Bloom in his controversial *The American Religion*; they are, rather, "intensely religious but devout in the American Religion, a faith that is old among us, and that comes in many guises and disguises, but that overdetermines much of our national life."[13]

According to Bloom, this "American Religion" is personal, eccentric, idiosyncratic, and *gnostic*, in that is it promises secret knowledge and the exultation of the individual, and he sees it everywhere from Christian Science to Mormonism. Bloom identifies the Pentecost of this new faith at the Cane Ridge Revival in the Kentucky town of that name which took place from August 6 to August 12, 1801. Unambiguously the largest such meeting held on the American frontier during the Second Great Awakening, it's estimated that possibly twenty thousand people attended at some point, a vast multitude baptized under the frontier stars in the heat of a Southern summer evening, the smell of tobacco and firewood permeating the obsidian darkness.

The debate over how "Christian" some of the sects which emerged from the Second Great Awakening were begs a lot about how we define religions, but it's fair to say that the anarchic freedoms unleashed by the First Amendment allowed for far more independence in spiritual exploration than ever would have been countenanced by a government with an official church. Regardless of the orthodoxy of these groups, they often found in the freedom of the American environment an opportunity to embrace a prophetic, millennial messianism. Traditions as varied as the Shakers, Mormonism, and the Spiritualists only connected insomuch as they emerged in roughly the same region, at the same juncture in history, and for similar sociocultural reasons. All were deeply enmeshed in messianic expectations. "Over the course of two and a half centuries," writes Adam Morris in *American Messiahs: False Prophets of a Damned Nation*, "numerous Americans have laid stakes to the claim of a divinely ordained salvation" and often they "seize on social injustices that directly contradict the primitive church that Christ's apostles built, and position themselves against American racism, class oppression and the subjugation of women" adhering to a millennialism based in a "more generous and humanistic approach: namely, that the Messiah might return in order to lead humankind through the process of reform and regeneration."[14]

A fascinating early example is the Public Universal Friend, a Rhode Island woman born as Jemima Wilkinson to Quaker parents who believed that she had been imbued with the essence of a genderless spirit after an illness in 1776. Transitioning the same year his own nation became a republic, the Public Universal Friend's career as a prophet and messiah began as he preached throughout southern New England and into Pennsylvania a gospel of racial emancipation and women's suffrage, while proclaiming the work of Revelation to be at hand. There had long been a countertradition of women and women-born messiahs, from the thirteenth-century Milanese noblewoman Guglielma whose followers believed her to be an incarnation of Christ, to the seventeenth-century English nonconformist preacher Anna Trapnel, and the Quaker renegade and founder of the Shakers Mother Anne Lee. Similarly, the Public Universal Friend's pronouncements drew a surprising number of adherents, women drawn to his egalitarian prophecies, but men as well. As with many sects that preach abstinence, the longevity of the group was tenuous, with his followers largely dissipating following the Public Universal Friend's death in 1819.

Far more enduring are the various denominations categorized under the banner of Mormonism, of which the Church of Jesus Christ of Latter-Day Saints based in Salt Lake City is the largest. With almost twenty million adherents throughout the world, Mormonism is arguably the most successful new religion since the advent of Sikhism in fifteenth-century Punjab, or even since Islam. Not uncoincidentally, its prophetic founder Joseph Smith was often known by critics as the "American Muhammad." Raised in the burned-over country of upstate New York in the small town of Palmyra, Smith had angelic visions as early as 1818—the same year as Miller's calculations—which ultimately revealed to him the Book of Mormon, an additional testament to Hebrew Scriptures and the New Testament which recounted the ancient New World arrival of the lost tribes of Israel and Christ's appearance to them following his resurrection.[15] Smith was inculcated in the same rationalist, deistic environment as was Miller; an enthusiast for the freedoms nourished by the First Amendment, the future prophet explored various Christian denominations, desiring to ascertain which one was true, before ultimately founding his own faith. As with Miller, and other religious leaders in the region, Smith was drawn to various hermetic philosophies, such as the eighteenth-century Swedish occult tradition of Swedenborgianism and Freemasonry.

From this mélange would arise his startlingly new vision, an original scripture which mapped the sacred onto American geography itself and held to a neo-gnostic belief in the divinization of individual believers. This was a distinctly American faith of individualism and self-creation, one that allowed every man to be a god, for as it reads in the Book of Mormon, "Adam fell that men might be; and men are, that they might have joy."[16] Fawn M. Brodie writes in *No Man Knows My History: The Life of Joseph Smith* that the prophet "was purely a Yankee product and that a great deal that was good in American folklore and thinking found its way into his writings and into his church. The cornerstone of his metaphysics was that virile concept which pervaded the whole American spirit . . . that man is capable of eternal progress towards perfection."[17]

To be clear, as with Muhammad, Smith declared himself to be prophetic, but not to be messianic, yet eschatology was as important to Mormonism as it was to all of the various religions which emerged from the Second Great Awakening. By its very nature as a "restorationist" faith—that is a movement which understood itself as restoring the original forms of apostolic Christianity—the recovery of the Book of Mormon itself could be understood as a millennial act, the beginnings of an end-times dispensation and the genesis of a new era in human understanding, a victory for the dove. Mormonism shares with much of orthodox Christianity a similar eschatological schedule; signs and portents signaling the Second Coming, tribulations, witnesses, and a millennium. There are differences as well, and Smith taught that many signs had already been fulfilled, portents which other Christians wouldn't necessarily have interpreted through an eschatological framework.

Bloom's claim that "what matters most about Joseph Smith is how American both the man and his religion have proved to be," is demonstrated with the Mormon founder's account of sacred history. Certain fulfilled signs that indicate the Second Coming include the discovery of America, the establishment of the United States, and the ratification of the US Constitution. Christ's Second Coming will precede the establishment of a New Jerusalem, which Smith believed would be placed roughly in the location of current-day Independence, Missouri, while proclaiming in an 1844 sermon that the "whole of America is Zion itself from north to south."[18] The Book of Mormon made explicit what had been alluded to, suspected, and wished for in American redeemer narratives back to the Puritans; Smith openly declared that this continent was the site for millennium, and endowed the political project of the Republic with religious significance, interpreting both the Declaration of Independence and the Constitution as divinely inspired documents.

Disputed by the LDS Church, but still taken as legitimate by many fundamentalist Mormon splinter groups, is the so-called "White Horse Prophecy," a prediction supposedly by Smith that at some future point the Constitution will be endangered, but that the nation shall be saved by the Mormon church. "You will see the Constitution of the United States almost destroyed," Smith is reported to have preached while at Nauvoo, Illinois, in 1843. "It will hang like a thread as fine as a silk fiber . . . I love the Constitution; it's made by the inspiration of God; and it will be preserved and saved by the efforts of the White Horse and by the Red Horse who will combine in its defense."[19] Drawing on language specifically indebted to Revelation, it's an example of Mormonism's spiritual vitality in combining Christianity with a divinized belief in America itself.

Most immediately during the Second Great Awakening, the Methodists and Baptists emerged as denominational victors as the burned-over country spread west, but as Bloom would argue, the real winner was the American God born at Cane Ridge, an ecstatic, boot-strapping individualist. "The American frontier worked like a universal solvent, erasing the vestiges of class and other forms of inherited hierarchy imported from the Old World," writes Grainger.[20] There was a surprising degree of racial and gender egalitarianism which defined the Second Great Awakening, as these revivals saw the emergence of both Black and women preachers, as well as denominations like the African Methodist Episcopal Church.

Most of those involved in the earliest decades of the revivals were adamantly postmillennialist doves; that is to say that they believed that both the individual and society could be improved upon through human intervention before Christ's return. A progressive political platform was frequently the result; directly related to the Second Great Awakening were any number of movements for liberal reform, including abolitionism, suffragism, temperance, and prison reform. Far from the stereotype of "fire and brimstone preachers" and conservative "holy rollers," many of those involved in organizing or attending such revivals had clearly progressive beliefs that were directly related to their postmillennial eschatology. In some ways this was actually a continuation of the old Puritan postmillennialism, except now filtered through the more emancipatory theology of the personal connection with salvation, with Ronald G. Walters describing in *American Reformers, 1815–1860* how there was an "antebellum process of dissociating religion from doctrinal complexity and fusing it and popular culture in powerful ways,"[21] the resulting being a potent rhetoric of justice and equality.

Miller represents a shift that would be as important as the transition from Calvinism to Arminianism in the abandonment of postmillennialism for premillennialism, in trading the dove for the dragon. When publishing his prediction about Christ's imminent return, Miller did not argue that we needed to prepare His way by abolishing slavery or reforming prisons (whatever his own or his followers opinions on those issues may have been). Christ was returning whatever we did, it was merely the job of the individual believer to get right with God beforehand. It was in many ways a more conservative faith, but also ironically one which represented a severance of politics and religion, at least for the time being; an adamantly *apocalyptic* as opposed to *millennial* faith, historically the nascent origin of much that would be termed "fundamentalist" by the turn of the century. Paul Boyer writes in *When Time Shall Be No More:*

Prophecy Belief in Modern American Culture that "earthbound concerns faded as the predicted date approached," even while he tries not to draw too much of a distinction "between a pessimistic, passive *pre*millennialism and an optimistic, activist *post*-millennialism."[22] However, Boyer admits that, by contrast to the progressives who emerged from the earlier awakenings, many "leading premillennialists did pronounce reform effort worthless—a bleak attitude that would survive and even intensify in the twentieth century."[23]

To the east of the frontier, not far from where the Pilgrims and Puritans first landed, a more genteel millennialism that believed in restoration of the world was also emerging, Though spoken of in the language of German philosophical idealism and Eastern religion more than Daniel and Revelation, Transcendentalism was no less denunciatory of injustices in American society than were its hotter corollaries on the Appalachian frontier. Arguably a branch of European Romanticism, the Transcendentalist movement associated with scholars like former Harvard professor and Unitarian minister Ralph Waldo Emerson, as well as the nature writer Henry David Thoreau, desired an expansive re-enchantment of an American landscape being altered by train tracks and telegraph lines. As with the reformers who gathered inspiration from the Second Great Awakening, the Transcendentalists pursued a vigorous political project dedicated to causes from abolition to suffrage. At intentional communities such as Amos Bronson Alcott's Fruitland in Harvard, Massachusetts, or Brooke Farm in Boston, founded by the Unitarians George and Sophia Ripley and satirized by former participant novelist Nathaniel Hawthorne in *The Blithedale Romance*, they imagined egalitarian communal living as apostolic in its purity, if inexpertly enacted in reality. Philip Gura, in *American Transcendentalism*, describes how this diverse gathering of the nation's first genuine cultural avant-garde wished to "hasten a secular millennium," whereby "rude American wilderness would blossom into an immense garden."[24]

Like the Puritans, the Transcendentalists' intellectual and sometimes literal ancestors, there was an ambivalence about nature and technology, millennium and apocalypse. A belief that the arc of progress would ever improve our lives, but a simultaneous fear of moving ever further from Eden, of the garden itself endangered by serpents threatening our fall. Leo Marx writes about the transformations of the American landscape in *The Machine in the Garden: Technology and the Pastoral Idea in America*, noting how "nothing quite like the event announced by the train in the woods had occurred before."[25] Authors such as Emerson and Hawthorne toggled between triumphant and despairing when they espied such changes, a trepidation that technology signaled an irreversible apocalypse at the moment the Transcendentalists tried to inaugurate millennium in New England, of how a "great world is invading the land, transforming the sensory texture of rural life . . . and threatening, in fact, to impose a new and more complete dominion over it," as Marx argues.[26] Unlike the Puritans, the Transcendentalists believed in, or attempted to believe in, a sacred, charged, pantheistic creation, yet that apocalyptic howling in the wilderness could still reverberate in Massachusetts's woods. By Walden Pond, where Thoreau famously made his hermitage, he would listen to the bestial shriek of the Fitchburg Railway line as it made its way through Concord. "We do not ride the railroad," wrote Thoreau in *Walden Pond*, "it rides upon us."[27]

Apocalypse Against Empire and Capital

Revolution and Resistance

Six months before the world didn't end in 1844, in April of that year within the Persian city of Shiraz, Sayyed Ali Muhammad Shirazi had the first of his religious visions in which it was revealed to him that he was the "Gate," or in Arabic the "Bab," who would herald the arrival of Shi'a Islam's messianic figure known as the hidden Twelfth Imam.[28] Shi'as' only recognized ultimate religious authority is an imam, who must be descended from the family of Muhammad, but Hasan al-Askari, the eleventh and last of those men in that position died in the ninth century without a clear line of succession. Among the denomination known as Twelvers, who constitute the overwhelming majority of Shi'a, it's believed that the twelfth imam ascended following al-Askari's death, but that he was graced by Allah with a supernaturally long life, and has ever since lived through a process called "Occultation," effectively in hiding, to return when the day of judgment approaches. Named Muhammad al-Mahdi, the twelfth imam's appearance signals the incipient arrival of the prophet and Jesus who will defeat Iblis and inaugurate the end of days.

It is a potent and powerful faith, as Abdulaziz Abdulhussein Sachedina explains in *Islamic Messianism: The Idea of the Mahdi in Twelver Shi'ism*, describing it as "a chiliastic vision of history expressed in terms of radical social protest in the face of political expression . . . [an] expectation for the end of tyranny and wickedness through the establishment of justice . . . a re-evaluation of present social and historic life."[29] Islamic messianism is both as similar and as different as Jewish and Christian messianism are from each other; unlike the beliefs of the former, Shi'a do not understand the twelfth imam as instituting a nationalist redemption and unlike the latter they do not understand the messiah as redeeming us of our sins, but rather the promise of "Islamic salvation lies instead in the historical responsibility of its followers, namely, the establishment of the ideal religio-political community."[30]

Certainly this was something which the Bab had faith in—more so. That the Bab would announce himself to be a gate of the twelfth imam, effectively the figure who transmits missives from the hidden holy man, was radical enough. Even more radical was when it became clear that this son of middle-class merchants believed himself to not just be heralding the arrival of the twelfth imam, but to actually be the Mahdi. Far more revolutionary was when in 1844 the Bab made a clear and decisive break with Islam. The Bab was indeed the imam, but that position was joined by other seminal religious founders—Moses, Zoroaster, Buddha, Jesus, and so on—as being a "Manifestation of God," the deliverer of an ongoing and progressive revelation to the respective communities of humanity. Included among those understood as "He Whom God Has Made Manifest," the Bab was the latest of messiahs to usher in a new dispensation in the form of Babism. Influenced by mystical strains of Islam, including Sufism and Ismailism, Babism also reflected the influence of Western occultism, particularly in the form of Victorian perennialism which understood all faiths to fundamentally be unitary, each religious founder expressing the ineffable divine truths in the language that a given society was capable of understanding. The Bab was clear however; none of these Manifestations of God should be seen as incarnations of the Lord, rather they were as mirrors are to the sun, fully reflecting the same divine light in different ways, and thus entirely intertwined with each other's' souls. "Every Manifestation is but a revelation of Thine Own Self," writes the Bab in *Him Who Shall Be Made Manifest*, "with each of Whom we have truly appeared and we bow down in adoration before Thee."[31]

Preaching the unity of all religions, the equality of races and sexes, and a rigorous but forgiving ethical code, Babism gathered perhaps a hundred thousand followers throughout Persia in only a few short years. A consummate prose stylist who investigated metaphysics with both subtlety and nuance, the letters of the Bab were consumed vociferously throughout the empire. Babism was particularly popular among women who were invested with a much more significant role and responsibility than was traditional. The ecumenical followers of the Bab—who emphasized that he was not the final dispensation—synthesized a tremendous number of disparate beliefs into their syncretic understanding, while translating egalitarianism, democracy, and pluralism in a Persian vernacular. Shi'a clerics were disturbed by the popularity of the Bab, and intense persecution followed, particularly in Tehran.

This period of violence culminated in the execution of the Bab by order of the shah in 1850, the initial survival of the prophet by a volley of bullets subsequently interpreted by his followers as a miracle, even while the second round would kill him. Into the power vacuum of the Bab's death emerged disagreements over the proper route that the faith should take, but unequivocally one follower of the Manifestation would emerge as the leader, the son of Persian nobles named Husayn ibn Ali. A steadfast follower of the Bab who was renowned for his erudition and eloquence, Ali would be forced into exile by the shah, living in the

Ottoman city of Baghdad when he had a series of mystical visions in 1863, after which he declared himself to be among "He Whom God Has Made Manifest," announcing that he was the fulfillment of the Bab's prophecy. Following this, he would take the name Bahaullah—"Glory of God."[32]

And so the same year that Abraham Lincoln signed the Emancipation Proclamation, in a pleasure garden by the Tigris River, Bahaullah initiated one of the fastest-growing and widely dispersed new religions in the world, the Bahai Faith. Among the pious, the teachings of the Bab and Bahaullah are understood as seamless, the beginnings of their faith marked to the start of the former's ministry, a doctrine which several million women and men still adhere to throughout the world. If the nineteenth century was a period of great religious syncretism, when spiritual geniuses within an increasingly globalized society manifested novel faiths that answered particularly contemporary maladies, then Bahaullah must be counted alongside Joseph Smith as a prophetic luminary.

They are truly modern prophets in all senses of that adjective, commensurate with scientific and technological progress, among the small number of people who founded major world religions of whom we have actual photographs. Still centered in the Middle East, particularly in Iran where members of the Bahai Faith face persecution, Bahaullah's new religion must also be understood as truly global and thus modern. Lil Osborne in the *Handbook of Islamic Sects and Movements* writes that the Bahai Faith has "spread throughout the globe, it has been embraced by a diverse community, comprising of urban workers, royalty, artists, and the lower classes . . . its emphasis on unity in diversity makes it likely to be of major significance in an ever more globally defined civilization."[33]

Bahaullah's perennialism is a novel attribute of his millennialism, though there are precursors to it in earlier movements, such as Zevi's claim that conversion to another faith somehow elevates all faiths. Even while the Persia of Bahaullah was relatively remote and impoverished, his religion's astounding success, even after his house arrest in the Ottoman city of Adrianople, speaks to the ways in which his ecumenical theology addressed increasing cultural connections throughout the globe. Today, with headquarters in Haifa, Israel, the Bahai Faith is "possibly the eighth largest religion in the world," as Osborne writes.[34] Notable as an example of what could be termed "religiously liberal millennialism," the Bahai Faith shares qualities with American Transcendentalism, albeit phrased in a different vocabulary, though both hew toward the dove over the dragon.

Indeed many of the intellectual descendants of the Transcendentalists, always drawn to Eastern mysticism, would be impressed by the teachings of Bahaullah when they were introduced to the United States by his son Abdul-Bahai, who spoke at the 1893 World Parliament of Religions held as part of Chicago's World Columbian Exposition.[35] Bahaullah's doctrine, with its insistence on racial and gender equality and its enthusiasm for a pacifistic world government, was subversive to both Persian religious authorities and the Western status quo, even while the Bahai faithful faced the bulk of their oppression from the former. During the nineteenth century, millennialism was frequently handmaid to anticolonial and anticapitalist resistance, often in far more violent a manner than that advocated for by the relatively pacifistic members of the Bahai Faith.

That millennialism and apocalypticism are fundamentally anticolonial makes innate sense based in a reading of the scriptural texts which provide the inspiration to such movements. While colonialism is a relatively modern form of oppression based in transoceanic conquest and the capitalist economy, oppression itself is depressingly universal. Apocalyptic scripture, by its very nature of imagining a world turned upside down, is fundamentally revolutionary. An apocalypse to further entrench the status quo scarcely deserves to be called an apocalypse; the only millennium worth extolling is the millennium for the poor, the disposed, the forgotten, and the tortured. In the Hebrew Scriptures, Daniel doesn't just castigate the Israelite's failures of faith, he writes against the Babylonians; in Revelation, John of Patmos provides not just a schedule for the end of days, he denounces the Romans. Even if written about civilizations that modern-day historians wouldn't recognize as "colonial," such apocalyptic texts already contained within them the nascent seeds of anti-imperialism, waiting to grow in the rocky soil of modernity. Bryan Wilson explains in the journal *Comparative Studies in Society and History* that the "goals of a millenarian movement are the awakening and preparation of men . . . to the fact that this world is to be transformed, often physically and always socially, and that this transformation will be sudden and soon."[36] Thus a multitude of millennial movements challenged colonial hegemony during the same century as Bahaullah, with more explosively violent methods, albeit with less enduring appeal.

The Cruzob Movement emerged on the Yucatan Peninsula during the middle of the nineteenth century, wherein the Maya believed that their gods would expel first the Spanish colonial government and then Mexican authorities, a theology which fueled an indigenous guerilla war which still has adherents.[37]

In 1856, a fifteen-year-old girl named Nonsqawuse of the South African Xhosa people had a vision of departed elders who informed her that her people must slaughter their cows, which had become infected with a lung sickness brought over by Dutch farmers, and that this sacrifice would expel European colonists from British Kaffraria. Encouraged by the British who elsewhere had already cynically deployed famine as a means of colonial subjugation, Nonsqawuse's visions tragically led to the exact opposite of what she prayed the Xhosa's delivery would be.[38]

More successful was the Mahdist State established in Sudan by the Nubian Sufi military leader Muhammad Ahmad bin Abd Allah, who had declared himself to be the Mahdi while expelling the Egyptians, Ottomans, and British. The Mahdist State, based on authoritarian principles of Sharia law, endured for fourteen years, until 1899 when Sudan was reconquered by an Anglo-Egyptian force.[39]

In the Mexican state of Chihuahua, a different revolutionary movement was bolstered by millennial enthusiasms during the same decade as the Mahdi State, when in 1891 rural peasants rose against the government in the Tomochic Rebellion, focusing their faith, hope, and belief in the indigenous folk healer Teresa Urrea, a messianic figure who combined both indigenous and Christian beliefs in her syncretic apocalypticism.[40]

"The function of new movements," writes Wilson, "is specifically to provide more satisfactory accommodation—psychic or social—for their adherent, and, in the case of revolutionist movements, to promises this in terms of a completely new dispensation."[41] Notably, for all of their sound and fury, none of these movements had any long-term success in demolishing the idols of colonialism and capitalism which oppressed those whom they represented.

Wilson writes that "Religiously inspired revolutionist movements might be classified in terms of the goals which they seek and the means by which they expect them to be realized," arguing that the major difference between revolution and apocalypse is the "fact that religious goals are in some sense supernatural, or that their attainment involves supernatural operation in human affairs."[42] A cynic might even argue that the relative failure of all the aforementioned movements lay in their undue faith in the supernatural, followers so anesthetized on the opiate of the masses that they irrationally sleepwalked their adherents into catastrophe. To this objection can be countered a response; that despite the enduring success of the American experiment, and the initial success of the French Revolution, radical political movements during the nineteenth century were also often as unsuccessful as their millenarian compatriots. Chief among nineteenth-century movements that erupted with optimistic fervor, only to end shortly in disappointment, were the massive revolutions of 1848, when calls for liberation and democracy rang throughout Europe from Dublin to Warsaw.

For many across the continent it seemed that a new political dispensation was at hand. In France, there was another revolution which overthrew the restored monarchy and declared the Second Republic; in Italy, not yet a unified country, revolutionaries fought to expel Austrian occupiers; the Young Irelander Revolution, enraged by British complacency during the Great Famine, agitated for independence from the United Kingdom; the "March Revolution" in Germany saw young partisans demand a unified nation based on democratic principles; throughout the vastness of the Hapsburg dynasty's Central European empire, there were movements for self-determination from Galicia to Hungary, against the monarchies, against the aristocrats, against the plutocracy. Yet, by

1849 the vast majority of these movements, which had erupted in stunning victory after victory, were now all but extinguished, revanchists quickly quashing what must have briefly felt like the eschaton itself.[43]

"A specter is haunting Europe," wrote a prophetic witness to these revolutions, "All the Powers of old Europe have entered into a holy alliance to exorcise this specter: Pope and Czar . . . French Radicals and German police-spies."[44] So began an incendiary pamphlet published in London at the height of the 1848 European Spring, and throughout those compact twenty-three pages the authors delivered similarly explosive turns of phrase, before concluding that the "proletarians have nothing to lose but their chains. They have a world to win."[45] Arguably the most enduring of events from 1848 was the publications of this thin book, a prophetic scripture of millenarian radicalism. Karl Marx and Friedrich Engels's *The Communist Manifesto* remains the most potent distillation of the millenarian perspective in the nineteenth century, and in keeping with its contention that the purpose of philosophy is not to critique the world but to change it, its influence in the subsequent century was nothing short of epoch-shifting. Historians, philosophers, and biographers argue about just how literally many of the positions in *The Communist Manifesto* are to be taken; whether Marx and Engels truly believed that revolution was providentially destined to succeed.

Obviously the manifesto can be contrasted with Marx's theoretical magnum opus *Das Kapital;* where the former is pithy, quotable, and short, the latter is turgid, complex, and theoretical; where the first reads as if dynamite has been tossed in a window, the later can feel like a brick hitting your toe. When writing *Das Kapital*, Marx sounded as dense and impenetrable as the German idealist philosopher George Wilhelm Friedrich Hegel; when he put pen to paper for the manifesto, however, he borrowed the tongue of Tom Paine. Partially this is because of the vastly different audiences Marx was writing for; *Das Kapital* is an explanation of complex philosophical and economic theories written for those already conversant in those fields, while *The Communist Manifesto* is designed to spur actual revolutionaries to action. As such, not only must nuance and subtilty be sacrificed upon the altar of muscular activism, but any sense of contingency or potential loss must also be mitigated. Equivocation is not the idiom of the manifesto.

Arguing as to the innate millenarianism of *Das Kapital* remains a controversial activity, especially among that dwindling cadre of orthodox Marxists who assert that their prophet's claim that "dialectical materialism" is a "scientific," "objective," and "empirical" understanding of social relations and class history. Indeed *Das Kapital* is written in the sober and measured language of analysis, so that it remains fair to be agnostic as to how much of the traces of the millenarian remain behind its ostensibly scientific perspective, but *The Communist Manifesto*, which promises the incipient unveiling of inevitable new order which will entirely remake the world, is almost classically millenarian, as is the variety of Marxism which would predominate in the twentieth century. If the American Revolution promised the dawn of a redeemer nation, then communism in its Marxist permutations declared the coming redeemer system. "Most modern thought about civil society, democracy, and modernity emphasizes the importance of 'secular' values in their emergence," writes Richard Landes in *Heaven on Earth: The Varieties of the Millennial Experience*, understanding religion as a "superstructure of superstitious opacity manipulated by priests and designed to justify the prime divider as either inevitable or necessary."[46]

Certainly that was Marx's stated claim about the nature of religion, but just as Paine (the child of nonconformist Quakers) rejected faith but couldn't actually escape such thinking, so too was the case with the author of *The Communist Manifesto*, descended from a long line of German rabbis. Just as the cause of the American Revolution was fundamentally religious and millennial, not in spite of its stated secularism but in part because of it, so too was this the case with Marxism. Despite protestations toward the "scientific" and regardless of his (often incredibly useful) method of analysis, Marx promulgated an ideology which was fundamentally millenarian in its disposition. None of that should be read as either a criticism or validation of the philosopher, but rather as a simple statement of fact—Karl Marx was the greatest and most important apocalyptic thinker of the nineteenth century.

Landes argues that "Marx's most important contributions to the millennial thought of his age concern his development of a 'scientific' reading of history—the historical dialectic—that resembles in some important ways the historical exegesis of the Bible carried out by the medieval monk, Joachim of Fiore . . . Marx offered a secular variant, a historical dialectic that inexorably drove toward collective salvation in Communism."[47] Just as Joachim had claimed that there was a tripartite division to history between the Ages of the Father, Son, and Holy Ghost, so did Marx see the teleological engine of progress as moving through the dialectic first explained by Hegel, between the thesis, antithesis, and synthesis, the internal contradictions of each age's dominant system pushing forth revolutionary change until the "final" system of socialism and then the promised withering away of the state.

Just as the Franciscan monk believed that this process of competing dispensations ending in millennium was inevitable, so too did Marx at least appear to claim that such predictions were baked into social relations themselves, even if he justified such claims with scientific rhetoric. As in both Christian and Jewish apocalypticism, popular conceptions of Marxism hold that in the past there was a perfected social arrangement—for the former it was in Eden and the latter the state of nature exemplified by hunter-gatherer primitive communism; in religion there was the fall and in Marxism the introduction of unequal social relations from feudalism through capitalism; and according to Scripture there will be a final apocalyptic confrontation before millennium and in *The Communist Manifesto* there will be revolution before the restoration of universal equality and freedom. Regardless of his claims to being scientific, Landes writes that "beneath all Marx's writings lies a radical—indeed prophetic—moral outrage at how man exploits his fellow man and a passionate desire to see an end to this evil,"[48] a fair appraisal from a scholar who is often highly critical of the philosopher. Irrelevant as to whether or not this system is accurate and useful or fallacious and dangerous, there remains a clear conclusion—Marxism is modern eschatology simply written in the language of scientific objectivity.

Marx was dead by the time the twentieth century arrived, the era which would see the consummation of his prophetic visions, often to catastrophic ends. During the nineteenth century he was read as a philosopher and critic, pamphleteer and journalist, but thirty-four years after his death Marx's theory would be converted into praxis by the Bolsheviks during the Russian Revolution, an enactment of his secular apocalypticism into the political realm, and one of several competing millenarianisms over the course of that bloody century. Not all of these millenarianisms derived from the same source, but whether totalitarian or democratic, libertarian or socialist, of the dragon or the dove, they all shared that broad theological expectation that a promised rupture in history would either restore or redeem the fallen world.

Marx had, perhaps inadvertently, resuscitated that obscure Sicilian monk Joachim of Fiore to his previous importance as a prophet of a particular variety of apocalyptic script. In *The Communist Manifesto* and arguably *Das Kapital* as well, Marx promulgated "left Joachitism," but it wasn't the only type of Joachimitism which would emerge in the twentieth century. Revanchists, reacting directly to the Marxist example, and inadvertently proving the dialectic as a legitimate process for comprehending history, inaugurated a "right Joachimitism," more popularly known as fascism. A nineteenth-century prophet of that incipient apocalypticism wrote with unnerving accuracy about what devastation lay ahead, Friedrich Nietzsche predicting in his 1888 autobiography *Ecce Homo* that "there will be wars, the likes of which have never been seen on earth before."[49] Such conflicts would make the French Revolution, the English Civil War, the Thirty Years' War, and the Crusades appear as mere preludes.

Ironically, Nietzsche didn't mention a contemporary war that was already among the most destructive the world had ever seen, an explicitly apocalyptic conflagration that exploded in China in 1850 and would continue for another fourteen violent years.[50] The rebellion against the Qing Dynasty by the group known as the Taiping Heavenly Kingdom had many causes, most notably resentment of the Han ethnic majority being oppressed by an imperial Manchu minority, as well as profound economic disparities which marked the regimented society. Yet the Taiping Rebellion is inextricably bound to obvious apocalyptic obsessions of a syncretic nature. Thomas H. Reilly argues in *The Taiping Heavenly Kingdom: Rebellion and Blasphemy of Empire* that the "rebel creed may have repelled certain groups, particularly those that wielded power in the established system, such as the gentry. A rebellion, like a revolution, is not a different party, after all."[51]

The movement's leader, Hong Xiuquan, was a failed civil servant born to an ethnically Hakka family in Guangzhou. Despairing over his professional failures, he would fortuitously meet a Connecticut-born Congregationalist minister named Edwin Stevens who would convert Hong to Christianity, or at least a version of it. American Protestant missionaries such as Stevens, fired with the zeal of the Second Great Awakening, arrived to win ever more souls to Christ. Yet the tracts distributed by these missionaries were often poorly translated into the local Cantonese, so that Hong developed his own idiosyncratic understanding of Christianity from a pamphlet entitled *Good Words for Exhorting the Age*.

After a series of mystical visions, Hong concluded that he was actually the celestial half-brother of Jesus Christ and that it was his responsibility to purge China of the "demon cults" of imperial veneration, even while he combined much of his new faith with Chinese traditional religion. As Reilly notes, the Taiping Rebellion was ultimately not a "Western religion, a foreign creed. The Taiping faith, albeit kindled by Anglo-American Protestantism, developed into a dynamic new Chinese religion, one whose conception of the title and position of the sovereign deity challenged the legitimacy of the imperial order. . . . A revival and restoration of the ancient classical faith."[52] More important than his iconoclasm was what Hong understood as his divine mandate to unseat the government. From the time of his 1836 vision until the start of the rebellion in 1850, Hong was able to assemble as many as fifty thousand followers through his utopian social tracts, attracted to his declaration that "When people of this earth keep nothing for their private use, but give all things to God for all use in common, then every place shall have equal shares, and everyone be clothed and fed."[53]

What the Qing first believed would be a simple peasant uprising burned on until 1864, when Hong perished, possibly from poisoning. The rebellion ended shortly after that, with the Qing barely victorious; Hong's corpse was beheaded, cremated, and his ashes shot from a canon. Along with Hong's death there were twenty million other fatalities—possibly as high as forty million deaths—during the Taiping Rebellion, making it among the bloodiest of conflicts ever fought, and a harbinger of what was to come. Contemporary war has often been defined not just by succession issues or even fighting over resources, but fighting over philosophies as well. The Taiping Rebellion could be claimed as not the last of ancient wars—waged with sword, pickax, and spear—but as the first modern war fought over abstract ideas. Nietzsche may have prophesized future apocalyptic wars as a variety of global hygiene, but in China such dispensations had already been initiated.

Wearily observing the start of the Taiping Rebellion in 1853, a London-based freelancer for the *New York Herald Tribune* observed that in "China the spinners and weavers have suffered greatly . . . and the community has become unsettled in proportion."[54] The journalist who authored that article was named Karl Marx. As he understood it, an oppressed people will only remain oppressed for so long, and the language in which their dissatisfaction is rendered will often be apocalyptic, and hell will follow with it.

A Beautiful Country

Abolitionism and Apocalypse

Like Christ, Nat Turner came not to send peace, but a sword; and like Christ, Nat Turner would be executed by the state in a place called Jerusalem, but rather than Judea this later Golgotha was in Southampton County, Virginia. Because Turner was literate, he was tasked by his master Thomas Moore to preach to others in bondage since the Bible is convenient for commanding subservience; after the failure of Turner's rebellion, the reading of Scripture by the enslaved was carefully circumscribed, since the Bible can also supply the language of freedom, liberation, and revolution.[55] Turner was already a mystic when at the age of twenty-four he encountered Christ while laboring in Moore's cotton fields. Having long taken to fits of prayer, meditation, and fasting, now Turner learned that the "Savior was about to lay down the yoke he had borne for the sins of men, and the great day of judgement was at hand."[56]

Turner was known for his piety among not just the enslaved whom he preached to, but also among the poor whites of Southampton County who sometimes called on him for spiritual edification. Now, he began to believe that the incipient apocalypse was upon America and that it was his righteous task to begin that work by wiping off the nation's incomparable and unspeakable sins of slavery with blood and fire. In 1828, Turner had another vision of the Holy Spirit, whom "instantly appeared to me and said the Serpent was loosened . . . and that I should take it on and fight against the Serpent, for the time was fast approaching when the first should be the last and the last should be first."[57] Daniel was written for the Jews oppressed by Babylon and Revelation by the Christians suffering under the yoke of Rome, but now both spoke to Turner about Black women and men who were enslaved by the new antichrist of America. Such visions were clear—it was Turner's task to rouse an army of those who were enslaved in southern Virginia and to burn a path through the fields and plantations of their oppressors, a fire which would not just guide Christ to earth but would singe away all inequity in the great apocalyptic conflagration.

Following the mass genocide of indigenous Americans and their death from successive waves of disease, European colonial powers kidnapped Africans and transported them to the Americas. From the sixteenth until the nineteenth century, Ibo, Yoruba, Wolof, and Mandinka peoples, among other mostly west African ethnic groups, were wrenched from their homes and enslaved in the New World; their descendants would not just be tortured and raped in the forge of slavery, but their very families split and broken apart, human beings reduced to mere commodity. Some estimates have the number of African women and men who were sent upon the Middle Passage at over twelve million people. A sizable percentage died at sea and their corpses were tossed into the ocean. By the time that Turner had his visions, there had been enslaved Africans in Virginia for 209 years.

The preacher was born into slavery, his surname the same as that of the first master who legally owned him. Few situations in human history have been so obviously unjust and evil that they would seem to merit the great cleansing promised of in apocalyptic scripture. The Bible's ambivalence is such that Turner had once been commanded to use it as if the whip of oppression, but now those same words transformed Scripture into a weapon of liberation. Kenneth S. Greenberg writes in *Nat Turner: A Slave Rebellion in History and Memory* how a "captive black prophet, wrestling the religion of white America out of its hands, had transformed it and had in turn been utterly changed . . . [into] an insurrectionary commander carrying out the sanguinary vengeance of a just God."[58] Turner's faith was that, by returning in small measure the violence that had been enacted upon his people for two centuries, there might be the beginnings of an apocalypse which would destroy the "peculiar institution" of slavery.

A solar eclipse across Virginia in February of 1831 was interpreted as if it was a black hand blotting out the sun; it convinced Turner that by Independence Day his army would march against the plantations of Southampton County. Unable to organize in time for the Fourth of July due to illness, the prophet regrouped with his followers a month later, when after an eerie, blue-green sunset—most likely dyed that hue from volcanic ash plumes off the faraway coast of Sicily—convinced Turner that the time was now for their insurrection (an example of how such material realities directly impact apocalypticism). Starting on the evening of August 21, 1831, an army of at least seventy enslaved men marched through the low country of Virginia along the border with North Carolina. Brandishing pickaxes, hatchets, knives, swords, and mallets, they traveled from plantation to plantation, killing masters, their families, and white overseers without regard to gender or age, though they did spare poor whites. Tellingly, a *Richmond Enquirer* report described the violence as reminding the author of a "parcel of blood-thirsty wolves rushing down the Alps; or rather like a former incursion of the Indians upon the white settlements."[59]

Two days later, the insurrection had killed at least sixty people, before the state militia defeated the remainder of Turner's army at Belmont Plantation; by late October the leader of the rebellion himself was discovered living among the Nottoway nation. During the interim, there was a flurry of state-sanctioned retaliatory violence against the Black population. Some fifty-six people were executed by Virginia, many who were not involved in the rebellion at all. A further two hundred innocent Black women and men were lynched by militias, human heads put on pikes lining the backcountry roads. Throughout the South there was palpable terror that such uprisings would become the norm, and ironically Turner's attempt to destroy the system served to make it more brutal, while in the North, where many people were often content to pretend that slavery was merely an issue below the Mason–Dixon Line, there was a hardening of attitudes toward free Blacks. The prophet's name became a byword throughout the antebellum United States, "the most famous slave insurgent in American history, the victim of a violent system who struck back with retributive violence," as Stephen B. Oates describes him in *The Fires of Jubilee: Nat Turner's Fierce Rebellion*.[60] After his arrest, Turner confessed, was tried, and executed; beheaded and flayed, his flesh was used as leather for souvenir purses and wallets. A few days before his November execution, he was asked by those who imprisoned him if he regretted the rebellion, to which Turner responded "Was Christ not crucified?"[61]

Turner's rebellion was as if the opening of John's seals in Revelation for people on both sides of the color line and both sides of the 39th parallel. For Southern aristocracy, so much of their own racialized identity was invested in the maintenance of a wicked system that they feared race war, plagued by paranoid visions of being murdered in their sumptuous beds by those whom they enslaved. Northern whites also feared the inevitability of a race war encouraged by the brutality of Southern slavery, while the minority of abolitionists felt that Turner's insurrection demonstrated the lengths to which an oppressed people will go to secure their own freedom. Stark divisions had separated the North and South since the colonial period; in matters of religion, economics, and politics the two were as if separate countries within an ostensibly united state.[62]

Shortly after the American Revolution, over the course of a few years, slavery was outlawed in varying stages across all of the states north of the Mason–Dixon line and the Ohio River (save for New Jersey), while only further entrenching in the South. There are clear economic and material reasons for these differences; Northern policy need not be interpreted as an issue of innate New England and mid-Atlantic virtue, yet the cultural and especially religious differences between the regions was also instrumental in this differing course regarding slavery. The tidewater South, settled by High Church Anglicans who sympathized with the

Royalist cause during the English Civil War, justified slavery through economic expediency but also by recourse to a fundamentally aristocratic conception of human hierarchy and power. In contrast, New England Congregationalist and mid-Atlantic nonconformists increasingly understood slavery as an affront to God, while more secular-minded writers saw it as a betrayal of the Revolution's Enlightenment values.

Increasingly this disjunct expressed itself in the framing of national origins and values. An abolitionist writing in 1857 exclaims that, as regards the original Massachusetts and Virginia colonies, "Here are two ideas, Liberty and Slavery—planted at about the same time, in the virgin soil of the new continent; the one in the North, the other in the South. They are deadly foes."[63] By contrast, the Southern apologist for slavery George Fitzhugh would compare Massachusetts and Virginia in 1860, declaring that the coming war was "between those who believe in the past, in history, in human experience, in the Bible, in human nature, and those who . . . foolishly, rashly, and profanely attempt to 'expel human nature,' to bring about a millennium."[64] For Southerners like Fitzhugh, heretical New England Puritanism had mutated into a score of new ideas from Unitarianism to Transcendentalism. Historian Jan C. Dawson, in *The Unusable Puritan Past: America's Puritan Tradition, 1830–1930*, explained that for Fitzhugh, and others like him, "Puritanism had been turned on its head. Something within Puritanism seemed to generate its opposite,"[65] so that religious orthodoxy gave way to calls of human liberty, threatening the slave system which Fitzhugh advocated. Consequently, in the leadup to the inevitable civil war, there were mutual excommunications of Southerner and Northerner, both seeing the other as anti-Christian and heretical.

A vast bulk of Northerners, no matter if they personally found slavery to be distasteful or not, viewed the system as a Southern malady, even while mostly New England abolitionists like William Lloyd Garrison advocated for secession from the infernal constitutional covenant which implicated all Americans in this evil. Two overreaching judicial and legal decisions swayed Northern political opinion to a more muscular approach—Congress's Fugitive Slave Act of 1850 and the Supreme Court's Dred Scott Decision of 1857, which stripped all Black women and men of US citizenship. Drawn into an immoral system which they had previously been able to ignore, many moderate Northerners felt themselves siding with the abolitionists, seeing the slavocracy as infringing upon their own political rights.

Religious and secular ideological positions hardened in this regard and though initially only a small subset of Northerners could be described as abolitionists, it's not unfair to say that a certain millennial fervor spread throughout New England and the mid-Atlantic, even while the war would ultimately be initiated by Southern secession. According to the demographer Kevin Phillips, to some controversy, in his study *The Cousins' Wars: Religion, Politics, and the Triumph of Anglo-America*, the American Civil War should be understood as an ideological and theological continuation of the same themes which motivated the American Revolution and the English Civil War. He argues that these conflicts were the "anvil on which some of the most lasting arrangements of English and American politics have been hammered,"[66] an ongoing mutual holy war fought between aristocratic Royalists and radical Republicans, with the latter winning each war, the result of which would be the reconsecration of the United States's perception of itself as a millennial redeemer nation.

Despite the overrepresentation of the Virginian planter class in the leadership of the American Revolution, it's true that the radical republican themes of the war were more congruent with the Puritan iconoclasm of New England, so that by the time of the American Civil War the burgeoning Confederate government justified itself as being conservative and more truly "European" than the United States. With some cause, the architects of secession, such as President Jefferson Davis, argued that their position was not dissimilar to the royals and aristocrats of Britain who would side with the Confederacy until the Emancipation Proclamation made it morally untenable. In keeping with the counterrevolutionary and anti-Enlightenment nature of the secessionist movement, the vice president of the Confederate States of America, Alexander H. Stephens, infamously intoned in an address at Savannah, Georgia, in 1861 that the "prevailing ideas entertained by . . . the leading statesmen at the time of the formation of the old Constitution were, that the enslavement of the African was in violation of the laws of nature; that it was wrong in principle, socially, morally, and politically," but that, by contrast, "Our new government is founded upon exactly the opposite ideas; its foundations are laid, its cornerstone rests, upon the great truth that the negro is not equal to the white man; that slavery, subordination to the superior race, is his natural and normal condition."[67]

This was a direct assault on the ideals of the Revolution justified by recourse to bogus science, but also by conservative religion. Southern ministers—every Christian denomination except for the American Roman Catholic Church would be split by the Civil War—argued that Northerners were fundamentally Yankee heretics, enraptured to chiliastic dreams of remaking the world and attempting to hasten the millennium. By contrast, such preachers claimed, Southern religion was conservative, traditional, ritualistic, hierarchical—a faith of order where the world would remain steadfastly upright.

After the Confederate loss, millennial fervor would develop among devotees of the pseudohistorical "Lost Cause" mythology, with their messianic claim that the "South will rise again," while the nascent Ku Klux Klan was arguably the origin of fascism as a political ideology constructed on an apocalyptic fusion of nostalgic pastoral romance and rank race hatred.[68] Even prior to the war there would be movements such as the shadowy Knights of the Golden Circle, who envisioned a massive slave-owning empire of unfreedom stretching from Washington DC to the north shore of South America, beliefs that could perhaps be categorized as millenarian, but during the Civil War itself the majority of millennial rhetoric was a steadfastly Union phenomenon.[69] For many Northerners, inheritors of a radical postmillennial religious tradition that understood our human task to increase justice, equality, and liberty, the blood-soaked plantations of the South were a reminder of the hypocrisy of the United States in claiming to be democratic. Phillips writes that, even in secular form, New England's "guiding political culture . . . [was] a Low Church, Calvinistic Protestantism . . . highly convinced . . . that it represented a chosen people and a manifest destiny,"[70] a consummation of the covenant that was both the Mayflower Compact and the American Revolution.

The difference in millennial inclinations between the Confederacy and the Union can be handily seen in the sentiments of their most famous musical anthems. Ohio-born songwriter Daniel Decauter Emmet's minstrel tune "Dixie," written on the eve of war in 1859, wasn't intended to be an anthem of the Confederacy, but during the war and after it has been cemented as a halcyon, gauzy pastoral which expresses Southern conceptions of their claimed values. Narrated from the perspective of an imagined enslaved man, "Dixie" reinforces the obviously untrue claim that slavery was a beneficial institution to those in bondage, while the lyrics emphasize the beauty of the landscape, the leisure of Southern life, and the Cavalier ethos. "I wish I was in the land of cotton," writes Emmet, "old times there are not forgotten."

Diametrically opposed to this vision is the millennial yearning for justice embodied by the Union anthem of Julia Ward Howe's "Battle Hymn of the Republic." Where "Dixie" is syrupy, maudlin, and sentimental, Howe's composition is righteous, prophetic, and apocalyptic. Echoing Revelation and Isaiah, Howe writes that "Mine eyes have seen the glory of the coming of the Lord; / He is trampling out the vintage where the grapes of wrath are stored; / He hath loosed the fateful lightning of His terrible swift sword: / His truth is marching on." The difference is obvious; the Confederacy a fundamentally glib regime whose saccharine rhetoric overlaid against the reality of human suffering only emphasizes its perfidy and wickedness, while the cause of the Union is that of the Lord Himself.

Howe's composition has the hallmarks of prophecy about it, the New York–born abolitionist retiring in Washington DC's Willard Hotel in the autumn of 1861 so that she "awoke in the gray of the morning twilight; and as I lay waiting for the dawn, the long lines of the desired poem began to twine themselves in my mind . . . I scrawled the verses almost without looking at the paper."[71] For the song's melody and partially the lyrics, Howe appropriated a Union camp song which she had heard earlier that day, a coarse but nonetheless urgently prophetic tune entitled "John Brown's Body." Referencing the subject of that march, Howe's version declares that "In the beauty of the lilies Christ was born across the sea / With a glory in His bosom that transfigures you and me; / As He died to make men holy, let us die to make men free." Two years since he was executed for organizing a failed raid on the military depot at Harper's Ferry, Virginia, in an attempt to initiate a widespread uprising of the enslaved throughout the South, in the minds of Northerners John Brown was now understood not as a fire-breathing madman, but rather a righteous martyr, if not a kind of suffering messiah.

Few figures in American millennialism, much less American history, are as endlessly fascinating as Brown. A Connecticut-born Midwestern settler who variously made his home in Pennsylvania, Ohio, and Kansas, Brown is the rare figure who broached absolutely no hypocrisy in his own thought. Deeply devout and an implacable foe of slavery, Brown shared none of the occasional racist condescension of his more well-heeled eastern abolitionist contemporaries and, rather than endlessly debating theoretical intricacies, he advocated direct action, which he took. While a Midwestern homesteader, during the period of violence known as Bleeding Kansas, Brown and his sons killed eight slave owners and catchers, while freeing those whom they held in bondage. Notorious among the genteel abolitionists of New England who feared the implications of Brown's violence, he was nonetheless respected by Black abolitionists such as the formerly enslaved Frederick Douglass and Harriet Tubman, even if they didn't always agree with his strategies.

The raid on Harper's Ferry cemented Brown's fame and notoriety, an attempt to capture the army's arsenal on the banks of the Potomac and to arm the enslaved while marching south, hoping to initiate a massive rebellion. "A few men in the right, and knowing that they are right, can overturn a mighty king," Brown wrote. "Fifty men, twenty men, in the Alleghenies would break slavery to pieces in two years."[72] He was overly optimistic, even while the raid at Harper's Ferry arguably was one of the sparks which conflagrated the Civil War only a year later. In late 1859 Brown and a small contingent of Black and white soldiers were able to take the arsenal relatively easily. However, a series of blunders and miscalculations meant the relatively quick defeat of the insurgents, and Brown's arrest and trial for treason, and ultimately his execution by the Commonwealth of Virginia, served as an acerbic catalyst. A man of steadfast courage and principle, Brown ascended the scaffold at Charles Town, Virginia, absolutely certain of his role in being an instrument of God and that a cleansing fire was awaiting the United States. Meteor of the Civil War, as the novelist Herman Melville referred to him, Brown declared in a statement that "I'm not quite certain that the crimes of this guilty land can never be purged away but with blood."[73]

Brown's "conflation of the Golden Rule, the Declaration [of Independence] and visions of apocalyptic violence was . . . made by someone who was descended on both sides from Revolutionary War soldiers and who was born into a Calvinistic family in a state that was among the first to emancipate slaves," explains David S. Reynolds in *John Brown, Abolitionist: The Man Who Killed Slavery, Sparked the Civil War, and Seeded Civil Rights*.[74] If the United States was mired in the contradictions of Enlightenment philosophy and Second Great Awakening values, of Republican virtue and religious enthusiasm, then Brown reconciled that paradox into the impetus of prophetic urgency. As Howe's framing of Brown's biography demonstrated, such a perspective was equivalent with the totality of what the Union was required to accomplish. Even frosty New England Transcendentalists were in awe of Brown's example, with Emerson describing him as that "new saint than whom none purer or more brave was ever led by love of men into conflict and death—the new saint awaiting his martyrdom, and who, if he shall suffer, will make the gallows glorious like the cross."[75]

Religion permeated nineteenth-century America, of course, especially in the afterglow of the Second Great Awakening, yet the same millennial urgency of Brown's language became more marked and pronounced among Northerners, who in the antebellum era would have been thought of as moderates or centrists. Lincoln, whom more radical abolitionists had initially despaired at being the Republican presidential nominee because of his presumed centrism, would intone at his second inaugural address that if "God will that it continue all the wealth piled by the bondsman's two hundred and fifty years of unrequited toil shall be sunk, and until every drop of blood drawn by the lash shall be paid by another drawn with the sword, as was said three thousand years ago, so still it must be said 'the judgements of the Lord are true and righteous altogether.'"[76]

Referencing that prophetic tradition which despises tyranny and exults liberty was a rhetorical mainstay of Lincoln, a man raised in no particular denomination and who at times seemed to fuse the Old Testament God with the rationalist being of the Deists. Yet he drew from the same apocalyptic wellspring as did Brown, his speeches holding a strange equilibrium between compassion and judgment, grace and damnation. Far more privy to the racist sentiments of the nineteenth century than was Brown, the Kentucky-born Lincoln still vociferously hated slavery, and despite the initial reputation for compromise and triangulation, his canny political brilliance was instrumental in the defeat of the Confederacy. The United States was a sin-permeated land that would be redeemed in blood, finally fulfilling its providential and messianic destiny, the country as the "last, best hope of earth," as Lincoln explain in an 1862 address to Congress.

A new national mission emerged from the Civil War, "practical abolitionism," ironically enforced by the Confederate insurrections themselves, for had secession not happened it's arguable that emancipation wouldn't have followed. Even after Lincoln's assassination—yet another martyrdom—the promise of radical Reconstruction was that the South and North might be reconfigured to fully embody the democratic ideals of the American Revolution. This was a short period, as the nation would suture her wounds at the expense of the formerly enslaved as institutionalized white supremacy became a bedrock of an unjust legal and political system.

Nor did the emancipation of the enslaved imply that other persecuted groups in the United States would see anything like justice, as the Union army that had previously fought Confederate traitors increasingly turned their attentions to the Indigenous peoples in the massive western interior of the continent. Explicitly genocidal, the various Prairie Wars waged against the Sioux, the Lakota, the Apache, and other groups in the second half of the nineteenth century generated a fierce and brave resistance, as well as fervent apocalypticism. During the earliest days of the Second Great Awakening, movements like the Longhouse Religion initiated by the Iroquois prophet Handsome Lake reinterpreted Christian eschatological narratives through Indigenous beliefs, promising a coming apocalypse in which the Indigenous peoples would be liberated from their white oppressors.[77] In the years after the Civil War, as conflict in the West became even more bloody, and a Pauite prophet named Wodziwob had a vision that "within a few moons there was to be a great upheaval or earthquake . . . the whites would be swallowed up, while the Indians would be saved."[78] Such were the beginnings of the enigmatic Ghost Dance tradition, an indigenous means of resistance that burnt its way across the West among an assortment of tribal groups throughout the 1870s and 1880s, fusing together apocalyptic rhetoric with traditional rituals and in keeping with the Sioux Chief Lame Deer's faith that this new practice could command a "new world into being."

By performing its titular ritual, the Ghost Dance participants believed that they were calling upon spiritual forces that would aid them in their resistance to white settlers and the government. "To invoke the Ghost Dance has been to call up an image of indigenous spirituality by turns militant, desperate, and futile," writes Louis S. Warren in *God's Red Son: The Ghost Dance Religion and the Making of Modern America*.[79] While literally true that the Indigenous peoples were often outgunned, the Ghost Dance provided a unifying ideology and poetics that contributed to a defensive spirit, and in the teachings of Wodziwob's successor-prophet Wovoka there was a language crafted to measure both that which had been lost, but also all of that which could be gained; a means of expressing a utopian and millennial yearning, of rolling back the "fences, the telegraph poles, the mines and factories. Underneath would be the wonderful old-new world," as Wovoka preached.[80] Such a dream was not so different from that of the saint of Harpers Ferry, because when Brown ascended that scaffold, and looked out onto the verdant Blue Mountains, for just a second he was able to see past the actual United States of Babylon, and rather stare into the potential Canaan of America, which was free of slavery, ethnic cleansing, technocratic dehumanization. Brown's last words were "This is a beautiful country."

CHAPTER NINE

Ending All Over Again

Modernity, Secularism, and Apocalypse

Assured of the Rapture

BILLY SUNDAY HAD an unremarkable hitting arm, though he was slightly better as a fielder than he ever was as a batter. However, his preaching voice was incomparable. Examine the statistics between two very different careers—in his tenure as a baseball player, starting in 1883 with the Chicago White Stockings and retiring seven years later with the Philadelphia Phillies, an interim with the Pittsburgh Alleghenies in the middle, Sunday had a lackluster batting average of .248. During his best season he ranked seventeenth in the American Association. Despite not being much of a ball player, audiences still enjoyed Sunday's easy athleticism, and he proved to be a fan favorite in the markets where he played.[1] That was perhaps the only similarity that Sunday the baseball player had with Sunday the traveling evangelist.

Compared to his mediocre athletics career, Sunday's stats as a preacher were astounding. First working as a minister at a Chicago YMCA in 1891, some five years after his born-again conversion experience Sunday would become the most celebrated itinerant evangelical preacher of the first twenty years of the twentieth century, enthralling crowds of thousands from Boston to Denver, extoling the saving grace of conservative Christianity and the imminent arrival of Christ to an astounding hundred million Americans over his four decade career. Matthew Avery Sutton writes in *American Apocalypse: A History of Modern Evangelicalism* that Sunday's "masterful blend of premillennialism with political engagement and American patriotism set precedents for subsequent generations of fundamentalists and evangelicals who sought to transform their culture."[2] He didn't achieve this by studying hermeneutics and writing exegesis. Sunday did it by pretending to run bases on stage and by knowing how to properly deploy the appropriate earthy vulgarity in his preaching. If his stint in the major leagues taught Sunday something, it was the value of keeping an audience's attention on you, even if you're not offering much in the way of runs.

At revivals, Sunday was known to prowl and pounce, to theatrically jab his arm into the air, and to smash his fist upon the pulpit of the al fresco wooden tabernacles paid for by the communities in which he would preach. "I have no interest," Sunday would tell the enraptured crowds, "in a God who does not smite." Born in Iowa to a first-generation German American bricklayer who had the fortuitous foresight to change the family name from the Teutonic "Sontag" to the almost ridiculously appropriate "Sunday," the preacher's father died in a Union Army camp in 1862. Consequently, the young Sunday was sent by his cash-strapped mother to be raised in a series of orphanages where he learned an American vernacular that had little to do with how ministers were educated in seminary. Staider clergy were sometimes scandalized by Sunday's popular sermons; when he talked about charity, he described gambling; when he denounced dipsomania, he told stories about drinking; and when extolling chastity, he talked about sex.

Sunday was the sort of preacher who, speaking to an audience that thrilled to such rhetoric, could denounce "weasel-eyed, hog-joweled, good-for-nothing, God-forsaken, iniquitous, rapacious buffoons and charlatans, and mountebanks and poltroons and marplots and moral perverts."[3] Managed by his wife Nell, Sunday became stupendously wealthy, known for fur coats and fedoras, a friend of presidents from Theodore Roosevelt to Herbert Hoover, of actors like Douglas Fairbanks, and captains of industry such as Nelson Rockefeller. Though no financial impropriety has ever been alleged against Sunday, he certainly didn't live a lifestyle in accordance with apostolic poverty. No theoretician or theologian, not even particularly a thinker, what Sunday really happened to be was a consummate American entertainer. His was the first of a new type—the mass media evangelist. What Sunday happened to be was dynamite.

Even if he didn't share poverty with that first generation of Christians, Sunday did have a similar sense that this was the last of days before Christ's imminent return. Sutton writes that "Sunday best exemplified the developing paradox of premillennialism: the call to exercise influence in politics and culture as aggressively as possible while preparing the world for the oncoming apocalypse";[4] the gospel of the dragon in keeping with the rising fortunes of a martial nation. Such was the context of the pinnacle of Sunday's career, when in 1917 he arrived to headline a series of New York City revivals intended to win soldiers for both Christ and the US Army. Over two-and-a-half months Sunday preached to a million-and-a-half women, men, and children within the Five Boroughs. A city that the preacher had compared to Sodom and Gomorrah was now a New Jerusalem. He announced a gospel where the army was composed of Christian soldiers in conflict with the antichrist of Kaiser Wilhelm II. "In these days, one is either a patriot or a traitor, in the cause of Jesus Christ, in the cause of the country," this was a war of "Germany against America, Hell against Heaven.... Either you are loyal or you are not, you are either a patriot or a black-hearted traitor."[5] His was an incendiary cocktail of nationalism and faith, not a uniquely American affliction, but certainly a virulent one.

While mainline Protestants became increasingly liberal, Sunday retreated into a strict conservatism, but it would be a categorical error to interpret religious fundamentalism as anything other than its own distinct aftereffect of modernity. As mainline Protestants either minimized the supernatural elements of Christianity or reinterpreted them as purely allegorical, conservatives returned to the "fundamentals" of the faith, or at least how they interpreted it. The creation of the world in seven days, the virgin birth, and the resurrection of Christ were all to be understood literally; as was the Lord's imminent return and the rapture, when the saved would be spared the tribulations of the end of days before the thousand-year millennium of God's rule on earth.

This premillennial dispensationalism, of the same variety which Miller taught, may have been understood as a return to first principles by fundamentalists, but it had little to do with the first century of Christianity and everything to do with beliefs held by reformers in the sixteenth century, or even evangelicals in the nineteenth. A belief that Christ would arrive after a tribulation when the wicked would rule became a defining feature of apocalypticism for many evangelicals and fundamentalists (not synonymous terms). Sutton explains that nothing about premillennialism was abstract for the fundamentalist; such beliefs "shaped how the faithful engaged with Christians and non-Christians alike. To believe that humankind was careening toward Armageddon, that signs of the last days were embedded in social and political changes, that long-term reform was futile, that global war was inevitable . . . had ramifications that extended far beyond the walls of their churches."[6]

Historians have debated how accurate the phrase "Fourth Great Awakening" is to refer to the period from the late nineteenth century through the late twentieth, when an emboldened and reactionary evangelical Christianity had a profound impact on culture and politics, but it is true that Sunday signaled the arrival of a new, muscular form of revival culture. Secular critics will often malign fundamentalism as a medieval vestige, but, like its revanchist cousin fascism, such extreme religious literalism is a cankered symptom of modernity. This is true in its ideology, its means of disseminating that theology, and its relationship to politics.

If Sunday was an exemplary evangelist for this cause, then its intellectual origins were with far more learned men. Starting in 1910, Lyman Stewart, cofounder of the Union Oil Company of California, convened a gathering of conservative Presbyterian, Baptist, and Methodist ministers who compiled a twelve-volume collection of ninety essays entitled *The Fundamentals: A Testimony of Truth*, from which "fundamentalism" derives its name.[7] Stewart's purpose was explicitly revanchist, an attempt to return to a pristine Christianity, at least as the oil tycoon defined it. Taking five years to complete the project, fundamentalism's primary intellectual target was modernity, specifically in the form of liberal Christianity. Insomuch as the movement was antiscientific (and it was), it was primarily such in its attacks on liberal Protestantism. More than Charles Darwin's theory of evolution, what fundamentalists blanched at was the discipline of study known as the Higher Criticism, the philologically inflected study of the origins of Scripture which first predominated in German universities and then spread to other countries, but which conservative ministers viewed as a threat to the Bible's status as the inerrant word of God.

During the last decades of the twentieth century, mainline Protestant ministers absorbed textual insights which complicated the authorship of the Bible, though for Stewart and his assembled clergy it was this development that heralded the greatest threat to faith. In 1907 Stewart would write that he wished to send "some kind of warning and testimony to the English-speaking ministers, theological teachers, and students, and English-speaking missionaries of the world . . . which would put them on their guard and bring them into right lines again."[8] According to this "new statement of the fundamentals of Christianity," not only was the Bible the inspired word of God to be interpreted as literal in all of its details, but for its compositors a firm commitment to its principles meant the dismissal of liberal Christianity, Darwinism, and secular Bible scholarship, as well as socialism, feminism, and Spiritualism. Ministers such as Louis Meyer, James Orr, and C. I. Scofield claimed that theirs was an undiluted gospel, rejecting the "natural view of the Scriptures" which contaminated faith with science, the result being as contributor Franklin Johnson wrote that liberalism "has been rising higher for three-quarters of a century. . . . It is already a cataract, uprooting, destroying, and slaying."[9]

Fundamentalists dismissed liberalism, but even more so theirs was a rejection of the secularized theology that existed at the core of liberalism in the form of postmillennialism. Fundamentalism was an assault of the dragon on the dove. *The Fundamentals* hewed to a vociferously premillennial eschatology, the better to discard the idea that there could ever be social, political, or cultural progress separate from supernatural intervention. As Boyer explains, premillennial dispensationalism was the "functional equivalent of the antigovernment, antireform ideology of laissez-faire advocates," the beginning of a strategically fruitful synthesis between Christian fundamentalism and right-wing politics mediated through the language of "sharp social criticism and skepticism about all efforts at betterment."[10]

For the fundamentalist, there was something heretical in believing that humans were capable of bettering their own lot, and besides, none of us would have to wait long for Christ to arrive and do the bettering for us. "More marvelous than the scenes at Pentecost, more startling than the fall of Jerusalem, more blessed than the indwelling of the spirit or the departure to be with the Lord," wrote the Presbyterian minister and professor at the Princeton Theological Seminary Rev. Charles R. Erdman in his contribution to *The Fundamentals*, "will be the literal, visible, bodily return of Christ. No event may seem less probable to unaided human reason; no event is more certain in the light of inspired Scripture."[11] Erdman is erudite and his rhetoric masterful, but his theology was reactionary. Not traditional per se, but radical, because though the early fundamentalists posed their position as the obvious historical essence of Christianity, their reactions to secularism and liberalism were steadfastly modern.

Twentieth-century Protestantism outside of the mainline denominations is often separated out into the evangelical and the fundamentalist, so that these differing (though often overlapping) terms are often treated as synonymous when they're not. *Evangelical* is a term that goes back to the earliest days of the Reformation; it was Luther's preferred term for "Protestant," which was initially a slur imposed by their critics. In a contemporary context, those who self-identify as evangelicals are marked by the immediacy of their faith and the style of their worship, but not necessarily their politics or even their theology. There are liberal and even left-wing evangelicals and their interpretive framework need not be literalist. In many ways, evangelicals are true inheritors of the Second Great Awakening, while fundamentalists are children of the Fourth Great Awakening.

A third related term, but with its own distinct definition, is *Pentecostalism*, an American innovation in Christianity that has become increasingly popular in the Global South. Traceable to the Holiness Movement within Wesleyan Methodism, Pentecostalism first emerged in working-class neighborhoods of Los Angeles, California, during the epic Azusa Street Revival which started in 1906 and continued for a flabbergasting nine more years.[12] Led by a Black preacher named William J. Seymour, the Azusa Street Revival was punctuated by the gift of glossolalia, that is speaking in tongues, as adherents believed that as the apostles had been graced with such at Pentecost, so too could believers in the modern day. Thrumming with a fervency of emotion extreme even by the standards of the Second Great Awakening, Pentecostals were known not just for speaking in tongues, but also prophecy and faith healing. That apocalyptic beliefs were consistent with this growing denomination of Christianity goes without saying; their eschatology was firmly premillennial. Randall J. Stevens writes in *The Fire Spreads: Holiness and Pentecostalism in the American South* that "a climate of expectancy prevailed" among charismatic Christians, as adherents "spent much of their time watching and waiting for signs of the fast-approaching apocalypse."[13]

Again, if there was anything which many evangelicals, Pentecostals, and fundamentalists shared with the earliest of Christians, it was this erroneous sense that millennium was imminent, for as Erdman described it, his "generation of believers will be living when Christ returns, and they will be translated, without the experience of death."[14] If there is a characteristic eschatological doctrine of fundamentalists which is fairly widely known, it's the novel belief in something called the rapture. Associated with the position of premillennial dispensationalism, the "rapture" refers to an event before the period of great tribulation when the antichrist shall reign on earth, when all of those who are saved in Christ will disappear, or ascend, or be transported to heaven, leaving the earth behind for both the damned and those survivors who may yet still be saved. This is the aspect of end-times belief which many secular people are most aware of, the slightly comical vision of a panoply of believers flying upwards to meet Jesus in the sky. Yet it's a relatively new belief, traceable to the nineteenth century and only gaining widespread popularity in the twentieth.[15] Even while believers justify their faith by recourse to Scripture, the exact mélange of doctrines which constitute premillennial dispensationalism has scant corollary in the ancient or early modern periods, despite there being antecedents for each individual aspect of such a belief system when isolated.

Following the rapture, believers hold that there will be a seven-year reign of the antichrist who will also be the head of a heretical church (predictably fundamentalists often conflated it with the Catholic Church). The Tribulation period, as it's known, will culminate in the battle of Armageddon, when Christ defeats the antichrist in battle at Megiddo. Upon the Lord's victory, Christ will reign for the requisite thousand years of millennium, and Satan will attempt a final doomed uprising at the end of that period, followed by the resurrection of the dead and the last judgment. "Prophecy belief is a way of ordering experience," writes Boyer. "It gives a grand, overarching shape to history, and thus ultimate meaning to the lives of individuals caught up in history's stream. . . . But if prophecy belief plays its private role for individuals, it has social ramifications as well. For it influences the worldview of those who embrace it."[16] Among fundamentalists there were certain narrative tropes, often variously interpreted but consistently present, which are central to their eschatological imagination, all of which increasingly had an impact on American political discourse. The antichrist, the mark of the beast, the tribulation—all are filtered through contemporary experience and understood in light of current events. Fundamentalist eschatology can't help but be modernist because it's obsessed with modernity, a reaction to our current condition, which constructs its own idol out of an imagined pure Christianity.

An example of how fundamentalist interpretation could be a powerful tool when overlaid against current events is in the common belief that following the rapture, but before Christ's return, a core of Jews will convert to Christianity and act as shock troops against the antichrist. Such prophetic obsession with the Jews was hardly new, but for nineteenth- and early twentieth-century evangelicals it was taken as a matter of course that a sign of the coming tribulation would be the return of Jews to their ancestral homeland. Consequently, when the contemporary State of Israel was declared in 1948, it was interpreted as confirming the accuracy of such predictions. Robert O. Smith explains in *More Desired Than*

Our Owne Salvation: The Roots of Christian Zionism that the "Protestant tradition of Judeo-centric prophecy interpretation . . . constructed Jews as essentially occidental and, as eventual converts to Protestant faith who would fight the enemies of Christendom, as standing on the correct side of the divine between civilization and savagism."[17] The conservative Christian embrace of Zionism, an attraction to an ideology that was Jewish and initially secular and socialistic, is flummoxing unless placed into the context of particular end-times narratives. Consequently, the most adamant American supporters of bellicose policies from Tel Aviv are not Jews, but evangelical Christians. It's a demonstration of the growing political power of Christian fundamentalists, as well as an embodiment of the strange disjunct of believing that nothing can be done to hasten the millennium while also precisely trying to do just that. Strange political alliances could form, such as that between evangelical Protestants and conservative Catholics when it came to matters of abortion, or between the former and Jews as regards US policies on Israel. Developing in parallel alongside the revivals which propelled Christian fundamentalism was the growth in ultra-Orthodox Judaism and Hasidic Judaism, which often harbors its own eschatological expectations about the construction of a Third Temple and the arrival of the Mashiach.

Conservative Christians, despite the political proficiency of men like Sunday, largely retreated from social engagement following the embarrassment of the infamous 1925 "Monkey Trial," in which a substitute teacher named John T. Scopes was convicted under Tennessee state law for teaching the theory of evolution. Though the jury returned a verdict which most fundamentalists should have been pleased with, the drubbing which they received in the popular press convinced many ministers that rather than a defeat of secularism, what was necessary was simply a retreat. Perhaps it's better to interpret that five-decade-long hiatus from politics as a regrouping rather than a retreat, even while fundamentalist Protestantism always lurked about the edges of respectable conservative politics. By the 1970s, largely in reaction to the counterculture of the New Left, fundamentalist and evangelical Christians found a new comfort with pursuing political power. A preacher like Billy Graham positioned himself publicly as largely apolitical, even though he was a lifelong conservative Republican. However, in the final quarter of the twentieth century, a new breed of evangelical minister flexed considerable political power, increasingly within the Republican Party as it moved to the right under President Ronald Reagan, who never had much use for faith himself, other than as a powerful strategic tool.

Evangelical psychologist James Dobson, though he was never ordained, established the organization Focus on the Family to pursue conservative political aims in 1977. The so-called Moral Majority of Baptist minister Jerry Falwell was founded in 1979, with a mission to promote prayer in schools, the illegalization of abortion and homosexuality, and opposition to the Equal Rights Amendment, among other right-wing causes. Broadcaster and Southern Baptist minister Pat Robertson's Christian Coalition was formed in 1987 to pursue a similar slate of policies. Despite the increasing overall secularism of the United States, writes Frances FitzGerald in *The Evangelicals: The Struggle to Shape America*, "since 1980 many evangelicals, led by the Christian right, have struggled to reverse the trend, and while they have not entirely succeeded, they have reintroduced religion into public discourse, polarized the nation, and profoundly changed American politics."[18] Long at the margins of political life, fundamentalist Christianity gained new urgency and power with Reagan's election, even as he had defeated Jimmy Carter, the first president to ever self-apply the term "born again" openly. In the unlikely personage of a divorced, agnostic, Hollywood actor, conservative Christians had found their savior.

Apocalypticism became a defining feature of this politically engaged fundamentalism, every opponent dismissed as the antichrist, every cultural development of which they disapproved evidence that the United States was a new Babylon, every political victory an indication of God's favor. Hal Lindsey's surprise 1971 bestseller *The Late Great Planet Earth* was an example of the mainstreaming of premillennial dispensationalism. Reading current events entirely through his own interpretations of Ezekiel, Daniel, and especially Revelation, Lindsey claimed that his readers were then living in the days before the tribulation, understanding the establishment of Israel as a sign of the imminent apocalyptic conflagration which would lead to the battle of Armageddon in which the Soviet Union and the United States would be engaged in a Manichean struggle, and where the European Union was the vehicle by which the antichrist would gain power. "As world events develop, prophecy becomes more and more exciting," gushes Lindsey. That sense of spectacle is yet another example of just how modern such fundamentalist apocalypticism is.[19] Invigorating, explosive, intoxicating, exciting—*entertaining*. The aesthetics of Lindsey's paperback were that of the Hollywood blockbuster, an action movie written in the vocabulary of eschatology whereby massive armies are about to clash in Levantine deserts and Christ himself prepares to return.

Even more incendiary was the sixteen-book fantasy Left Behind series by Baptist minister Tim LaHaye and writer Jerry B. Jenkins, the first book of which was published in 1995 in clear anticipation of the coming calendrical millennium. Paperback novels designed for beaches and airports, the Left Behind books describe the world after the rapture has occurred, as a multiracial and multiethnic (but not really) cast of characters must grapple with this new reality. No theological text has had the reach of LaHaye and Jenkins's series; Bruce David Forbes and Djeanne Halgren Kilde explain in *Rapture, Revelation, and the End Times: Exploring the Left Behind Series* that the "books are intended to convince readers that in real life, Jesus' return and the commencement of the end times may happen at any minute, so it is necessary to embrace immediately the particular style of Christianity represented in the books . . . the novels are intended as a wake-up call for non-believing readers."[20] Over sixty-five million copies of the Left Behind books have been sold.

The plot is pulpy in the extreme, with characters that have names like Rayford Steel and Buck Williams. As American as those antagonists' names are, they are to be contrasted with the nefarious Romanian Nicolae Carpathia, an appropriately foreign antichrist, who first becomes secretary general of the United Nations and later facilitates an anti-Christian New World Order with a Pope Peter II being declared Pontifex Maximus of the syncretic Enigma Babylon One World Faith. The Tribulation Force, of which Steel and Williams are members and that has a name consciously fit for an action movie, must battle this wicked and satanic one-world government, with LaHaye and Jenkins indulging every imaginable trope of reactionary politics, including antisemitism, anti-Catholicism, and Islamophobia. At the conclusion, those who allied with Carpathia literally explode as Christ punishes them for their perfidy. "But this show, this shower of fire and ice and blood, reminded him yet again that God is faithful," write LaHaye and Jenkins. "He keeps his promises."[21] A dark gospel, for sure, based on vengeance, suffering, cruelty. A particularly American gospel, for there is something of the blockbuster about it. Conversion facilitated through entertainment has been a strategic gambit for evangelical Christians since the Pentecostal megachurch preacher Aimee Semple MacPherson had Hollywood costume designers stage her pageants, since Billy Sunday would pretend to slide into home plate while preaching atop the wooden tabernacle, since the boozy carousing of the Cane Ridge Revival.

Such apocalypticism benefits from mass media, so that the success of the Christian Right must take into account the material circumstances of their means of communication. Dobson, Falwell, and Robertson were all masters of television, as McPherson was of the radio, and Sunday the public-speaking tour upon the "Sawdust Trail." By the time Reagan became president, his own apostasy was irrelevant to conservative Christian leaders who understood that an actor was the greatest weapon to have in their arsenal. Reagan rewarded them for their support handily. Yet there are grave risks in mistaking myth for reality. Reagan's secretary of the interior James Watt, who had opened up some eighty million acres of previously protected public land for mining, drilling, and logging, was a vocal premillennial dispensationalist. Before Congress in 1981, Watt responded to a question about the preservation of the environment by saying "I do not know how many future generations we can count on before the Lord returns."[22] That same year, an article written by NASA scientist James Hansen published in the peer-reviewed journal *Science* concluded that "anthropogenic carbon dioxide warming should emerge from the noise level of natural climate variability by the end of the century, and there is a high probability of warming."[23] Despite believing that human interference can't bring about the millennium, premillennial dispensationalists have ironically done much to ensure the apocalypse.

Lasting a Thousand Years

Totalitarianism and Apocalypse

In his youth, the Austrian writer and occultist Guido von List claimed that he had turned away from the crucifix of his family's Catholic faith and rather embraced the staff of Wotan. Von List believed that the religion of the ancient Germanic pagans was virile, muscular, and strong, in contrast to the weak supplications of Christianity, with its emphasis on meekness and humility, most of all with its distinctly Semitic origins. By contrast, von List advocated for the resurrection of old gods, for the expulsion of Christian influences in the Germanic-speaking lands, and for what he imagined to be a racially pure nation which would be sustained by this new faith that in his mind was the oldest of all. This was a Romantic project, a nationalist project, a *Volkisch* project which abandoned the dreams of universal brotherhood in favor of the provincial pleasures of mere blood and soil. Growing his beard out to prodigious, Odinesque lengths, von List looked every bit the pagan chieftain while developing a rancorously vile ideology in pseudoscholarly works like *Secret of the Runes* from 1908 and *The Religion of the Aryo-Germanic Folk* published in 1920, among dozens of others. Therein he denounced democracy, feminism, and multiculturalism, while extolling the supposed virtues of monarchism and militarism, all of this shot through with an anti-Christian animus, and especially a poisonous antisemitism. Regardless, despite having traded Moses and Christ for Odin and Thor, von List was still amenable to that Abrahamic conception of a time succeeding time, of a time that ends time.

For von List, this was not millennium, but rather Valhalla, writing in *Secret of the Runes* that in the "course of uncounted generations all men will become Einherjar [apotheosized Nordic warriors], and that state—willed and preordained by the godhead—of general liberty, equality, and fraternity will be reached. This is that state which sociologists long for and which socialists want to bring about by false means."[24] This millennium, this Valhalla, that von List claimed was a utopia, would see the subjugation of every race in the world under the yoke of Aryan rule, it would see the embrace of absolute rulers and the rejection of any religion which emphasized grace, mercy, forgiveness. Wotonism was a symptom of modernity insomuch that von List needed a modernity to react against, but he vociferously rejected the revolutionaries of 1789, claiming that democrats "are not able to comprehend the esoteric concept that lies hidden in the triad: liberty, equality, fraternity, concepts which must first ripen and mature in order that someday it can be picked like a fruit from the World Tree."[25] According to von List, "liberty, equality, fraternity" meant the exact opposite of how they were interpreted by revolutionaries, for they rather stood for bondage, exploitation, and genocide. He dreamt of a Teutonic realm purged of all foreign influence; on the 1,500-year anniversary of the Gothic defeat of the Romans at Carnuntum in 1875, a young von List and his friends had a drunken bacchanal underneath the ruins of a triumphal arch. There, in the morning, von List buried eight wine bottles beneath what was known as the "Heathen's Gate," the destroyed Roman arch on that Alpine field. He arranged them in the shape of a swastika.[26]

Among German-speaking reactionaries at the turn of the twentieth century there was a vogue for a constructed fantasy of pre-Christian Teutonic culture and religion, an imagined paganism which by its very nature became a repository for extreme right-wing political beliefs. Syncretic by their nature, absorbing a variety of different beliefs from Rosicrucianism to Hermeticism, Theosophy to Gnosticism, such thinkers combined these discrete intellectual strains into a scarcely comprehensible mélange, so that German nationalist occultists believed in an upcoming apocalyptic confrontation that would see the northern European peoples dominating the world. *Volkisch* nationalist groups proliferated during the first decades of the twentieth century, spawning a variety of new religious movements that for what they lacked in numbers they'd unfortunately make up for in influence. Philosophies with strange names proliferated, and groups associated with new faiths such as Arisophy, Armanism, Theozoology, Germanenordern, and the Secret Society Order of the New Templars advocated an apocalyptic perspective which, as Olav Hammer explains in his contribution to *The Occult World*, understood "world history as the struggle of Aryan and non-Aryan races, where the Aryans' superiority . . . was threatened by racial degeneration."[27]

Despite their own hatred of Christianity and Judaism, this eschatological belief of the various *Volkisch* groups was clearly indebted to traditional millenarian thought, even as it twisted it to a specifically racist orientation. One occultist sect was the Study Group for Germanic Antiquity, whose anodyne name is rarely used in favor of the group's entirely more esoteric sounding title—the Thule Society.[28] Founded in 1918, just as it was clear that the Central Powers were losing the Great War, the Thule society took its name from the capital of the mythic northern kingdom of Hyperborea, seeing in the frosty environs of the edge of Europe the forge where the master race was molded. Conceived of by an eccentric Prussian named Rudolf von Sebottendorg who was attracted to both Sufism and Nordic mythology, the Thule Society was vehemently anticommunist, antidemocratic, and antisemitic, its founder committed to the belief that since Germans lacked unity of faith they "must therefore bring out another unity, that of race, if you want to achieve anything."[29] The Thule Society, with a little under two thousand members, had several of its leaders arrested for their role in attempting to assassinate the leaders of the Bavarian government; later they purchased the *Munich Observer* newspaper, and in 1919 they founded a political party with the innocuous name of the German Workers Party. Less than a year later, the Thule Society's political party would have the phrase "National Socialist" appended to it by a member who'd joined shortly after its formation and who would ultimately sever that original connection to the occult group after he took leadership of the organization—Adolph Hitler.

Much debate has been had over the extent of the role which the various occult *Volkisch* groups in general and the Thule Society in particular had in the development of Nazism. That some of the Nazi high command, including leader of the Foreign Policy Office Alfred Rosenberg, *Reichsführer* of the Schutzstaffel Heinrich Himmler, deputy *Führer* Rudolf Hess, and minister of propaganda Joseph Goebbels, were enthusiastic neo-pagans and occultists is incontrovertible, though Hitler himself, despite having been baptized Catholic, seems to have been an atheist. Much of the occult symbolism which proliferated in those prewar groups would be incorporated into Nazi imagery, but whether or not it's accurate to literally connect Hitler's party to the cracked metaphysics of the Thule Society, the former certainly imbibed an eschatological view of themselves as a millennial vanguard who would usher in a new dispensation. Nicholas Goodricke-Clarke writes in *The Occult Roots of Nazism: Secret Aryan Cults and Their Influence on Nazi Ideology* how the fascists "fused several German intellectual traditions into a millenarian vision of the new fatherland," having envisioned a "pan-German racist and hierarchical paradise" where the "entire plant was her natural colony," but first an "apocalyptic battle would be released upon the corrupt and resistant world, in order to attain this racist millennium."[30]

Hitler may have viewed his own pseudobiological theories as based in objective science, but the apocalyptic orientation of Nazism more generally was as obvious as the self-designation of their government being a "Third Reich." Here again we see the old Joachimite tripartite division, the idea that history seamlessly separates into three epochs, with the final period a messianic age. Just as Joachim of Fiore saw sacred history as divided between an Age of the Father, an Age of the Son, and an Age of the Holy Spirit, so did Hitler separate German history between a First Reich commensurate with the thousand years of the Holy Roman Empire from the ninth century onward, a Second Reich which was equivalent with the German Empire that reigned between 1871 and its collapse at the end of the First World War, and his own Third Reich, which, as if to confirm the obvious millennial associations, was a "Thousand-Year Reich," though in reality it only lasted for twelve.

Nazism as both a totalizing and totalitarian creed is by definition a religion; that is to say that it generates a sense of transcendent meaning and communal belonging among its adherents, no matter how cankered its perspectives are. Like fundamentalism and the other variants of broad fascism which Nazism can be categorized amongst, it was a dogma that reacted to modernity and posited its own counter-eschatology, a millennium not of universal democracy but rather of slavery, and yet one which its adherents claimed was a state of societal perfection. Nazism's apocalyptic orientation was steadfastly of the dragon, positing purification through violence. David Reddles argues in *Hitler's Millennial Reich: Apocalyptic Belief and the Search for Salvation* that eschatological faith shaped "Hitler's messianic self-perception, propelled the formation, growth, and success of the Nazi movement, and ultimately gave impetus to what the Nazis termed the Final War and the Final Solution—World War II and the Holocaust."[31]

Because so much of the religiosity of the Nazis was expressed through a constructed fantasy of Teutonic paganism, it can be easy to overlook the clear apocalyptic overtones of the regime's ideology, yet Reddles makes clear that for those committed to that monstrous project, Hitler was posited as a messiah, the Jews and other "undesirables" as a demonic force to be destroyed, with the gas chamber and crematorium as a means of supposedly purging the world. Just as medieval Joachimites saw the Age of the Spirit as a cleansing through tribulation, so did the Nazis understand the Third Reich as eliminating decadence and degeneracy while establishing racial purity. Gregor Strasser, an important Nazi theoretician who would be murdered in 1934 during the Hitler-ordered purge known as the Night of the Long Knives, bemoaned the "dreadful hopelessness in the souls of humanity, a disintegration of all firm values.... The core itself is eaten away and had to a great extent already gone missing."[32] For these men, notes Reddles, it was a "time of apocalypse or salvation in a millennial Third Reich. Hitler and his disciples came to believe that they were not only fortunate witnesses to the birth of a New Age but divinely chosen to help bring it into being."[33]

Overemphasizing the pagan aspects of Nazism can serve to obscure just how much of Hitler and Germany's antisemitism was derived from twenty centuries of Christian anti-Judaism. Fevered Christian nightmares about the apocalypse had often featured Jews as a nefarious, undifferentiated entity who conspired against their gentile neighbors and were collectively guilty of deicide. Nothing demonstrates Nazism's ultimate Christian origins more than its antisemitism. Ancient German paganism wasn't anti-Jewish; it would scarcely make sense to blame the Jews for the death of a God whom those Teutons themselves didn't believe in. Apocalypticism is the other element of Nazism that evidences its continuity with the ancient hatreds and prejudices of European Christendom, even while the millennialism offered by Hitler was particularly jaundiced and cancerous. Christians within Nazi Germany responded to Hitler in different ways; the Vatican officially entered into a 1933 treaty with Berlin known as the *Reichsconkordat* wherein the former was granted official recognition provided that it didn't politically agitate against the state. Despite that grotesque compromise, thousands of nuns and priests resisted the Nazis and would die in the concentration camps. The Nazis reacted more favorably to Protestantism, seeing Luther's Reformation as a quintessentially German rebellion against that which was foreign, and a majority of party members belonged to Protestant denominations rather than the Catholic Church.

There were exemplary manifestations of evangelical resistance to Nazism, none more so than in the form of the Confessing Church, a group of Protestant ministers and their flock who correctly understood Nazism to be a form of idolatry, with the Lutheran minister Dietrich Bonhoeffer, who was executed at the Flossenbürg Concentration Camp in 1945, as perhaps the most notable and noble martyr of Christian resistance to the Third Reich. Most Christians weren't as admirable as Bonhoeffer, however, with the movement known as the "German Christians" an example of how religious authorities often acquiesced with state power.[34] A centralized and hierarchically structured Protestant denomination that was organized by the Nazi party known as the National Reich Church was tasked by Rosenberg with the elimination of the Old Testament, the promulgating of the claim that Jesus was an Aryan, and placing on the altar of every church a copy of Hitler's *Mein Kampf*. Doris L. Borgen writes in *Twisted Cross: The German Christian Movement in the Third Reich* how "German Christians phrased their affirmation of... [Hitler's goals] in the language of the apocalypse."[35] Not only did the German Christians attempt to eliminate their faith of any elements of Judaism, but they also rejected the traditional morality of Christianity as an imposition of a Semitic "herd" mentality onto the virile German psyche. The pastors and party officials involved in the construction of the National Reich Church consented to the minister Adolf Bartels's belief that Judaism must somehow be purged from its historical and theological relationship to the church, that a "deep connection between Christianity and Germanness can only be achieved when it is released from this unnatural connection."[36]

Among the German Christians there was a sense that Hitler was the fulfillment of the Reformation, if not a type of messiah himself, while the members of the Confessing Church rather felt that *der Führer* was more likely identified with a different eschatological character. What all of these various denominations and movements demonstrate is how much of World War II can be understood through the lens of competing eschatology, all the more so because, true to Nietzsche's prophecy at the turn of the twentieth century, World War II would be the most violent conflagration in human history, with fifty million dead during the years of conflict, including eleven million who perished in the

Holocaust. These years were an example of not just the horrors of irrationality and evil, but of the very specific dangers which apocalyptic zeal can engender.

"World War II and the Holocaust should be seen as examples of an induced apocalypse," writes Reddles.[37] The attempted destruction of European Jewry and the subsequent murder of six million Jewish women, men, and children was a conscious, deliberate, organized action of the Nazi state and it was undertaken for specifically millennial reasons. Reddles's observation about the apocalyptic nature of the Third Reich's policy isn't just a comment about its violence, but also about its intentions. It speaks to the organizational goals of Hitler and his state, as well as the irrationality of the Holocaust itself. In the waning days of the war, instead of diverting precious resources to the front, the Nazis used train lines and fuel to transport innocent people to their murder. As a matter of military strategy this was nonsensical; as an issue of fervent and insane belief, it was perfectly consistent with the apocalyptic faith of the Nazis. This was, after all, precisely what Hitler had promised to do since the beginning of his political career, and in that regard, he was nothing if not honest.

Such nihilism was a twisted variety of belief forged through anti-belief, an eschaton which compelled meaning, reason, and truth themselves to be sacrificed within the gas chamber in a ritual of mechanized and industrial barbarity. Nazism in this regard isn't a repudiation of Western values, disturbingly, but rather a consummation of them; its apocalypse the fullest willing of the death drive which often sporadically burst forth in popular enthusiasms from the Rhineland massacres onward, but which always remained implicit within European civilization. According to the philosopher George Steiner, the Holocaust was an attempt to destroy the abstract, the transcendent, the universal, and the cosmopolitan in favor of the idols of racialized blood and nationalistic soil by attacking the Jews as a symbol of those first set of values, claiming that "When it turned on the Jew, Christianity and European civilization turned on the incarnation—albeit an incarnation often wayward and unaware—of its own best hopes."[38] The Holocaust thus signified not millennium, but anti-millennium.

Nihilism is the operative mode of fascism, not just of Nazism as a particular subset of fascism, but every manifestation of such totalitarian politics from Spain to Japan. The Spanish Falangist creed of "Long Live Death!" coined by José Millán-Astray, the founder of the Spanish Legion and loyal lieutenant to General Francisco Franco, encapsulates the central faith of that later political philosophy, as does the Italian fascist and Futurist artist F. T. Marinetti's contention that "War is the hygiene of the world."[39] Militarism, authoritarianism, oppression, not as means to an end but as ends unto themselves. This aspect of fascism is best explained by Umberto Eco's rubric in his celebrated essay from *The New York Review of Books* on the phenomenon he identifies as "Ur-Fascism," writing that such a dogma is based on an irrational "cult of *action for action's sake.*

Action being beautiful in itself, it must be taken before, or without, any previous reflection. Thinking is a form of emasculation."[40]

The middle of the twentieth century saw the emergence of the most virulent and destructive form of apocalypticism in fascism, even if it's not commonly interpreted as such. Dreams of national glory and resurrected empires and the interdependence of the business class and the state are certainly features of fascism, but ultimately its central characteristic is this valorization of death and a desire to immanentize the eschaton, not in the establishment of a utopia but as pure dystopia. Eco explains that in fascism there is "an Armageddon complex. Since enemies have to be defeated, there must be a final battle. . . . But such a 'final solution' implies a further era of peace . . . which contradicts the principle of permanent war. No fascist leader has ever succeeded in solving this predicament."[41] Fascism, as understood in this interpretation, isn't just an apocalyptic movement—it's apocalypse itself, unceasing and unending, the dragon forever swallowing its own tail.

What distinguishes World War II is that it was such a complete battle between contrasting and opposing eschatologies. Every major power among the Allies and the Axis fundamentally had an understanding of teleology and they each fought for different millenniums, but where the definition of perfection was often completely different. The most obvious example of this is in the Soviet Union, as millennial a state as has ever existed, the embodiment of Marx's own Joachimite dialectics from the previous century. Just as the Nazis believed that theirs was a third dispensation, so too did the Soviet communists adhere to that Marxist faith which held that the collectivization of the economy and the common ownership of the means of production would eventually lead to the withering away of all class differences and the state. As such, fascism was inarguably a revanchist response to the Bolshevik Revolution, an attempt from the capitalist class to marshal reactionary politics to their own benefit and to violently respond to the communists.

If during the Russian Revolution, which convulsed through the capitals of Europe in a manner not seen since 1789, the Bolsheviks desired to create a new man through the overthrow of capitalism, to bring about a millennium on earth, then the fascists sought to create an answer to that millennium with their own compelled eschaton. Perhaps it's an anemic interpretive matrix that reduces fascism and Soviet totalitarianism into the same system but through a mirror, yet in addition to the brutality of these respective systems their biggest similarity lay in the sense that they were vanguards for the transformation of history itself, that they could in some sense bring about a new Edenic age. Fascists were as obsessed with race as communists were with class, and both saw in their respective millenniums an elimination of difference as being the means for bringing about the eschaton.

The faith which emerged most victoriously from the ashes of the most violent war in human history was also the millennial system which was the oldest of the three. Before Marxism or fascism there was that *novum ordum* of Thomas Paine, the eschatological system of liberal democracy as filtered through the American myth. President Franklin Delano Roosevelt, in his Third Inaugural Address of 1941, said that "democracy alone has constructed an unlimited civilization capable of infinite progress in the improvement of human life," a revolutionary and also unmistakably millennial assertion, in direct contraposition to the millennial assertions of an Adolf Hitler. Roosevelt specifically conflated this millennial faith in freedom with the American experience, for he said in that same speech that this has been the "New World in all tongues, to all peoples, not because this continent was a new-found land, but because all those who came here believed they could create upon this continent a new life—a life that should be new in freedom."

Whether or not the historical particulars are accurate is incidental; what Roosevelt offers was as religious and millennial a creed as those being promulgated by the United States's military adversaries during World War II. With great irony then, it was only this final eschatology, the American millennialism, that would produce that ingenious mechanism which made an actual apocalypse a possibility. Such an Armageddon, however, would be initiated not by God, but by a human hand lingering above a button. America is she who ushered in the potential for an actual end of the world, who made apocalypse not something which humanity needed to wait for, but rather something which humanity could now choose.

The Destroyer of Worlds

The Nuclear Age Begins

The entire mythological framework of apocalyptic fears—the four horsemen and the Whore of Babylon, the unbreaking of the seals and the blowing of the trumpet—all of that moved from the realm of religion into that of reality at precisely 5:29 a.m. on the morning of July 16, 1945, when a false dawn arose over Alamogordo, New Mexico. No longer figuration and metaphor, allegory and symbol, but rather the explicable technical process of nuclear fission releasing energy heretofore hidden within the atom. Before the advent of nuclear weapons, apocalypse remained a fantasy of poets and prophets, an aspect of legend and myth, but after the successful detonation of the first atomic bomb in the scrub of the southwestern desert during the waning days of World War II apocalypse became something that was very real, the beginning of a system of coldly rational madness when every human on earth would forever live with the possibility that the entire planet could be irradiated in a brief nuclear war. Albert Einstein, whose theory of special relativity explained the mechanism which made this weapon possible, opined in a 1946 editorial for *The New York Times* that nuclear capability has "altered profoundly the nature of the world as we know it, and the human race consequently finds itself in a new habitat."[42] Never before did people exist under a Sword of Damocles such as this, where humanity itself was capable of enacting an apocalypse. Never before did each individual have in their mind the knowledge that a government could decide—or an accident could trigger—the extinction of humanity in a few minutes time.

History thus divides before and after 1945 in a manner that no other event matches in significance, certainly not the birth of Christ. Now every fevered nightmare from Daniel and Revelation could become simply an issue of technical knowhow and political decisions. The bomb which was detonated at Trinity had 18.6 kilotons of power, enough to vaporize the platform upon which it sat and to crystalize the desert sand into glass for hundreds of meters about ground zero, but insignificant by later nuclear standards. That which incinerated the civilian population of Hiroshima a few months later was actually a little less powerful, for as many people died during the firebombing of Tokyo as did in the atomic attacks. The same year as Hiroshima and Nagasaki, scientists at the Los Alamos National Laboratory, where the weapon was invented, calculated that it would only take around a hundred hydrogen bombs released during a hypothetical world war—such a device had yet to be built—to destroy civilization.[43] The first hydrogen bomb was tested by the United States in 1952. Today there are around 15,000 thermonuclear weapons possessed by nine different nations. According to a 1957 article in *The Atlantic*, when the British prime minister Winston Churchill was first informed of what had happened in New Mexico, he declared that the "atomic bomb is the Second Coming in Wrath."[44]

J. Robert Oppenheimer, the brilliant but troubled physicist who directed the Manhattan Project, turned toward a different set of ancient texts than did Churchill. Famously, when Oppenheimer saw the blinding flash of light released at Trinity and heard the subsequent sonic boom as the mushroom cloud plumed upward, he claimed that "We knew the world would not be the same. A few people laughed, a few people cried, most people were silent. I remembered the line from the Hindu scripture the *Bhagavad Gita*. Vishnu . . . says, 'Now I am become Death, the destroyer of worlds.' I supposed we all thought that one way or another."[45] The Trinity test is a fulcrum in any history of apocalypticism, because now the subject has moved from theory to praxis. Ingrained among everybody alive is the knowledge of an ever-present possibility of nuclear Armageddon. We are intellectually capable of being skeptical or dismissing any number of religious concepts—the atheist can deny God, the skeptic can doubt miracles, the rationalist can question the supernatural—but only the fool can pretend that apocalypse isn't real.

With the Manhattan Project humanity finally fully confirmed a theological concept, even if it required us to become God to do so. It necessitated Oppenheimer and his colleagues to sign their names to that Faustian bargain. If apocalypse wasn't real it would be necessary to invent it, and so we did. Out of the radioactive ash of the conclusion of history's most apocalyptic war, humanity's relationship to judgment day was irrevocably altered. Now that such coiled potential for utter and complete devastation existed, there would forever be a latent violence at the core of every single second following that early-morning test at Alamogordo. Apocalypse became, whether stated or not, whether conscious or not, the preoccupation and concern of every single human being, regardless of doctrine or creed. "We have somehow managed to avert our attention from the pervasive impact of the bomb on . . . our collective experience," writes Paul Boyer in *By the Bomb's Early Light: American Thought and Culture at the Dawn of the Atomic Age*, and he's right.[46] It is a symptom of madness and folly, the better paradoxically to keep everyone sane, whereby selective amnesia is required simply to function, lest one be overwhelmed by the awareness that all which stands between any of us and the complete eradication of all life on earth are a few shadowy apparatchiks in the militaries of a little under a dozen nations.

Boyer argues that in the half-decade after Trinity the United States developed roughly two different cultural responses to the atomic bomb. The first was an unalloyed enthusiasm for such weaponry and the American hegemony and supposed security which they assured. The second was a terror at the possibility of total devastation. As a parable, there is the account of a worried conversation and some back-of-the-envelope calculations made by two physicists who worked on the Manhattan Project. Hans Bethe and Edward Teller, both of Jewish background and respectively German and Hungarian refugees from Nazi Europe, were instrumental in the development of first the atomic bomb and then later the hydrogen bomb. Teller had become concerned that when the first atom bomb was detonated, so intense would the heat have been that it could potentially trigger a runaway nuclear fusion reaction throughout the atmosphere, engulfing and destroying the entire planet. In 1942, Teller went to Oppenheimer with his concerns, who in turn went to Arthur Compton, the director of the Chicago Laboratory where the Manhattan Project was inaugurated, who then enlisted the assistance of Bethe. With little of the panic exhibited by the other men, Bethe did a few quick calculations and decided that there was less than a one in three million chance that the Trinity test would consume the planet in a thermonuclear fireball.[47]

When interviewed for the *American Weekly* in 1959 by novelist Pearl S. Buck, Compton said that his concerns about the possibility of such a chain reaction were that it "would be the ultimate catastrophe. Better to accept the slavery of the Nazis than to run the chance of drawing the final curtain on mankind!"[48] Meanwhile, between nervous Teller and assured Bethe, there was a reversal as regards fears concerning nuclear weapons. Teller became the most steadfast champion of their use, from battlefield tactical nukes to deploying them to clear construction debris, while Bethe developed into an eloquent champion of disarmament and a leader in the Emergency Committee of Atomic Scientists, despite the latter being the one who had been relatively sure from some envelope math that they would not destroy the world in 1945.

In the wider culture there was a similar split between Teller's nuclear evangelism and Bethe's Casandra-like warnings about the atomic specter. The decades after World War II saw a perverse enthusiasm for all things nuclear, from the candy known as Atomic Fireballs to the strange recreation of Las Vegas tourists paying premium for hotel rooms in view of Nevada desert weapons testing, the shadow of the mushroom cloud rising over the Sands Casino and Caesar's Palace. Of course the potential horror of World War III also meant suburban families building fallout shelters in their backyards and young children undergoing warning drills during which they would huddle under their desks, as if a bit of wood and metal could protect them from a thermonuclear shockwave. Boyer explains that very quickly after the end of the war, "contemporary observers understood that a profoundly unsettling new culture factor had been introduced—that the bomb had transformed not only military strategy and international relations, but the fundamental ground of culture and consciousness,"[49] what the columnist Anne O'Hare McCormick described in *The New York Times* the day after the first attack on Japan as "an explosion in man's minds as shattering as the obliteration of Hiroshima."[50]

Apocalyptic imagery permeated atomic rhetoric within hours of Hiroshima's destruction. Harry Truman's address to the American people claimed that the United States now had the ability to harness the "basic power of the universe," while two days after Hiroshima the president would exclaim in a radio address that "We thank God that it has come to us . . . we pray that He may guide us to use in His ways and for His purposes."[51] Compton, who had been so alarmed about the possibility of setting the atmosphere on fire, would change his mind much as Teller did, telling an audience organized by the Episcopal Church in 1946 that "Atomic power is ours, and who can deny that it was God's will that we should have it?"[52] Furthermore, according to Compton, lest he be accused of merely speaking rhetorically, nuclear power was a gift of the Lord to help humanity more rapidly "become the children of God."[53]

Whether this view was uttered by the president or a physicist, the atom bomb was seen as an explosive mechanism of God's grace, a benediction bestowed upon his redeemer nation. This view was expressed not just by presidents and physicists, but country musicians as well, such as Fred Kirby in his bizarre hit written the day of Hiroshima and entitled "Atomic Power," in which he denounces those cities that "paid a big price for their sins . . . scorched from the face of the earth," as the pilots of the *Enola Gay* were, in his mind, "the mighty hand of God" who rained upon Hiroshima and Nagasaki as if they were Sodom and Gomorrah the "mighty brimstone fire."

Fear and horror were psychologically the more comprehensible responses, especially once the full scale of devastation was made apparent and the implications for such weaponry in a potential World War III became obvious to people. The British novelist Martin Booth poignantly expressed the horror of this new reality in his book *Hiroshima Joe*, about a fictional British POW who was witness to August 6, 1945, when sixty thousand women, children, and men were incinerated within a minute, and twice that number having perished from radiation sickness and burns in the following days. Booth's main character observes the flattening of whole city blocks, humans charred to ash, shadows burnt into sidewalks, and children with long strips of burned flesh hanging from their bodies; scenes from Revelation, "what no man should be made to see . . . fearing what we all must fear."[54] Journalist John Hersey had no need to fictionalize in his account *Hiroshima*, first published in *The New Yorker* in 1946. Hersey describes people whose "eyebrows . . . were burned off and skin hung from their faces and hands. . . . Some were vomiting as they walked. Many were naked or in shreds of clothing," for whom "their faces were wholly burned, their eye sockets were hollow, the fluid from their melted eyes had run down their cheeks."[55]

All of those nightmares of prophets and visions of divines, the warnings of poets and priests, had come to pass in this Japanese city. The existentialist philosopher Albert Camus, writing in the French Resistance newspaper *Combat* the day after the first attack, argued that "Our technical civilization has just reached its greatest level of savagery. We will have to choose, in the more or less near future, between collective suicide and the intelligent use of our scientific conquests. . . we are given a new source of anguish; it has all the promise of being our greatest anguish ever."[56]

We are all children of Trinity in that regard. As close as we are to that rupture in history, it's difficult to fully grapple with the effect it has had on our collective consciousness, yet whether or not a causal connection can be made between the atom bomb and the eschatological madness which followed, it is true that an eruption of apocalyptic paranoia and fear defined the second half of the twentieth century onward. The threat of actual, verifiable, measurable, objective Armageddon irrevocably altered the human condition, so that fears of the end weren't merely theological, but now political and personal as well. Among Christian fundamentalists, nuclear weapons were a prophetic sign that the work of Revelation was at hand, the invention of an actual means to destroy all life on earth an indication that the Bible's fulfillment was near. Charles B. Strozier and Laura Simich in the journal *Political Psychology* write that "it is a tenet of fundamentalist theology that humans have strayed from God's path and that this rotten, evil world will soon end in a great firestorm of apocalyptic destruction and Jesus will return to remake it."[57] While emphasizing that adherents of such a belief don't personally welcome nuclear destruction per se, Strozier and Simich both claim that atomic weapons were at least viewed as a divine tool that would bring to fruition the warnings and promise of Revelation.

Conducting a series of interviews with members of four separate fundamentalist "end times" churches in the New York City area, Strozier and Simich concluded that the nuclear threat was particularly conducive to validating beliefs in premillennial dispensationalism because of the sudden spectacular violence which such weaponry implies; nuclear flames as hot as the dragon's breath. Fundamentalist leadership often welcomed the idea of nuclear war, even if their flocks were more ambivalent about that possibility. Falwell's 1983 tract, rather bluntly titled *Nuclear War and the Second Coming of Christ*, claimed that his two main subjects were "indelibly intertwined," while Robertson in his 1982 book *The Secret Kingdom* identified Gog and Magog as the Soviet Union, claiming that World War III will involve the USSR's invasion of Israel, with Revelation having provided "a vision of nuclear bombing."[58] Preaching before a group of evangelical businessmen in 1980, some of whom had connections to the arms industry, Robertson gushed about the potential for nuclear war, declaring that "This is the real thing. This isn't a drill. This isn't a warm-up . . . God says you're in my army. Get ready."[59]

Simich and Strozier conclude that as enthusiastic as televangelists often seemed to be for the potential of nuclear war, rank-and-file members of fundamentalist churches often had a far more studied understanding of the threat. They record a pastor at an Assembly of God Church in Manhattan as anxiously saying that there is now the "Potential [for destruction] . . . more than ever," while a Baptist named Isaac who belonged to a congregation in the Bronx notes that "For the first time in history. . . we have the ability to destroy everything."[60] Interpreted through that apocalyptic lens, much of the fundamentalist response to atomic weaponry can't be siloed from the wider culture, but must rather be understood as connected to society's reaction to the possibility of complete and total nuclear war. Both psychologists conclude that "concern with end-time among fundamentalists is part of a culture in which the scientific possibility of a nuclear end haunts everyone's imagination."[61] It could be argued that if anything, nuclear weaponry had only changed the mechanism of an apocalypse which fundamentalists had always believed was approaching, but that now Hiroshima made all of us—nonbelievers as well—adamant adherents to apocalypticism, since we could see the photographs of mushroom clouds and read the descriptions of incinerated cities.

It is telling that only two decades after the advent of the nuclear age there was a flowering of American counterculture during the self-declared "Age of

Aquarius." While grossly overstated in numbers, the mélange of occult, supernatural, theurgic beliefs which motivated a certain subsection of the 1960s youth culture should be understood as in part manifesting both anxiety over nuclear weapons and millennial expectations and utopian yearnings. Drawn to practices as diverse as shamanism and astrology, the latter of which the name "Aquarian Age" came from, much of the 1960s counterculture was attracted to the idea that a great shifting was underway, that a new epoch of human understanding and consciousness was incipient. "When the Moon is in the seventh house and Jupiter aligns with Mars, then peace will guide the planets and love will steer the stars," read the lyrics of Gerome Ragni and James Rado's 1967 ersatz hippie Broadway musical *Hair* with its enthusiastic declaration that "This is the dawning of the Age of Aquarius!"

Christian fundamentalism and the Aquarian counterculture might appear diametrically opposed, but both understood modernity as undergoing a rupture, with either apocalypse, millennium, or both quickly approaching, and as potentially being brought about by a nuclear war which would wipe away the old way of doing things and inaugurate a new epoch. Fundamentalists may have been of the dragon and Aquarians of the dove, but they were clearly two sides of a related apocalypticism. These two reactions are the inheritors of a nineteenth-century religious enthusiasm, with the fundamentalists a continuation of the Millerite views on premillennial dispensationalism and the hippies the second coming of the Spiritualists who were attracted to their own heterodox and occult ideas a century before.

Of course, the 1960s counterculture was a complicated and diverse movement and it's hard to conflate all of the different attributes of it into any kind of single system, much less reduce the often vehemently secular political wing of the New Left and the attendant Black Power movement, antiwar movement, or second-wave feminism in with the California New Age focused on healing crystals and astrological charts. Yet at least among the Aquarian counterculture, there was a sense of millennial planetary realignment as both a means of humanity's redemption from the threat of nuclear weapons and the dawning of this new age of peace, love, and understanding.[62] This was the creed advocated succinctly by former Harvard psychologist and evangelist for psychedelic drugs Timothy Leary when he advised people in his 1968 *The Politics of Ecstasy* "to turn on, tune in and drop out . . . to detach yourself from involvement in secular, external social games."[63] Deep in its core, this was the dogma of a religious movement, a type of New Age Great Awakening which created an alternative society with different values and rules, all in an attempt not to overthrow humanity but to save it. As with the Spiritualists of the nineteenth century or the Münster communards of the sixteenth, there was inevitably a dark undercurrent which existed simultaneously alongside the optimism and idealism of the Aquarians, as perhaps should be expected whenever any group of people imagines the demise of one way of being and the birth of another.

Prefacing her celebrated piece about the San Francisco Haight-Ashbury counterculture with an epigraph from W. B. Yeats's apocalyptic poem "The Second Coming," essayist Joan Didion writes in her 1967 *Slouching Towards Bethlehem* that "The center was not holding. It was a country of bankruptcy notices and public-auction announcements and commonplace reports of casual killings and misplaced children and abandoned homes and vandals who misspelled even the four-letter words they scrawled. . . . People were missing. Children were missing. Parents were missing."[64] Any revolutionary potential during the Summer of Love was extinguished on the eve of the paranoid, anxious, rambling 1970s, the utopian promise of the Flower Power generation snuffed out at the Altamont Free Concert in 1969 where the Hell's Angels biker gang would beat audience members to death as the Rolling Stones played "Sympathy for the Devil." Or perhaps that generational promise was murder, with the killing of actress Sharon Tate in Los Angeles that same year. That last crime was perpetrated by followers of a two-bit hustler and aspiring rock musician named Charles Manson, who'd positioned himself as an erstwhile cult leader of the so-called Manson Family, some roughly hundred followers largely drawn from troubled backgrounds. Adherents of Manson murdered Tate and her friends at a house party in the wealthy Los Angeles neighborhood of Benedict Canyon, and then a few days later they killed a wealthy older couple, Lena and Rosemary LaBianca, in the same area.

Responsible for several other slayings, Manson fused together the aesthetics of the hippie counterculture with an ideology that could charitably be described as nihilistic and fascistic. In lieu of the tribulation, Manson taught his acolytes that society would collapse during a period known as "Helter Skelter," drawing the name from a Beatles song which he believed prophesied a coming race war between whites and Blacks. According to followers of Manson, such as murderer Charles Denton "Tex" Watson, the cult leader had mapped the book of Revelation onto lyrics from the Beatles' "White Album" and *Abbey Road*, claiming that in the coming race war all white people would be killed and afterwards the surviving Manson Family, now numbering the 140,000 who would be saved during the Tribulation according to some interpretations of Revelation, would emerge from hiding to rule over all Black people.[65]

Manson offered his own warped apocalyptic exegesis of *The Beatless*, with the prosecuting attorney from his murder trial Vincent Bugliosi recounting in his true crime classic *Helter Skelter: The True Story of the Manson Murders* how the cult leader interpreted the four horseman of the apocalypse to be John, Paul, George, and Ringo, the "locusts" mentioned by Patmos to be a reference to the band, and the issuing of "fire and brimstone" in the last book of the New

Testament to have "referred to the spoken words, the lyrics of the Beatles' songs, the power that came out of their mouths."[66] In perpetrating the murder of Tate, her friends, and the elderly LaBiancas, Manson tried to leave misleading clues, such as racially inflammatory graffiti written in the blood of his victims, to convince people that the crimes had been perpetrated by Black radicals and thus to hasten the coming race war. Chaos and apocalypse were Manson's main creed, the "Will of God," as he said in a 1981 interview with Geraldo Rivera from prison, being "whatever you wanna call it . . . you call it Jesus, call it Mohammad, call it goobybob, call it nuclear mind, call it blow the world up. . . . Whatever you wanna call it, it's still music to me."[67] With his grizzled visage and his long hair and beard, Manson may have affected the appearance of an apostolic prophet, but like other countercultural figures he was a product of pure modernity, a child of the nuclear age.

One of the strangest phenomena to emerge out of the ash of Hiroshima was the assortment of new millennial religions that are often collectively known as UFO cults. Replacing the rapture with extraterrestrial abduction, the millennium with technological perfection, and Jesus Christ with aliens riding upon a spaceship, cults which claimed that creatures from outer space would bring utopia to earth notably proliferated after the dawning of the nuclear age, an attempt to grapple with the overwhelming power of science and technology in our contemporary moment and of the seeming omnipotence of such weapons themselves. "That flying saucers and their inhabitants have come to be invested with religious meaning should not, therefore, be surprising," writes James R. Lewis in *The Gods Have Landed: New Religions from Other Worlds*. "This religious meaning can be [both] manifested in . . . explicitly religious organizations. . . . It can also be manifested less obviously, in the forms of certain themes and patterns that—when cloaked in the guise of flying machines—are not immediately recognized as religious, but which fulfill religious functions."[68]

Sects like the Aetherius Society, the Unarius Academy of Science, the Raelians, Scientology, the Universe People, and Heaven's Gate maintain a diversity of heterodox beliefs which in some aspect focused on alien intelligence. Heaven's Gate, a relatively minor group led by Marshall Applewhite, an army veteran and son of a Presbyterian minister, dominated headlines in 1997 after he and thirty-eight of his followers committed suicide in anticipation of the arrival of messianic aliens being transported upon the Comet Halle-Bop. As with many of the new religions associated with the apocalyptic connotations of unidentified flying objects, Heaven's Gate had West Coast connections.

If California gestated the utopian enthusiasms of the counterculture, then such UFO cults weren't the only aberration in that millennial project. Unlike the explicitly racist Manson, the charismatic Pentecostal preacher Jim Jones and his Peoples Temple ostensibly promoted a gospel of racial reconciliation and social justice. The first white man to adopt a Black child in the state of Indiana, Jones would alight for northern California whose social liberalism was seemingly more conducive to his initial politics. Fusing the ecstatic worship of Pentecostalism with an explicitly left-wing ideology, Jones's unusual belief system saw him advocating communal living, the abolishment of private property, and ultimately claiming to be both the reincarnation of Jesus Christ and Vladimir Lenin, preaching that if "you're born in capitalist America, racist America, fascist America, then you're born in sin. But if you're born in socialism, you're not born in sin," or as Morris describes him in *American Messiahs: False Prophets of a Damned Nation*, the minister who was a "holy rolling Marxist."[69]

The Peoples Temple had a surprising degree of mainstream political success in the environs around San Francisco, with Jones even being appointed to the city's Housing Authority Commission. Regardless of the progressive politics expressed from the pulpit, Jones oversaw his flock in an increasingly authoritarian manner. Fearing a coming nuclear exchange between the United States and the Soviet Union, he relocated hundreds of his followers to the rainforests in Guyana where they worked to build a communal utopia named Jonestown after its leader. There an unhinged Jones became convinced of his divine anointing and in 1978 he both compelled and forced 909 of his followers to drink cyanide-laced Flavor Aid in an act of "revolutionary suicide," the largest act of mass religious violence in American history until the terrorist attacks of September 11, 2001.

Almost a thousand women, children, and men died in the jungles of Guyana, many of whom we have come to understand had been coerced or openly forced into ending their lives. As with Manson, Jones was a narcissistic sociopath whose convoluted ideology was most aptly summarized as simply being an attraction to absolute power. Americans were rightly horrified by the violence of the Tate–LaBianca murders and the Peoples Temple mass suicide, but when Manson told a *Rolling Stone* interviewer in 1970 that "Anything you see in me is in you . . . I am just a mirror," there was a cracked sort of logic to his characteristic logorrheic ramblings.[70] Manson, Jones, Applewhite—as different as they all were, their scandalous and very visible violence was a reflection of the all-consuming, incipient violence that had defined humanity's existential condition ever since that New Mexico spring morning in 1945. Their madness was but a mote in the eye of the international order's all-consuming insanity when the Promethean fire of the atom was brought among the fallen exiles of Eden.

A year after the 909 deaths at Jonestown, a computer error at North American Aerospace Defense Command in Colorado Springs alerted responders that there were 2,200 Soviet nuclear-tipped intercontinental ballistic missiles incoming, with the president having seven minutes to decide whether or not to retaliate. There was a minute to spare before it was substantiated that the alert was a false alarm.[71] Had the United States responded to this false alert, the death toll would have been a few billion people in the following hour, a fiery sixty minutes constituting the entirety of World War III. This wasn't the only nuclear close call. Both human and computer error were responsible for potential nuclear launches: in 1960 when a Norwegian moonrise was interpreted by radar as a massive Soviet missile strike; in 1983 a Korean Air Lines flight 007 was shot down over Russia, having strayed into Soviet airspace and been read by a satellite early-warning system as the beginning of an American attack; and of course the week-long Cuban Missile Crisis in 1963. The individual and select madness of the twentieth century must always be understood in light of the ongoing threat of nuclear extinction, where dark prophets like Manson and Jones are but children of Oppenheimer, that destroyer of worlds. Faith in technology had brought humanity to the nuclear precipice, but each time such close calls came to bear, it was individual human wisdom which prevented the unthinkable, as close to a hopeful parable as can be derived from that sordid century.

CHAPTER TEN

Hoofbeats of the Horsemen

The Future and Apocalypse?

Imagining the End

Postapocalyptic Literature

IN THE MIDDLE of the 2020s, climate change has led to deadly heatwaves in the western United States, along with attendant droughts and wildfires, temperature highs supplanting record after record, over and over again. American infrastructure is crumbling while the federal government is interested in selling off public land to developers. Even whole communities have become privatized, as the extreme deprivations of neoliberal economic policies continue to fray the social contract. Unemployment, inflation, crime, and drug abuse are rampant, pandemics spread unchecked throughout the population, and diseases which experts had previously believed eliminated have seen a resurgence due to an irrational vaccine hesitancy among many in the public. Disinformation proliferates, and citizens increasingly turn toward bizarre alternative belief systems and conspiracy theories. Private mercenaries guard heavily armed compounds in which the wealthy cordon themselves away from the rest of the nation, while the police either fail to prevent crime or brutalize the public they've supposedly sworn an oath to protect. Gun violence is endemic throughout the country, with mass shootings every single day, often targeting the most helpless of people in schools and neighborhoods. Political extremism is on the rise, particularly reactionary ideologies which trade in noxious racist beliefs, and a strengthening Christian Nationalist vanguard sees its candidates elected to statewide positions and even federal office, further eroding the separation of church and state. The presidential standard bearer of this toxic movement is a glib and blunt celebrity candidate, a strutting and demagogic aspiring authoritarian who summarizes his own political beliefs with the slogan "Make America Great Again."

This is the world described by the seminal Black Afrofuturist science fiction author Octavia Butler in her dystopian classic *Parable of the Sower* and its sequel *Parable of the Talents*. Though critically acclaimed when first published in 1993, Butler's magnum opus had disappointing sales, readers possibly uninterested in such a depressing and unrealistic novel published a year after the United States had just elected a young and optimistic president who promised that the already booming economy could easily go green, and that the information super highway led to a technological future. "That's all anybody can do right now. Live. Hold out. Survive," says the father of Laura Olamina, the narrator and main character of Butler's novel. "I don't know whether good times are coming back again. But I know that won't matter if we don't survive these times."[1]

Parable of the Sower is more of a pre-apocalyptic novel than a postapocalyptic one, its resonance being that it describes a society which seems in the process of rapid collapse, but which is still inexpertly functioning. Butler's novel brilliantly describes a type of *hypernormalization*, whereby people are aware that everything is worse than it was before, but they're able to delude themselves into thinking that this is only a temporary predicament.[2] Narrated by Lauren Olamina, the fifteen-year-old daughter of a Baptist minister and professor, the first half of the novel is set in a gated community outside of Los Angeles, where a multiracial neighborhood of once middle-class residents have to increasingly rely on each other in defense against the extreme violence of marauding gangs. The second half of the novel follows Lauren, who in addition to being stricken with a condition known as "hyperempathy," has developed her own burgeoning religion called Earthseed based on the premise that "God is Change," as she helps lead a group from southern California toward Oregon, Washington, and Canada, where they believe conditions will be less horrific.

Butler, who died in 2006, would never live to see one of her novels on *The New York Times* bestseller list, but in 2020, some twenty-seven years after it was written, *Parable of the Sower* finally became a bestseller. It would seem that readers were now willing to pay attention for some reason. Rebecca Onion, in a 2020 article for *Slate*, hypothesizes that the parable novels "resonate right now because the apocalypse they describe is not singular but a series of them. There's no major event that wracks the United states, just an accumulation of serious problems (climate change, inequality), and second-order crises (hunger, war, an epidemic of abuse of dangerous designer drugs)."[3] Part of what's so striking about both *Parable of the Sower* and *Parable of the Talents* is this slow accumulation of horrors, as Butler eschews the Hollywood pyrotechnics of other postapocalyptic texts that deal in asteroid strikes, nuclear war, or a zombie pandemic. "I was not trying to prophesize," Butler told interviewer Joshunda Sanders of *In Motion Magazine* in 2004, "Matter of fact I was trying to give warning."[4]

There is, to be clear, a variety of complicated and at times contradictory reasons for why postapocalyptic literature is both written and read—to warn, to entertain, to inform, to titillate—and despite Butler's protestations, certainly to prophesize. If authors are weather vanes of current events, picking up vibrations and rhythms not immediately detectable by the rest of us, then *Parable of the Sower* has a despairing prediction for the remainder of our century. An ethical function of dystopian fiction, from George Orwell's *Nineteen Eighty-Four* to Margaret Atwood's *The Handmaid's Tale*, has been to provide a warning about future possibilities, but Butler's prescience is inextricably connected to her genre of Afrofuturism. Mark Dery, the critic who coined that neologism in his essay "Black to the Future" from the 1994 collection *Flame Wars: The Discourse of Cyberculture*, explains that Afrofuturism is "Speculative fiction that treats African-American themes and addresses African-American concerns in the contexts of twentieth-century technoculutre."[5] In the parable novels Lauren is Black, as are a majority of the characters, but far more important is that Butler's fears are born specifically from a deep understanding of marginalization, the awareness that it's always been the apocalypse for some group of people, somewhere. Perhaps even more importantly, Butler's own political positions as a Black writer and a feminist ensure that despite how grim both books are (a third was planned, but she died before the trilogy could be completed), there is a variety of hope as well, a spirit of resistance that imagines alternative and even utopian ways of organizing society.

Often categorized as a subset of science fiction—or "speculative fiction" if the critic is feeling high-minded –postapocalyptic literature became increasingly popular in the decades leading up to the turn of the millennium, its pertinence only increasing as a series of catastrophes from terrorism to economic collapse, authoritarianism to pandemics, are reflected within such works. "The end approaches, but the apocalypse is long lived," wrote the French philosopher Jacques Derrida in 1984, opining in the *Oxford Literary Review* how the inescapable theological "unveiling" of Revelation had seen itself supplanted by the idea of the end of days as a process.[6] Now, rather than Gabriel's trumpet, a final moment which by definition abolishes time, we have the long, grueling, seemingly never-ending horror of social collapse and nuclear winter. The Left Behind books are strictly speaking not postapocalyptic literature (even while the authors imitate some of the popular tropes of that genre), rather they're pretribulation novels, explicitly religious agitprop. Works such as Butler's, by contrast, are penned with a different purpose in mind. *The Parable of the Sower* and *The Parable of the Talents* were written with an ear to the ground, picking up on the distant rumblings of the hoofbeats of the four horsemen of the apocalypse as they ride in from the west.

Apocalyptic literature can be traced back to the period of the Babylonian exile, but postapocalyptic literature is a distinctly modern genre, emergent when theological conjectures were supplanted by the measurable and certain possibility that all life could be destroyed by technological means alone. "The question remains and comes back," writes Derrida, "what can be the limits of demystification?"[7] That is to say, in what manner has the red horse of war appeared in Nevile Shute's 1957 nuclear warning *On the Beach*, the black horse of pestilence in Stephen King's 1978 novel about the extinguishing super-flu *The*

Stand, the white horse of conquest in William Gibson's 1984 cyberpunk dystopia *Neuromancer*, and the pale horse of death across the entirety of the genre? And what grim fascinations draw so many to read of the destruction of life over and over, to watch the immolation of our most famous monuments and landmarks on the movie screen, or to read of nuclear war and genocide, cannibalism and torture, in comics?

Postapocalyptic literature, in that it concerns itself with themes like the end of civilization or the extinction of humanity, clearly exists in a relationship to apocalypticism. Because by definition such texts are recounted from the perspective of survivors, the name of the genre itself is paradoxical, for a truly postapocalyptic work could be only rendered in silence. As such, the genre may evidence a form of postsecularized religion, but in and of itself what's most notable about the genre's existence are the ways in which its development and popularity so obviously coincides with humanity's ability to no longer just dream of the end of days, but to enact them as well. Postapocalyptic literature, like nightmares, serves to sort through the subconscious detritus too terrifying to fully comprehend in our waking hours.

To categorize explicitly scriptural narratives, from Noah's Ark to the destruction of Sodom and Gomorrah, as postapocalyptic, is nonsensical, but those works' tropes about hearty survivors of global cataclysm being charged with rebuilding the planet do prefigure much of the genre. The earliest examples of literary texts that could be interpreted as postapocalyptic emerge during the early nineteenth century, including Romantic poems such as Lord Byron's *The Prisoner of Chillon* and Mary Shelley's novel *The Last Man*, from, respectively, 1816 and 1826. Shelley, already a visionary who inaugurated science fiction more generally with her celebrated *Frankenstein*, explored in *The Last Man* a late twenty-first century depopulated of people because of a virulent plague, describing the "shores of deserted earth, while the sun is high, and the moon waxes or wanes, angels, the spirits of the dead, and the ever-open eye of the Supreme, will behold the tiny bark . . . the LAST MAN."[8] H. G. Wells's *The Time Machine*, published in 1895, more famously prefigures many of the same themes which would preoccupy authors of postapocalyptic fiction, in his tale of his nameless Victorian physicist who builds a contraption capable of propelling him almost a million years into the future. There, in the remnants of a society that had collapsed millennia ago, he discovers that humanity has evolved into two branches—the carefree, innocent, elven Eloi, and the grotesque, laboring, subterranean Morlocks. Reflecting both the vogue for Darwinian evolution and Marxian theorization about class war, *The Time Machine* is as much trenchant social satire as it is an account of apocalypse.

It is crucial to note that genuine, full-throated, and clearly postapocalyptic fiction of the variety written by Shelley and Wells arose in the nineteenth century, when technological progress, from the combustion engine to electricity, indicated to many an irrevocable and perhaps sinister shift. Even more crucial is that, in some respects, those Victorian science fiction writers were *correct* in their intimation that the locomotive and telegraph, the light bulb and phonograph, represented a point of no return, that technological and environmental collapse would perhaps be the inevitable result of burning coal dug from the ground. Geologists have argued that the earliest days of the Industrial Revolution, in the midst of Shelley's writing of *The Last Man*, define the inauguration of the Anthropocene, the epoch whereby humanity became capable of shaping our environment as much as our environment is capable of shaping us.[9] The very beginnings of anthropogenic climate change can be traced to the nineteenth century, with scientists noting that the burning of fossil fuels, first coal and later oil, would release carbon dioxide into the atmosphere and create a runaway warming effect for the planet. But it was the twentieth century in which nightmares of the end of the world—or perhaps wish fulfillments for the urge to death—would proliferate in books and comics, television and film, video games and music.

"The apocalypse is everywhere right now," writes Mark Payne in *Flowers of Time: On Postapocalyptic Fiction*, arguing that the contemporary popularity of the form is because "Postapocalyptic fiction is political theory in fictional form. Instead of producing arguments in favor of a particular form of life, it shows what it would be like to live that life."[10] Inevitably postapocalyptic fiction is haunted by the pastoral, by the fantasy that civilization and all of its degradation can be erased. What it holds is the promise of a do-over; at their best such works express a utopian yearning, though at their worst there can be a sadistic glee at wanton destruction, what Ursula Heise dismisses as "apocaholism."[11] The unstated fantasy of the zombie film is to acquire the freedom to finally murder your next-door neighbor.

As with any literary theory which relies too heavily on narratological conventions, it may be impossible to derive much of a unified theory of postapocalyptic fiction beyond the rather prosaic observation that an upswell of interest in these stories which feature "small groups of beleaguered survivors . . . banding together to outsmart zombies or crazed survivalists, and generally doing their best to get by on a planet ravaged by pollution, consumerism, and reckless resource extraction" as Payne describes them,[12] evidences an awareness of our actual dire circumstances regarding planetary survival, as we're all pursued by those twin demons of climate collapse and nuclear holocaust. Then there is Butler's claim about postapocalyptic fiction being written to warn people, the Cassandra Effect of the would-be prophets who can sense the gathering doom while everyone else merrily continues in their quotidian existence. As uncanny as it can be to read Butler's novels in the decade in which they were set and to have the sense that the author was able to understand future trends better than sociologists and economists, it's not a rare quality of the best of the genre. For example, one of the most powerful of stories concerning nuclear war was published in *The Saturday Evening Post* in 1937, eight years before Hiroshima. Stephen Vincent Benet, who is most celebrated for his Faustian parable "The Devil and Daniel Webster," prefigured the template of much postapocalyptic fiction with "The Place of the Gods," though the story is normally anthologized as "By the Waters of Babylon."[13]

Benet's story follows the coming-of-age trial of a young man who is a member of a hunter-gatherer tribe called only "the Hill People," tasked by his priest father to travel into the ruins of a city known as the "Place of the Gods" to scavenge for metal. Crossing the river Ou-dis-son which separates the domain of the Hill People from the skeletal flooded metropolis that is overgrown with foliage, the narrator clambers through the remnants of what had obviously been a sophisticated civilization, now long perished. With an unsettling prescience, Benet's language recalls accounts of cities destroyed in nuclear conflagration; as the narrator first espies the ruined towers, he recounts how "Very great they were, and wonderful and broken—broken in the time of the Great Burning when the fire fell out of the sky."[14] As the story progresses, it becomes clear to the reader that this isn't some Aztec or Mayan city overgrown in the jungle, but rather the remains of New York; the towers are skyscrapers, the "temple" in the heart of the metropolis is Grand Central Station. "We shall go to the Place of the Gods—the place new-york," concludes Benet, "We shall look for the images of gods . . . the gods Lincoln and Biltmore and Moses."[15] Inspired by the aftermath of the Luftwaffe's attack on Guernica, Benet's story shares narrative and thematic qualities with other works of nuclear fiction which would become common, evoking later science fiction classics from Walter Miller's 1959 *A Canticle for Leibowitz* to the massive film franchise based on Pierre Boulle's 1963 novel *Planet of the Apes*.

Benet's story warns of the inevitable decline of American civilization, envisioning a far-future community that exists in a stereotypically indigenous state of nature, where technology and science are only understood through the language of myth. This cyclical understanding of civilization—of rise and fall and perhaps rise again—was certainly not novel with Benet; the story shows the clear evidence of the German historian Oswald Spengler's reactionary philosophy as expressed in *The Decline of the West* published fifteen years before, whereby the inevitable conclusion of any peoples is that the "whole pyramid of cultural man vanishes. It crumbles from the summit, first the world-cities, then the provincial forms, and finally the land itself. . . . At the last, only the primitive . . . remains, alive, but robbed of its strongest and most promising elements."[16] Decline, obviously, is a theme traceable back to antiquity itself, with its myth of a Golden Age, but Benet's mention of the "Great Burning" eerily has more of Hiroshima and Nagasaki about it than Sodom and Gomorrah.

Canticle for Leibowitz is one of the most celebrated of postapocalyptic narratives, in which Miller had the benefit (if that word can be used) of nuclear hindsight, his classic published a bit over a decade after the conclusion of World War II. Like Benet, Miller imagines a future more primitive than our present, and in this regard he has the example to draw upon of the medieval world looking back on classical antiquity, but he also appropriates the Spenglerian cycles of rise, fall, rise, and fall again. The narrative is divided into three distinct parts—respectively titled "Fiat Homo," "Fiat Lux," and "Fiat Voluntas Tua"—with each set at three wildly different future ages. Miller's novel begins some five centuries into the future, after a nuclear holocaust has returned humanity to a Dark Age and our current era is spoken of in the hushed incompleteness of myth. He envisions the church as being the primary repository of knowledge in a manner similar to that same role during the Middle Ages. Just as philosophy and literature would be copied down by monks in scriptoria after the long eclipse of Rome's fall, so too would the church be responsible once again for preserving humanity's cultural posterity. The characters of *A Canticle for Leibowitz* are haunted by the ancient nuclear calamity which they're incapable of fully understanding, where they "visualized a Fallout as half-salamander, because, according to tradition, the thing was born in the Flame Deluge, and as half-incubus who despoiled virgins in their sleep, for, were not the monsters of the world still called 'children of the Fallout?'"[17]

The primary character in "Fiat Homo" is a monk in the Order of Leibowitz, named for a Jewish electrical engineer who converted to Catholicism and sought refuge in a Cistercian abbey in the Utah desert following the "Flame Deluge" which destroyed the world. Brother Francis Gerard, a novice in the Order of Leibowitz, holds Lenten vigil in the irradiated landscape menaced by roving gangs of mutants; he will ultimately be involved in the successful canonization proceedings for the founder of his abbey, though the monk will be murdered in the desert as he returns from "New Rome" (implied to be Salt Lake City). By the early fourth millennium of "Fiat Lux," culture has returned to a relatively high degree of development, roughly corresponding to the Renaissance in our timeline, but with scholars during this new period able to build on a higher level of knowledge preserved at the abbey, so that the section ends with the reinvention of the light bulb. Throughout the middle portion of the narrative, Miller details the rise of nation-states out of the chaos of the previous Dark Ages, the return of learning, and a new philosophical rationalism which encourages empirical science and its attendant technological innovations. By "Fiat Voluntas Tua," in the year 3781, civilization has now surpassed the level where it was when nuclear war initiated a precipitous fall, much as in the twentieth century we had advanced not just beyond the Middle Ages and the Renaissance, but classical Rome as well. Now the Order of Leibowitz exists in a world not just where nuclear weapons have been reinvented, but also of starships and space colonization. Nation-states have coalesced into massive globe-spanning hegemons, the equivalent of superpowers in Miller's day, with everyone precipitously balanced during a cold war between the Atlantic Confederacy and the Asian Coalition.

A Canticle for Leibowitz ends just as that cold war flares into a second apocalyptic nuclear conflagration, with the monks of Leibowitz departing earth in a starship, and the hope that this cycle of history might be broken amidst the stars. "Are we doomed to do it again and again?" asks Miller, "Have we no choice but to play the Phoenix in an unending sequence of rise and fall? Assyria, Babylon, Egypt, Greece, Carthage, Rome, the Empires of Charlemagne and the Turk: Ground to dust and plowed with salt."[18]

If *Canticle for Leibowitz* expressed nuclear anxieties by reenacting historical societal traumas of civilizational collapse, then the cultural memory of pandemic lodged deep within the collective psyche makes it a common subject of postapocalyptic writing as well. Pandemic is almost as much of a mainstay of the genre as is nuclear war—the fourteenth-century Black Death transposed onto our contemporary moment. Horror writer Stephen King's massive 1978 *The Stand* is one of the most notable examples of that conceit, largely eschewing the faux-medical language of works like Michael Crichton's 1969 *The Andromeda Strain* or Robin Cook's 1987 *Outbreak* in favor of an explicitly theological allegory about the battle between good and evil amidst the ashes and rubble of civilization. A genetically engineered biological weapon known as the "super flu" escapes from containment, killing an astounding 99 percent of the population over the course of one summer. Following the virtual extinction of humanity, King's protagonists are sorted into Manichean camps, with the angelic heading toward Boulder, Colorado, drawn by dream visions sent by the 106-year-old daughter of slaves named Mother Abigail, and the wicked compelled to Las Vegas by the mysterious and demonic drifter Randall Flagg. In his 1994 nonfiction *Danse Macabre*, King explained the partial impetus for *The Stand*, writing that he had wanted to craft an epic which did for the United States what J. R. R. Tolkien's fantasy classic *The Lord of the Rings* did for England, that his purpose was to write about the Captain Trips pandemic as an explicitly mythopoeic story. Certainly the contention that "Life was such a wheel that no man could stand upon it for long. And it always, at the end, came round to the same place again" has its resonances with the medieval cult of Fortuna so in vogue during the years of the Black Death.[19]

The Stand, as a novel about pestilence, is intimately concerned with physicality, with the way in which the plague makes the body fail, the eruption of sores and boils, the coughing up of phlegm and blood. Captain Trips, as with the Black Death, is marked by a horrific rapidity, so scores of decomposing corpses are left in the streets of Manhattan and the fields of Maine, and the infected fill fleeing cars lining the Lincoln Tunnel and are scattered throughout hospital halls. Apocalypse provides an incongruous union of the abstract and the concrete; to envision a time when there shall be no time is the height of metaphysical speculation, yet the end of the world frequently dwells on the specifics of bodily pain, on those four horsemen bringing pestilence, famine, and war.

The highly unusual subset of postapocalyptic fiction dealing in zombies perhaps most literalizes the indignity of being a body, of imagining the severity of base appetites in a crowd of soulless corpses somehow animated with *élan vital.* Originally, the concept of the zombie was drawn from Haitian Voudon, the syncretic faith of West African religious beliefs and Catholicism, where the creature was more an alchemically enslaved person than a reanimated corpse, but it was the filmmaker George Romero who brilliantly reimagined the monster in his pentalogy that began with the 1968 B-movie masterpiece *Night of the Living Dead.* Inaugurating not just his own franchise, but a cultural phenomenon that over the decades has proliferated in popularity across works like Danny Boyles's 2002 horror film *28 Days Later* and the comic book series *The Walking Dead,* which ran from 2002 until 2019 and was adapted into a popular cable television series, Romero transformed the lumbering zombies of Voudon into a seemingly viral-infected creature of no conscience but pure rage, a resurrected corpse whose only desire is to feast on the flesh of the living. Romero's filmography is cagey on the cause of the zombie apocalypse; *Night of the Living Dead* attributes it to "radiation from Venus," while in *28 Days Later* the sufferers are infected with a "rage virus." Reasons are incidental, however, as the tagline of the original film in Romero's franchise made the religious implications of his apocalypse clear—"When there's no more room in hell, the dead will walk the earth."

Zombie films have been theorized from multiple critical perspectives; Romero's original films often evidence a politically countercultural commitment. The hero of *Night of the Living Dead* was a Black man, a notable fact in a film made in the violent summer of 1968. *Dawn of the Dead,* meanwhile, was filmed in a shopping mall in Monroeville, Pennsylvania, and has often been interpreted as a smart critique of American consumer culture. There is, of course, the aspect of pure violent spectacle in zombie films which, beyond the exceptions of literary works like Max Brooks's 2006 *World War Z: An Oral History of the Zombie War* or Colson Whitehead's *Zone One,* is so clearly cinematic.

Apocalypse has often been a topic for summer blockbusters, and audiences delight in seeing wanton destruction and gross suffering, our monuments and cities destroyed, pulverized, incinerated, whole populations eradicated. The director Roland Emmerich is the great master of this sort of entertainment, particularly in his spectacularly popular 1996 popcorn flick *Independence Day,* in which massive alien spacecraft leading an invasion force destroy the Empire State Building, the White House, and the US Bank Tower, while also obliterating the rest of New York, Washington DC, and Los Angeles. The highest-grossing film of that year, with the largest preopening to date and the quickest to make 150 million dollars at the box office, *Independence Day* is a totem of the mid-1990s, of American triumphalism between the collapse of the Soviet Union and the turn of the millennium, when enemies had to be imagined. After the terrorist attacks of September 11, 2001, brought about by an Islamic fundamentalist apocalyptic death cult, there was some hand wringing among the punditocracy that the sort of escapist fantasy offered by Emmerich's films would cease to have appeal to Americans traumatized by seeing actual skyscrapers implode on live television, and yet Emmerich lucratively took on climate change in 2004's *The Day After Tomorrow* and the Mayan apocalypse in *2012*, from that same year.

If apocalypse has long been fodder for suburban movie theaters, the turn of the actual millennium saw a new respect for the literary possibilities of the genre, as such narratives migrated from their cordoned siloes of genre fiction into more critically acclaimed literary fiction. Emily St. John Mandel's 2014 pandemic novel *Station Eleven*, about a traveling troupe of Shakespearean performers amidst the collapse of civilization, received accolades normally reserved for conventional literary fiction, as did Lauren Groff's novel *Arcadia* from two years earlier, which was set in what was then the near future and involved that decade ending with a fast-moving, contagious respiratory illness that kills millions of people.

No work contributed more to the new-found respect for postapocalyptic fiction, however, than the famously taciturn and critically acclaimed author Cormac McCarthy's relentlessly despairing 2006 novel *The Road*, which went on to become the rare science fiction book to win a Pulitzer Prize for Fiction. Taking place after an unnamed calamity has rendered the world almost completely inhospitable to life, *The Road* features an unnamed father and his young son making their way across a burnt, blighted, and devastated landscape—bereft of other humans except for marauding cannibals—in an attempt to reach the coast where they believe there will be a greater chance of long-term survival. In unsparing, unsentimental, and characteristically minimalist prose, McCarthy's postapocalypse is almost parable without referent, allegory without cipher, as much a sentiment, a mood, a nightmare as it is a narrative, with his elegant descriptions of the "cold and the silence. The ashes of the late world carried on the bleak and temporal winds to and fro in the void. Carried forth and scattered and carried forth again. Everything uncoupled from its shoring. Unsupported in the ashen air. Sustained by a breath, trembling and brief."[20]

That imagining the end has become such a preoccupation during a moment where the end itself seems less remarkable to imagine isn't surprising. If postapocalypse functions as entertainment or warning, titillation and prophecy, then in the waning days of the Anthropocene it offers us something else—recognition.

To reduce postapocalypse to escapism, especially during this period in our history, seems slightly delusional. It's hard to take your mind off of climate change, pandemic, and authoritarianism in a darkened movie theater where you have to sit at least six feet away from your closest fellow audience member. There is the possibility that postapocalypse offers us a mirror as much as it does a phantasmagoria. Critic Frederic Jameson famously observed in *The Seeds of Time* that it is "easier to imagine the end of the world than to imagine the end of capitalism," and he's correct of course—all of those survivors in postapocalyptic narratives foraging for Campbell's soup and cans of Coca Cola.[21] "We can now revise that and witness the attempt to imagine capitalism by way of imagining the end of the world," Jameson writes.[22]

Yet there is another possibility in postapocalypse, not just relentless destruction and despair, but the possibility of the world being reenergized, of being born again, of the dove emerging from the dragon. Just as every millennium necessitates an apocalypse, so every apocalypse may reveal a millennium. There is the possibility of inequity and injustice being eliminated, of a new birth of freedom. Apocalypse can be the mother of Utopia. As despairing as Butler's *The Parable of the Sower* is, the author never loses sight of the radical possibilities of the moment, of redemption, emancipation, and liberation as available within any second, even as the world burns. Because despite the heat and fire, this world is still capable of beauty, where Butler describes a "glint of water . . . visible in the distance through the trees and bushes. The world is full of painful stories. Sometimes it seems as though there aren't any other kind and yet I found myself thinking how beautiful that glint of water was through the trees."[23]

Assured of the Singularity

Techno-Utopianism

Gary Kasparov, the Russian-born World Chess Champion and among the most brilliant strategists to ever play the game, lost to an IBM supercomputer named Deep Blue in 1997. It's assumed chess requires cunning and guile, empathy and elegance, but Deep Blue was able to simply beat Kasparov with nothing but his programming, no soul but algorithm. Losing a chess game is a prosaic affair, except when the person who has lost is the greatest player in the world and the winner isn't conscious and lacks all interiority. Kasparov wrote in *How Life Imitates Chess* that the game is a "unique cognitive nexus, a place where art and science come together in the human mind, and are then refined and improved by experience,"[24] a description of an emphatically human activity, except of course it apparently isn't. Six games were played in this New York City rematch in 1997, a year after Kasparov had roundly defeated Deep Blue, except this time the computer outright won two of the six games and played the grandmaster to three draws. In that final game of the set, Deep Blue sacrificed a knight, somewhere making the decision in its wiring that the elimination of this piece was justified. Kasparov assumed that it was a mistake, that the computer wasn't capable of the artful error in service of the greater strategy. He was wrong, and his defenses became scrambled. Deep Blue beat the greatest player of the game in only twenty moves.

This is a fable about man versus machine, with Kasparov as the nebbish John Henry, except the locomotive in this version drives over him. Pundits were equally disturbed and triumphant; the iconic American company IBM had bested a Russian chess master less than a decade after the fall of the Soviet Union, yet it also heralded that mankind's unique genius was being supplanted by the computers programed by that same corporation. Reflecting on his loss to Deep Blue some twenty years later in his book *Deep Thinking: Where Machine Intelligence Ends and Human Creativity Begins*, Kasparov notes that by 2017 "you can download any number of free chess apps for your phone that rival any human Grandmaster. You can easily imagine a robot in my place . . . circling inside the tables and defeating thirty-two of the world's best human players at the same time."[25] In just two decades, Deep Blue's vanquishing of Kasparov had become almost unimpressive. The difference was due to something called Moore's law, and for an assortment of Silicon Valley prophets who could variously be called techno-utopians or Transhumanists, it signaled either the emergence of an apocalyptic dragon, of a millennial dove, or both.

The earliest "computer," in any modern sense of the word, goes back almost two hundred years to 1833 and mathematician Charles Babbage's "Analytical Engine," a mechanical contraption that calculated by using punch cards, and which set the basic template for such technology well into the twentieth century. The first analog computer which was powered by electricity was a device used on a US Navy submarine as early as 1938, yet throughout the duration of World War II the word "computer" was defined as a person who literally "computes" numbers together (a task that in government laboratories was often given to teams of young women). During the war, the British operated a computer laboratory at Bletchley Park, the site of the famed Enigma machine designed by Alan Turing, father of contemporary computer science, which was instrumental in cracking German military codes. The Cold War necessitated massive government and corporate funding of computer technology which directly led to the cybernetic revolution, the development of devices as distant from Babbage's machine as a spaceship is from a kite.

Many of these contraptions were massive—the US government's ENIAC machine, or the Electronic Numeric Integrator and Computer, as designed by mathematician John von Neumann in 1945, took up several floors of an office building on the campus of the University of Pennsylvania. It's computational abilities were infinitesimally less than those of an average cellphone today, a testament to the significance of semiconductors, transistors, and integrated circuits, all perfected within a few decades after the war. Gordon Moore, the director of research at Fairchild Semiconductors, wrote about general trends in computing technology for *Electronics* magazine in 1965, defining his titular law by explaining that "complexity for minimum component costs has increased at a rate of roughly a factor of two per year . . . this rate can be expected to continue, if not to increase."[26]

Moore's law is not an inviolate dictate of the universe, it is merely the observation of a trend, though its discoverer has yet to be proven wrong. The implications of Moore's article were that computers would continue to get smaller and more powerful at an increasing rate, as has been borne out since 1965. The implications have been staggering, not just technologically, but economically, socially, politically, and culturally as well. From the age of ENIAC to that of the iPhone, the cybernetic revolution has seen the invention of personal computers, the proliferation of the internet and all of its attendant alterations to everyday life, the rise of smartphones, social media, virtual reality, and artificial intelligence.

Deep Blue is now primitive in comparison to deep fakes and deep machine learning, when programs like Generative Pre-Trained Transformers are able to produce text that reads like it was written by a human, or where the application Dall-E can manufacture in a matter of seconds visual images that look as if they were painted by a person. It is an exponential improvement in technological advancement that has happened so rapidly that most adults living today can mark these tremendous changes in the course of our own lives. Following the upward chart graphed by an application of Moore's law, it's been argued among a minority of computer scientists, though an influential minority, that we're decades away from a moment in which our computer systems become so advanced that we're no longer capable of understanding them ourselves; that artificial intelligence will have ascended through its own efforts to a transcendent level of comprehension, at which point humanity itself will be functionally obsolete.

For the faithful who believe in this messianic "technological Singularity," as it is known, the question becomes whether the new digital gods of silicon will be benevolent to their creators or not. Swedish philosopher Nick Bostrom, in his book *Superintelligence: Paths, Dangers, Strategies* (blurbed by Bill Gates), asks if the "internet might one day 'wake up'? Could the internet become something more than just the backbone of a loosely integrated collective superintelligence—something more like a virtual skull housing an emerging unified super-intellect?"[27] Exploring both the benefits and dangers of this computerized deity, Bostrom predicts that around the year 2040 we will have reached the technological Singularity, forever changing what it means to be human, to be conscious. For believers in a coming technological Singularity, whether it bodes an apocalyptic overthrow of humanity by our silicon slaves or the arrival of a millennial moment in which our machines surpass our intelligence and usher in a new dispensation in consciousness, the Kasparov defeat still stands as a testament to the coming shift: the first moment that human genius could be shown to be limited, to be potentially obsolete, when compared to the algorithms and programs which structure our machines. Deep Blue announced itself as a prophet for the Singularity.

What might the Singularity be like? Proponents have claimed that with its seemingly infinite calculating power, an artificial intelligence that's virtually omnipotent would be able to simulate realities within its mind, that it could bode a form of digital immortality for all of us, as our consciousness are downloaded as software, perhaps even the simulation and thus resurrection of the dead. Engineer and futurist Ray Kurzweil, one of the most prominent evangelists for the Singularity, claims in the documentary *Transcendent Man* that the coming decades bode an artificial intelligence–generated virtual reality that "will have all of the features of real reality plus a lot more that you can choose from millions of virtual environments."[28] In this brave new world, you can be "someone else, you don't have to pick the same boring body every time; you can be different people and different situations and over time our biological bodies will become obsolete."[29] Kurzweil has even claimed to interviewers that he believes the Singularity will not just preserve and expand human consciousness in the form of software, but that it will be able to recreate the dead, such as his own father, whom he told an ABC interviewer in 2011 will be "more like my father than my father would be, were he to live."[30]

Those who adhere to this faith in the Singularity maintain that we are approaching an eschaton that will see the expansion of consciousness, the resurrection of the dead, and the triumph of the living spirit over dead matter (or at least the triumph of our minds as software). Resonances to Christian eschatology couldn't be clearer, even while the vast majority of such techno-utopians maintain that their metaphysics are strictly materialist and their epistemology totally scientific. Hans Moravec, a computer scientist and researcher at Carnegie Mellon University, as well as another prominent advocate for the imminent arrival of the Singularity, maintains that "we are most likely to find ourselves reconstituted in the minds of superintelligent successors, or perhaps in dreamlike worlds (or AI programs) where psychological rather than physical rules dominate," as he argued in a 1998 paper entitled "Simulation, Consciousness, Existence" which was uploaded to CMU's Field Robotics Center's website.[31] Asked by journalist Ed Regis, who interviewed Moravec for his account *Great Mambo Chicken and the Transhuman Condition: Science Slightly Over the Edge*, what the difference was between his own beliefs and those of his wife who was a born-again Christian, Moravec confessed the similarities. Regis writes that both Moravec and his wife "were really, at bottom, interested in the same thing, which is to say, true immortality, life everlasting in the form of pure consciousness."[32] In lieu of the day of judgment there would instead be the Singularity, but ironically the result would be indistinguishable.

Singularitarianism is strongly related to other attendant movements which believe that the future will see an inevitable superhuman emergence, such as the aforementioned transhumanists. That grouping of thinkers, which arguably includes figures like Bostrom, Kurzweil, and Moravec, claim that any number of technologies are just on the horizon, from cryonics to the "downloading" of minds, but the result will be a type of simulated paradise which shall be constructed by our machines themselves. This shift is what Kurzweil in *The Age of Spiritual Machines: When Computers Exceed Human Intelligence* describes as a "spiritual process that will make us more godlike."[33]

Journalist Meaghen O'Gieblyn, who was raised as an evangelical Christian but has since left the faith, notes the clear parallels in *God, Human, Animal, Machine: Technology, Metaphor, and the Search for Meaning*, describing Kurzweil's writing as being like "all classic works of revelation . . . unfolded with the kind of elegant simplicity that is easily mistaken for truth."[34] She compares the diagrams in *The Age of Spiritual Machines* to the premillennial dispensationalist charts examined by her fellow seminarians when she was the Moody Bible Institute, seeing Kurzweil's belief that in "Each era we were moving closer and closer to this point of culmination, when intelligence would merge with the universe and we would become divine" as a secularized eschatology.[35] That belief in the Singularity strains scientific credulity, despite the protestations of its enthusiasts, and that it so clearly mirrors Abrahamic beliefs about the end of time is of no accounting to most of its proponents who claim the utmost rationalism. Arguably such Silicon Valley fervency is its own variety of American Great Awakening, perhaps not so different from those revivals of the past.

Singularitarianism would seem a fringe belief, except it's been promoted by a number of influential figures. Bostrom, Kurzweil, and Moravec are all well-published scholars at respected institutions. Despite its anodyne name, the Machine Intelligence Research Institute in Berkeley, founded by computer scientist Eliezer Yudkowsky and funded with Silicon Valley endowments, is explicitly tied to work related to the Singularity. Business magnates like Elon Musk and Peter Thiel have, to varying degrees and with some predictable inconsistency, promoted theories that could be broadly considered techno-utopian. Regardless of how bizarre or unlikely the Singularity would seem to most, *belief* in the Singularity has proven to be hugely influential, at least because of who happens to believe in it.

Longtermism is a particular iteration of techno-utopian faith, ostensibly born from utilitarian social philosophies that go back to the eighteenth century but smoothed over by the greater knowledge of our own era. Associated with the Scottish philosopher William MacAskill, longtermism emerged from a variety of staid, ethically scrupulous utilitarianism which demanded, among other things, that people donate as much of their surplus income as possible to alleviate the suffering of other people. For thinkers like MacAskill, capitalism could be a useful tool for acquiring surplus profit and using it to improve the greatest possible number of lives, such as by buying mosquito nets for communities in developing countries to help prevent malaria, or funding vaccination efforts in impoverished nations. Followers of MacAskill argued that jobs which promised the largest salaries—careers in finance or technology—could be used to acquire the wealth that would then be distributed to improve the greatest number of lives. MacAskill argues in *Doing Good Better: How Effective Altruism Can Help You Make a Difference* that "innovators only collect 2 percent of the value they generate; that is, for every dollar an innovative company makes in profit, society has benefitted by fifty dollars. By becoming an innovative entrepreneur, you are, on average, producing benefits to society that far exceed your paycheck,"[36] an assertion that was bound to flatter those who work at Google, Apple, Facebook, and Microsoft.

Unsparing, unsentimental, and committed to their own version of a rigorous rationality, utilitarians like MacAskill understand philanthropy not as a sentimental exercise, but a logical one. In his 2022 book *What We Owe the Future*, MacAskill's utilitarianism is pushed to its final logical conclusion, arguing that the principle that that which is good is anything which increases happiness for the greatest number of people must also be extended to future generations of those not yet born. Influenced by Singularitarianism, longtermism developed a new logic, whereby the primary good is to ensure the coming of the digital eschaton. Gone are the mosquito nets, in comes the robot millennium. Bostrom has argued that those living in the present day have a moral duty to ensure our survival because trillions of future digital souls depend on us, we who are worth infinitely less than these silicon angels. Such rapturous sentiments are expressed by MacAskill in *What We Owe the Future*, of "ecstasy so great that I would have sacrificed all the rest of my life for a few hours of this joy."[37] Longtermism, as detailed by Emile P. Torres in *Salon*, has grown out of the effective altruism community, which has an endowment of forty-six billion dollars, regardless of how marginal their beliefs may be among the wider public.

The theology of Silicon Valley is strongly connected to the politics of Silicon Valley. Religious enthusiasms as mediated through politics—the American sectarianism of today—was inevitably shaped by the spectacular technological success of the second half of the twentieth century. Enthusiasts for the life-improving potential of technology during the halcyon days of the early cybernetic revolution often expressed political commitments that were strongly countercultural, if not in some sense anarchic. Centered in 1960s California, computer scientists absorbed much of the same Aquarian tendencies of other subcultures during that time and place. Stewart Brand, the hippy publisher of the alternative lifestyles magazine *The Whole Earth Catalogue*, influenced the early technicians of the personal computer revolution, such as Apple founder Steve Jobs. Much of hacker culture, with its "do it yourself" politics of self-sufficiency, saw in the potential of technology not the surveillance capitalism which would ultimately grow from it, but rather an alternative history which understood computers as devices of personal emancipation, a means to assault an entrenched status quo that instead became a status quo in and of itself.

Brand should be understood as a figure of the 1960s Left; an associate of the psychedelic advocate and inventor of the Electric Kool-Aid Acid Test Ken Kesey, as well as a fellow traveler to countercultural groups like the Merry Pranksters, friend to the Grateful Dead, and special adviser to California governor Jerry Brown. He was a man who believed that computers signaled a "realm of intimate, personal power . . . power of the individual to conduct his own education, find his own inspiration, shape his own environment, and share his adventure with whoever is interested,"[38] as Brand wrote, a utopian description of the World Wide Web's possibilities written in *The Whole Earth Catalogue* more than three decades before the internet became omnipresent. In the prologue to the first issue of that publication, Brand enthused "We are as gods and might as well get good at it."[39] The desire for apotheosis couldn't help but have an aristocratic tendency, and Brand's computer enthusiasms, no matter how much they were channeled in the cause of a type of political liberation, inevitably also enshrined a cult of individuality. The result is that the countercultural politics of the early computer revolution would be supplanted by a different faith, a type of libertarian neoliberalism that, if no more rational, would ultimately prove to be far more destructive.

That wealthy tech executives would embrace a politics that rejects regulation and eschews governmental intervention isn't surprising, for that tends to be true of all executives, regardless of industry. Yet the countercultural individualism of a Brand also exists in entirely more revanchist permutations as well, none more so than among the partisans of what's called the Dark Enlightenment, an ethos wholly of the dragon. An inchoate philosophical movement associated with the English theorist Nick Land and the American blogger Curtis Yarvin (who wrote under the pseudonym Mencius Moldbug), the movement promotes what's sometimes termed "Neo-Reaction," an antiliberal, antidemocratic, antifeminist, and anti-egalitarian ideology that at best engages in a sentimental monarchism and that prefigures a type of internet-inflected fascism.[40]

True to the name of the movement, those who identify as being among the Dark Enlightenment see the eighteenth century as a nadir in human thought and would rather prefer a society, politics, and culture that reinscribes aristocratic hierarchies. Yarvin, in particular, advocates for a "techno-monarchy," arguing that the computer programmers and their algorithms should be atop a rigid hierarchy rather than what they see as an ill-defined sentiment for "the people." Having made his own money from computer programing, Yarvin was attracted to the extreme libertarianism of economists like Moses Rothbard and Ludwig von Mieses, ultimately concluding that the natural superiority of certain exemplary men was hampered by a nexus of influences to which he gave the notably religious name of "The Cathedral." This was a union of government, media, and education that Yarvin claims constrains the truly exceptional and that in throwing off democracy these exalted men could ascend to their proper place in the hierarchy. On a blog that often countenanced slavery, engaged in abject racism, and denounced democracy, Yarvin would eulogize Steve Jobs by writing "And yet—there is a God in this World. . . . In everything. . . . The real work of a real King . . . who served God, or right at least, could bend small armies to obey. . . . So near we are to salvation; so infinitely far away."[41]

In Land there is a similar dark millennial yearning, especially in his embrace of "accelerationism," the belief that a vanguard must actively work to encourage societal chaos so that they can harness that disorder in the entire rebuilding of culture. Like Yarvin, Land has little regard for the Enlightenment and even less for democracy, advocating instead for a type of technologically inflected fascism. As with the Singulatarians, Land sees the coming decades as promising the virtual abolishment of the human in favor of the technological, albeit his gospel is of an entirely darker variety. Accelerationism promises a reverse millennium, the rejection and abolishment of both progress and modernity in favor of a return to the properly hierarchical structure of society that was understood as the de facto means of organization prior to the widespread embrace of democratic ideals. "The current time is a period of transition," writes Land in *Time in Transition*, "with a distinctive quality, characterizing the end of an epoch. Something—some age—is coming quite rapidly to an end."[42]

Sharing with Marxists the dogma that the contradictions of the system irrevocably mean its ultimate demise, right-wing accelerationists such as Land think that our current culture is decadent and depraved, doomed to collapse. Aphoristic, gnomic, and obscure, Land's philosophy shrieks a certain prophetic nihilism, a reactionary fusion of millennialism and apocalypse which sees the destruction of the political and social order built over the past four centuries swept away by despots and strongmen, monarchs and dictators. Except this is an antimodernity that will benefit from the advancements of modernity, an aristocracy of artificial intelligence and cyborgs, robots and computers. As Land writes in *Meltdown*, "Nothing human makes it out of the near future."[43]

The Arc of History and the Fourth Turning

Twenty-First-Century American Politics

"The road ahead will be long," intoned President-Elect Barack Obama on November 4, 2008, to a crowd of thousands in Chicago's Grant Park. "Our climb will be steep. We may not get there in one year or even in one term. But, America, I have never been more hopeful than I am tonight that we will get there. I promise you, we as a people will get there," Obama said, though it was unclear where the "there" was that everyone would get to. Eight years later, the just-nominated Republican candidate for the presidency, Donald Trump, would stand on the dais at the Republican National Convention in Cleveland and intone that "I alone can fix it." After he was inaugurated, Trump spoke before the Capitol Building that his supporters would later lead an assault on, and he described a violent, apocalyptic nation mired in what he termed "American carnage," while promising that "we will make American great again."

Between those two men, between those two years, there is a veritable history of competing millennialisms and apocalypticisms, of action and reaction, of the conflict between the dove and the dragon, and of the turning of the world. The century wasn't even a decade old when Obama was elected as the first Black president of the United States and for some hopeful pundits his success and popularity was verification that America was "postracial," that the divisions and contradictions that so cleaved the culture would be reconciled by the former junior senator from Illinois, who had eloquently said in the 2004 Democratic National Convention speech which launched his national career that "there is not a liberal America and a conservative America—there is the United States of America." A sentiment that, as admirable and optimistic as it may have been, was proven patently false as Trump rode racial animus, culture-war politics, and white aggrievement directly into the White House a bit more than a decade later.

Obama is the postmillennial president and Trump the premillennial one; the two embody contradictory eschatologies that have endured throughout American history. In opposite ways, the election of both Obama and Trump signaled the continuing return of history and for the latter certainly a return of ideology. The political scientist Francis Fukuyama infamously argued in his 1992 book *The End of History and the Last Man* that "What we may be witnessing is not just the end of the Cold War . . . but the end of history as such. . . . That is, the end point of mankind's ideological evolution and the universalization of Western liberal democracy as the final form of human government."[44] While admitting that Fukuyama's controversial contention has often been misinterpreted, in its most literal formulation he was clearly incorrect, even while doing the 1990s saw markets opening in the former Soviet Union, the acceptance of a hegemonic Pax Americana, and a period of relative peace and prosperity. It certainly felt as if history had paused. What's even more interesting is the eschatology of Fukuyama's claim—it implies that millennium is real, that we'd already reached it in the form of neoliberal free markets with the combination of relatively progressive social policy and supply-side economics.

History, of course, rather rapidly started again on September 11, 2001, when the attack on the United States by an al-Qaeda enraptured to Wahabi apocalypticism killed almost three thousand people in New York and Washington DC. The result was the emergence of another type of American millennialism in the form of the aggressive foreign policy of neoconservative hawks who promoted disastrous military intervention in Afghanistan and Iraq. John Gray argues in *Black Mass: Apocalyptic Religion and the Death of Utopia*, that neoconservatism, which in his mind is functionally equivalent to neoliberalism, "claimed the world is converging on a single type of government and economic system—universal democracy, or a global free market. . . . This belief that humanity was on the brink of a new era was only the most recent version of apocalyptic beliefs that go back to the most ancient times."[45] Yet the failures of that very ideology—first in the debacle of Iraq and then in the hideous stock market crash of 2008—are the direct context that led to the elections of both Obama and Trump.

As a symbol, Obama was the consummation of a hopeful, progressive, postmillennial faith in America as a universalist redeemer nation with intellectual roots back to the Puritans. "What's more, we are the first nation to be founded for the sake of an idea," Obama said in his 2011 State of the Union Address, "the idea that each of us deserves the chance to shape our own destiny," a variation on the belief of America as a covenantal nation, while in his 2004 DNC address he gave expression to a sense of American exceptionality when he claimed that "in no other country on earth is my story even possible." Insomuch as Obama's presidency engaged theological sentiments, it engaged this secularized, liberal version of American civil religion, where the election of a Black man—in a nation whose foundational metaphysic was based in white supremacy—could be understood as a millennial expression of American society moving ever closer to a perfection. The oft-quoted phrase "the arc of the moral universe is long, but it bends towards justice," is a favorite of Obama's, and is often attributed to Martin Luther King Jr., but was first said in a variation by the Congregationalist minister and Antebellum abolitionist Theodor Parker. The sentiment is pure postmillennialism, it embodies a certain optimism which Obama's election inculcated among many for whom he was a visible reminder of American exceptionalism. For some liberals, Obama's election wasn't merely a repudiation of the disastrous George

W. Bush years, but it was an exoneration of the nation itself, the final culmination of the millennial faith that went back to Paine. Yet Obama's ascendancy was also in many ways a rebuke by voters against neoliberal excess. Ironically then, the forty-fourth president ran to the left, but governed at the center, and if his supporters intended Obama's election as a rejection of Wall Street and the Pentagon they'd be disavowed of that idealism shortly.

Two opposing eschatological groups would emerge from the Obama years; one an aborted postmillennial movement and the other the morning star for a noxious premillennial dispensationalism which would later mutate into the assortment of authoritarian far-right groups that would coalesce around Trump. As concerns the first, the Occupy Wall Street movement was both a protest and a glimmering of alternative ways of organizing society, establishing Lower Manhattan's Zucotti Park as an anarchic autonomous zone for two months in the autumn of 2011, before New York's billionaire mayor Michael Bloomberg had the protesters forcefully expelled by the NYPD. Mere blocks from Wall Street, Occupy's immediate impetus was the complete lack of consequences for the investors who were responsible for the Great Recession, as well as the extreme economic stratification in American society, as aptly summarized by the slogan coined by the radical anthropologist David Graeber which is perhaps the movement's most enduring contribution—"We are the 99%"—in other words, the vast majority of people who don't control the wealth are oppressed by the 1 percent who do.[46]

More than just an economic protest, Occupy also modeled a different way of understanding power, with Zucotti Park transformed into an egalitarian community where decision-making was intended to be shared horizontally rather than vertically. The encampment most clearly evoked the various dissenting groups of the seventeenth century, Occupy appearing as if postmodern Levellers, with Zucotti Park an urban St. George's Hill, or perhaps as a type of politically radical Cane Ridge Revival. Nathan Schneider, an activist and theorist who participated in Occupy, writes in his observation *Thank You, Anarchy: Notes from the Occupy Apocalypse* that he "felt like I was witnessing a glimpse of how Paul described his early church: the holding of all things in common, a single-minded asceticism, and local cells miraculously spreading throughout the known world,"[47] a harbinger of millennium in the midst of the economic collapse of the Great Recession.

The inorganic Tea Party arose at the same time, with a similar sense of antinomian theatricality in terms of activism (and costumes). Though it was also protesting the Obama administration (albeit for entirely different reasons), this right-wing movement was funded largely by billionaire donors and would mutate into something entirely apocalyptic as opposed to millennial. Largely bolstered by financial backing from wealthy conservatives like the petrochemical magnates David and Charles Koch, the Tea Party (an acronym for "Taxed Enough Already") harnessed populist sentiment to advance libertarian economic policies, though a not insignificant portion of beliefs which it tapped into were specifically racist reactions to the election of the first Black president. Central to the Tea Party mythos was an uncomplicated and schmaltzy patriotism which relied heavily on imagery related to the American Revolutionary War, as evidenced by its rather obvious name.

As conceived of by its architects, the Tea Party was primarily a means to advance the supply-side economics that had held sway in the United States since the Reagan administration, which Obama was scarcely a threat to in any substantial way, but the movement's trappings—the ruffled wigs and tricornered hats, the Gadsden flags and sloganeering, the fife and drums—evidenced a darker, chthonic, Dionysian impulse just beneath the surface, one which the initial funders were either unaware of or indifferent toward. "Something more was going on," writes Jill Lepore in *The Whites of Their Eyes: The Tea Party's Revolution and the Battle Over American History*, "something not about taxation or representation but about history itself."[48] Returning to an Edenic past, a standard conservative eschatology, the Tea Party constructed a Revolution which "bore almost no resemblance" to the event itself, as Lepore notes. Yet in and of itself the Tea Party wasn't exactly apocalyptic, though many of its most fervent supporters would move on to more extreme reactionary ideologies.

"Make America Great Again," deceptively simple and completely unoriginal, was still a potent form of political rhetoric that tapped into a mass apocalyptic urge for a type of restoration which was invisible to a number of Beltway pundits. There would be no Trump without the Tea Party, but the former jettisoned much of the libertarian rhetoric of the latter (even if he maintained and extended those policies) because he intuitively understood that the appeal of such a movement had nothing to do with fiscal policy and everything to do with cultural resentments. Trump's slogan was predicated on two fantasies: that there was a halcyon past and that he'd be the one to return the nation there. Where the Tea Party, as well as mainstream Republicans for that matter, had often hidden racist appeals underneath codewords and inuendo, Trump is zestfully and gleefully a naked bigot, whose mocking rejection of liberal pieties was read by his supporters as transgressive liberation, in an odd way not dissimilar to the flouting of convention that made past apocalyptic figures briefly powerful.

For being such a religiously disinterested and personally faithless man, Trump captured the imaginations of white evangelical Christians, who viewed him as a blunt instrument to smash liberalism, comparing him to Cyrus or even King David. "As one evangelical pastor explained it," writes Kristin Kobes Du Mez in *Jesus and John Wayne: How White Evangelicals Corrupted a Faith and Fractured a Nation*, "Jesus might have preached a gospel of peace, but the Book of Revelation showed that the suffering Messiah turned into the conquering Messiah."[49] Whatever misgivings this voting bloc may have had about a multiple divorced New York real estate billionaire who slept with porn stars were quickly justified away as Trump delivered his political promises to them. Besides, dark apocalyptic currents always thrummed through Trump's rhetoric, his simple but potent message being that the United States was continually assaulted by any number of perfidious forces, first Hispanic immigrants, then Muslims, after that "Globalists" (a not so thinly veiled antisemitic dog whistle), followed by Black Lives Matter protestors, then the LGBTQ community, and whoever else the president would be able to mobilize outrage against. His depiction of the nation was irredeemably dark, as opposed to the sunny optimism of Reagan, the last celebrity president. During his 2017 inauguration address, Trump portrayed the nation as being in a state of bloody "American carnage," despite an overall drop in violent crime, and, as he'd promised during his nominating speech the summer before, he was the one chosen to rectify such anarchy, a creed both antidemocratic and messianic.

The antidemocratic and the messianic would be fused in both Trump's governance and the perception of him among his zealous supporters. Regarding that first attribute, Trump was the most patently authoritarian president in contemporary memory, an aspiring tyrant who bore far more similarity to autocrats like Turkey's Recep Tayyip Erdoğan, Hungary's Viktor Orbán, or Russia's Vladimir Putin than he did to any American executive. As a reactionary, he feigned indifference to the traditional supply-side economics of the Republican Party, at times sounding almost progressive on those issues (albeit none of that was ever yielded tangible legislation), but his focus was entirely on an anti-immigrant, anti-Muslim, antiliberal revanchism. In the months after taking office, a particularly toxic contingent of supporters known as the alt-right, an assortment of intellectual dilletantes and fascist provocateurs such as the white supremacists Richard Spencer and Milo Yiannopoulos, were promoted by a mass media eager to explain the appeal of Trumpism. Many of these figures shared connection to Steve Bannon, a former Hollywood producer and the editor of the extreme right-wing website Breitbart.com, who ensconced himself within the White House where he briefly served as chief strategist and on the National Security Council, before he was fired by the infamously fickle president. With connections to the international fascist movement throughout the world, Bannon styled himself as an intellectual vanguard, a theorist of Trumpism, and much of his thinking was explicitly apocalyptic in orientation, telling a reporter for *The Daily Beast* in 2016 that "I want to bring everything crashing down, and destroy all of today's establishment."[50]

Central to much of Bannon's thinking, inchoate though it may be, are the writings of two crackpot pseudohistorians named William Strauss and Neil

Howe who, in their 1997 book *The Fourth Turning*, advanced a providential history of American politics based in cycles of generations. Entirely unfalsifiable, and thus unscientific, the Strauss–Howe generational theory claims that all of Western history can be explained by recourse to a cyclical movement based in the dispositions and experiences of individual generations. Strauss and Howe posit the existence of periods which they call *saeculum*, roughly eight to ten decades long, when there is relative national unity on questions of political value, but which are occasionally interrupted by twenty-five-year "turnings," triggered by some sort of social, political, or economic crisis, a type of paradigm shift in which a new *saeculum* is inaugurated. According to the writers, the United States has experienced several since the Revolution (which itself was a turning), including during the Civil War and roughly seventy years later during the Great Depression. With all of the certainty of an Adventist adding up the years of a dispensation, Strauss and Howe predicted that a fourth turning was approaching, writing with apocalyptic import that "Sometime before the year 2025, America will pass through a great gate in history, commensurate with the American Revolution, Civil War, and twin emergencies of the Great Depression and World War II."[51] Bannon was transfixed by *The Fourth Turning*; he saw in it a prophecy of his own movement, with Trump a tool to destroy the liberal consensus that had dominated Washington since the Roosevelt administration, and thus lead to the "deconstruction of the bureaucratic state," as the strategist bragged.[52]

Bannon, in many ways, draws his political inspiration from an avowedly European rather than American conservative tradition, even while it's obvious that there are forerunners to much of his thought in domestic nativism, xenophobia, and authoritarianism. Yet he's also credibly just a small node on an international trend toward reactionary totalitarianism throughout the West, oftentimes dressed up in intellectual obfuscation and apocalyptic imagery. This is the domain of Bannon's eastern corollary, the Russian philosopher Aleksander Dugin, who is also an adviser to Putin, who gushed, in his 1997 *Foundations of Geopolitics*, over the possibility of a "genuine, true, radically revolutionary and consistent, fascist fascism," seeing a revived Czarist power as a final kingdom before the eschaton, and governing accordingly.[53] Both Bannon's influences like Dugin and his alt-right acolytes were drawn to cyclical thinking derived from a quasi-dispensationalist understanding of historiography. Many on the alt-right, from Bannon to Spencer, shared an enthusiasm for the same sort of reactionary occultism that had been a hallmark of the Thule society. Bannon, for example, was a staunch advocate for reading twentieth-century racist occultists like the Italian Julius Evola and the French philosopher Alain de Benoist. Apocalypticism was a shock current through the writings of these sorts of figures, yet what they promised was not an Edenic millennium, but a cataclysmic race war followed by white global dominance, of a dragon devouring all the doves.

Despite such a hideous goal, the so-called "alt-right" was white supremacist fascism and neo-Nazism made respectable for the mass media, more of a marketing job than a novel political phenomenon, but all the more terrifying for how it had ensconced itself at the center of the Trump administration. Their preferred medium of communication, however, was different from past survivalist and militia groups in that they made full use of the internet, from Twitter to Reddit boards, to express their positions in a quasi-ironic and meme-heavy style, an anarchic rhetoric that called to mind the 1960s counterculture as much as the Ku Klux Klan. The effect was intentionally disorienting, where the purpose was to, in Bannon's memorable and earthy phrase, "flood the zone with shit."

The sorts of views which Bannon was attracted toward, it should be obvious, are antidemocratic, with Evola writing in *Civilta Americana* in 1945 that "America is the final stage of modern Europe," desiring both the downfall of Paine's nation and praying for a future that is feudal, aristocratic, monarchical, and hierarchical.[54] "There is a necessary correspondence between the most advanced stages of a historical cycle and the most primitive," predicted Evola, seeing in the degeneration of the United States the possibility of a fascist future.[55] Well-educated fascists like Evola and Benoist, and their "interested" readers like Bannon, share an eschatological orientation with gutter racists like the author of the virulently white supremacist novel *The Turner Diaries*, widely read by neofascists and self-published by William Luther Pierce in 1978. Whether educated or not, fascists have a blood lust for violence and a desire for pogrom against those whom they consider unworthy of life, their wicked "dream of a white world" that will "rule over the earth for all time to come."

If the antidemocratic impulses attracted Bannon and the alt-right to Trump, than the messianism is somehow an even more unique and disturbing aspect of his political popularity (though certainly this is not exclusive either). Nominally Presbyterian, though strongly influenced by the prosperity gospel of positive thinking inculcated by the celebrity pastor Norman Vincent Peele, Trump was an odd choice for an evangelical religious cult of devotion, and yet the combination of naked power and antiliberal diatribe made him irresistible to many conservative Christians. Du Mez writes that "evangelical support for Trump was no aberration, nor was it merely a pragmatic choice. It was, rather, the culmination of evangelicals embrace of militant masculinity, an ideology that enshrines patriarchal authority and condones the callous display of power, at home and abroad."[56]

Many scholarly observers, albeit not enough in the mainstream press in 2016, correctly identified correspondences between the growing MAGA movement and fascism, but the line of American revivalism through Trump's incendiary rallies is instrumental in understanding not just how the he captured the imagination of evangelical voters, and in many ways constructed his own distinctly apocalyptic religion out of those former Christians. Journalist Jeff Sharlet, after observing and talking to participants at dozen of Trump rallies, describes in a 2020 *Vanity Fair* feature how the former president "has fused his penchant for self-pity with the paranoia that runs like a third rail through Christian conservatism, the thrilling promise of 'spiritual war' with dark and hidden powers."[57]

Sharlet is, in part, writing about the most troubling and surprising apocalyptic cult to achieve widespread popularity in the twenty-first-century United States, a movement known as QAnon. Directly emerging from the Trumpist movement, though absorbing a variety of influences, QAnon is an explicitly apocalyptic religion that endows Trump with a messianic significance, affirming that he is fighting a spiritual war against "demon worshippers" who've infiltrated government, media, and the Democratic Party. Adherents interpret so-called "Q Drops," internet missives from someone who claims to have a high-level security clearance (designated by the letter "Q," hence the name), as well as parsing the often orthographically unique Tweets of Trump for secret codes. Those who believe in QAnon—perhaps as high as 20 percent of Americans share some tenets with this belief system—await the "Coming Storm," the eschaton whereby Trump will overthrow the demonic usurpers and bring about American greatness. The movement, closely related to the growth in right-wing paramilitary groups like the Proud Boys, the Three Percenters, and the Oath Keepers, was involved in the siege on the US Capitol, the attempted coup of January 6, 2021. A few months before that event, Adrienne LaFrance in *The Atlantic* warned that QAnon was "much more than a loose collection of conspiracy-minded chat-room inhabitants," but rather a destructive new apocalyptic religion, "united in mass rejection of reason, objectivity, and other Enlightenment values. And we are likely closer to the beginning of its story than the end."[58]

The simultaneous rejection of Enlightenment values while benefiting from technological advancements which can be attributed to those same values is a hallmark of the fascist project, and such characteristics are abundantly apparent in the Christian theological movement known as Dominionism. While QAnon—born in internet chatrooms—is arguably only marginally Christian, perhaps more of a fusion of fundamentalism, neo-paganism, and cult of personality, Dominionism is unequivocally Christian and born out of seminaries; but both reject the idea of objective and universal truths in favor of a cult of irrationality. The danger of apocalypticism has always been the siren's call of the self-fulfilling prophecy, so that the perils of Dominionism shouldn't be minimized, as sociologists Philip S. Gorski and Samuel L. Perry write in *The Flag and the Cross: White Christian Nationalism and the Threat to American Democracy*, arguing that such beliefs are "Fast becoming the San Andreas Fault of American politics," where a "deeper, existential debate over American identity underlies them all. There will be another eruption—and soon. Will this be 'the big one'? The one that finally topples the centuries-old structures of American democracy?"[59] Dominionists certainly hope so.

Theologians like R. J. Rushdoony and evangelists such as Francis Schaeffer believed that only faith should be the guide for how to properly constitute society and that there was a coming moment when a pious Christian minority would have "dominion" over the formerly secular government of the United States, a position aptly summarized by the evangelical writer George Grant in his 1987 *The Changing of the Guard: Biblical Principles for Political Action*, in which he claims that "Christians have an obligation, a mandate, a commission, a holy responsibility to reclaim the land for Jesus Christ—to have dominion in civil structures, just as in every other aspect of life and godliness. . . . But it is dominion we are after. Not just a voice."[60]

Dominionism may have been inaugurated by Calvinists like Rushdoony, but it's quickly become conducive to the political theology of a movement of charismatic Christians who refer to themselves as the New Apostolic Reformation. Claiming that since their variety of faith is neither Catholic nor Protestant, thus signifying a "New Reformation," these primarily Pentecostal Christians believe that they're engaged in spiritual warfare against demons, where the domain of politics becomes explicitly theological. Tracing back to the missionary and evangelist C. Peter Wager, who organized a conference in 1996 that is often identified as the beginning of the movement, those associated with the New Apostolic Reformation believe that they have a role in the coming spiritual war. According to their developing dogma, they are capable of interpreting signs and wonders and of effecting their own miraculous powers, so that their goal is to establish the United States as a Christian theocracy. Drawing from Dominionism, those associated with the NAR believe in something called the "Seven Mountain Mandate," or the "Seven Mountain Prophecy," a program for achieving absolute political power. According to this mandate, there are seven societal spheres that believers must achieve control over—the church, families, education, media, entertainment, business, and government—and that hegemony in each of those domains is necessary for the implementation of theocracy.

"The average reader might be inclined to think that such extremism means that these figures cannot be taken seriously or don't represent the mainstream of a religious movement," writes John Weaver in *The New Apostolic Reformation: History of a Modern Charismatic Movement*, yet in the United States there are some ten million people affiliated with the movement.[61] Politicians such as former Minnesota representative Michelle Bachman, former Texas governor Rick Perry, and former Alaska governor and one-time Republican vice presidential nominee Sarah Palin all have connections to the NAR. The faithful, according to New Apostolic Reformation minister, evangelist, and faith healer Paula White, is to "play a critical role in Armageddon as the United States stands alongside Israel in the battle against Islam."[62] White would later have the official position of "Spiritual Adviser" in the first administration of Donald J. Trump.[63] In February of 2025, she would become the first director of the so-called "White House Faith Office."[64]

Epilogue

Monsters of the Anthropocene

> *Is that all there is?*
> *Is that all there is?*
> *If that's all there is my friends,*
> *then let's keep dancing,*
> *let's break out the booze and have a ball.*
> —Peggy Lee, "Is That All There Is?" (1969)

FOUR CENTURIES AGO, somebody starving in the drought-afflicted Elbe region in what is today the Czech Republic anonymously chiseled onto the stone of the receding river bank a warning. Here, along the river where one day American and Soviet troops would meet on their dual approach to Berlin, a graffito made by an unknown hand marks 1616 as the oldest year recorded on one particular "Hunger Stone," for on that surface there is a *memento mori* which reads "Wenn du mich sicht, dann weine." In the summer of 2018, which at that point was among the hottest recorded, though that standard has been broken in every subsequent year, the Elbe once again receded to the point where observers could read that ominous missive—"If you see me, weep."[1]

That same summer, the United Nations released its latest iteration of the Intergovernmental Report on Climate Change. Authored by ninety-one scientists, representing forty countries and based on over six thousand peer-reviewed scientific studies, the conclusions of the commission are horrifying. According to Coral Davenport at *The New York Times*, the climatologists discovered that if "greenhouse gas emissions continue at the current rate, the atmosphere will warm up by as much as 2.7 degrees Fahrenheit" by 2040, radically earlier than had been thought, meaning that anyone reading this will bear witness to "inundating coastlines and intensifying droughts and poverty."[2] In the summer of 2023, scientists writing in the journal *Nature* concluded that of the nine "planetary boundaries" which regulate the parameters of life on earth, including criteria such as biosphere integrity and ocean acidification, seven had already been crossed.

It's estimated that, because of the mass burning of fossil fuels, the average temperature throughout the world rose a single degree Celsius during the nineteenth century. It rose another degree during the twentieth century and today that rate has increased in a feedback loop powered by the melting of Arctic tundra and the release of previously trapped methane gas alongside industrial carbon dioxide. Physicist Joseph Fourier, writing in an 1837 edition of *The American Journal of Science Arts*, had already hypothesized that industrial exhaust "must produce variations in the mean temperature," while in 1856 Eunice Newton Foote wrote in *The American Journal of Science* that an "atmosphere of... [carbon dioxide] would give to our earth a high temperature."[3]

If those were minority opinions then, and they by no means necessarily were, then it was definitely confirmed by 1977, when a climatologist named James Black reported that "there is general scientific agreement that the most likely manner in which mankind is influencing the global climate is through carbon dioxide released from the burning of fossil fuels."[4] Black delivered that report before the management committee of EXXON, who purposefully buried those conclusions and continued to fund lobbyists, think tanks, and politicians who vociferously denied the reality of anthropogenic climate change. And so, rather than with the breaking of seals and the blowing of trumpets, apocalypse was announced as a footnote in a buried corporate report.

Climate change is a special case when considering the history of apocalypticism, both because inevitably the issues which it raises—civilizational collapse, biodome destruction, and perhaps human extinction—so obviously call to mind the same imagery and rhetoric, tropes and themes, of past end-times prophecies, but also because in this particular case the issue happens to be real. Comparable only to nuclear war, but arguably even dwarfing the long-term implications of that unthinkable possibility, climate change signals the culmination of apocalypse at human hands, the end of the world as rendered not by the supernatural means, but because of our economic system's rapacious avarice.

Yet if apocalypticism is phrased in the rhetoric of visionary metaphor and symbol, then the current climate crisis is rendered in the language of arid climatology and geology, a distinction which makes a huge difference. Apocalypse as a concept is by necessity supernatural, so that, when discussing the cataclysmic implications of climate change, words like "degradation," "catastrophe," "decline," and even "collapse" may be more literally appropriate. However, for all of us living within this moment, that's perhaps a distinction without a difference. After all, whether or not hell is real, murder surely is. "I can't speak the language of science" writes the essayist Paul Kingsnorth in *Confessions of a Recovering Environmentalist*, "without a corresponding poetry."[5] Today our data may be unassailably empirical, but our emotions are very much apocalyptic.

Within two decades of this writing, massive hurricanes and wildfires will be the norm, coastal cities will be inundated and perhaps abandoned, the planet's sixth great extinction will continue unabated. The social, cultural, and economic effects of climate change will be recorded not on hunger stones, but in pandemics, wars, famines, and genocides exacerbated by the effects of higher temperatures. Alterations to human behavior which might hasten the worst effects of climate change are technically possible, though the authors of the IGCR doubt such change is politically feasible, as it would require direct action on the part of the industrial economies of the world, something with "no documented historic precedent." Myles Allen of Oxford University explained that "we need to reverse emissions trends and turn the world economy on a dime"[6] if we're to stave off an ecological apocalypse which we now understand isn't centuries in the future, but rather mere decades, if not years.

We already see the effects in the increasing ferocity of storms, the droughts not just in the developing world, but increasingly in North America and Europe as well, and in the wildfires, which have burnt their way across the west. As the world's temperature rises we see an equivalent political slow burn, nations increasingly moving toward the delusional reactionary nationalisms as a means of punishing refugee populations often affected either directly by climate change or by the civil strife made possible by it, for as Mark Fishcetti describes the Syrian civil war in *Scientific American*, "Human-induced drying in many societies can push tensions over a threshold that provokes violent conflict."[7] Fischetti noted the propensity toward climate war only a few years before Russia, inspired by millennial dreams of restored greatness, invaded sovereign Ukraine, the agricultural bread basket of Europe.

Roy Scranton in *We're Doomed: Now What?* writes that as the "gap between the future we're entering and the future we once imagined grows ever wider, nihilism takes root in the shadow of our fear. . . . [Y]ou can see it in the pull to nationalism, sectarianism, war, and racial hatred."[8] This is the recently spoken of "polycrisis," a political and social description of the preponderance of crises which humanity now faces, from climate change to reinvigorated pandemics, increased military bellicosity and economic stratification, many of which are existential threats. Does this describe "apocalypse?" In one sense literally no, since even if the entire biome collapses, even if billions of humans perish in the coming century, populations of people will still survive, and "nature" certainly will, having faced any number of extinctions in the past. Perhaps the question then becomes "How useful is the language of apocalypse, the imagery, the symbolism, the allegory?" Perhaps such language spurs people to action, though it seems to have had perilously little effect in that regard as concerns the behavior of the most consequential of decision-makers. By contrast, maybe such language engenders a sense of defeatism, a belief in the inevitability of collapse which is collectively paralyzing. At the same time, such a transition as implied by the current crisis necessitates and implies a coming organizational shift in society, but that could either result in a hideous fascism or in something genuinely utopian. What's worrying at this point in our history is that we have ample experience in being able to see the dragon, but perilously little in even being able to imagine the dove.

Right now we're at an impasse—there is a new global, political, and spiritual reawakening from the activist movement Extinction Rebellion to Pope Francis's encyclical *Laudato si'* that attempts to imagine a more equitable future—but there are also the enthusiasms of the Lords of Capital, none more so than the confidence men of Silicon Valley, praying to Moloch's final incarnation in the form of the techno-utopian singularity, their creed being nothing less than Faust's injunction—"Am I a god? Light fills my mind." It's not technology that's the problem—it's the doctrine that technology is more than a tool, that in fact we're tools for it. If a reading of this book demonstrates anything, it's that that every century has a contingent of people, both smaller and larger depending on circumstance, who are convinced that they're living in the last days. The metaphysical irony of our situation is that today we may actually be living in the last days, and it's not a conclusion rendered through scriptural exegesis or dispensation charts but by simply examining the untenable amount of greenhouse gas in the atmosphere.

At the very outset of working on this book which you're now reading, I sat with my son after he'd fallen asleep on the last day of the year 2021 and I doom-scrolled through social media on my phone. There I came across an acutely disturbing and arresting image, later to be swallowed in the maw of the ever-churning digital cacophony, as is the wont of our jaundiced age. It was taken earlier that New Year's Eve night, a photo of a group of exhausted doctors in Colorado working in a Covid ward, all wearing personal protective equipment, looking out the window of their hospital at the entire horizon of the Rockies burning with an unprecedented winter wildfire inching ever closer to them. The central economic, political, ethical, and spiritual question of the remainder of this century—no matter how much time we actually might have left—is how to prevent that apocalypse which we spent so many millennia frightened of, but which now seems so near to moving from myth to reality, like a line of fire moving swiftly across the mountains. If apocalypse has always appealed to the human need for narrative finality projected onto all of reality, the question is will there be another chapter, and another chapter, and another chapter, or rather if this is actually all that there shall be?

ACKNOWLEDGMENTS

In addition to all of the scholars who've made this work possible and who are represented in the endnotes and bibliography, I'd like to make special mention of my colleagues in the English Department of Carnegie Mellon University. Thanks must go to Marian Aguiar, Jane Bernstein, Jon Klancher, Peggy Knapp, Jane McCafferty, Kathy Newman, David Shumway, Jeffrey Williams, Stephen Wittek, and James Wynn. In particular, special thanks among the faculty are due to Andreea Ritivoi, Christopher Warren, and Sharon Dilworth for imagining a space for the public humanities at CMU. Finally, my eternal gratitude is for my family, my mother Janet and brother Jacob, and especially my wife Meg and my two boys Finn and Milo.

NOTES

INTRODUCTION

1. Lawrence James, *Imperial Warrior: The Life and Times of Field Marshall Viscount Allenby 1861–1936* (Weidenfeld & Nicolson, 1993), 140.
2. Edmund Allenby, "Proclamation of Martial Law in Jerusalem," in *Standing Orders and General Instructions for the Information of Officers* (Headquarters, Occupied Enemy Territory Administration, 1918), 91.
3. Both the memo and the *Punch* cartoon are described in Hatem Bazian, "Revisiting the British Conquest of Jerusalem," *Al Jazeera*, December 14, 2014, https://www.aljazeera.com/opinions/2014/12/14/revisiting-the-british-conquest-of-jerusalem.
4. Bazian, "Revisiting the British Conquest of Jerusalem."
5. C. Brad Faught, *Allenby: Making the Modern Middle East* (Bloomsbury, 2020), 99.
6. "Welcome to the Megiddo Expedition!" Tel Aviv University, October 14, 2021, https://www.themegiddoexpedition.com/post/exciting-updates-about-the-2022-season.
7. Unless otherwise indicated, all scriptural quotations are from the King James Version of the Bible. There are, for sure, many more accurate translations in terms of verisimilitude to the original Hebrew, Aramaic, and Greek, but in tracing the cultural influence of biblical rhetoric in the anglophone world, the King James is by far the most important and impressive from a literary standpoint.
8. Revelation 16:14.
9. Revelation 20:8–9.
10. Richard G. Kyle, *Apocalyptic Fever: End-Times Prophecies in Modern America* (Wipf & Stock, 2012), 98.
11. Karen Armstrong, *A Short History of Myth* (Canongate, 2004), 1.
12. Northrop Frye, *The Great Code: The Bible and Literature* (Houghton Mifflin Harcourt, 1981), 136.

CHAPTER ONE: IN THE BEGINNING WAS THE END

1. Daniel L. Smith-Christopher, *The Religion of the Landless: The Social Context of the Babylonian Exile* (Wipf & Stock, 2015), 81.
2. James Kugel, *The Bible as It Was* (Belknap Press, 1997), i.
3. Jack Miles, *God: A Biography* (Vintage, 1996), 53.
4. Robert Alter, *The Art of Biblical Poetry* (Basic Books, 2011), 29.
5. Joel S. Badsen, *The Composition of the Pentateuch: Reviewing the Documentary Hypothesis* (Yale University Press, 2012), 216.

6. Robert A. Kraft, "The Codex and Canon Consciousness," in *The Canon Debate: On the Origins and Formation of the Bible*, ed. Lee Martin McDonald and James A. Sanders (Hendrickson Publishers, 2002), 229.
7. Kugel, *The Bible as It Was*, 12.
8. Uwe Becker, "The Book of Isaiah: Its Composition History," in *The Oxford Handbook of Isaiah*, ed. Lena-Sofia Tiemeyer (Oxford University Press, 2020), 41.
9. Kugel, *The Bible as It Was*, 12.
10. Carl G. Cereti, "Myths, Legends, Eschatologies," in *The Wiley Blackwell Companion to Zoroastrianism* (Wiley Blackwell, 2015), 259.
11. Mary Boyce, *Zoroastrians: Their Religious Beliefs and Practices* (Routledge, 2000), 1.
12. Jeffrey Burton Russell, *The Devil: Perceptions of Evil from Antiquity to Primitive Christianity* (Cornell University Press, 1987), 87.
13. Pablo Vasquez, trans., *The Sacred Gathas of Zarathustra and the Old Avestan Canon: A Modern Translation of Ancient Wisdom* (Mantra Books, 2022).
14. Mahnaz Moazami, "Millennialism, Eschatology, and Messianic Figures in Iranian Tradition," *Journal of Millennial Studies* (Winter 2000): 14.
15. Boyce, *Zoroastrians*, 120.
16. Geza Vermes, *The Complete Dead Sea Scrolls in English* (Penguin, 2012), 1.
17. As quoted in James C. VanderKam, *The Dead Sea Scrolls Today* (Eerdmans, 2010), 9.
18. Melvin Konner, *Unsettled: An Anthropology of the Jews* (Viking, 2003), 59.
19. Israel Carmi, "Radiocarbon Dating of the Dead Sea Scrolls," in *The Dead Sea Scrolls: Fifty Years After Their Discovery, 1947–1997*, ed. Lawrence Schiffman, Emanuel Tov, and James VanderKam (IES, 2000), 881.
20. Vermes, *The Complete Dead Sea Scrolls in English*, 412.
21. Vermes, *The Complete Dead Sea Scrolls in English*, 411.
22. Anathea E. Portier-Young, *Apocalypse Against Empire: Theologies of Resistance in Early Judaism* (Eerdmans, 2014), xxii.
23. Portier-Young, *Apocalypse Against Empire*, xxii.
24. As quoted by Peter Schäfer in *The History of the Jews in Antiquity* (Routledge, 1995), 191.
25. John Joseph Collins, *Daniel: With an Introduction to Apocalyptic Literature* (Eerdmans, 1984), 49.
26. Daniel 2:34.
27. Daniel 2:34.
28. Daniel 7:10–11.
29. Paul Boyer, *When Time Shall Be No More: Prophecy Belief in American Culture* (Harvard University Press, 1992), 133.
30. Gershom Scholem, *The Messianic Idea in Judaism: And Other Essays on Jewish Spirituality* (Schocken Books, 1971), 1.
31. Konner, *Unsettled*, 97.
32. Dvir Raviv and Chaim ben David, "Cassius Dio's Figures for the Demographic Consequences of the Bar Kokhba War: Exaggeration or Reliable Account?," *The Journal of Roman Archeology* 34, no. 2 (2021): 585–607.

CHAPTER TWO: HELL FOLLOWED WITH HIM

1. Peter France, *A Place of Healing for the Soul* (Grove Press, 2002), 1.
2. Pheme Perkins, *Reading the New Testament: An Introduction* (Paulist Press, 1989), 19.
3. As quoted in Edward Champlin, *Nero* (Harvard University Press, 2003), 121–122.
4. Milton S. Terry, *The Sibylline Oracles: Translated from the Greek into English Blank Verse* (Eaton & Mains, 1899), 109.
5. D. R. Hillers, "Revelation 13:8 and a Scroll from Murabba'at," *Bulletin of the American Schools of Oriental Research* 170 (1963), 65.
6. "Book of Revelation," in *The Oxford Dictionary of the Christian Church*, ed. F. L. Cross (Oxford University Press, 2005), 1239.
7. Elaine Pagels, *Revelations: Visions, Prophecy, and Politics in the Book of Revelation* (Penguin, 2012), 1.
8. "Book of Revelation," in *Oxford Dictionary of the Christian Church*, 1402.
9. Bart Ehrman, *Jesus: Apocalyptic Prophet of the New Millennium* (Oxford University Press, 1999), 112.
10. John W. Marshall, *Parables of War: Reading John's Jewish Apocalypse* (Wilfrid Laurier University Press, 2001), 2.
11. Marshall, *Parables of War*, 5.
12. David L. Barr, "Violence in the Apocalypse of John," in *The Oxford Handbook of the Book of Revelation*, ed. Craig Koester (Oxford University Press, 2020), 336.
13. Kristofer Widhom and Bernard McGinn, "Antichrist: An Interview with Bernard McGinn," *Cabinet Magazine* 5 (Winter 2001–2002).
14. A good overview is Bernard McGinn, *Antichrist: Two Thousand Years of the Human Fascination with Evil* (Columbia University Press, 1999).
15. Elisabeth Schüssler, *Revelation: Vision of a Just World* (Fortress Press, 1991), 11.
16. A riveting account is in Matthew Gabriel and David M. Perry, *Bright Ages: A New History of Medieval Europe* (HarperCollins, 2021), 9.
17. Jerome, *The Saint Jerome Collection* (Aeterna Press, 2016), 753.
18. John Kelly, *The Great Mortality: An Intimate History of the Black Death, the Most Devastating Plague of All Time* (Harper Perennial, 2006), 44.
19. Paulus Orosius, *The Seven Books of History Against the Pagans* (The Catholic University of America Press, 1964), 336.
20. Ehrman, *Jesus*, x.
21. Tertullian, *The Five Books Against Marcion* (T&T Clarke, 1870), 170.
22. David Bentley Hart, *That All Shall Be Saved: Heaven, Hell, and Universal Salvation* (Yale University Press, 2017), 68.
23. James Carroll, *Constantine's Sword: The Church and the Jews* (Houghton Mifflin Harcourt, 2001), 58.
24. Diarmaid MacCulloch, *Christianity: The First Three Thousand Years* (Viking, 2010), 129.
25. An excellent introduction is Hans Jonas, *The Gnostic Religion: The Message of the Alien God and the Beginnings of Christianity* (Beacon Press, 2001).

26. Walter Schmithals, *The Apocalyptic Movement, Introduction and Interpretation* (Abingdon Press, 1975), 108.
27. "The Apocalypse of Adam," trans. George W. McRae, in *Nag Hamadi Codex*, vol. 5 (Brill, 1996).

CHAPTER THREE: THE FIRST MILLENNIUM APPROACHES

1. Reza Aslan, *No God But God: The Origins, Evolution, and Future of Islam* (Random House, 2011), 300.
2. An interesting discussion of the meteorite hypothesis is in Maria Golia, *Meteorite: Nature and Culture* (Reaktion Books, 2015).
3. Aziz Al-Azmeh, *The Emergence of Islam in Late Antiquity: Allah and His People* (Cambridge University Press, 2014), 219.
4. Al-Azmeh, *The Emergence of Islam in Late Antiquity*, 219.
5. Quoted in Hava Lazarus-Yafeh, *Some Religious Aspects of Islam: A Collection of Articles* (Brill, 1981), 120–124.
6. Karen Armstrong, *Muhammad: A Prophet for Our Times* (HarperOne, 2007), 1.
7. It is worth consulting Christian Julien Robin, "South Arabia, Religions in Pre-Islamic," in *Encyclopedia of the Qur'an*, ed. Jane Dammen McAuliffe (Brill, 2006), 5:84–94.
8. Jean-Pierre Filiu, *Apocalypse in Islam* (University of California Press, 2011), 21.
9. Todd Lawson, *The Quran, Epic and Apocalypse* (OneWorld, 2017), 29.
10. Aslan, *No God But God*, 12.
11. Michael Cook, "Eschatology and the Dating of Traditions," in *Hadith: Origins and Developments*, ed. Harald Motzki (Routledge, 2016), 217.
12. Jan-Olaf Blichfeldt, *Early Mahdism: Politics and Religion in the Formative Period of Islam* (Brill, 1985).
13. Filiu, *Apocalypse in Islam*, 14.
14. Stephen J. Shoemaker, *The Apocalypse of Empire: Imperial Eschatology in Late Antiquity and Early Islam* (University of Pennsylvania Press, 2018), 149.
15. Shoemaker, *The Apocalypse of Empire*, 149.
16. Bede, *Ecclesiastical History of the British People*, quoted in *Medieval Sourcebook* (Fordham University, 1996).
17. Patrick Wormald, "Bede and the 'Church of the English,'" in *The Times of Bede: Studies in Early English Christian Society and Its Historian*, ed. Stephen Baxter (Blackwell, 2006), 207.
18. E. G. Richards, *Mapping Time: The Calendar and Its History* (Oxford University Press, 2000), 351.
19. *Bede: The Reckoning of Time*, trans. Faith Wallis (Liverpool University Press, 2004), lxxxv.
20. Bonnie Blackburn and Leofranc Holford-Strevens, "Calendar and Chronology," in *The Oxford Companion to the Year* (Oxford University Press, 1999), 767.
21. David Ewing Duncan, *Calendar: Humanity's Epic Struggle to Determine a True and Accurate Year* (Harper Perennial, 1999), 110.
22. J. Patrick, "General Chronology," in *The Catholic Encyclopedia* (Robert Appleton Company, 1908).

23. Duncan, *Calendar*, xvii.
24. Much of this is explicated in Stephen Jay Gould, *Questioning the Millennium: A Rationalist's Guide to a Precisely Arbitrary Countdown* (Harmony, 1997).
25. Baruch S. Davidson, "What Is the Significance of the Year 6000 in the Jewish Calendar?," Chabad.org, accessed January 13, 2025, https://www.chabad.org/library/article_cdo/aid/607585/jewish/Significance-of-the-year-6000.htm.
26. "Vedic Time System," Vedic Knowledge Online, accessed January 13, 2025, http://veda.wikidot.com/vedic-time-system.
27. Vyasa Valmiki, *Delphi Collected Sanskrit Epics* (Delphi Classics, 2018) Section 1809.
28. Ibid.
29. J. Brockington, *The Sanskrit Epics* (Brill, 1998), 26.
30. Wendy Doniger, *The Hindus: An Alternative History* (Penguin, 2010), 57.
31. Linda Schele and David Freidel, *A Forest of Kings: The Untold Story of the Ancient Maya* (Harper Perennial, 1993), 59–75.
32. F. Kent Reilly III, "Mesoamerican Religious Beliefs: The Practices and Practitioners," in *The Oxford Handbook of Mesoamerican Archeology*, ed. Deborah L. Nicholes and Christopher Poole (Oxford University Press, 2016), 773.
33. Tim Whitmarsh, *Ancient Greek Literature* (Wiley Blackwell, 2006).
34. Hesiod, *Works and Days*, accessed January 13, 2025, https://www.perseus.tufts.edu/hopper/text?doc=Perseus%3Atext%3A1999.01.0132%3Acard%3D109.
35. Hesiod, *Works and Days.*
36. Hesiod, *Works and Days.*
37. Whitmarsh, *Ancient Greek Literature* 38..
38. The reference to Innocent III can be found in John Victor Tolan, *Saracens: Islam in the Medieval European Imagination* (Columbia University Press, 2002), 194. The reference to Müntzer is in Gould, *Questioning the Millennium*, 48. The reference to Newton can be found in Stephen D. Snobelen, "A Time and Times and the Dividing of time: Isaac Newton the Apocalypse and AD 2060," in *The Canadian Journal of History* 38 (December 2003): 537–551.

CHAPTER FOUR: THE BROKEN SEAL

1. Jay Asher and Jessica Freeburg, *Piper* (Razorbill, 2017), 1.
2. Wolfgang Mieder, *Tradition and Innovation in Folk Literature* (Routledge, 2015), 46.
3. Mieder, *Tradition and Innovation in Folk Literature*, 49.
4. Anthony Bridge, *The Crusades* (Granada Publishing, 1980), 243.
5. Thomas Asbridge, *The Crusades: The Authoritative History of the War for the Holy Land* (Ecco, 2011), 533.
6. C. Krey August, *The First Crusade: The Accounts of Eyewitnesses and Participants* (Princeton University Press, 1921), 42–43.
7. Stephen O'Shea, *Sea of Faith: Islam and Christianity in the Medieval Mediterranean World* (Walker, 2007), 7.
8. Jay Rubenstein, *Nebuchadnezzar's Dream: The Crusades, Apocalyptic Prophecy, and the End of History* (Oxford University Press, 2019), xix.

9. Jonathan Riley Smith, *The First Crusaders, 1095–1131* (Cambridge University Press, 1997).
10. Carroll, *Constantine's Sword*, 266.
11. Carroll, *Constantine's Sword*, 59.
12. Israel Jacob Yuval, *Two Nations in Your Womb: Perceptions of Jews and Christians in Late Antiquity and the Middle Ages* (University of California Press, 2008), 142.
13. Yuval, *Two Nations in Your Womb*, 4.
14. Yuval, *Two Nations in Your Womb*, 4.
15. Rubenstein, *Nebuchadnezzar's Dream*, 23.
16. Jonathan Phillips, *Holy Warriors: A Modern History of the Crusades* (Random House, 2010), 31.
17. Richard Fletcher, *The Cross and the Crescent: The Dramatic Story of the Earliest Encounters Between Christians and Muslims* (Penguin, 2005), 1.
18. Phillips, *Holy Warriors*, 29.
19. Niall Christie, ed. and trans., *The Book of the Jihad of 'Ali ibn Tahir al-Sulami* (Routledge, 2015), 220.
20. Quoted in Mary Franklin Brown, *Reading the World: Encyclopedic Writing in the Scholastic Age* (University of Chicago Press, 2012), 271.
21. Francisco Bethencourt, *The Inquisition: A Global History* (Cambridge University Press, 2007), 110.
22. Stephen O'Shea, *The Perfect Heresy: The Revolutionary Life and Death of the Medieval Cathars* (Walker & Company, 2000).
23. Michael Frassetto, *Heretic Lives: Medieval Heresy from Bogomil and the Cathars to Wyclif and Hus* (Profile, 2007), 1.
24. Norman Cohn, *The Pursuit of the Millennium: Revolutionary Millenarians and Mystical Anarchists of the Middle Ages* (Oxford University Press, 1970), 39.
25. Andrew McCall, *The Medieval Underworld* (Trafalgar Square, 1979), 219.
26. Quoted in Henry Hart Milman's *History of Latin Christianity: Including that of the Popes to the Pontificate of Nicholas V* (John Murray, 1864), 13.
27. O'Shea, *The Perfect Heresy,* 7.
28. Sean Martin, *The Cathars: The Most Successful Heresy of the Middle Ages* (Chartwell Books, 2006), 16.
29. Martin, *The Cathars*, 36.
30. "Bernard Gui on the Albigensians," Internet Medieval Source Book, Fordham University, accessed January 13, 2025, https://sourcebooks.fordham.edu/source/gui-cathars.asp.
31. Martin, *The Cathars*, 36.
32. Martin, *The Cathars,* 122–123.
33. Frassetto, *Heretic Lives,* 14.
34. Andrew Phillip Smith, *The Lost Teachings of the Cathars: Their Beliefs and Practices* (Watkins Publishing, 2015), 51.
35. "Cathar Text and Rituals," The Gnostic Society Library, accessed December 30, 2024, http://gnosis.org/library/Interrogatio_Johannis.html.
36. Walter L. Wakefield, "Notes on Some Antiheretical Writings of the Thirteenth Century," *Franciscan Studies* 27, no. 1 (1967): 285–321.

37. Rene Weis, *The Yellow Cross: The Story of the Last Cathars' Rebellion Against the Inquisition, 1290–1329* (Vintage, 2002), xli.
38. W. A. Sibly, *The Chronicle of William of Puylaurens: The Albigensian Crusade and Its Aftermath* (The Boydell Press, 2003), 127–128.
39. John V. Tolan, *Saint Francis and the Sultan: The Curious History of a Christian–Muslim Encounter* (Oxford University Press, 2009), 11.
40. Cohn, *The Pursuit of the Millennium*, 37.
41. Jennifer Kolpacoff Deane and Anne E. Lester, *Between Orders and Heresy: Rethinking Medieval Religious Movements* (University of Toronto Press, 2022).
42. Decima Langworthy Douie, *The Nature and the Effect of the Fraticelli* (AMS Press, 2021).
43. Frassetto, *Heretic Lives,* 132.
44. Douie, *The Nature and the Effect of the Fraticelli*, 73.
45. David Burr, *Olivi's Peaceable Kingdom. A Reading of the Apocalypse Commentary* (University of Pennsylvania Press), 1993.
46. "PETRUS IOHANNIS OLIVI: Selections from the Apocalypse Commentary," Internet Medieval Source Book, Fordham University, accessed January 13, 2025, https://www2.kenyon.edu/projects/margin/olivi.htm.
47. Julia Anne Wannenmacher, ed., *Joachim of Fiore and the Influence of Inspiration: Essays in Memory of Marjorie E. Reeves (1905–2003)* (Routledge, 2016).
48. Bernard McGinn, *Visions of the End: Apocalyptic Traditions in the Middle Ages* (Columbia University Press, 1998), 129.
49. McGinn, *Visions of the End*, 130.
50. Dick Harrison, *Stora döden: den värsta katastrof som drabbat Europa* (Oldfront, 2000).
51. Cohn, *The Pursuit of the Millennium*, 131.
52. Cohn, *The Pursuit of the Millennium*, 134.
53. Mark Wheelis, "Biological Warfare at the 1346 Siege of Kaffa," *Emerging Infectious Diseases* 8, no. 9 (2002): 971–975.
54. Ibn Battutah, *The Travels of Ibn Battutah* (Picador, 2002), 120–121.
55. Lewis Dowell III, "Origins: A Study of the Black Death in Fourteenth Century Eurasia," PhD diss. University of Aberdeen, 2012, https://www.academia.edu/4905081/Origins_A_Study_of_the_Black_Death_in_Fourteenth_Century_Eurasia.
56. Quoted in Kelly, *The Great Mortality*, 25.
57. Kelly, *The Great Mortality*, 226.
58. Giovani Boccaccio, *The Decameron*, accessed January 13, 2025, https://uwaterloo.ca/communication-arts/performances/dramaturgy-and-archives/concord-floral-dramaturgy-hub/decameron.
59. William M. Bowsky, "Plague in Siena: An Italian Chronicle Agnolo di Tura del Grasso, 1349," in *The Black Death: A Turning Point in History?*, ed. William M. Bowsky (University of California, 1971), http://onala.free.fr/ditura1349.pdf.
60. Kelly, *The Great Mortality*, xiv.
61. James Clark, *The Dance of Death in the Middle Ages and the Renaissance* (Jackson, Son, & Company, 1950).
62. Hans Holbein, *The Dance of Death* (Penguin, 2017).

63. Juliet Barker, *1381: The Year of the Peasant's Revolt* (Belknap Press, 2014).
64. From a sermon delivered at Blackheath, June 12, 1381.
65. Samuel K. Cohn Jr., *Popular Protests in Late Medieval English Towns* (Cambridge University Press, 2012), 113.
66. Frassetto, *Heretic Lives,* 184.
67. "Who Coined 'Government of the People, by the People, for the People'?", *Washington Post,* Letters to the Editor, March 31, 2017, https://www.washingtonpost.com/opinions/who-coined-government-of-the-people-by-the-people-for-the-people/2017/03/31/12fc465a-0fd5-11e7-aa57-2ca1b05c41b8_story.html.

CHAPTER FIVE: REBIRTHING THE END

1. George Gemistos Plethon, "Fifth Monthly Hymn, To Apollo," trans. Manuela Simeoni, accessed January 13, 2025, http://www.giornopaganomemoria.it/plethon07apollo.html.
2. Stuart M. McManus, "Byzantines in the Florentine Polis: Ideology, Statecraft and ritual during the Council of Florence," *The Journal of the Oxford University History Society* 6 (2009): 4–6.
3. Niketas Siniossoglou, *Radical Platonism in Byzantium: Illumination and Utopia in Gemistos Plethon* (Cambridge University Press, 2016), 39.
4. Roger Crowley, *1453: The Holy War for Constantinople and the Clash of Islam and the West* (Hachette, 2006), 115.
5. Aphrodite Papayianni, "*He Polis healo:* The Fall of Constantinople in 1453 Post-Byzantine Popular Literature," *Al-Masaq: Islam and the Medieval Mediterranean* 22, no. 1 (2010): 27–44.
6. Papayianni, "*He Polis healo.*"
7. Siniossoglou, *Radical Platonism in Byzantium,* 2.
8. Jakob Burkhardt, *The Civilization of the Renaissance in Italy* (Penguin, 1990), 217.
9. Anthony Gottlieb, *The Dream of Reason: A History of Western Philosophy from the Greeks to the Renaissance* (W. W. Norton, 2016), 427.
10. Paul Oskar Kristeller, "The Platonic Academy of Florence," *Renaissance News,* 14, no. 3 (1961): 147–159.
11. Marsilio Ficino, "Five Questions Concerning the Mind," accessed January 13, 2025, https://www.sjsu.edu/people/cynthia.rostankowski/courses/HUM120AF14/s3/Marsilio-Ficino.pdf.
12. Frances Yates, *Giordano Bruno and the Hermetic Tradition* (University of Chicago Press, 1991), 18.
13. Yates, *Giordano Bruno and the Hermetic Tradition,* 17.
14. The standard work is Keith Thomas, *Religion and the Decline of Magic: Studies in Popular Belief in Sixteenth and Seventeenth-Century England* (Penguin, 2003).
15. Thomas, *Religion and the Decline of Magic,* 282.
16. "Precursors of Nostradamus?," Propheties on Line, last updated February 9, 2003, http://www.propheties.it/nostradamus/medieval/mirabilis-english/mirabilis-english.htm.

17. J. Britnell and D. Stubbs, "The *Mirabilis liber*, Its Compilation and Influence," *Journal of the Warburg and Courtauld Institutes* 49 (1986): 126.
18. Nostradamus, *The Prophecies: A Dual-Language Edition with Parallel Text* (Penguin, 2013), xxiv.
19. Nostradamus, *The Prophecies*, v.
20. Nostradamus, 5.
21. Nostradamus, 313.
22. The first reference is quoted in James Randi, *The Mask of Nostradamus* (Prometheus Books, 1993), 236, and the second reference is in Michael Servetus, *The Restoration of Christianity* (1553).
23. Rob Hatfield, "Botticelli's *Mystic Nativity*, Savonarola and the Millennium," *Journal of the Warburg and Courtauld Institutes* 58 (1995): 88–114.
24. David Weinstein, *Savonarola: The Rise and Fall of a Renaissance Prophet* (Yale University Press, 2011).
25. Girolamo Savonarola, as quoted in *A Guide to Righteous Living and Other Works* (The University of Toronto Press, 2003), 17.
26. Savonarola, *A Guide to Righteous Living and Other Works*, 63.
27. Weinstein, *Savonarola*, 76.
28. Ann Christiansen Remp, "Girolamo Savonarola (1452–1498): Fashioning of a Prophet and a New Jerusalem in Late Fifteenth-Century Florence," master's thesis, Eastern Michigan University, 2021, https://commons.emich.edu/cgi/viewcontent.cgi?article=2463&context=theses.
29. Quoted in Weinstein, *Savonarola*, 143.
30. Quoted in Philip and David Schley Schaff, *History of the Christian Church*, vol. V (C. Scribner's. 1910), 688.
31. Julia Stimac, "Marsilio Ficino, Astrology, and Renaissance Magic," PRPH Books, June 10, 2020, https://www.prphbooks.com/blog/ficino-astrology-magic.
32. Alison McQueen, *Political Realism in Apocalyptic Times* (Cambridge University Press, 2018), 76.
33. Schaff, *History of the Christian Church*, vol. V, 715.
34. Abbas Hamdani, "Columbus and the Recovery of Jerusalem," *Journal of the American Oriental Society*, *99*, no. 1 (1979): 39–48.
35. Brian A. Catlos, *Kingdoms of Faith: A New History of Islamic Spain* (Basic Books, 2018), 1.
36. James H. Sweet, "The Iberian Roots of American Racist Thought," *The William and Mary Quarterly* 54, no. 1 (1997): 143–166.
37. Hamdani, "Columbus and the Recovery of Jerusalem," 39–48.
38. Christopher Columbus, *The Diario of Christopher Columbus' First Voyage to America* (1492–1493), 291.
39. Tzvetan Todorov, *The Conquest of America: The Question of the Other* (Oxford University Press, 1999), 15.
40. Carol Delaney, "Columbus' Ultimate Goal: Jerusalem," *Comparative Studies in Society and History* 48 (2006), 260.
41. Arnold K. Garr, *Christopher Columbus: A Latter-Day Saint Perspective* (Religious Studies Center, Brigham Young University, 1992), 63–69, https://rsc.byu.

edu/christopher-columbus-latter-day-saint-perspective/later-years-book-prophecies-final-voyage.

42. Edmundo O'Gorman, *The Invention of America: An Inquiry into the Historical Nature of the New World and the Meaning of History* (The University of Indiana Press, 1961).
43. O' Gordman, *The Invention of America*, 1.
44. Quoted in Delaney, "Columbus' Ultimate Goal: Jerusalem," 260.
45. Quoted in Jan Willem Schulte Nordholt, *The Myth of the West: America as Last Empire* (Eerdmans, 1995), 68.
46. Christoph Mauntel, "The T-O Diagram and Its Religious Connotations: A Circumstantial Case," in *Geography and Religious Knowledge in the Medieval World*, ed. Christoph Mauntel (deGruyter, 2001), 57–82.
47. Toby Lester, "The Waldseemüller Map: Charting the New World," *Smithsonian Magazine*, December 2009, https://www.smithsonianmag.com/history/the-waldseemuller-map-charting-the-new-world-148815355.
48. Edward Simon, "Bradstreet and Trans-Atlantic Non-Conformism in the American-Prophetic Mode," in *Prophecy and Eschatology in the Trans-Atlantic World, 1550–1800*, ed. Andrew Crome (Palgrave-Macmillan, 2016), 83.
49. The previous three examples are all cited by Nordholt, *The Myth of the West*, 60.
50. A thorough discussion of this is engaged in Edward Simon, *The American Strand: Directional Poetics and Apocalypse in the Early Modern Trans-Atlantic* (Lehigh University, 2017).
51. Nordholt, *The Myth of the West*, 41.
52. Charles C. Mann, *1493: Uncovering the New World that Columbus Created* (Vintage, 2012), 14.
53. Mann, *1493*, 14.
54. Mann, *1493*, 14.
55. Kevin Gosner, *Soldiers of the Virgin: The Moral Economy of a Colonial Maya Rebellion* (University of Arizona Press, 1992), 3.
56. Gosner, *Soldiers of the Virgin*, 126.
57. John Beverley, "Tupac Amaru Rebellion," in *Historical Companion to Postcolonial Literatures: Continental Europe and Its Colonies* (Edinburgh University Press, 2008), 549.
58. As quoted in Greil Marcus, *A New Literary History of America* (Belknap Press, 2009), 6.
59. As quoted in Greil Marcus, *A New Literary History of America*, 6.
60. Miguel Leon-Portilla, *Broken Spears: The Aztec Account of the Conquest of Mexico* (Beacon Press, 2006), 22.
61. Leon-Portilla, *Broken Spears*, 23.
62. Brad S. Gregory, *The Unintended Reformation: How a Religious Revolution Secularized Society* (Belknap Press, 2015), 2.
63. Diarmaid MacCulloch, *All Things Made New: The Reformation and Its Legacy* (Oxford University Press, 2016), 4.

64. "Martin Luther: The Tower Experience, 1519," Fordham University Modern History Sourcebook, accessed January 13, 2025, https://sourcebooks.fordham.edu/mod/1519luther-tower.asp.
65. "Martin Luther: The Tower Experience, 1519," Fordham University Modern History Sourcebook, accessed January 13, 2025, https://sourcebooks.fordham.edu/mod/1519luther-tower.asp.
66. Carlos M. N. Eire, *Reformations: The Early Modern World, 1450–1650* (Yale University Press, 2018), vii.
67. Diarmaid MacCulloch, *The Reformation: A New History* (Penguin, 2005), 62.
68. Marc Greengrass, *Christendom Destroyed: Europe 1517–1648* (Penguin, 2015), 5.
69. Greengrass, *Christendom Destroyed*, 6.
70. Martin Luther, *Table Talk* (Frankfurt, 1569), 330.
71. Angela Serratore, "They Saw the Signs," *Lapham's Quarterly*, December 20, 2012, https://www.laphamsquarterly.org/roundtable/they-saw-signs.
72. Til-Holger Borchert and Joshua P. Waterman, *The Book of Miracles* (Taschen, 2017).
73. Greengrass, *Christendom Destroyed*, 5.
74. John R. Franke, "Reformation Amillennialism: Salvation Now, Salvation Forever," Christianity Today, accessed January 13, 2025, https://www.christianitytoday.com/history/issues/issue-61/reformation-amillennialism-salvation-now-salvation-forever.html.
75. Kenneth Scott Latourette, *A History of Christianity* (Prince, 1975), 720.
76. William R. Estep, *The Anabaptist Story* (Eerdmans, 1995), 1.
77. Michael G. Baylor, *The German Reformation and the Peasant's War: A Brief History with Documents* (Bedford/St. Martin's, 2012).
78. *A Sincere Admonition to All Christians to Guard Against Insurrection and Rebellion* (1522), in *Luther's Works*, vol. 45, ed. Walter I. Brandt (Fortress, 1962), 68.
79. Quoted in James M. Stayer, *The German Peasants' War and Anabaptist Community of Goods* (McGill-Queen's University Press, 1991), 109.
80. Albert Toscano, "Preface," in *Wu Ming Presents Thomas Müntzer Sermon to the Princes* (Verso, 2010), viii.
81. Stephen Greenblatt, *Learning to Curse: Essays in Early Modern Culture* (Routledge, 2015), 149.
82. Quoted in "Albrecht Durrer," in *The Catholic Encyclopedia: An International Work of Reference on the Constitution, Doctrine, Discipline, and History of the Catholic Church* (The Encyclopedia Press, 1909), 211.
83. Cohn, *The Pursuit of the Millennium*, 254.
84. Cohn, *The Pursuit of the Millennium*, 258.
85. Cohn, *The Pursuit of the Millennium*, 262.
86. Cohn, *The Pursuit of the Millennium*, 272.
87. Cohn, *The Pursuit of the Millennium*, 272.
88. Thomas Nashe, *The Unfortunate Traveller and Other Works* (Penguin, 1972), 278.
89. Nash, *The Unfortunate Traveller and Other Works*, 286.
90. Nash, *The Unfortunate Traveller and Other Works*, 280.

CHAPTER SIX: THE WHORES OF BABYLON

1. Tate Gallery, *The Pre-Raphaelites* (Tate Gallery/Penguin, 1984), 99.
2. Claire Ridgway, "St Bartholomew's Day Massacre 1572 – Primary Source Accounts," The Tudor Society, accessed January 13, 2025, https://www.tudorsociety.com/st-bartholomews-day-massacre-1572-primary-source-accounts.
3. Mack Holt, *The French Wars of Religion, 1562–1629* (Cambridge University Press, 2005), 236.
4. F. Fernadez-Armesto and D. Wilson, *Reformation: Christianity and the World 1500–2000* (Bantam Press, 1996), 236–237.
5. Adrianne Streete, *Apocalypse and Anti-Catholicism in Seventeenth-Century Drama* (Cambridge University Press, 2017), 38.
6. John Lothrop Motley, *The Rise of the Dutch Republic* (Bickers & Sons, 1883), 471.
7. Peter H. Wilson, *The Thirty Years War: Europe's Tragedy* (Belknap Press, 2011), 261.
8. Wilson, *The Thirty Years War*, 262.
9. MacCulloch, *The Reformation*, 536.
10. MacCulloch, *The Reformation*, 536.
11. Christopher Marlowe, *The Jew of Malta* (Dover, 2003), 1.
12. John Demos, *The Enemy Within: 2,000 Years of Witch-Hunting in the Western World* (Viking, 2008), 253.
13. *The Malleus Maleficarum*, accessed January 13, 2025, https://pages.uoregon.edu/dluebke/Witches442/442MalleusMaleficarum.html.
14. John Foxe, *Book of Martyrs: Select Narratives* (Oxford University Press, 2009), 154.
15. Quoted in Tryntie Helfferich, *The Essential Thirty Years War: A Documentary History* (Hackett, 2015), 15.
16. Geoffrey Parker, *The Thirty Years War* (Routledge, 1997), 189.
17. John Theibault, "The Rhetoric of Death and Destruction in the Thirty Years War," *The Journal of Social History*, 27, no. 2 (1993): 271–290.
18. Walter Kurschner, "Aus dem Kirchenbuch von Reichensachsen (und Langenhain) von 1639–1653," *Archiv für Hessische Geschichte und Altertumskunde* NF 9 (1913): 53.
19. Mark Lila, *The Stillborn God: Religion, Politics, and the Modern West* (Vintage, 2008), 4.
20. Gordon Goodwin, "Geddes, Jenny," in *Dictionary of National Biography*, vol. 21. (Smith, Elder & Co., 1890).
21. Michael Braddick, *God's Fury, England's Fire: A New History of the English Civil War* (Penguin, 2009), xxiv.
22. Eamon Duffy, *The Stripping of the Altars: Traditional Religion in England, 1400–1580* (Yale University Press, 2005), 52.
23. Martin Luther, "Martin Luther Against Henry King of England," Anglican History, February 7, 2025, https://anglicanhistory.org/lutherania/against_henry.html
24. Paul Kenneth Christianson, *Reformers and Babylon: English Apocalyptic Visions from the Reformation to the Eve of Civil War* (University of Toronto Press, 1978), 13.
25. John Knox, *The First Blast of the Trumpet Against the Monstrous Regiment of Women* (Edinburgh, 1558), 11.

26. Bernard Capp, "The Political Dimension of Apocalyptic Thought," in *The Apocalypse in English Renaissance Thought and Literature: Patterns, Antecedents, and Repercussions*, ed. C. A. Patrides and Joseph Wittreich (Manchester University Press, 1984), 96.
27. Capp, "The Political Dimension of Apocalyptic Thought," 95.
28. Christopher Hill, *Antichrist in Seventeenth Century England* (Verso, 1990), 51.
29. Hill, *Antichrist in Seventeenth Century England*, 51.
30. Andrew Bradstock, *Radical Religion in Cromwell's England: A Concise History from the English Civil War to the End of the Commonwealth* (I. B. Tauris, 2011), viii.
31. Bradstock, *Radical Religion in Cromwell's England*, xxiii.
32. Quoted in Philip Baker, ed., *The Putney Debates* (Verso, 2007).
33. Bradstock, *Radical Religion in Cromwell's England*, viii.
34. Quoted in Bradstock, *Radical Religion in Cromwell's England*, xxvi.
35. Gerrard Winstanley, *The True Levellers Standard Advanced* (London, 1649).
36. Winstanley, *A Declaration from the Poor Oppressed People of England* (1649).
37. Letter from Cromwell to Speaker Lenthall, September 17, 1649.
38. Abraham Nelson, *A Perfect Description of Antichrist, and his False Prophet: Wherein is Plainly Shewed that Oliver Cromwell was Antichrist* (1654).
39. "The True Emblem of Antichrist," The British Museum, February 7, 2025, https://www.bmimages.com/preview.asp?image=01613769610
40. Christopher Hill, *The World Turned Upside Down: Radical Ideas During the English Revolution* (Penguin, 1984), 341.
41. Quoted in Padraig Lawlor, "Oliver Was So Drunk with the Philtre of His Power; He Had Grown Corrupt: Sir Henry Vane's Political Theology," *Political Theology* 20, no. 7 (2019): 556–573.
42. Gershom Scholem, *Sabbatai Sevi: The Mystical Messiah* (Princeton University Press, 1973), ix.
43. Kaufmann Kohler and Henry Malter, "Shabbathai Zebi B. Mordecai," in *The Jewish Encyclopedia*, ed. Isidore Singer (Funk & Wagnalls, 1906).
44. Scholem, *Sabbatai Sevi*, xii.
45. Scholem, *Sabbatai Sevi*, 201.
46. Kohler and Malter, "Shabbathai Zebi B. Mordecai."
47. Matt Goldish, *The Sabbatean Prophets* (Harvard University Press, 2004), 1.
48. Kohler and Malter, "Shabbathai Zebi B. Mordecai."
49. Isaac Bashevis Singer, *Satan in Goray* (Farrar, Strauss & Giroux, 1996).
50. Scholem, *Sabbatai Sevi*, 7.
51. Yitzhak Luria, "Hymn for the Third Meal," accessed January 13, 2025, https://www.poetryfoundation.org/poetrymagazine/poems/55432/hymn-for-the-third-meal.
52. Scholem, *Sabbatai Sevi*, 8.
53. Scholem, *Sabbatai Sevi*, 9.
54. Harry Charles Lukach, The City of Dancing Dervishes and Other Sketches and Studies from the Near East (Macmillan, 1914), 189–190.
55. Steven Nadler, *Menasseh ben Israel, Rabbi of Amsterdam* (Yale University Press, 2018), 3.

56. Zvi Ben-Dor Benite, *The Ten Lost Tribes: A World History* (Oxford University Press, 2013), 24.
57. Goldish, *The Sabbatean Prophets*, 2.
58. "Ask with Joy," Chabad.org, accessed January 13, 2025, https://www.chabad.org/library/article_cdo/aid/1407567/jewish/Ask-With-Joy.htm.
59. "Thirty-Six Aphorisms of the Baal Shem Tov," Chabad.org, accessed January 13, 2025, https://www.chabad.org/library/article_cdo/aid/3073/jewish/36-Aphorisms-of-the-Baal-Shem-Tov.htm.
60. Bernard Bailyn, *The Barbarous Years—The Peopling of British North America: The Conflict of Civilizations, 1600–1675* (Vintage, 2013), 31.
61. Marcin Kilarski, *A History of the Study of the Indigenous Languages of North America* (John Benjamins, 2021), 25.
62. Alan Taylor, *American Colonies: The Settling of North America* (Viking, 2001), 169.
63. William Bradford, *Of Plymouth Plantation*, 70.
64. Lynn Ceci, "Fish Fertilizer: A Native North American Practice?" *Science* 188, no. 4183 (1975): 26–30.
65. Bailyn, *The Barbarous Years*, 31.
66. "William Bradford on the Great Sickness Among New England Indians (1633)," accessed January 13, 2025, https://www.westshore.edu/personal/mwnagle/US1/NativeAmerDocs/Bradford-sickness.htm#:~:text=For%20it%20pleased%20God%20to,ground%20for%20want%20of%20burial.
67. Simon, *Directional Poetics and Apocalypse in the Early Modern Trans-Atlantic*, 1.
68. Perry Miller, "The Shaping of the American Character," *The New England Quarterly* 28, no. 4 (1955): 435–454.
69. Abram C. van Engen, *City on a Hill: A History of American Exceptionalism* (Yale University Press, 2020), 3.
70. *Collectanea Anglo-Poetica* (Chetham Society, 1873), 128.
71. Sacvan Bercovitch, *The American Jeremiad* (The University of Wisconsin Press, 1978), 8.
72. Perry Miller, *Errand into the Wilderness* (Belknap Press, 1956), 1.
73. Samuel Danforth, "A Brief Recognition of New-England's Errand into the Wilderness" (1670).
74. Andrew Crome, "The Restoration of the Jews in Transatlantic Context," in *Prophecy and Eschatology in the Transatlantic World* (Palgrave Macmillan, 2016), 127–150.
75. The first reference is in Richard Drinnon, *Facing West: The Metaphysics of Indian Hating* (Oxford University Press, 1997), xxvi, while the second reference is from Daniel K. Richter, *Facing East from Indian Country: A Native History of Early America* (Harvard University Press, 2003), 252.
76. Jill Lepore, *The Name of War: King Philip's War and the Origins of American Identity* (Vintage, 1999), 72.
77. Benjamin Thompson, *New-England's Crisis* (1894).
78. Quoted by Edward Simon in "The Remembrance of Amalek," *The Revealer*, March 22, 2016, https://therevealer.org/the-remembrance-of-amalek.
79. Increase Mather, "A Brief History of the Warr with the Indians in New-England (1676): An Online Electronic Text Edition," Libraries at University of

Nebraska-Lincoln, accessed January 13, 2025, https://digitalcommons.unl.edu/cgi/viewcontent.cgi?article=1034&context=libraryscience.

80. Joseph Tyson III, "The Monks of the Wissahickon: Part 1," *Schuylkill Valley Journal Online* 2021.
81. Edward Benton-Banai, *The Mishomis Book - The Voice of the Ojibway* (St. Paul: Red School House Publishers, 1988).

CHAPTER SEVEN: VISIONS OF THE LAST JUDGMENT

1. A good introduction is Paul Collins, *The Trouble with Tom: The Strange Afterlife and Times of Thomas Paine* (Bloomsbury, 2009).
2. Thomas Paine, *The Age of Reason* (Liberal & Scientific Publishing Co., 1877), 143.
3. Peter Manseau, *One Nation, Under Gods: A New American History* (Back Bay Books, 2016), 6.
4. Jon Butler, *Awash in a Sea of Faith: Christianizing the American People* (Harvard University Press, 1992), 165.
5. Leonard Woolsey Bacon, *A History of American Christianity* (Christian Literature Co., 1897), 230.
6. Roger Finke and Rodney Stark, *The Churching of America, 1776–2005: Winners and Losers in Our Religious Economy* (Rutgers University Press, 2005), 29.
7. Leigh Eric Schmidt, *The Church of Saint Thomas Paine: A Religious History of American Secularism* (Princeton University Press, 2021), 4.
8. All quotations from Thomas Paine are in *Commonsense* (Dover, 2016), 2.
9. "Origin and Meaning of the Motto on the Reverse Side of the Great Seal," GreatSeal.com, accessed January 13, 2025, http://www.greatseal.com/mottoes/seclorum.html.
10. Craig Nelson, *Thomas Paine: Enlightenment, Revolution, and the Birth of Modern Nations* (Penguin, 2007), 8.
11. David Hackett Fischer, *Albion's Seed: Four British Folkways in America* (Oxford University Press, 1989), 6.
12. Gordon Wood, *The Radicalism of the American Revolution* (Vintage, 1993), 112.
13. Wood, *The Radicalism of the American Revolution*, 158.
14. Alan Taylor, *American Revolution: A Continental History, 1750–1804* (W. W. Norton, 2016), 452.
15. J. Hector St. John de Crèvecœur, *Letters from an American Farmer and Sketches of Eighteenth-Century America* (Penguin, 1981), 66.
16. Crèvecœur, *Letters from an American Farmer and Sketches of Eighteenth-Century America*, 9.
17. Benedict Anderson, *Imagined Communities: Reflections on the Origin and Spread of Nationalism* (Verso, 2016), 6.
18. Robert N. Bellah, *The Broken Covenant: American Religion in Time of Trial* (University of Chicago Press, 1992), 2.
19. Robert N. Bellah, "Civil Religion in America," accessed January 13, 2025, http://www.robertbellah.com/articles_5.htm.
20. Ernest Tuveson, *Redeemer Nation: The Idea of America's Millennial Role* (University of Chicago Press, 1980), vii.

21. William Blake, *America: A Prophecy* (1793), 2003rosen1805.pdf (loc.gov).
22. Blake, *America: A Prophecy.*
23. Stephen C. Behrendt, "'This Accursed Family': Blake's 'America' and the American Revolution," *The Eighteenth Century* 27, no. 1 (1986): 26–51.
24. William Hogeland, *The Whiskey Rebellion: George Washington, Alexander Hamilton, and the Frontier Rebels Who Challenged America's Newfound Sovereignty* (Scribner, 2006).
25. Paul Finkelman (Winter 2000). "Garrison's Constitution. The Covenant with Death and How It Was Made". Prologue Magazine. 32 (4).
26. Thomas Hartwell Horne and Samuel Davidson, *An Introduction to the Critical Study and Knowledge of the Holy Scriptures* (Cambridge University Press, 1818), 30.
27. Jeremy D. Popkin, *New World Begins: A History of the French Revolution* (Basic Books, 2019), 367.
28. Quoted in Popkin, *New World Begins*, 368.
29. Ruth Scurr, *Fatal Purity: Robespierre and the French Revolution* (Henry Holt, 2006), 293.
30. "On the Principles of Political Morality," Marxists.org, February 7, 2025, https://www.marxists.org/history/france/revolution/robespierre/1794/political-morality.htm
31. Emmet Kennedy, *A Cultural History of the French Revolution* (Yale University, 1989), 345.
32. Simon Schama, *Citizens: A Chronicle of the French Revolution* (Vintage, 1999).
33. Eric Voegelin, *The New Science of Politics*, in *The Collected Works of Eric Voegelin,* vol. 5, *Modernity Without Restraint* (University of Missouri Press, 1999), 185.
34. Mona Ozouf, "Revolutionary Calendar," in *Critical Dictionary of the French Revolution*, ed. François Furet and Mona Ozouf (Harvard University Press, 1989), 538–547.
35. Immanuel Kant, "What Is Enlightenment?," accessed January 13, 2025, http://www.columbia.edu/acis/ets/CCREAD/etscc/kant.html.
36. Susan Juster, *Doomsayers: Anglo-American Prophecy in the Age of Revolution* (University of Pennsylvania Press, 2006), viii.
37. From a letter to Jean d'Alembert of November 26th, 1762.
38. John Gray, *Black Mass: Apocalyptic Religion and the Death of Utopia* (Farrar, Strauss & Giroux, 2006), 2.
39. Gray, *Black Mass*, 2.
40. Juster, *Doomsayers*, 136.
41. Edmund Burke, Letter to a Member of the National Assembly of France (1791).
42. Slavoj Žižek, *In Defense of Lost Causes* (Verso, 2017), 159.
43. Juster, *Doomsayers*, 137.
44. Pawel Maciejko, *The Mixed Multitude: Jacob Frank and the Frankist Movement* (University of Pennsylvania Press, 2011).
45. Maciejko, *The Mixed Multitude: Jacob Frank and the Frankist Movementi*, 185.
46. Silvana Greco, *Moses Dobruska and the Invention of Social Philosophy. Utopia, Judaism, and Heresy Under the French Revolution* (De Gruyter, 2022).

47. Pawel Maciejko, *The Mixed Multitude: Jacob Frank and the Frankist Movement, 1755–1866* (University of Pennsylvania Press, 2011), 253.
48. Martin Munro, *Tropical Apocalypse: Haiti and the Caribbean End Times* (University of Virginia Press, 2015), 1971.
49. "From Thomas Jefferson to St. George Tucker, 28 August 1797," The National Archives, Accessed February 7, 2025, https://founders.archives.gov/documents/Jefferson/01-29-02-0405
50. Phillippe Girard, *Toussaint Louverture: A Revolutionary Life* (Basic Books, 2016), 1.

CHAPTER EIGHT: A TERRIBLE SWIFT SWORD

1. David L. Rowe, *God's Strange Work: William Miller and the End of the World* (Eerdmans, 2008), xiii.
2. *Wm. Miller's Apology and Defence* (Joshua V. Himes, 1845), 24, 32–53.
3. *Wm. Miller's Apology and Defence*, 6.
4. *Wm. Miller's Apology and Defence*, 11–12.
5. Rowe, *God's Strange Work*, xiv.
6. Rowe, *God's Strange Work*, xiv.
7. Hiram Edson, "Experience in the Advent Movement" (undated transcript), in *George Knight, 1844 and the Rise of Sabbatarian Adventism: Reproduction of Original Historical Documents* (Review & Herald Publishing Association, 1994), 9.
8. Edson, 9.
9. Alexis de Tocqueville, *Democracy in America: And Two Essays on America* (Penguin, 2003), 348.
10. Nathan O. Hatch, *The Democratization of American Christianity* (Yale University Press, 1991), 3.
11. Hatch, *The Democratization of American Christianity*, 4.
12. Brett Malcolm Grainger, *Church in the Wild: Evangelicals in Antebellum America* (Harvard University Press, 2019), 14.
13. Harold Bloom, *The American Religion: The Emergence of the Post-Christian Nation* (Simon & Schuster, 1992), 37.
14. Adam Morris, *American Messiahs: False Prophets of a Damned Nation* (W.W. Norton, 2019), 1.
15. Fawn M. Brodie, *No Man Knows My History: The Life of Joseph Smith* (Vintage, 1995).
16. The Book of Mormon, 2 Nephi 2.
17. Brodie, *No Man Knows My History*, ix.
18. "A Witness and a Warning," The Church of Jesus Christ of Latter Day Saints, Accessed February 7, 2025, https://www.churchofjesuschrist.org/study/general-conference/1979/10/a-witness-and-a-warning?lang=eng
19. Richard Abanes, *One Nation Under Gods: A History of the Mormon Church* (Basic Books, 2003), xvii.
20. Grainger, *Church in the Wild*, 14.
21. Ronald G. Walters, *American Reformers, 1815–1860* (Hill & Wang, 1997), 22.

22. Paul Boyer, *When Time Shall Be No More: Prophecy Belief in Modern American Culture* (Belknap Press, 1994), 83.
23. Boyer, *When Time Shall Be No More*, 83.
24. Philip Gura, *American Transcendentalism: A History* (Hill & Wang, 2008), 203.
25. Leo Marx, *The Machine in the Garden: Technology and the Pastoral Idea in America* (MIT Press, 1965), 31.
26. Marx, *The Machine in the Garden*, 32.
27. Henry David Thoreau, *Walden* (Thomas Y. Crowell and Company, 1910), 120.
28. Abbas Amanat, *Resurrection and Renewal: The Making of the Babi Movement in Iran, 1844–1850* (Cornell University Press, 1889), 1.
29. Abdulaziz Abdulhussein Sachedina, *Islamic Messianism: The Idea of the Mahdi in Twelver Shi'ism* (SUNY Press, 1980), 1.
30. Abdulaziz Abdulhussein Sachedina, *Islamic Messianism*, 2.
31. "Two Alwah ('Scriptural Tables') of the Bab Addressed to the Babi Messiah Figure Man Yuzhiru-hu Allah, 'He Whom God Shall Make Manifest,'" Hurqalya Publications: Center for the Shayki and Babi Bahai Studies, Accessed February 8, 2025, https://hurqalya.ucmerced.edu/node/4461.
32. Hassan Balyuzi, *Bahá'u'lláh: King of Glory* (George Ronald, 2000).
33. Lil Osborne, *Handbook of Islamic Sects and Movements* (Brill, 2021), 319.
34. Osborne, *Handbook of Islamic Sects and Movements,* 402.
35. "First Public Mentions of the Bahá'í Faith," Bahá'í Information Office of the UK (1998).
36. Bryan Wilson, "Millennialism in Comparative Perspective," *Comparative Studies in Society and History* 6, no. 1 (October 1963): 93–114.
37. Don E. Dumond, *The Machete and the Cross: Campesino Rebellion in Yucatan* (University of Nebraska Press, 1997).
38. Adam Ashforth, "The Xhosa Cattle Killing and the Politics of Memory," *Sociological Forum* 6, no. 3 (1991): 581–592.
39. P. M. Holt, *The Mahdist State in the Sudan 1881–1898: A Study of Its Origin, Development, and Overthrow* (Oxford University Press, 1958).
40. Paul Vanderwood, *The Power of God against the Guns of Government: Religious Upheaval in Mexico at the Turn of the 19th Century* (Stanford University Press, 1986), 36.
41. Wilson, "Millennialism in Comparative Perspective," 93–114.
42. Wilson, "Millennialism in Comparative Perspective," 93–114.
43. Michael Rappaport, *1848: Year of Revolution* (Basic Books, 2010).
44. Karl Marx and Friedrich Engels, *The Communist Manifesto* (Penguin, 2011), 1.
45. Marx and Engels, *The Communist Manifesto,* 1.
46. Richard Landes, *Heaven on Earth: The Varieties of the Millennial Experience* (Oxford University Press, 2011), 229.
47. Landes, *Heaven on Earth,* 378.
48. Landes, *Heaven on Earth,* 295.
49. Friedrich Nietzsche, *Ecce Homo* (Penguin, 1992), 108.
50. Carl S. Kilcourse, *Taiping Theology: The Localization of Christianity in China, 1843–64* (Palgrave Macmillan, 2016).

51. Thomas H. Reilly, *The Taiping Heavenly Kingdom: Rebellion and Blasphemy of Empire* (University of Washington Press, 2004), 3.
52. Reilly, *The Taiping Heavenly Kingdom*, 3.
53. "Leaders of the Taiping Rebellion," Facts and Details, Accessed February 8, 2025, https://factsanddetails.com/china/cat2/sub4/entry-7448.html
54. "Revolution in China and in Europe," Marxists.org, Accessed February 8, 2025, https://www.marxists.org/archive/marx/works/1853/06/14.htm
55. Richard H. Brodhead, "Millennium, Prophecy and the Energies of Social Transformation: The Case of Nat Turner," in *Imagining the End: Visions of Apocalypse from the Ancient Middle East to Modern America*, ed. A. Amanat and M. Bernhardsson (I. B. Tauris, 2002), 212–233.
56. Quoted in Kevin C. Julius, *The Abolitionist Decade, 1829–1838* (McFarland, 2004), 80.
57. "Nat Turner Explains Why He Led His Insurrection," Digital History, Accessed February 8, 2025, https://www.digitalhistory.uh.edu/disp_textbook.cfm?smtID=3&psid=505
58. Kenneth S. Greenberg, *Nat Turner: A Slave Rebellion in History and Memory* (Oxford University Press, 2004), 82.
59. Quoted in Maisha Wester, "Slave Narratives and Slave Revolts," in *The Palgrave Book of the Southern Gothic*, ed. Susan Castillo Street and Charles L. Crow (Palgrave Macmillan, 2016), 247.
60. Stephen B. Oates, *The Fires of Jubilee: Nat Turner's Fierce Rebellion* (Harper Perennial, 2004), ix.
61. Oates, *The Fires of Jubilee*, 57.
62. Oates, *The Fires of Jubilee*, 127.
63. Quoted in Jill Lepore, *The Story of America: Essays on Origins* (Princeton University Press, 2012), 22.
64. Lepore, *The Story of America*, 78.
65. Jan C. Dawson, *The Unusable Puritan Past: America's Puritan Tradition, 1830–1930* (Scholar's Press, 1984) 63.
66. Kevin Phillips, *The Cousins' Wars: Religion, Politics, and the Triumph of Anglo-America* (Basic Books, 1998), xiv.
67. Alexander Stephens, "The Cornerstone Speech" (1861).
68. Consult James Q. Whitman, *Hitler's American Model: The United States and the Making of Nazi Race Law* (Princeton University Press, 2017), 3.
69. Jimmie Hicks, "Some Letters Concerning the Knights of the Golden Circle in Texas, 1860–1861," *Southwestern Historical Quarterly* 65 (July 1961): 80–86.
70. Phillips, *The Cousin's War*, xv.
71. Benjamin Soskis, "A Fiery Gospel," Slate.com, November 17, 2011, https://slate.com/culture/2011/11/julia-ward-howes-battle-hymn-of-the-republic-how-it-changed-america.html.
72. Quoted in Richard Josiah Hinton, *John Brown and His Men: With Some Accounts of the Roads They Traveled to Reach Harper's Ferry* (Funk & Wagnalls, 1894), 426.
73. "John Brown's Holy War," Public Broadcasting Corporation, Accessed February 8, 2025, https://www.pbs.org/wgbh/americanexperience/features/brown-hanging/

74. David S. Reynolds, *John Brown, Abolitionist: The Man Who Killed Slavery, Sparked the Civil War, and Seeded Civil Rights* (Vintage, 2006), 25.
75. Ralph Waldo Emerson, *The Complete Works of Ralph Waldo Emerson: Society and Solitude*, vol. 7 (Houghton, Mifflin, 1903–1904), https://quod.lib.umich.edu/e/emerson/4957107.0007.001?id=N99907.P433N2;note=ptr;rgn=div1;view=trgt.
76. "Lincoln's Second Inaugural Address," National Parks Service, Accessed February 8, 2025, https://www.nps.gov/linc/learn/historyculture/lincoln-second-inaugural.htm
77. Manseau, *One Nation, Under Gods*, 285.
78. James Mooney, *The Ghost Dance Religion and Wounded Knee* (1896, reprint Constable, 1973), 702.
79. Louis S. Warren, *God's Red Son: The Ghost Dance Religion and the Making of Modern America* (Basic Books, 2017), 4.
80. John Fire/Lame Deer and Richard Erdoes, *Lame Deer, Seeker of Visions* (Simon & Schuster, 1972), chap. 14.

CHAPTER NINE: ENDING ALL OVER AGAIN

1. Details on Sunday's baseball career can be found in Wendy Knickerbocker, *Sunday at the Ballpark: Billy Sunday's Professional Baseball Career 1883–1890* (Scarecrow Press, 2000)
2. Matthew Avery Sutton, *American Apocalypse: A History of Modern Evangelicalism* (Belknap Press, 2017), 41.
3. Sutton, *American Apocalypse*, 41.
4. Sutton, *American Apocalypse*, 41.
5. Quoted in Glenn Watkins, *Proof Through the Night: Music and the Great War* (University of California Press, 2003), 276.
6. Sutton, *American Apocalypse*, 32.
7. Gabriel A. Almond, R. Scott Appleby, and Emanual Sivan, *Strong Religion: The Rise of Fundamentalisms Around the World* (University of Chicago Press, 2003).
8. Paul Rood, "The Untold Story of The Fundamentals," Biola Magazine, September 2, 2014, https://www.biola.edu/blogs/biola-magazine/2014/the-untold-story-of-the-fundamentals.
9. Franklin Johnsons, "The Fallacies and the Perils of the Higher Criticism," in *The Fundamentals of the Christian Faith*, ed. Edward D. Andrews and Reuben Archer Torrey (Christian Publishing House, 2022), 83.
10. Boyer, *When Time Shall Be No More*, 96.
11. Quoted in *The Union Seminary Review* (1915).
12. Marne L. Campbell, "'The Newest Religious Sect Has Started in Los Angeles': Race, Class, Ethnicity, and the Origins of the Pentecostal Movement 1906–1913," *The Journal of African American History* 95, no. (2010): 1–25.
13. Randall J. Stevens, *The Fire Spreads: Holiness and Pentecostalism in the American South* (Harvard University Press, 2008), 138.
14. "The Coming of Christ," Blue Letter Bible, Accessed February 8, 2025, https://www.blueletterbible.org/Comm/torrey_ra/fundamentals/85.cfm

15. John L. Bray, *The Origin of the Pre-Tribulation Rapture Teaching* (John L. Bray Ministry, 1982), 24–25.
16. Boyer, *When Time Shall Be No More*, xi.
17. Robert O. Smith, *More Desired Than Our Owne Salvation: The Roots of Christian Zionism* (Oxford University Press, 2013), 6.
18. Frances FitzGerald, *The Evangelicals: The Struggle to Shape America* (Simon & Schuster, 2017), 2.
19. Hal Lindsey, *The Late Great Planet Earth* (Zondervan, 1970), 89.
20. Bruce David Forbes and Djeanne Halgren Kilde, *Rapture, Revelation, and the End Times: Exploring the Left Behind Series* (Palgrave Macmillan, 2004), 2.
21. Tim LaHaye and Jerry B. Jenkins, *Left Behind: Soul Harvest – The World Takes Sides* (Tyndale, 1998), 412
22. Stephanie Mecimer, "Evangelicals Love Donald Trump for Many Reasons, But One of Them Is Especially Terrifying," *Mother Jones*, January 23, 2020, https://www.motherjones.com/politics/2020/01/evangelicals-are-anticipating-the-end-of-the-world-and-trump-is-listening.
23. J. Hansen et al., "Climate Impact of Increasing Atmospheric Carbon Dioxide," *Science* 213 (1981): 957–966, https://pubs.giss.nasa.gov/abs/ha04600x.html.
24. Guido von List, *Secret of the Runes (Guido-von-List-Bücherei 1)*, trans. Stephen E. Flowers (Destiny Books, 1908), 109.
25. Guido von List The Secret of the Runes *(Guido-von-List-Bücherei 1).* Translated by Flowers, Stephen E. Rochester, (Destiny Books, 1988) 109.
26. Nicholas Goodrick-Clarke, *The Occult Roots of Nazism: Secret Aryan Cults and Their Influence on Nazi Ideology* (Tauris Parke, 2004), 35.
27. Olav Hammer, "The Theosophical Current in the Twentieth Century," in *The Occult World*, ed. Charles Partridge (Routledge, 2016), 352.
28. Nicholas Goodrick-Clarke, *Black Sun: Aryan Cults, Esoteric Nazism and the Politics of Identity* (New York University Press, 2002).
29. Quoted in Mark Sedgewick, *Against the Modern World: Traditionalism and the Secret Intellectual History of the Twentieth Century* (Oxford University Press, 2004), 96.
30. Goodrick-Clarke, *The Occult Roots of Nazism*, 98.
31. David Reddles, *Hitler's Millennial Reich: Apocalyptic Belief and the Search for Salvation* (New York University Press, 2008), 13.
32. Reddles, *Hitler's Millennial Reich*, 43.
33. Reddles, *Hitler's Millennial Reich*, 70.
34. Doris L. Bergen, *Twisted Cross: The German Christian Movement in the Third Reich* (University of North Carolina Press, 1996).
35. Bergen, *Twisted Cross*, 27.
36. "The German Christian Movement," The Bell Society, Accessed February 8, 2025, https://richardwsymonds.wordpress.com/2021/02/27/february-27-2021-deutsche-christen-the-german-christian-movement-1932-1945/
37. Reddles, *Hitler's Millennial Reich*, 6.
38. George Steiner, *In Bluebeard's Castle: Some Notes Towards the Redefinition of Culture* (Faber and Faber, 1971), 45.

39. "The Dictator's Playbook," the Public Broadcasting System, Accessed February 8, 2025, https://www.pbs.org/video/benito-mussolini-pluih0/
40. Umberto Eco, "Ur-Fascism," *The New York Review of Books,* June 22, 1995.
41. Ibid.
42. Albert Einstein, "The Real Problem Is in the Hearts of Men," accessed January 13, 2025, http://scarc.library.oregonstate.edu/omeka/scripto/transcribe/11181/20791#transcription.
43. "How Many Nuclear Bombs Would it Take to Totally Screw Humanity?" IFL Science, Accessed on February 8, 2025, https://www.iflscience.com/how-many-nukes-would-it-take-to-totally-screw-humanity-48281
44. "Foreign Relations of the United States: Diplomatic Papers, The Conference of Berlin (The Potsdam Conference), 1945, Volume II," US Department of State, Office of the Historian, accessed January 13, 2025, https://history.state.gov/historicaldocuments/frus1945Berlinv02/d710a-59.
45. J. R. Oppenheimer, "Now I Am Become Death . . ." (video) (Atomic Archive, 1965), archived from the original on May 16, 2008.
46. Paul Boyer, *By the Bomb's Early Light: American Thought and Culture at the Dawn of the Atomic Age* (The University of North Carolina Press, 1994), vii.
47. Ross Pomeroy, "The Fear That a Nuclear Bomb Could Ignite the Atmosphere," Real Clear Science, September 12, 2019, https://www.realclearscience.com/blog/2019/09/12/the_fear_that_a_nuclear_bomb_could_ignite_the_atmosphere.html.
48. Arthur Compton, later quoted in *The Bulletin of Atomic Scientists* (1975), 21.
49. Boyer, *By the Bomb's Early Light*, xxi.
50. Boyer, *By the Bomb's Early Light*, xi; quoted in Allan M. Winkler's "The 'Atom' and American Life," *The History Teacher* 26, no. 3 (1993): 317–337.
51. "Radio Report to the American People on the Potsdam Conference," The Presidency Project, Accessed February 8, 2025, https://www.presidency.ucsb.edu/documents/radio-report-the-american-people-the-potsdam-conference#:~:text=It%20is%20an%20awful%20responsibility,way%20of%20life%20over%20another.
52. Quoted in Brendan Cooper, *Dark Airs: John Berryman and the Spiritual Politics of Cold War American Poetry* (Peter Lang, 2009), 49.
53. Ibid.
54. Martin Booth, *Hiroshima Joe* (Picador, 2003), 441.
55. John Hersey, *Hiroshima* (Vintage, 1989), 69.
56. Albert Camus, "On the Bombing of Hiroshima," in *Between Hell and Reason: Essays from the Resistance Newspaper Combat, 1944–1947* (Wesleyan University Press, 1991), 49.
57. Charles B. Strozier and Laura Simich, "Christian Fundamentalism and Nuclear Threat," *Political Psychology* 12, no. 1 (1991): 81–96.
58. Pat Robertson and Bob Slosser, *The Secret Kingdom: Your Path to Peace, Love, and Financial Security* (W. Pub Group, 1992), front matter.
59. Quoted by Lary Jones, "Apocalyptic Eschatology in the Nuclear Arms Race," *Transformation* (5:1, 1988), 25.
60. Stozier and Simich, *Political Psychology,* 81.

61. Stozier and Simich, *Political Psychology*, 96.
62. Timothy Miller, *Hippies and American Values* (University of Tennessee Press, 1991).
63. Timothy Leary, *The Politics of Ecstasy* (Ronin Publishing, 1998), frontmatter.
64. Joan Didion, "Slouching Towards Bethlehem," *The Saturday Evening Post*, June 14, 2017, https://www.saturdayeveningpost.com/2017/06/didion.
65. Vincent Bugliosi and Curt Gentry, *Helter Skelter (a Manson Scenario): The True Story of the Manson Murders*, 25th anniv. ed. (W. W. Norton, 1994).
66. Bugliosi, *Helter Skelter*, 239.
67. Charles Manson interview with Geraldo Rivera, *The Geraldo Show,* Rialto Theater, May 9th, 1988.
68. James R. Lewis, *The Gods Have Landed: New Religions from Other Worlds* (SUNY Press, 1995), xii.
69. Morris, *American Messiahs*, 5.
70. David Felton and David Dalton, "Charles Manson: The Incredible Story of the Most Dangerous Man Alive," *Rolling Stone,* June 25, 1970.
71. Union of Concerned Scientists, "Close Calls with Nuclear Weapons," April 2015, https://www.ucsusa.org/sites/default/files/attach/2015/04/Close%20Calls%20with%20Nuclear%20Weapons.pdf.

CHAPTER TEN: HOOFBEATS OF THE HORSEMEN

1. Octavia Butler, *Parable of the Sower* (Warner Books, 2000),
2. A concept and term coined by Alexei Yurchak in *Everything Was Forever, Until It Was No More: The Last Soviet Generation* (Princeton University Press, 2005), 52.
3. Rebecca Onion, "Why So Many Readers Are Turning to Octavia Butler's Apocalypse Fiction Right Now," Slate.com, September 19, 2020, https://slate.com/culture/2020/09/octavia-butler-parable-of-the-sower-talents-pandemic.html.
4. Octavia E. Butler, "A Few Rules for Predicting the Future," Common Good Collective, accessed January 1, 2025, https://commongood.cc/reader/a-few-rules-for-predicting-the-future-by-octavia-e-butler.
5. Mark Dery, "Black to the Future: Interviews with Samuel R. Delany, Greg Tate, and Tricia Rose," *The South Atlantic Quarterly* 92, no. 4 (Fall 1993): 736.
6. Jacques Derrida, "Of an Apocalyptic Tone Recently Adopted in Philosophy," *Oxford Literary Review* 6, no. 2 (1984): 3–37.
7. Jacques Derrida, "Of an Apocalyptic Tone Recently Adopted in Philosophy," *Oxford Literary Review* (6:2, 1984), 159.
8. Mary Shelley, *The Last Man* (Wordsworth Classics, 2004), 375.
9. Jan Zalasiewicz et al., "Are We Now Living in the Anthropocene?," *GSA* 18, no. 2 (2008): https://www.geosociety.org/gsatoday/archive/18/2/pdf/i1052-5173-18-2-4.pdf.
10. Mark Paynes, *Flowers of Time: On Postapocalyptic Fiction* (Princeton University Press, 2020), 1–2.
11. Ursula Heise, "What's the Matter with Dystopia," Public Books, February 1, 2015, https://www.publicbooks.org/whats-the-matter-with-dystopia.
12. Payne, *Flowers of Time*, 1.

13. Stephen Vincent Benet (July 31, 1937). "THE PLACE OF THE GODS". *Saturday Evening Post.* 210 (5). July 31, 1937.
14. "Thirteen O'Clock – By the Waters of Babylon," Fadedpage.com, Accessed on February 8, 2025. https://www.fadedpage.com/showbook.php?pid=20110103
15. "Thirteen O'Clock – By the Waters of Babylon," Fadedpage.com, Accessed on February 8, 2025. https://www.fadedpage.com/showbook.php?pid=20110103
16. Oswald Spengler, *The Decline of the West: Perspectives of World History* (George Allen, 1928), 105.
17. William Miller, *A Canticle for Leibowitz* (Spectra, 1984), 17.
18. Miller, *A Canticle for Leibowitz*, 264.
19. Stephen King, *The Stand* (Anchor, 2012), 1, 155.
20. Cormac McCarthy, *The Road* (Knopf Doubleday, 2006), 11.
21. Fredric Jameson, "Future City," *New Left Review* 21 (May/June 2003): https://newleftreview.org/issues/ii21/articles/fredric-jameson-future-city.
22. Fredric Jameson, "Future City," *New Left Review* 21 (May/June 2003): https://newleftreview.org/issues/ii21/articles/fredric-jameson-future-city.
23. Octavia Butler, *Parable of the Sower* (Warner Books, 2000),
24. Gary Kasparov, *How Life Imitates Chess* (Bloomsbury, 2007), 4.
25. Gary Kasparov, *Deep Thinking: Where Machine Intelligence Ends and Human Creativity Begins* (Public Affairs, 2017), 2.
26. Gordon E. Moore, "Cramming More Components onto Integrated Circuits," *Electronics Magazine*, April 19, 1965: 114–117.
27. Nick Bostrom, *Superintelligence: Paths, Dangers, Strategies* (Oxford University Press, 2014), 49.
28. Barry Ptolemy, *Transcendent Man* (Ptolemaic Productions and Therapy Studios, 2009).
29. Ptolemy, *Transcendent Man*.
30. ABC News, "Futurist Ray Kurzweil Says He Can Bring His Dead Father Back to Life Through a Computer Avatar," August 10, 2011, https://abcnews.go.com/Technology/futurist-ray-kurzweil-bring-dead-father-back-life/story?id=14267712.
31. Hans Moravec, "Simulation, Consciousness, Existence," accessed February 6, 2025, https://www.organism.earth/library/document/simulation-consciousness-existence.
32. Ed Regis, *Great Mambo Chicken and the Transhuman Condition: Science Slightly Over the Edge* (Basic Books, 1991), 6.
33. Ray Kurzweil, *The Age of Spiritual Machines: When Computers Exceed Human Intelligence* (Penguin, 2000), 56.
34. Meaghen O'Gieblyn, *God, Human, Animal, Machine: Technology, Metaphor, and the Search for Meaning* (Penguin Random House, 2021), 49.
35. Meaghen O'Gieblyn, *God, Human, Animal, Machine: Technology, Metaphor, and the Search for Meaning* (Penguin Random House, 2021), 49.
36. William MacAskill, *Doing Good Better: How Effective Altruism Can Help You Make a Difference* (Penguin Random House, 2015), 170.
37. William MacAskill, *What We Owe the Future* (Basic Books, 2022), 217.

38. Carole Cadwalladr, "Stewart Brand's Whole Earth Catalog, the Book That Changed the World," *The Guardian*, May 5, 2013, https://www.theguardian.com/books/2013/may/05/stewart-brand-whole-earth-catalog.
39. Stewart Brand, *The Whole Earth Catalogue* (1968), 1.
40. Andrew Jones, "From NeoReactionary Theory to the Alt-Right," in *Critical Theory and the Humanities in the Age of the Alt-Right*, ed. Christine M. Battista and Melissa R. Sande (Palgrave Macmillan, 2019), 101–120.
41. "Thos. Carlyle on Steve Jobs," Mencius Moldbug, October 6, 2011, https://www.unqualified-reservations.org/2011/10/thos-carlyle-on-steve-jobs.
42. Nick Land, *Time in Transition* (2011).
43. "Nick Land," Wikiquote, Accessed February 8, 2025. https://en.wikiquote.org/wiki/Nick_Land
44. Francis Fukuyama, *The End of History and the Last Man* (Simon & Schuster, 1992), 201.
45. Gray, *Black Mass*, 1.
46. Sian Cain, "David Graeber, Anthropologist and Author of Bullshit Jobs, Dies Aged 59," *The Guardian*, September 3, 2020, https://www.theguardian.com/books/2020/sep/03/david-graeber-anthropologist-and-author-of-bullshit-jobs-dies-aged-59.
47. Nathan Schneider, *Thank You, Anarchy: Notes from the Occupy Apocalypse* (University of California Press, 2013), 162.
48. Jill Lepore, *The Whites of Their Eyes: The Tea Party's Revolution and the Battle Over American History* (Princeton University Press, 2010), 7.
49. Kristin Kobes Du Mez, *Jesus and John Wayne: How White Evangelicals Corrupted a Faith and Fractured a Nation* (Liveright, 2020), 185.
50. Ronald Radosh, "Steve Bannon, Trump's Top Guy, Told Me He Was 'a Leninist,'" The Daily Beast, August 22, 2016, https://www.thedailybeast.com/steve-bannon-trumps-top-guy-told-me-he-was-a-leninist.
51. William Straus and Neil Howe, *The Fourth Turning: What the Cycles of History Tell Us About America's Next Rendezvous with History* (Broadway Books, 1997), 6.
52. Gregory Krieg, "Steve Bannon, Trump's Top Guy, Told Me He Was 'a Leninist,'" CNN.com, March 30, 2017, https://www.cnn.com/2017/03/30/politics/trump-bannon-administrative-state/index.html.
53. Ed Simon, "The Would-Be Czar's Dark Prophet," History News Network, March 6, 2022, https://historynewsnetwork.org/article/182605.
54. Ed Simon, "The Would-Be Czar's Dark Prophet," History News Network, March 6, 2022, https://historynewsnetwork.org/article/182605.
55. Julius Evola, *Civilta Americana* (Quaderni di testi evoliani, 1945).
56. Du Mez, *Jesus and John Wayne*, 3.
57. Jeff Sharlet, "'He's the Chosen One to Run America': Inside the Cult of Trump, His Rallies Are Church and He Is the Gospel," *Vanity Fair*, June 18, 2020, https://www.vanityfair.com/news/2020/06/inside-the-cult-of-trump-his-rallies-are-church-and-he-is-the-gospel.
58. "The Big Story: The Sprawling Universe of QAnon," virtual event, *The Atlantic*, May 28, 2020, https://www.theatlantic.com/live/sprawling-universe-qanon-2020.

59. Philip S. Gorski and Samuel L. Perry, *The Flag and the Cross: White Christian Nationalism and the Threat to American Democracy* (Oxford University Press, 2022), 104.
60. George Grant, *The Changing of the Guard: Biblical Principles for Political Action* (Dominion, 1987), 192.
61. John Weaver, *The New Apostolic Reformation: History of a Modern Charismatic Movement* (McFarland, 2016), 2.
62. Elle Hardy "The 'modern apostles' who want to reshape America ahead of the end times". The Outline. March 19, 2020.
63. Elle Hardy "The 'modern apostles' who want to reshape America ahead of the end times". The Outline. March 19, 2020.
64. Monica Sager "Who is Paula White-Cain? Trump's Pick to Lead White House Faith Office". *Newsweek*. Retrieved February 8, 2025.

EPILOGUE

1. Ruairi Casey, "'If You See Me Weep': Hunger Stones Auguring Drought in Europe," AlJazeera.com, November 29, 2022, https://www.aljazeera.com/features/2022/11/29/if-you-see-me-weep-hunger-stones-auguring-drought-in-europe.
2. Coral Davenport, "Major Climate Report Describes a Strong Risk of Crisis as Early as 2040," *New York Times*, October 7, 2018, https://www.nytimes.com/2018/10/07/climate/ipcc-climate-report-2040.html#:~:text=The%20authors%20found%20that%20if,and%20intensifying%20droughts%20and%20poverty.
3. "First Paper to Link CO2 and Global Warming, by Eunice Foote (1856)," The Public Domain Review, October 3, 2019, https://publicdomainreview.org/collection/first-paper-to-link-co2-and-global-warming-by-eunice-foote-1856.
4. Neela Banerjee et al., "Exxon's Own Research Confirmed Fossil Fuels' Role in Global Warming Decades Ago," Inside Climate News, September 16, 2015, https://insideclimatenews.org/news/16092015/exxons-own-research-confirmed-fossil-fuels-role-in-global-warming.
5. Paul Kingsnorth, *Confessions of a Recovering Environmentalist* (Graywolf, 2017), 80.
6. Davenport, "Major Climate Report Describes a Strong Risk of Crisis as Early as 2040."
7. Mark Fischetti, "Climate Change Hastened Syria's Civil War," *Scientific American*, March 2, 2015, https://www.scientificamerican.com/article/climate-change-hastened-the-syrian-war.
8. Roy Scranton, *We're Doomed: Now What?* (Soho Press, 2018), 3.

BIBLIOGRAPHY

Abanes, Richard. *One Nation Under Gods: A History of the Mormon Church*. Basic Books, 2003.

Al-Azmeh, Aziz. *The Emergence of Islam in Late Antiquity: Allah and His People*. Cambridge University Press, 2014.

Allenby, Edmund. "Proclamation of Martial Law in Jerusalem." In *Standing Orders and General Instructions for the Information of Officers*. Headquarters, Occupied Enemy Territory Administration, 1918.

Almond, Gabriel A. R., Scott Appleby, and Emanual Sivan. *Strong Religion: The Rise of Fundamentalisms Around the World*. University of Chicago Press, 2003.

Alter, Robert. *The Art of Biblical Poetry*. Basic Books, 2011.

Amanat, Abbas. *Resurrection and Renewal: The Making of the Babi Movement in Iran, 1844–1850*. Cornell University Press, 1989.

Anderson, Benedict. *Imagined Communities: Reflections on the Origin and Spread of Nationalism*. Verso, 2016.

"The Apocalypse of Adam." In *Nag Hamadi Codex*. Vol. 5. Translated by George W. McRae. Brill, 1996.

Armstrong, Karen. *Muhammad: A Prophet for Our Times*. HarperOne, 2007.

Armstrong, Karen. *A Short History of Myth*. Canongate, 2004.

Asbridge, Thomas. *The Crusades: The Authoritative History of the War for the Holy Land*. Ecco, 2011.

Asher, Jay, and Jessica Freeburg. *Piper*. Razorbill, 2017.

Ashforth, Adam. "The Xhosa Cattle Killing and the Politics of Memory." *Sociological Forum* 6, no. 3 (1991): 581–592.

Aslan, Reza. *No God But God: The Origins, Evolution, and Future of Islam*. Random House, 2011.

August, C. Krey. *The First Crusade: The Accounts of Eyewitnesses and Participants*. Princeton University Press, 1921.

Bacon, Leonard Woolsey. *A History of American Christianity*. Christian Literature Co., 1897.

Badsen, Joel S. *The Composition of the Pentateuch: Reviewing the Documentary Hypothesis*. Yale University Press, 2012.

Bailyn, Bernard. *The Barbarous Years—The Peopling of British North America: The Conflict of Civilizations, 1600–1675*. Vintage, 2013.

Baker, Philip, ed. *The Putney Debates*. Verso, 2007.

Balyuzi, Hassan. *Bahá'u'lláh: King of Glory*. George Ronald, 2000.

Barker, Juliet. *1381: The Year of the Peasant's Revolt*. Belknap Press, 2014.

Barr, David L. "Violence in the Apocalypse of John." In *The Oxford Handbook of the Book of Revelation*, edited by Craig Koester. Oxford University Press, 2020.

Battutah, Ibn. *The Travels of Ibn Battutah*. Picador, 2002.

Baylor, Michael G. *The German Reformation and the Peasant's War: A Brief History with Documents*. Bedford/St. Martin's, 2012.

Bazian, Hatem. "Revisiting the British Conquest of Jerusalem." *Al Jazeera*, December 14, 2014. https://www.aljazeera.com/opinions/2014/12/14/revisiting-the-british-conquest-of-jerusalem.

Becker, Uwe. "The Book of Isaiah: Its Composition History." In *The Oxford Handbook of Isaiah*, edited by Lena-Sofia Tiemeyer. Oxford University Press, 2020.

Bede, *Ecclesiastical History of the British People*. In *Medieval Sourcebook*, edited by Paul Halsall. Fordham University, 1996. https://origin-rh.web.fordham.edu/halsall/basis/bede-book1.asp.

Behrendt, Stephen C. "'This Accursed Family': Blake's 'America' and the American Revolution." *The Eighteenth Century* 27, no. 1 (Winter 1986): 26–51.

Bellah, Robert. *The Broken Covenant: American Religion in Time of Trial*. University of Chicago Press, 1992.

Ben-Dor Benite, Zvi. *The Ten Lost Tribes: A World History*. Oxford University Press, 2013.

Bercovitch, Sacvan. *The American Jeremiad*. The University of Wisconsin Press, 1978.

Bergen, Doris L. *Twisted Cross: The German Christian Movement in the Third Reich*. The University of North Carolina Press, 1996.

Bethencourt, Francisco. *The Inquisition: A Global History*. Cambridge University Press, 2007.

Beverley, John. "Tupac Amaru Rebellion." In *Historical Companion to Postcolonial Literatures: Continental Europe and Its Colonies*, edited by Prem Poddar, Rajeev S. Patke, and Lars Jensen. Edinburgh University Press, 2008.

Blackburn, Bonnie, and Leofranc Holford-Strevens, "Calendar and Chronology." In *The Oxford Companion to the Year*, edited by Bonnie J. Blackburn and Leofranc Holford-Stevens. Oxford University Press, 1999.

Blichfeldt, Jan-Olaf. *Early Mahdism: Politics and Religion in the Formative Period of Islam*. Brill, 1985.

Bloom, Harold. *The American Religion: The Emergence of the Post-Christian Nation*. Simon & Schuster, 1992.

"Book of Revelation." In *The Oxford Dictionary of the Christian Church*, edited by F. L. Cross. Oxford University Press, 2005.

Booth, Martin. *Hiroshima Joe*. Picador, 2003.

Borchert, Til-Holder, and Joshua P. Waterman. *The Book of Miracles*. Taschen, 2017.

Bostrom, Nick. *Superintelligence: Paths, Dangers, Strategies*. Oxford University Press, 2014.

Boyce, Mary. *Zoroastrians: Their Religious Beliefs and Practices*. Routledge, 2000.

Boyer, Paul. *By the Bomb's Early Light: American Thought and Culture at the Dawn of the Atomic Age*. The University of North Carolina Press, 1994.

Boyer, Paul. *When Time Shall Be No More: Prophecy Belief in American Culture*. Harvard University Press, 1992.

Braddick, Michael. *God's Fury, England's Fire: A New History of the English Civil War.* Penguin, 2009.

Bradford, William. *Of Plymouth Plantation.* 1651.

Bradstock, Andrew. *Radical Religion in Cromwell's England: A Concise History from the English Civil War to the End of the Commonwealth.* I. B. Tauris, 2011.

Bray, John L. *The Origin of the Pre-Tribulation Rapture Teaching.* John L. Bray Ministry, 1982.

Bridge, Anthony. *The Crusades.* Granada, 1980.

Britnell. J., and D. Stubbs, "The *Mirabilis liber*, Its Compilation and Influence." *Journal of the Warburg and Courtauld Institutes* 49 (1986): 126–149.

Brockington, J. *The Sanskrit Epics.* Brill, 1998.

Brodhead, Richard H. "Millennium, Prophecy and the Energies of Social Transformation: The Case of Nat Turner." In *Imagining the End: Visions of Apocalypse from the Ancient Middle East to Modern America*, edited by A. Amanat and M. Bernhardsson. I. B. Tauris, 2002.

Brodie, Fawn M. *No Man Knows My History: The Life of Joseph Smith.* Vintage, 1995.

Brown, Mary Franklin. *Reading the World: Encyclopedic Writing in the Scholastic Age.* University of Chicago Press, 2012.

Bugliosi, Vincent, and Curt Gentry. *Helter Skelter (a Manson Scenario): The True Story of the Manson Murders.* 25th anniversary ed. W. W. Norton, 1994.

Burke, Edmund. Letter to a Member of the National Assembly of France. 1791.

Burkhardt, Jakob. *The Civilization of the Renaissance in Italy.* Schweighauser'sche Verlagsbuchhandlung, 1860.

Burr, David. *Olivi's Peaceable Kingdom. A Reading of the Apocalypse Commentary.* University of Pennsylvania Press, 1993.

Butler, Jon. *Awash in a Sea of Faith: Christianizing the American People.* Harvard University Press, 1992.

Butler, Octavia. *Parable of the Sower.* Warner Books, 2000.

Campbell, Marne L. "'The Newest Religious Sect Has Started in Los Angeles': Race, Class, Ethnicity, and the Origins of the Pentecostal Movement 1906–1913." *The Journal of African American History* 95, no. 1 (Winter 2010). https://doi.org/10.5323/jafriamerhist.95.1.0001.

Camus, Albert. "On the Bombing of Hiroshima." In *Between Hell and Reason: Essays from the Resistance Newspaper Combat, 1944–1947.* Wesleyan University Press, 1991.

Capp, Bernard. "The Political Dimension of Apocalyptic Thought." In *The Apocalypse in English Renaissance Thought and Literature: Patterns, Antecedents, and Repercussions*, edited by C. A. Patrides and Joseph Wittreich. Manchester University Press, 1984.

Carmi, Israel. "Radiocarbon Dating of the Dead Sea Scrolls." In *The Dead Sea Scrolls: Fifty Years After Their Discovery, 1947–1997,* edited by Lawrence Schiffman, Emanuel Tov, and James VanderKam. IES, 2000.

Carroll, James. *Constantine's Sword: The Church and the Jews.* Houghton Mifflin Harcourt, 2001.

Catlos, Brian A. *Kingdoms of Faith: A New History of Islamic Spain.* Basic Books, 2018.

Ceci, Lynn. "Fish Fertilizer: A Native North American Practice?" *Science* 188, no. 4183 (1975): 26–30.

Cereti, Carl G. "Myths, Legends, Eschatologies." In *The Wiley Blackwell Companion to Zoroastrianism*, edited by Michael Stausberg, Yuhan Sohrab-Dinshaw Vevaina, and Anna Tessmann. Wiley Blackwell, 2015.

Christianson, Paul Kenneth. *Reformers and Babylon: English Apocalyptic Visions from the Reformation to the Eve of Civil War*. University of Toronto Press, 1978.

Christie, Niall (ed. and trans.) *The Book of the Jihad of 'Ali ibn Tahir al-Sulami*. Routledge, 2015.

Clark, James. *The Dance of Death in the Middle Ages and the Renaissance*. Jackson, Son, & Co., 1950.

Cohn, Norman. *The Pursuit of the Millennium: Revolutionary Millenarians and Mystical Anarchists of the Middle Ages*. Oxford University Press, 1970.

Cohn, Samuel K., Jr. *Popular Protests in Late Medieval English Towns*. Cambridge University Press, 2012.

Collectanea Anglo-Poetica. The Chetham Society, 1873.

Collins, John Joseph. *Daniel: With an Introduction to Apocalyptic Literature*. Eerdmans, 1984.

Collins, Paul. *The Trouble with Tom: The Strange Afterlife and Times of Thomas Paine*. Bloomsbury, 2009.

Columbus, Christopher. *The Diario of Christopher Columbus' First Voyage to America*. 1492–1493.

Cook, Michael. "Eschatology and the Dating of Traditions." In *Hadith: Origins and Developments*, edited by Harald Motzki. Routledge, 2016.

Cooper, Brendan. *Dark Airs: John Berryman and the Spiritual Politics of Cold War American Poetry*. Peter Lang, 2009.

Crèvecœur, J. Hector St. John de. *Letters from an American Farmer and Sketches of Eighteenth-Century America*. Penguin, 1981.

Crome, Andrew. "The Restoration of the Jews in Transatlantic Context." In *Prophecy and Eschatology in the Transatlantic World*, edited by Andrew Crome. Palgrave Macmillan, 2016.

Crowley, Roger. *1453: The Holy War for Constantinople and the Clash of Islam and the West*. Hachette Books, 2006.

Dawson, Jan C. *The Unusable Puritan Past: America's Puritan Tradition, 1830–1930*. Scholar's Press, 1984.

Deane, Jennifer Kolpacoff, and Anne E. Lester. *Between Orders and Heresy: Rethinking Medieval Religious Movements*. University of Toronto Press, 2022.

Delaney, Carol. "Columbus' Ultimate Goal: Jerusalem." *Comparative Studies in Society and History* 48 (2006): 260–292.

Demos, John. *The Enemy Within: 2,000 Years of Witch-Hunting in the Western World*. Viking, 2008.

Derrida, Jacques. "Of an Apocalyptic Tone Recently Adopted in Philosophy." *Oxford Literary Review* 6, no. 2 (1984): 3–37.

Derry, Mark. "Black to the Future: Interviews with Samuel R. Delany, Greg Tate, and Tricia Rose." *The South Atlantic Quarterly* 92, no. 4 (1993): 735–778.

Doniger, Wendy. *The Hindus: An Alternative History*. Penguin, 2010.
Douie, Decima Langworthy. *The Nature and the Effect of the Fraticelli*. AMS Press, 2021.
Drinnon, Richard. *Facing West: The Metaphysics of Indian Hating*. Oxford University Press, 1997.
Duffy, Eamon. *The Stripping of the Altars: Traditional Religion in England, 1400–1580*. Yale University Press, 2005.
Du Mez, Kristin Kobes. *Jesus and John Wayne: How White Evangelicals Corrupted a Faith and Fractured a Nation*. Liveright, 2020.
Dumond, Don E. *The Machete and the Cross: Campesino Rebellion in Yucatan*. University of Nebraska Press, 1997.
Duncan, David Ewing. *Calendar: Humanity's Epic Struggle to Determine a True and Accurate Year*. Harper Perennial, 1999.
Edson, Hiram. "Experience in the Advent Movement" (undated transcript). In *George Knight, 1844 and the Rise of Sabbatarian Adventism: Reproduction of Original Historical Documents*. Review & Herald Publishing Association, 1994.
Ehrman, Bart. *Jesus: Apocalyptic Prophet of the New Millennium*. Oxford University Press, 1999.
Eire, Carlos M. N. *Reformations: The Early Modern World, 1450–1650*. Yale University Press, 2018.
Estep, William R. *The Anabaptist Story*. Eerdmans, 1995.
Evola, Julius. *Civilta Americana*. Quaderni di testi evoliani, 1945.
Faught, C. Brad. *Allenby: Making the Modern Middle East*. Bloomsbury, 2020.
Fernadez-Armesto, F., and D. Wilson. *Reformation: Christianity and the World 1500–2000*. Bantam Press, 1996.
Filiu, Jean-Pierre. *Apocalypse in Islam*. University of California Press, 2011.
Finke, Roger, and Rodney Stark. *The Churching of America, 1776–2005: Winners and Losers in Our Religious Economy*. Rutgers University Press, 2005.
Fischer, David Hackett. *Albion's Seed: Four British Folkways in America*. Oxford University Press, 1989.
FitzGerald, Frances. *The Evangelicals: The Struggle to Shape America*. Simon & Schuster, 2017.
Fletcher, Richard. *The Cross and the Crescent: The Dramatic Story of the Earliest Encounters Between Christians and Muslims*. Penguin, 2005.
Forbes, Bruce David, and Djeanne Halgren Kilde. *Rapture, Revelation, and the End Times: Exploring the Left Behind Series*. Palgrave Macmillan, 2004.
Foxe, John. *Book of Martyrs: Select Narratives*. Oxford University Press, 2009.
France, Peter. *A Place of Healing for the Soul*. Grove Press, 2002.
Frassetto, Michael. *Heretic Lives: Medieval Heresy from Bogomil and the Cathars to Wyclif and Hus*. Profile, 2007.
Frye, Northrop. *The Great Code: The Bible and Literature*. Houghton Mifflin Harcourt, 1981.
Fukuyama, Francis. *The End of History and the Last Man*. Simon & Schuster, 1992.
Gabriel, Matthew, and David M. Perry. *Bright Ages: A New History of Medieval Europe*. HarperCollins, 2021.
Girard, Phillippe. *Toussaint Louverture: A Revolutionary Life*. Basic Books, 2016.

Goldish, Matt. *The Sabbatean Prophets*. Harvard University Press, 2004.

Golia, Maria. *Meteorite: Nature and Culture*. Reaktion Books, 2015.

Goodrick-Clarke, Nicholas. *Black Sun: Aryan Cults, Esoteric Nazism and the Politics of Identity*. New York University Press, 2002.

Goodrick-Clarke, Nicholas. *The Occult Roots of Nazism: Secret Aryan Cults and Their Influence on Nazi Ideology*. Tauris Parke, 2004. Originally published in 1985.

Goodwin, Gordon. "Geddes, Jenny." In *Dictionary of National Biography*. Vol. 21. Smith, Elder & Co., 1890.

Gorski, Philip S., and Samuel L. Perry. *The Flag and the Cross: White Christian Nationalism and the Threat to American Democracy*. Oxford University Press, 2022.

Gosner, Kevin. *Soldiers of the Virgin: The Moral Economy of a Colonial Maya Rebellion*. University of Arizona Press, 1992.

Gottlieb, Anthony. *The Dream of Reason: A History of Western Philosophy from the Greeks to the Renaissance*. W. W. Norton, 2016.

Gould, Stephen Jay. *Questioning the Millennium: A Rationalist's Guide to a Precisely Arbitrary Countdown*. Harmony, 1997.

Grainger, Brett Malcolm. *Church in the Wild: Evangelicals in Antebellum America*. Harvard University Press, 2019.

Grant, George. *The Changing of the Guard: Biblical Principles for Political Action*. Dominion, 1987.

Gray, John. *Black Mass: Apocalyptic Religion and the Death of Utopia*. Farrar, Strauss & Giroux, 2006.

Greco, Silvana. *Moses Dobruska and the Invention of Social Philosophy. Utopia, Judaism, and Heresy Under the French Revolution*. De Gruyter, 2022.

Greenberg, Kenneth S. *Nat Turner: A Slave Rebellion in History and Memory*. Oxford University Press, 2004.

Greenblatt, Stephen. *Learning to Curse: Essays in Early Modern Culture*. Routledge, 2015.

Greengrass, Marc. *Christendom Destroyed: Europe 1517–1648*. Penguin, 2015.

Gregory, Brad S. *The Unintended Reformation: How a Religious Revolution Secularized Society*. Belknap Press, 2015.

Gura, Philip. *American Transcendentalism: A History*. Hill & Wang, 2008.

Hamdani, Abbas. "Columbus and the Recovery of Jerusalem." *Journal of the American Oriental Society* 99, no. 1 (1979): 39–48.

Hammer, Olav. "The Theosophical Current in the Twentieth Century." In *The Occult World*, edited by Charles Partridge. Routledge, 2016.

Harrison, Dick. *Stora döden: den värsta katastrof som drabbat Europa*. Oldfront, 2000.

Hart, David Bentley. *That All Shall Be Saved: Heaven, Hell, and Universal Salvation*. Yale University Press, 2017.

Hatch, Nathan O. *The Democratization of American Christianity*. Yale University Press, 1991.

Hatfield, Rob. "Botticelli's *Mystic Nativity*, Savonarola and the Millennium." *Journal of the Warburg and Courtauld Institutes* 58 (1995): 88–114.

Helfferich, Tryntie. *The Essential Thirty Years War: A Documentary History*. Hackett, 2015.

Hersey, John. *Hiroshima*. Vintage, 1989.
Hicks, Jimmie. "Some Letters Concerning the Knights of the Golden Circle in Texas, 1860–1861." *Southwestern Historical Quarterly* 65 (July 1961): 80–86.
Hill, Christopher. *Antichrist in Seventeenth Century England*. Verso, 1990.
Hill, Christopher. *The World Turned Upside Down: Radical Ideas During the English Revolution*. Penguin, 1984.
Hillers, D. R. "Revelation 13:8 and a Scroll from Murabba'at." *Bulletin of the American Schools of Oriental Research* 170 (1963): 65.
Hinton, Richard Jossiah. *John Brown and His Men: With Some Accounts of the Roads They Traveled to Reach Harper's Ferry*. Funk & Wagnalls, 1894.
Hogeland, William. *The Whiskey Rebellion: George Washington, Alexander Hamilton, and the Frontier Rebels Who Challenged America's Newfound Sovereignty*. Scribner, 2006.
Holbein, Hans. *The Dance of Death*. Penguin, 2017.
Holt, Mack. *The French Wars of Religion, 1562–1629*. Cambridge University Press, 2005.
Holt, P. M. *The Mahdist State in the Sudan 1881–1898: A Study of Its Origin, Development, and Overthrow*. Oxford University Press, 1958.
Horne, Thomas Hartwell, and Samuel Davidson. *An Introduction to the Critical Study and Knowledge of the Holy Scriptures*. Cambridge University Press, 1818.
James, Lawrence. *Imperial Warrior: The Life and Times of Field Marshall Viscount Allenby 1861–1936*. Weidenfeld & Nicolson, 1993.
Jerome, *The Saint Jerome Collection*. Aeterna Press, 2016.
Johnsons, Franklin. "The Fallacies and the Perils of the Higher Criticism." In *The Fundamentals of the Christian Faith*, edited by Edward D. Andrews and Reuben Archer Torrey. Christian Publishing House, 2022.
Jonas, Hans. *The Gnostic Religion: The Message of the Alien God and the Beginnings of Christianity*. Beacon Press, 2001.
Jones, Andrew. "From NeoReactionary Theory to the Alt-Right." In *Critical Theory and the Humanities in the Age of the Alt-Right*, edited by Christine M. Battista and Melissa R. Sande. Palgrave Macmillan, 2019.
Julius, Kevin C. *The Abolitionist Decade, 1829–1838*. McFarland, 2004.
Juster, Susan. *Doomsayers: Anglo-American Prophecy in the Age of Revolution*. University of Pennsylvania Press, 2006.
Kasparov, Gary. *Deep Thinking: Where Machine Intelligence Ends and Human Creativity Begins*. Public Affairs, 2017.
Kasparov, Gary. *How Life Imitates Chess*. Bloomsbury, 2007.
Kelly, John. *The Great Mortality: An Intimate History of the Black Death, the Most Devastating Plague of All Time*. Harper Perennial, 2006.
Kennedy, Emmet. *A Cultural History of the French Revolution*. Yale University Press, 1989.
Kilarski, Marcin. *A History of the Study of the Indigenous Languages of North America*. John Benjamins, 2021.
Kilcourse, Carl S. *Taiping Theology: The Localization of Christianity in China, 1843–64*. Palgrave Macmillan, 2016.

King, Stephen. *The Stand*. Anchor, 2012.

Knickerbocker, Wendy. *Sunday at the Ballpark: Billy Sunday's Professional Baseball Career 1883–1890*. Scarecrow Press, 2000.

Knox, John. *The First Blast of the Trumpet Against the Monstrous Regiment of Women*. Edinburgh, 1558.

Kohler, Kaufmann, and Henry Malter. "Shabbathai Zebi B. Mordecai." In *The Jewish Encyclopedia*, edited by Isidore Singer. Funk and Wagnalls, 1906.

Konner, Melvin. *Unsettled: An Anthropology of the Jews*. Viking, 2003.

Kraft, Robert A. "The Codex and Canon Consciousness." In *The Canon Debate: On the Origins and Formation of the Bible*, edited by Lee Martin McDonald and James A. Sanders. Hendrickson Publishers, 2002.

Kristeller, Paul Oskar. "The Platonic Academy of Florence." *Renaissance News* 14, no. 3 (1961): 147–159.

Kugel, James. *The Bible as It Was*. Belknap Press, 1997.

Kurschner, Walter. "Aus dem Kirchenbuch von Reichensachsen (und Langenhain) von 1639–1653." *Archiv für Hessische Geschichte und Altertumskunde* NF 9 (1913).

Kurzweil, Ray. *The Age of Spiritual Machines: When Computers Exceed Human Intelligence*. Penguin, 2000.

Kyle, Richard G. *Apocalyptic Fever: End-Times Prophecies in Modern America*. Wipf & Stock, 2012.

Landes, Richard. *Heaven on Earth: The Varieties of the Millennial Experience*. Oxford University Press, 2011.

Latourette, Kenneth Scott. *A History of Christianity*. Prince, 1975.

Lawlor, Padraig. "'Oliver Was So Drunk with the Philtre of His Power; He Had Grown Corrupt': Sir Henry Vane's Political Theology." *Political Theology* 20, no. 7 (2019): 556–573.

Lawson, Todd. *The Quran, Epic and Apocalypse*. OneWorld, 2017.

Lazarus-Yafeh, Hava. *Some Religious Aspects of Islam: A Collection of Articles*. Brill, 1981.

Leon-Portilla, Miguel. *Broken Spears: The Aztec Account of the Conquest of Mexico*. Beacon Press, 2006.

Lepore, Jill. *The Name of War: King Philip's War and the Origins of American Identity*. Vintage, 1999.

Lepore, Jill. *The Story of America: Essays on Origins*. Princeton University Press, 2012.

Lepore, Jill. *The Whites of Their Eyes: The Tea Party's Revolution and the Battle Over American History*. Princeton University Press, 2010.

Lewis, James R. *The Gods Have Landed: New Religions from Other Worlds*. SUNY Press, 1995.

Lila, Mark. *The Stillborn God: Religion, Politics, and the Modern West*. Vintage, 2008.

Lindsey, Hal. *The Late Great Planet Earth*. Zondervan, 1970.

Lukach, Harry Charles. The City of Dancing Dervishes and Other Sketches and Studies from the Near East. Macmillan, 1914.

Luther, Martin. *Table Talk*. Frankfurt, 1569.

MacAskill, William. *Doing Good Better: How Effective Altruism Can Help You Make a Difference*. Penguin Random House, 2015.

MacAskill, William. *What We Owe the Future*. Basic Books, 2022.

MacCulloch, Diarmaid. *All Things Made New: The Reformation and Its Legacy*. Oxford University Press, 2016.

MacCulloch, Diarmaid. *Christianity: The First Three Thousand Years*. Viking, 2010.

MacCulloch, Diarmaid. *The Reformation: A New History*. Penguin, 2005.

Maciejko, Pawel. *The Mixed Multitude: Jacob Frank and the Frankist Movement*. University of Pennsylvania Press, 2011.

Mann, Charles C. *1493: Uncovering the New World That Columbus Created*. Vintage, 2012.

Manseau, Peter. *One Nation, Under Gods: A New American History*. Back Bay Books, 2016.

Marcus, Greil. *A New Literary History of America*. Belknap Press, 2009.

Marlowe, Christopher. *The Jew of Malta*. Dover, 2003.

Marshall, John W. *Parables of War: Reading John's Jewish Apocalypse*. Wilfrid Laurier University Press, 2001.

Martin, Sean. *The Cathars: The Most Successful Heresy of the Middle Ages*. Chartwell Books, 2006.

Marx, Leo. *The Machine in the Garden: Technology and the Pastoral Idea in America*. MIT Press, 1965.

Mauntel, Christoph. "The T-O Diagram and Its Religious Connotations: A Circumstantial Case." In *Geography and Religious Knowledge in the Medieval World*, edited by Christoph Mauntel. De Gruyter, 2001.

McCall, Andrew. *The Medieval Underworld*. Trafalgar Square, 1979.

McCarthy, Cormac. *The Road*. Knopf Doubleday, 2006.

McGinn, Bernard. *Antichrist: Two Thousand Years of the Human Fascination with Evil*. Columbia University Press, 1999.

McGinn, Bernard. *Visions of the End: Apocalyptic Traditions in the Middle Ages*. Columbia University Press, 1998.

McManus, Stuart M. "Byzantines in the Florentine Polis: Ideology, Statecraft and Ritual During the Council of Florence." *The Journal of the Oxford University History Society* 6 (2009): 4–6.

McQueen, Alison. *Political Realism in Apocalyptic Times*. Cambridge University Press, 2018.

Mieder, Wolfgang. *Tradition and Innovation in Folk Literature*. Routledge, 2015.

Miles, Jack. *God: A Biography*. Vintage, 1996.

Miller, Perry. *Errand into the Wilderness*. Belknap Press, 1956.

Miller, Perry. "The Shaping of the American Character." *The New England Quarterly* 28, no. 4 (1955): 434–454.

Miller, Timothy. *Hippies and American Values*. University of Tennessee Press, 1991.

Miller, William. *A Canticle for Leibowitz*. Spectra, 1984.

Milman, Henry Hart. *History of Latin Christianity: Including That of the Popes to the Pontificate of Nicholas V.* John Murray, 1864.

Moazami, Mahnaz, "Millennialism, Eschatology, and Messianic Figures in Iranian Tradition." *Journal of Millennial Studies* (Winter 2000): 14.

Mooney, James. *The Ghost Dance Religion and Wounded Knee*. Reprint, Constable, 1973. Originally published 1896.

Moore, Gordon E. "Cramming More Components onto Integrated Circuits." *Electronics Magazine*, April 19, 1965: 114–117.

Morris, Adam. *American Messiahs: False Prophets of a Damned Nation*. W. W. Norton, 2019.

Motley, John Lothrop. *The Rise of the Dutch Republic*. Bickers & Sons, 1883.

Munro, Martin. *Tropical Apocalypse: Haiti and the Caribbean End Times*. University of Virginia Press, 2015.

Nadler, Steven. *Menasseh ben Israel, Rabbi of Amsterdam*. Yale University Press, 2018.

Nashe, Thomas. *The Unfortunate Traveller and Other Works*. Penguin, 1972.

Nelson, Abraham. *A Perfect Description of Antichrist, and his False Prophet: Wherein is Plainly Shewed that Oliver Cromwell was Antichrist*. 1654.

Nelson, Craig. *Thomas Paine: Enlightenment, Revolution, and the Birth of Modern Nations*. Penguin, 2007.

Nordholt, Jan Willem Schulte. *The Myth of the West: America as Last Empire*. Eerdmans, 1995.

Nostradamus, *The Prophecies: A Dual-Language Edition with Parallel Text*. Penguin, 2013.

Oates, Stephen B. *The Fires of Jubilee: Nat Turner's Fierce Rebellion*. Harper Perennial, 2004.

O'Gieblyn, Meaghen. *God, Human, Animal, Machine: Technology, Metaphor, and the Search for Meaning*. Penguin Random House, 2021.

O'Gorman, Edmundo. *The Invention of America: An Inquiry into the Historical Nature of the New World and the Meaning of History*. The University of Indiana Press, 1961.

Oppenheimer, J. R. "Now I Am Become Death . . ." (video). Atomic Archive, 1965. Archived from the original on May 16, 2008.

Osborne, Lil. *Handbook of Islamic Sects and Movements*. Brill, 2021.

O'Shea, Stephen. *The Perfect Heresy: The Revolutionary Life and Death of the Medieval Cathars*. Walker & Co., 2000.

O'Shea, Stephen. *Sea of Faith: Islam and Christianity in the Medieval Mediterranean World*. Walker, 2007.

Ozouf, Mona. "Revolutionary Calendar." In *Critical Dictionary of the French Revolution*, edited by François Furet and Mona Ozouf. Harvard University Press, 1989.

Pagels, Elaine. *Revelations: Visions, Prophecy, and Politics in the Book of Revelation*. Penguin, 2012.

Paine, Thomas. *The Age of Reason*. Liberal & Scientific Publishing Co., 1877.

Paine, Thomas. *Commonsense*. Dover, 2016.

Papayianni, Aphrodite. "*He Polis healo:* The Fall of Constantinople in 1453 Post-Byzantine Popular Literature." *Al-Masāq: Journal of the Medieval Mediterranean* 22, no. 1 (2010): 27–44.

Parker, Geoffrey. *The Thirty Years War*. Routledge, 1997.

Patrick, J. "General Chronology." In *The Catholic Encyclopedia*. Robert Appleton, 1908.

Paulus Orosius, *The Seven Books of History Against the Pagans*. The Catholic University of America Press, 1964.

Paynes, Mark. *Flowers of Time: On Postapocalyptic Fiction*. Princeton University Press, 2020.

Perkins, Pheme. *Reading the New Testament: An Introduction*. Paulist Press, 1989.

Phillips, Jonathan. *Holy Warriors: A Modern History of the Crusades*. Random House, 2010.

Phillips, Kevin. *The Cousins' Wars: Religion, Politics, and the Triumph of Anglo-America*. Basic Books, 1998.

Popkin, Jeremy D. *New World Begins: A History of the French Revolution*. Basic Books, 2019.

Portier-Young, Anathea E. *Apocalypse Against Empire: Theologies of Resistance in Early Judaism*. Eerdmans, 2014.

Ptolemy, Barry. *Transcendent Man*. Ptolemaic Productions and Therapy Studios, 2009.

Randi, James. *The Mask of Nostradamus*. Prometheus Books, 1993.

Rappaport, Michael. *1848: Year of Revolution*. Basic Books, 2010.

Raviv, Dvir, and Chaim ben David. "Cassius Dio's Figures for the Demographic Consequences of the Bar Kokhba War: Exaggeration or Reliable Account?" *The Journal of Roman Archeology* 34, no. 2 (2021): 585–607.

Reddles, David. *Hitler's Millennial Reich: Apocalyptic Belief and the Search for Salvation*. New York University Press, 2008.

Regis, Ed. *Great Mambo Chicken and the Transhuman Condition: Science Slightly Over the Edge*. Basic Books, 1991.

Reilly III, F. Kent. "Mesoamerican Religious Beliefs: The Practices and Practitioners." In *The Oxford Handbook of Mesoamerican Archeology*, edited by Deborah L. Nicholes and Christopher Poole. Oxford University Press, 2016.

Reilly, Thomas H. *The Taiping Heavenly Kingdom: Rebellion and Blasphemy of Empire*. Seattle: University of Washington Press, 2004.

Reynolds, David S. *John Brown, Abolitionist: The Man Who Killed Slavery, Sparked the Civil War, and Seeded Civil Rights*. Vintage, 2006.

Richards, E. G. *Mapping Time: The Calendar and Its History*. Oxford University Press, 2000.

Richter, Daniel K. *Facing East from Indian Country: A Native History of Early America*. Harvard University Press, 2003.

Robin, Christian Julien. "South Arabia, Religions in Pre-Islamic." In *Encyclopedia of the Qur'an*, Vol. 5, edited by Jane Dammen McAuliffe. Brill, 2006.

Rowe, David L. *God's Strange Work: William Miller and the End of the World*. Eerdmans, 2008.

Rubenstein, Jay. *Nebuchadnezzar's Dream: The Crusades, Apocalyptic Prophecy, and the End of History*. Oxford University Press, 2019.

Russell, Jeffrey Burton. *The Devil: Perceptions of Evil from Antiquity to Primitive Christianity*. Cornell University Press, 1987.

Sachedina, Abdulaziz Abdulhussein. *Islamic Messianism: The Idea of the Mahdi in Twelver Shi'ism*. SUNY Press, 1980.

Savonarola, Girolamo. *A Guide to Righteous Living and Other Works*. The University of Toronto Press, 2003.

Schaff, Philip, and David Schley Schaff. *History of the Christian Church.* Vol. V. C. Scribner's, 1910.

Schama, Simon. *Citizens: A Chronicle of the French Revolution.* Vintage, 1999.

Schele, Linda, and David Freidel. *A Forest of Kings: The Untold Story of the Ancient Maya.* Harper Perennial, 1993.

Schmidt, Leigh Eric. *The Church of Saint Thomas Paine: A Religious History of American Secularism.* Princeton University Press, 2021.

Schmithals Walter. *The Apocalyptic Movement, Introduction and Interpretation.* Abingdon Press, 1975.

Schneider, Nathan. *Thank You, Anarchy: Notes from the Occupy Apocalypse.* University of California Press, 2013.

Scholem, Gershom. *The Messianic Idea in Judaism: And Other Essays on Jewish Spirituality.* Schocken Books, 1971.

Scholem, Gershom. *Sabbatai Sevi: The Mystical Messiah.* Princeton University Press, 1973.

Schüssler, Elisabeth. *Revelation: Vision of a Just World.* Fortress Press, 1991.

Scranton, Roy. *We're Doomed: Now What?* Soho Press, 2018.

Scurr, Ruth. *Fatal Purity: Robespierre and the French Revolution.* Henry Holt, 2006.

Sedgewick, Mark. *Against the Modern World: Traditionalism and the Secret Intellectual History of the Twentieth Century.* Oxford University Press, 2004.

Servetus, Michael. *The Restoration of Christianity.* 1553.

Shelley, Mary. *The Last Man.* Wordsworth Classics, 2004.

Shoemaker, Stephen J. *The Apocalypse of Empire: Imperial Eschatology in Late Antiquity and Early Islam.* University of Pennsylvania Press, 2018.

Sibly, W. A. *The Chronicle of William of Puylaurens: The Albigensian Crusade and Its Aftermath.* The Boydell Press, 2003.

Simon, Edward. *The American Strand: Directional Poetics and Apocalypse in the Early Modern Trans-Atlantic.* Lehigh University, 2017.

Simon, Edward. "Bradstreet and Trans-Atlantic Non-Conformism in the American-Prophetic Mode." In *Prophecy and Eschatology in the Trans-Atlantic World, 1550–1800*, edited by Andrew Crome. Palgrave-Macmillan, 2016.

A Sincere Admonition to All Christians to Guard Against Insurrection and Rebellion (1522). In *Luther's Works.* Vol. 45. Edited by Walter I. Brandt. Fortress, 1962.

Singer, Isaac Bashevis. *Satan in Goray.* Farrar, Strauss & Giroux, 1996.

Siniossoglou, Niketas. *Radical Platonism in Byzantium: Illumination and Utopia in Gemistos Plethon.* Cambridge University Press, 2016.

Smith, Andrew Phillip. *The Lost Teachings of the Cathars: Their Beliefs and Practices.* Watkins Publishing, 2015.

Smith, Jonathan Riley. *The First Crusaders, 1095–1131.* Cambridge University Press, 1997.

Smith, Robert O. *More Desired Than Our Owne Salvation: The Roots of Christian Zionism.* Oxford University Press, 2013.

Smith-Christopher, Daniel L. *The Religion of the Landless: The Social Context of the Babylonian Exile.* Wipf & Stock, 2015.

Snobelen, Stephen D. "A Time and Times and the Dividing of Time: Isaac Newton the Apocalypse and AD 2060." *The Canadian Journal of History* 38 (December 2003): 537–551.

Spengler, Oswald. *The Decline of the West: Perspectives of World History*. George Allen, 1928.

Stayer, James M. *The German Peasants' War and Anabaptist Community of Goods*. McGill-Queen's University Press, 1991.

Steiner, George. *In Bluebeard's Castle: Some Notes Towards the Redefinition of Culture*. Faber & Faber, 1971.

Stephens, Alexander. "The Cornerstone Speech." 1861.

Stevens, Randall J. *The Fire Spreads: Holiness and Pentecostalism in the American South*. Harvard University Press, 2008.

Straus, William, and Neil Howe's Howe. *The Fourth Turning: What the Cycles of History Tell Us About America's Next Rendezvous with History*. New York: Broadway Books, 1997.

Streete, Adrianne. *Apocalypse and Anti-Catholicism in Seventeenth-Century Drama*. Cambridge: Cambridge University Press, 2017.

Sutton, Matthew Avery. *American Apocalypse: A History of Modern Evangelicalism*. Belknap Press, 2017.

Sweet, James H. "The Iberian Roots of American Racist Thought." *The William and Mary Quarterly* 54, no. 1 (January 1997): 143–166.

Tate Gallery. *The Pre-Raphaelites*. Tate Gallery/Penguin, 1984.

Taylor, Alan. *American Colonies: The Settling of North America*. Viking, 2001.

Taylor, Alan. *American Revolution: A Continental History, 1750–1804*. W. W. Norton, 2016.

Terry, Milton S. *The Sibylline Oracles: Translated from the Greek into English Blank Verse*. Eaton & Mains, 1899.

Tertullian. *The Five Books Against Marcion*. T&T Clarke, 1870.

Theibault, John. "The Rhetoric of Death and Destruction in the Thirty Years War." *The Journal of Social History* 27, no. 2 (1993): 271–290.

Thomas, Keith. *Religion and the Decline of Magic: Studies in Popular Belief in Sixteenth and Seventeenth-Century England*. Penguin, 2003.

Tocqueville, Alexis de. *Democracy in America: And Two Essays on America*. Penguin, 2003.

Todorov, Tzvetan. *The Conquest of America: The Question of the Other*. Oxford University Press, 1999.

Tolan, John Victor. *Saint Francis and the Sultan: The Curious History of a Christian–Muslim Encounter*. Oxford University Press, 2009.

Tolan, John Victor. *Saracens: Islam in the Medieval European Imagination*. Columbia University Press, 2002.

Toscano, Alberto. "Preface." In *Wu Ming Presents Thomas Müntzer Sermon to the Princes*. Verso, 2010.

Tuveson, Ernest. *Redeemer Nation: The Idea of America's Millennial Role*. University of Chicago Press, 1980.

Tyson III, Joseph. "The Monks of the Wissahickon: Part 1." *Schuylkill Valley Journal Online* 2021. https://www.svjlit.com/features/the-monks-of-the-wissahickon-pt-1-by-joseph-tyson-1.

Valmiki, Vyasa. *Delphi Collected Sanskrit Epics*. Delphi Classics, 2018.

Vanderwood, Paul. *The Power of God Against the Guns of Government: Religious Upheaval in Mexico at the Turn of the 19th Century*. Stanford University Press, 1986.

van Engen, Abram C. *City on a Hill: A History of American Exceptionalism*. Yale University Press, 2020.

Vasquez, Pablo (trans.) *The Sacred Gathas of Zarathustra and the Old Avestan Canon: A Modern Translation of Ancient Wisdom*. Mantra, 2022.

Vermes, Geza. *The Complete Dead Sea Scrolls in English*. Penguin, 2012.

Voegelin, Eric. *The New Science of Politics*. In *The Collected Works of Eric Voegelin*. Vol. 5, *Modernity Without Restraint*. University of Missouri Press, 1999.

von List, Guido. *Secret of the Runes*. Guido-von-List-Bücherei 1. Translated by Stephen E. Flowers. Destiny Books, 1908.

Wakefield, Walter L. "Notes on Some Antiheretical Writings of the Thirteenth Century." *Franciscan Studies* 27, no. 1 (1967): 285–321.

Walters, Ronald G. *American Reformers, 1815–1860*. Hill & Wang, 1997.

Wannenmacher, Julia Anne, ed. *Joachim of Fiore and the Influence of Inspiration: Essays in Memory of Marjorie E. Reeves (1905–2003)*. Routledge, 2016.

Warren, Louis S. *God's Red Son: The Ghost Dance Religion and the Making of Modern America*. Basic Books, 2017.

Watkins, Glenn. *Proof Through the Night: Music and the Great War*. University of California Press, 2003.

Weaver, John. *The New Apostolic Reformation: History of a Modern Charismatic Movement*. McFarland, 2016.

Weinstein, David. *Savonarola: The Rise and Fall of a Renaissance Prophet*. Yale University Press, 2011.

Weis, Rene. *The Yellow Cross: The Story of the Last Cathars' Rebellion Against the Inquisition, 1290–1329*. Vintage, 2002.

Wester, Maisha. "Slave Narratives and Slave Revolts." In *The Palgrave Book of the Southern Gothic*, edited by Susan Castillo Street and Charles L. Crow. Palgrave Macmillan, 2016.

Wheelis, Mark. "Biological Warfare at the 1346 Siege of Kaffa." *Emerging Infectious Diseases* 8, no. 9 (2002): 971–975.

Whitman, James Q. *Hitler's American Model: The United States and the Making of Nazi Race Law*. Princeton University Press, 2017.

Whitmarsh, Tim. *Ancient Greek Literature*. Wiley Blackwell, 2006.

Widhom, Kristofer, and Bernard McGinn. "Antichrist: An Interview with Bernard McGinn." *Cabinet Magazine* 5 (Winter 2001–2002). https://www.cabinetmagazine.org/issues/5/widholm_mcginn.php.

Wilson, Bryan A. "Millennialism in Comparative Perspective." *Comparative Studies in Society and History* 6, no. 1 (October 1963): 93–114.

Wilson, Peter H. *The Thirty Years War: Europe's Tragedy*. Belknap Press, 2011.

Winstanley, Gerrard. *A Declaration from the Poor Oppressed People of England*. 1649.
Winstanley, Gerrard. *The True Levellers Standard Advanced*. 1649.
Wm. Miller's Apology and Defence. Joshua V. Himes, 1845.
Wood, Gordon. *The Radicalism of the American Revolution*. Vintage, 1993.
Wormald, Patrick. "Bede and the 'Church of the English.'" In *The Times of Bede: Studies in Early English Christian Society and Its Historian*, edited by Stephen Baxter. Blackwell, 2006.
Yates, Frances. *Giordano Bruno and the Hermetic Tradition*. University of Chicago Press, 1991.
Yurchak, Alexei. *Everything Was Forever, Until It Was No More: The Last Soviet Generation*. Princeton University Press, 2005.
Yuval, Israel Jacob. *Two Nations in Your Womb: Perceptions of Jews and Christians in Late Antiquity and the Middle Ages*. University of California Press, 2008.
Žižek, Slavoj. *In Defense of Lost Causes*. Verso, 2017.

INDEX